WRITING RED

WRITING RED

An Anthology of American Women Writers, 1930–1940

Edited by Charlotte Nekola
and Paula Rabinowitz

Foreword by Toni Morrison

THE FEMINIST PRESS
at The City University of New York
New York

To our families

Library of Congress Cataloging in Publication Data

Writing red.

   1. American literature—Women authors. 2. American
literature—20th century. 3. Social problems—Literary
collections. 4. Women—Literary collections.
5. Feminism—Literary collections. I. Nekola,
Charlotte. II. Rabinowitz, Paula.
PS509.S5W75 1987   810'.8'09287   87-25023
ISBN 0-935312-77-3
ISBN 0-935312-76-5 (pbk.)

This publication is made possible, in part, by public funds from the New York
State Council on the Arts.

Cover and text design: Paula Martinac
Cover art: On the Street by Isabel Bishop (1932). Collection of Mrs. Paul Wachs;
courtesy of Midtown Galleries, New York

CONTENTS

Part II POETRY 125

Part III   REPORTAGE, THEORY, AND ANALYSIS   187

FOREWORD

The embrace of women and politics has always had an uneasy history. From Antigone to Angela Davis, patriarchal reactions to that participation have been to trivialize, to rage, to dismiss, or bury. The possibility that one half of the population should get interested in exercising the power the other half takes for granted, or that a female intelligence is keen enough to analyze and fully engage the political issues of the day is still a startling prospect in some quarters. It conjures up defensive language and frightening images—as though Scylla were in league with Charybdis and the navigation of historical waters had been completely denied all male voyagers. Fortunately, efforts to diminish the perceptiveness with which women have entered the political terrain have not always succeeded. A substantial part of feminist scholarship has chosen to investigate that perception and its consequences.

Even so, it is surprising that the literary histories of a singularly radical period in the United States, the 1930s, have, until now, rested on the work of men. Suffrage, as Paula Rabinowitz tells us, has been assumed to have been followed by a feminist void, until, in the wake of the Civil Rights movement, women again turned their attention toward national and, inevitably, feminist politics. The error of that assumption is revealed in these pages, and is nothing less than redemption for the hundreds of women writers who "immersed themselves," as Charlotte Nekola reminds us, "in political struggles far removed from personal and domestic realms," and who " . . . added gender as another element of political analysis and explored the complex relationships among sex, work, and class."

When women take noncompetitive notice of other women, when their sensitivity to the plight of each other traverses the lines that separate them—class, race, religion, nationality—extraordinary things can happen: poor women see through the bars rich women are caged in; Black women understand the "privileges" of light skin as destructive to the whole race; mothers recognize the dependence of capitalist bosses on prolific child-bearing; female office workers perceive the oppressive complexities of gender and power at the workplace; middle-class women respond to strikers with compassion and intelligence. In these and other kinds of experiences represented in this collection, we see clearly that the "1930s radicalism [that] appears to be a masculine preserve" is in fact peopled with questioning, caring, socially committed women writers.

The publication of *Writing Red* is itself testimony to this alert, feminist generosity: a pair of women scholars (who are also friends) search and excavate buried or dusty records for the work of other women whose interests in social issues both preceded and affected their own; they are encouraged in this work by other women; they find a publishing haven in a women's press. By making it possible for the women writers of the 1930s to live once more in their political context, Charlotte Nekola and Paula Rabinowitz have widened the circle. (And I am personally pleased about the modest contribution that the Schweitzer Chair at the State University of New York at Albany was able to make.)

In praise of this anthology, perhaps I may be forgiven for misappropriating some lines at the close of Muriel Rukeyser's "Absalom." The poem is about the triumph of a mother who has made the death of her miner son *count.*

> *I come forth by day, I am born a second time,*
> *I force a way through, and I know the gate*
> *I shall journey over the earth among the living.*

In *Writing Red* these long neglected voices are born a second time, and *count.*

Toni Morrison
Schweitzer Professor of Humanities
State University of New York at Albany

PREFACE

There it was again—another graduate seminar that promised an intensive look at a literary era, the 1930s, yet did not include one woman writer on the reading list. It was 1980. Naturally, the course introduced some examples of proletarian literature by, for example, Jack Conroy and John Dos Passos. Surely there were some women writers? The instructor knew of no names but thought some might be found. Critical works on the period mentioned a few women writers, and the stacks of the University of Michigan library yielded up a very dusty copy of Tess Slesinger's 1934 novel *The Unpossessed*. At that point, this book began. The more we read, the more amazed we were at the range of political issues taken on by women in this era. Here were many women "writing red"—writing with great passion from a radical political perspective.

Muriel Rukeyser's poem "Fifth Elegy: A Turning Wind" (reprinted in this volume) talks about "nightwalking in stranger cities." That captures our experience in making this anthology. Despite our "comprehensive" education in United States literature, we had not known that an entire generation of women wrote literature that addressed those issues central to our own politics: gender, race, class, and international relations. We did not know about this immensely vocal group of women who traveled the United States and the world in search of answers to the problems of their unsettling times: hunger, racism, inhuman working conditions, fascism, revolution. We were also surprised to find a literature concerned with women's issues that we thought had not surfaced until the 1960s and 1970s: the politics of marriage, enforced sterilization, the double day of women workers.

We were also fascinated by the almost complete silence in literary history about the existence of these works. It was only little more than fifty years ago that these women wrote. How was it possible that they had dropped out of sight so quickly? Finding these relatively recent works meant combing through thousands of yellowed pages of 1930s periodicals, pamphlets, and now out-of-print collections of short fiction, poetry, and political reportage. The more we found, the more impressed we were by another omission in the records: there were certainly many more women thinking and writing in revolutionary ways than we could find in print. As it was, we found a wealth of material to choose from.

In the beginning, we felt we were working on one of America's best-kept secrets. Since then, other writers of and about the period have shared our interest in exploring and reviving the works of these women. But not all. In the process of contacting authors and heirs for permission to reprint works in this book we encountered a few who were reluctant at first to be associated with a volume entitled *Writing Red*. Some had suffered, or had seen their friends and relatives suffer, the outrages of the McCarthy era. For them, this persecution remained a bitter memory. For others, the political enthusiasms of the past had long since been replaced by other philosophies and interests. Most, however, were delighted to have their works from the 1930s available to a new generation of readers. Nevertheless, we should like to emphasize that our title is not intended to suggest that the writers included in this book were adherents to any one "party line." "Writing red" refers, instead, to a very loosely defined group of women writers who, to a greater or lesser degree, contributed to and were themselves moved by the intellectual, literary, and political energy of the left during that turbulent decade.

Writing Red is the first comprehensive collection of women's writings of the 1930s in three major genres: short fiction; poetry; reportage, theory, and analysis. These works are almost entirely absent from the standard literary canon and are still not well represented even in new feminist literary anthologies and histories. This volume includes works by known authors, such as Tillie Olsen, Margaret Walker, Josephine Herbst, and Meridel Le Sueur; and writers whose names are mostly unknown to readers of today: Marita Bonner, Ella Winter, Joy Davidman, Mary Inman. In addition, there are anonymous workers' narratives and contributions by obscure poets and writers who may have published only one or two works in *Working Woman,* the *Crisis, Opportunity,* or *New Masses,* never to be heard from again. *Writing Red* both restores these works to their place within U.S. literary radicalism and shows that women writers do have, as Deborah Rosenfelt says, a "radical tradition" of their own.

We would first like to thank the authors in this volume for their remarkable contributions to the literature of the United States. Their courage, activism, and vision from half a century ago bring us sustenance today. Each of us has also been fortunate in receiving institutional support for this project. As the Schweitzer Chair in Humanities at the State University of New York at Albany, Toni Morrison extended a Schweitzer Fellowship in Humanities to Charlotte Nekola, in part for this project. Her generous assistance and friendship offered us time as well as intellectual support. The Horace Rackham School of Graduate Studies at the University of Michigan gave Paula Rabinowitz substantial support for a dissertation examining sexuality and politics in more than forty novels by women literary radicals of the 1930s. Our editors at The Feminist Press, Florence

Howe and Joanne O'Hare, guided us through the maze of assembling an anthology with much dedication and imagination.

Deborah Rosenfelt, Elaine Hedges, Rosalyn Baxandall, and Alan Wald read and commented on various parts of the manuscript. We found these selections with assistance from librarians at the Labadie Collection of the University of Michigan library, the Tamiment Library of New York University, and the New York Public Library. We thank each other for a friendship sustained, in part, by this book; while each of us has written separate introductions for the various sections, we both read and chose all of the selections collaboratively. And, finally, we owe special thanks to our families and friends.

WRITING RED

Women and U.S. Literary Radicalism

PAULA RABINOWITZ

The images of the 1930s—the hunger marches, the breadlines, the militant labor struggles, the mass demonstrations in New York City's Union Square, and the vast, dusty fields of Arkansas and Oklahoma—have been etched into our cultural memory. The bleak statistics of the Great Depression that American writers and artists engraved in their stories, poems, novels, plays, dances, woodcuts, and paintings include the stock market loss of over thirty billion dollars in the few weeks between October 24 and November 13, 1929; the nearly 30 percent unemployment by 1933; the dust storms ravaging millions of acres from Amarillo, Texas, to Pierre, South Dakota, throughout the mid-1930s; and the more than half a million workers who staged sit-down strikes across the nation between September 1936 and May 1937. This personal and creative confrontation with hunger and politics changed, for a time, the relationships between politics, culture, and personal commitment for intellectuals in the United States. Artists and writers worked in every media, using a variety of stylistic and formal techniques, but they shared an urge to document, to record, to report, and, ultimately, to change the world in much of their work during the 1930s.

The influence of Marxism had grown among American intellectuals during the 1920s through the translation of works by Marx, Engels, Lenin, and Trotsky (including Trotsky's 1923 work of literary criticism, *Literature and Revolution*), the establishment of the Communist Party in America (CPUSA), as well as the publication of independent radical journals such as V. F. Calverton's *Modern Monthly*. As fascism shadowed Europe and America, Marxist theory appeared to explain a world racing from prosperity to poverty and from one world war to another. Furthermore, the vision of the Soviet Union as a society developing a new culture consolidated the influence of the CPUSA among disaffected American intellectuals. While the primary goals of Party work during the 1930s were to organize industrial workers, the unemployed, and minorities and to fight fascism, the CPUSA also attempted to foster a new aesthetic in American arts. Proletarianism, a cultural movement of, by, and for workers (nobody was ever quite certain which), was to usher in "Soviet America," much as Proletcult signaled a revolutionary aesthetic in the Soviet Union during the 1920s.[1]

Because the Depression was marked by massive unemployment and farm foreclosures, the misery of the 1930s is often shrouded in a masculine cloak: the landscape is crowded by millions of men in the breadlines, at the plant gates, or, defiantly, sitting on the plant floor. According to Milton Meltzer, when the "jobless lined up in the street for free soup or bread . . . they were always men; the hungry women stayed away."[2] In 1932, Meridel Le Sueur published her first piece for the *New Masses,* entitled "Women on the Breadlines," as a corrective to the widespread perception that poverty was a peculiarly masculine experience in Depression America.[3]

This anthology of women's writings from the 1930s continues Le Sueur's project. Supplementing The Feminist Press's reprint series "Novels of the Thirties," *Writing Red* corrects the failure of most collections from the 1930s to include a substantial amount of writing by women. A quick glance through these anthologies—*The American Writer and the Great Depression* (1966); *Years of Protest* (1967); *New Masses: An Anthology of the Rebel Thirties* (1969); *Writers in Revolt: The Anvil Anthology* (1973); and *Social Poetry of the 1930s: A Selection* (1978)— suggests women appear more frequently than Tillie Olsen's calculation of "one out of twelve" as the ratio of published women authors to men.[4] However, these more recent anthologies recapitulate the one-in-seven ratio of the International Publishers' anthology *Proletarian Literature in the United States* (1935), which included only nine women out of selections by sixty-five authors.[5] Likewise, much of the prevailing scholarship about literary radicalism has been institutional, focusing on what Josephine Herbst called the "head-boys" who edited journals, wrote criticism, and prescribed the aesthetic and political outlines of the Left literary movement.[6] Thus, 1930s literary radicalism appears to be a masculine preserve.

Even recent feminist attempts to recover lost women writers have, for the most part, ignored the 1930s as a fertile era of women's literary production. The prevailing depiction of the rise, fall, and subsequent rise of waves of feminist activity places the 1930s within the great hiatus between suffrage and the publication of Betty Friedan's *The Feminine Mystique* in 1963.[7] This model diminishes the significance of women's confrontation with issues of economic and racial exploitation that is typical of their writing during the 1930s. Moreover, even if few feminist organizations survived the Great Depression, some discussions about female sexuality, women's work, and gender ideology continued within the CPUSA under the amorphous rubric of "the woman question."[8] Inside or outside the

CPUSA, women's writing in the 1930s indicates a desire to explore the complex relationships among sexual, gender, racial, and class oppressions, a project that should resonate for many feminist scholars today.[9]

THE EARLY 1930s: PROLETARIAN CULTURE AND GENDER IDEOLOGY

When, in 1929, Michael Gold urged young writers to "go Left," he was associating the genre of proletarian literature with the horizons of the West which Horace Greeley had imagined for young men a century earlier.[10] A few years later, V. F. Calverton repeated the metaphor, connecting the West and the Left, in his call for intellectuals to join the young writers of the "mine, mill and farm" and travel "Leftward Ho!"[11] This use of the image of the West invoked the connection between the proletarian aesthetic and popular American imagery. It also suggested that the Left, like the West, was a wild place—brutal, rugged, and certainly no place for a lady. Gold was more specific in his vision:

> A new writer has been appearing; a wild youth of about twenty-two, the son of working class parents, who himself works in the lumber camps, coal mines, steel mills, harvest fields and mountain camps of America. He is sensitive and impatient. He writes in jets of exasperated feeling and has no time to polish his work. He is violent and sentimental by turns. He lacks self confidence but writes because he must.[12]

According to Philip Rahv, the new writer would create a new literature freed of the " 'nice and waterish' diet of emasculated unsocial writing."[13] In 1936, Michael Gold proudly proclaimed the newly formed *Partisan Review and Anvil* "the child of roughneck Father Anvil and his thoughtful college bride . . . a vigorous male, retaining the best features of both parents; papa's earthy directness and mom's erudition and sensibility."[14] By linking the proletariat, and its culture, with masculinity, the metaphors of gender permeated the aesthetic debates of male literary radicals throughout the 1930s.

Gold had asserted that only "if he has vigor and guts" could a son of the working class write revolutionary fiction and thus "explore" that "wonderful virgin field."[15] Nevertheless, women authors did venture into those male preserves—lumber camps, steel mills, harvest fields, and coal mines—for their writings, finding a landscape populated not only by heroic male workers but by their mothers, sisters, wives, lovers, and daughters as well. Women's labor created a different terrain, one marked by childbirth, domestic work, and unorganized labor, as depicted in Agnes Smedley's novel *Daughter of Earth*.[16] Walt Carmon criticized *Daughter of Earth* in the *New Masses,* however, suggesting that it "took its bias from the bitterness of a woman, and was therefore "marred as [a] class novel."[17] As a working-class author, Smedley could still be praised for writing a "proletarian" novel; however, by suggesting that sexuality was constitutive of female class consciousness, Smedley implied divisions within the working class that were unacknowledged within CPUSA rhetoric. Women's desire to chart new territory in prose or poetry was often criticized when it included a "flesh and blood reality" different from that found in the "large, heroic and self-confident" confrontation with the masculine workplace.[18]

The equation of literary and political vitality with masculinity created a series of obstacles to any woman who wanted to write revolutionary literature. Female intellectuals sympathetic to the Left were particularly vulnerable to attack. Zelda Leknorf wrote to the *New Masses* after reading Meridel Le Sueur's "I Was Marching"—a story about a middle-class intellectual woman who joins the workers' movement—that she "wanted to scream and tear at my face which shrieked guilt" at the sight of striking mill workers in New Bedford, because she stood apart from them. She accuses herself of "cowardice that lay beneath my flabby indolence and intellectual luxuriance" and says that "I sat back gaping and superciliously discussing and criticizing tactics and maneuvers of the Party. . . . The ghastly futility of our plight is overwhelming."[19]

Because the proletariat was conceived of as masculine, Zelda Leknorf's plight as a bourgeois intellectual woman positioned her hopelessly outside of the working class. In effect, intellectual women on the Left were permanently estranged from historical change. Only by disfigurement, tearing her face, could she overcome her guilt and actively enter the struggle. The editors' criticism of her "hysterical self-flagellation" did little to aid Leknorf and her sisters' entrance into the movement of literary radicalism.[20] Like Mrs. Phillips, the bourgeois woman in Josephine Johnson's *Jordanstown* (1937) who is sympathetic to the poor and who desires an "air-conditioned mind" to avoid contemplating her contradictory position, the intellectual woman appeared unable to "bridge the chasm" between herself and the workers.[21]

In her 1981 study of Tillie Olsen and the "radical tradition," Deborah Rosenfelt paints a complex portrait of the dilemmas involved in being a female, a radical, and a writer.[22] She points to a series of contradictions endemic to 1930s literary radicalism that posed particularly difficult constraints on some women writers. Communist intellectuals experienced a conflict between the value of theory and the historical importance of militant action, which resulted in naming themselves "cultural workers."[23] For example, Meridel Le Sueur, in her essay "The Fetish of Being Outside," attempted to reconcile this contradiction by arguing that "belief is the action, the function of the writer."[24] However, because the Party stressed the revolutionary potential of the mostly male industrial labor force, its female members also felt a disparity between a theory that named and criticized sexual inequality and an institution that reproduced male dominance within its hierarchic structure.

Despite a program that included women's full equality, the CPUSA in the 1930s was a masculine preserve—male-dominated in person, in politics, and in metaphor. Women associated with the Party were often patronized by the male leadership. In 1931, Josephine Herbst wrote Katherine Ann Porter that she was being kept out of a "talkfest" with John Herrmann, Mike Gold, Malcolm Cowley, and others with "the same gentle stay-in-your-place which may, or may not be the home," when they departed for a bar without her, "full of a masculine importance." Upon Herrmann's return, Herbst told him that "as long as the gents had bourgeois reactions to women they would probably never rise very high in their revolutionary conversations."[25] Similarly, Meridel Le Sueur felt that the CPUSA expected those women who rose to leadership to live like men, and those who remained within the rank and file to act as the "Party's housekeepers."[26] In 1976, looking back, Peggy Dennis criticized the Party leadership for its "explicit, deliberate, and reprehensible sexism."[27] Esther Allen remembered that when her husband brought home a group of comrades to discuss politics, she "had to feed them and keep trotting out for drinks." She'd yell, "While you sit on your ass making the revolution, *I'm* out in the kitchen like a slavey. What we need is a revolution in this *house*."[28]

Throughout the early 1930s, however, a number of challenges to "male supremacy" were raised by women organizers in trades that were predominated by a female labor force. The *Party Organizer,* the internal organ for rank-and-file members of the CPUSA, featured a column entitled "Work Among Women" which often included articles castigating the Party for its failure to be creative about organizing women into leadership positions. For instance, the author of one piece challenged the leadership to include women as delegates rather than assigning women to do the "technical work" such as typing; she noted that "the women are organized in women's councils and mothers' leagues, instead of being drawn into the unemployed branches."[29]

Thus, the CPUSA could not ignore the special concerns facing women as workers and even as a "sex class."[30] For instance, the pages of the *Working Woman,* the organ of the CPUSA Women's Commission, provide a fascinating illustration of the feeble attempts to link class and gender within an official Party publication. One issue of the magazine contained an article on the position of women in the Soviet Union which suggested that not only had equality under the law been achieved there but that economic equality as well as sexual equality had become institutionalized. The next column ran an editorial calling for women to organize antiwar committees to fight against war and fascism. In addition, a letter to a birth control clinic was reprinted, in which a desperate woman pleads for "the knowledge" that will keep her from getting pregnant. The editorial response suggests that while wealthy women can afford doctors who will prescribe contraceptive devices or perform abortions, working-class women are "kept in ignorance of this important information by bosses, who want a large supply of labor for industry and plenty of docile workers to get killed or maimed in war for them." It goes on to urge women to fight for free birth control clinics. In another section of the journal, Gwen Bard's "Fashion Letter" provides a pattern for trimming "any old dress" with grosgrain ribbon; she concludes her directions: "You know of course, that these ideas are not offered as little dabs of cheer to try to make us content with our lot. . . . Our first task is to align ourselves with men workers in the day-to-day fight for better conditions."[31]

The editors exhorted their readers to submit letters or testimonials of their experiences as working women, farm women, or working-class housewives. In one case, a contest was held for the best response to a letter in which a woman complained that her husband would not allow her to attend meetings. Sixteen prizes were being offered, ranging from a "Hamper of White Rose canned products," for first prize, to "Three large glossy photos of Lenin, Stalin, and Marx," for sixteenth, suggesting, perhaps, that *Working Woman* understood its readers' priorities. Articles analyzing popular cultural icons of romance, such as Hollywood movies and dime magazines, connected capitalist exploitation of workers to the ideology of women's sexual surrender. Stories by "One Who Knows" exposed the sleazy experiences of Orbach's saleswomen or of Hollywood extras. Juxtaposed with these articles were brief and poignant remembrances by black women sharecroppers or white miners' wives who recalled an eviction or a strike in muted, simple language. Some of these are reprinted in this volume.

The ideal of a synthesis of literature and politics, of popular and literary forms, and of class and gender which characterized *Working Woman* may have reached its most ridiculous point in the collectively written story "Stockyard Stella," serialized during 1935.[32] This story raises (but does not resolve) the problems of sexual harassment and of male and female leadership within a militant workers' organization. The story constructs a narrative as indebted to *True Romance* magazine as to the novel *Cement,* prompting Ann Barton, an editor of *Working Woman,* to call it "the first American proletarian love story."[33]

While *Working Woman* was aimed specifically at a female audience, even the *New Masses,* the Party's influential journal of politics and culture, edited by Michael Gold, periodically commissioned articles to address its women readers. Both Rebecca Pitts and Grace Hutchins, whose pieces are included in Part 3, analyzed sexuality in relation to American culture and to Communism. According to Pitts, the "specific dilemma involved in being a woman . . . is social rather than biological." Because the sex act is based on a "psychology of power," it cannot be satisfying for women; neither can work be productive because of economic exploitation by employers. Even professional women, she argues, are subjected to a false choice between marriage and work, resulting in psychological deformity. For Pitts, "only Communism offers women the right to be an independent, productive worker. . . . Only Communism likewise offers woman another right (so closely related to that of independent work): the right to a freer, more natural sex happiness."[34] As usual in Party-sanctioned discussions about women, the final delivery of the goods was dependent upon the working-class struggle, because to champion feminist concerns over those of the proletariat—to privilege gender over class—implied one was "still a suffragette."[35] Pitts's assertion that her claim had already been proven in the Soviet Union where women were liberated as workers, and thus, as sexual beings, was suspect by 1935 when Stalin had abolished many of the most progressive elements of the 1926 Family Code by making abortion and homosexuality illegal and by curtailing divorce. Pitts's article could not forestall the challenge Ann Weedon posed later in the year when she accused both the *New Masses* and the Communist Party of male dominance and of insensitivity to women's issues.[36] Six months later, in an article entitled "Women and the *New Masses,*" Pitts tried to refute Weedon by pointing to the magazine as a vision of an ideal community of commited intellectuals, "something to believe in" (as she had earlier characterized the CPUSA), but she failed to answer or explain the persistent exclusion of women within the Party leadership.[37]

Women, and the representation of woman, were used in different ways quite cynically, Elsa Dixler argues in her comprehensive 1974 study of "The Woman Question," depending upon the prevailing line from Moscow.[38] During the Third Period, when the Party followed an ultra-leftist line, open discussions of sexual freedom dominated the discussion about women within Party literature. As the effects of Stalinism spread, especially through the increasing repression of sexual freedom in the Soviet Union, and as the Popular Front era attempted to insert the CPUSA into mainstream America, the emphasis shifted away from radical challenges of "male supremacy" and toward an accommodation with women's traditional roles as wives and mothers. By the end of the decade, talking about "husband trouble" in the women's pages of the *Daily Worker* meant developing a strategy to get wives to join the Ladies' Auxiliary rather than criticizing the male dominance of the Party or of working-class men.*

In a more recent study, Robert Shaffer confirms Dixler's findings within the pages of the *Working Woman* and in the two most sustained works of feminist theory produced by Party women: Grace Hutchins's *Women Who Work* (1935) and Mary Inman's *In Women's Defense* (1939) (selections from both appear in this volume).[39] He notes that although the rhetoric of the early 1930s was militantly radical in its feminist programs, the sectarianism and extreme leftism of the Party made it difficult for large numbers of working-class women to become members. However, with the shift to the Popular Front line in 1935, which significantly tempered feminist rhetoric, an actual increase in female membership and female organizational power took place. Because many women headed the unemployed councils in their neighborhoods and organized support for the "mothers of Spain," women's Party membership rose significantly during the late 1930s to reach almost 40 percent; but their orientation emphasized economic and anti-fascist, not feminist, programs. Thus, while the Party never really stressed feminist programs during the 1930s, the early years of the decade had seen a surge of demands resonant with feminist goals; by the end of the decade, despite an increase in women's participation, the Party's rhetoric curtailed any radically feminist language.

Many of the women authors associated with the Party maintained a keen feminist critique in their writing, despite changes in Party line. Meridel Le Sueur's literary project included an attempt to feminize proletarian fiction with stories about forced sterilization, prostitution, pregnancy in jail, rape, unemployed women, and women's militancy. Myra Page's novels and reportage focused on the connections between "white chauvinism" and "male supremacy." The sophisticated world of bohemian and radical culture was unmasked in the fiction of Tess Slesinger and

---

*The final verse of Woodie Guthrie's "Union Maid" (New York: Ludlow Music, 1961) provides a concise example of this tendency from the 1930s:

You gals who want to be free,
just take a little tip from me:
Get you a man who's a union man
and join the Ladies Auxiliary;
Married life ain't hard
when you've got a union card,
A union man has a happy life
when he's got a union wife.

Words and music by Woody Guthrie. © Copyright 1961, 1963. Ludlow Music, Inc., New York. Used by permission.

Josephine Herbst and in *We Too Are Drifting,* Gale Wilhelm's novel about the lesbian bohemia of San Francisco. Poems entitled "Lines for an Abortionist's Office," "This Body Politic," and "Babies Are Luxuries" linked the devastation of the Depression to women's problematic relationship to the medical establishment and the restrictions on their sexuality. Thus, women's response to literary radicalism included the complicated factors of history, economics, and new aesthetic positions influencing men's writings, but gender and sexuality informed women's revolutionary writing as well.

THE LATE 1930s: THE POPULAR FRONT AND THE CELEBRATION OF MOTHERHOOD

Although Kenneth Burke was widely criticized at the 1935 American Writers' Congress for suggesting that "people," rather than "worker," better described the audience and subject of literary radicalism, his speech actually prophesied the changing rhetoric of the Popular Front.[40] The new rightward shift tempered the urgency to develop a proletarian aesthetic and culture to usher in "Soviet America." Instead, a new emphasis on populist traditions resurrected heroes of America's past and stressed continuity with its history. Earl Browder's 1936 assurance that "Communism is twentieth-century Americanism" signaled to those wavering liberals that an alliance with the Party against fascism would not threaten their middle-class identification. At the same time, Spain fired the imagination of literary radicals, and the reverence formerly accorded workers was given to the Loyalists fighting the first battle against fascism. Such changes in Communist political doctrine were invariably translated into aesthetic and critical terms for leftist authors. The Party disbanded the John Reed Clubs responsible for promoting proletarian culture; they were replaced by the League of American Writers, whose membership was made up of established liberal authors, rather than the left-wing and working-class writers who had been nourished by the John Reed Clubs. What was gained in flattening out party line to attract a broader spectrum of intellectuals to the Left was lost in the dissipation of voices from among the younger working-class writers who retreated into "silences" after the John Reed Clubs were disbanded.[41]

As early as 1933, writers had been soft-stepping around the issues of Stalinist tactics. For instance, in *Red Virtue: Human Relationships in the New Russia,* Ella Winter comments on the practice Soviet parents had of naming their children after revolutionary heroes or phrases, such as Spartacus or Diamata. She notes coyly "an amusing illustration of changing conditions in the USSR . . . the child whose parents enthusiastically named him Lentrozin. Trotsky is one of the worst renegades and now

Zinoviev has been exiled. Only the first syllable of the boy's name is good Communism now."[42] This breezy dismissal of brutal political struggles did not reflect the feelings of all Communists; many agonized over shifts in line. However, most of the literary radicals associated with the Party accepted the inconsistencies because of a sense of allegiance to the USSR as the only socialist nation and active opponent of fascism, and because Marxism still provided some valid theories for understanding capitalism, even if its practical application could at times be found wanting.

The Popular Front sought to make the Party more benign by an emphasis on American traditions; however, its emergence at a time when more sinister events were occurring within the Soviet Union masked some of the horrors of Soviet domestic and foreign policy. Two crucial dramas were being played out in Spain and Moscow that tested the allegiance of intellectuals to the Party. For a time, the Spanish Civil War appeared to be the successful proving ground for the Popular Front. The Loyalists, consisting of a broad coalition of Socialists, Anarcho-Syndicalists, Communists, separatists, and liberals, embodied the alliances that would make the Popular Front strong. Despite the fact that the Soviet Union was the only nation to provide the Loyalists with arms and supplies, however, information was leaking out through various journalists that the Party was preventing a social revolution in Spain because the USSR feared that such a revolution would alienate the support of liberal, bourgeois nations.

At the same time that intellectuals were being courted in America, they were being tried for treason in the Soviet Union, as the Moscow Trials continued to provide a vehicle for Stalin's consolidation of power. The information coming from witnesses questioned the image of the Soviet Union as the future of political culture for those same intellectuals adhering to the Popular Front. Trotskyists, dissident communists, and anarchists were being jailed, executed, and assassinated by Communists in Spain and in Siberia, and anyone supporting them was denounced as a "renegade."[43] For some intellectuals, disillusioned with the Party's inconsistencies and brutalities, Trotskyism was emerging as a leftist alternative to the Party's rigid insistence on the inseparability of literary practice and Soviet policy. *Partisan Review,* once the journal of the New York John Reed Club, became, under the editorship of Philip Rahv and William Phillips, the literary expression of this divergent tendency.

Despite grave political, ideological, and aesthetic differences between the Trotskyist and Stalinist literary radicals, one similarity prevailed within their changing aesthetic positions. For both groups, the male intellectual (either as a representative of an American populist tradition, for the Popular Frontists; or as estranged political and social critic, for the *Partisan Review* group) had replaced the worker as the emblem of literary radicalism. The proletarian cultural ideal placed the militant worker as chief architect of the new culture. The Popular Front replaced the image of the class-conscious worker with an ongoing American tradition of rebellion. Tom Paine, Walt Whitman, and Ernest Hemingway were united in a panorama of "the people," all of whom, it might be noted, are male and white. While the Trotskyist literati disparaged this folksy image of the intellectual, they elevated the male modernist to cultural arbiter.

With the abandonment of proletarianism after the Party shifted line, a critique of male supremacy within and without the Party, minimal as it was during the Third Period, gave way to a celebration of motherhood during the Popular Front era. As the Party sought to fit itself into mainstream American culture, it adopted images of wholesome family life that conformed to stereotypes of Mom and apple pie. This meant that the open discussions of working-class sexuality, limited as they were by the gender prescriptions of Rahv and Gold, became politically suspect. In 1936, one male reader wrote to the editors of the *New Masses* complaining that proletarian novels were "centered around smutty vulgar sex stories" that one could not read "without becoming disgusted with the gaudy sex descriptions."[44] Ironically, the metaphors of gender that had prescribed proletarian literature as masculine had, nevertheless, employed a rhetoric borrowed from feminist and Freudian sources. Thus, women's literary radicalism had used the openings provided by proletarianism to address sexuality and gender as well as class and race. By the middle of the decade, however, the conservative party line regarding gender and sexuality had tempered much of the critical rhetoric, reducing the use of sexual and gender metaphors which, offensive on one level, had been liberating nevertheless.

As early as 1934, in a satirical piece published in the *Modern Quarterly,* Lauren Gilfillan claimed that "when Woman is a Communist today she has been driven to it by her Motherly Instincts."[45] By 1939, Ruth McKenney's story "Rehearsal for May Day" appeared in the *New Masses*.[46] It follows a family preparing to attend a May Day parade. The mother readies her children for the demonstration as though they were on the way to church; her behavior hints that the family who marches in May together, stays together. The implication that woman is a natural Communist because of her ability to mother children informed much of Meridel Le Sueur's work. In a 1941 article she wrote: "Women who have never read a book understand it [antiwar and anti-fascism work]. It is written in the book of flesh."[47] In 1937, La Pasionaria (Dolores Ibarruri, one of the leaders of the Spanish Communist Party) appealed to the "mothers and women in America" to aid the Spanish Loyalists "because you must understand all the better what our struggle symbolizes."[48] This appeal for support pleads that the war in Spain is really a fight for the children.

By claiming that women's maternity determines women's political responses, the Party was subscribing again to a regressive notion of gender. The metaphors of gender first used by the proletarian critics had described the bourgeoisie as feminine, implying that only the virility of the working class possessed sufficient strength to fight capitalism. The ideology of the Popular Front tempered this somewhat; however, it produced a sentimental portrait of motherhood as a natural well for political consciousness. The implications for women were identical: gender was fixed through biology; male sexuality or maternity determined one's political and literary efficacy.

Despite this glorification of motherhood, a role that had earlier been seen as a burden for working-class women, Mary Inman wrote a long piece of Marxist feminist theory, *In Women's Defense* (1939), arguing that housewives constitute the "pivot of the system" to be destroyed: capitalism. Because the family reproduces laborers by raising children, and housework, as unpaid labor, aids an employer by producing emotionally stable workers, Inman declares housework to be productive labor. She analyzes how capitalism contributes to "manufacturing femininity" because female dependence benefits both the economic system and individual men. She is careful to differentiate the oppressions experienced by working-class and middle-class women; yet she is sensitive to the constrictions that gender places on all women's lives. Rather than castigate the middle-class woman as a parasite of a parasite, she understands the precarious privileges that class position determine for the middle-class woman who must remain within the restrictions of bourgeois femininity. Asserting that the "double standard is fascism in the bedroom," Inman describes how female sexuality is curbed when bourgeois male protection is needed to safeguard middle-class women from working-class male rapaciousness. The double standard becomes "the code of a class . . . on which to hang a whole contemptuous philosophy of women." For this challenge to the CPUSA's ready acceptance of traditional femininity, Inman was taken to task by the Party leadership.[49]

The year 1939 proved a crucible for many leftist intellectuals as the Stalin-Hitler pact negated much of the previous five years of cultural and political work. The League of American Writers was paralyzed over how to react to the Stalin-Hitler pact. Several prominent figures, such as Granville Hicks, left the Party; others who remained were so stunned that they withdrew politically and intellectually.[50] With the war in Europe already in progress, and America's entrance an inevitability, the images that had sparked the revolutionary literature of the early years in the decade—hunger, unemployment, working-class struggle—became increasingly blurred. Nevertheless, two of the most important novels by female literary radicals—Josephine Herbst's *Rope of Gold* and Meridel Le Sueur's *The Girl*—were completed in 1939, suggesting, again, that women writers maintained a different perspective than many of their male contemporaries. Both novels are set during the 1930s and openly confront such controversial topics as the Party's attitude toward women, intellectuals, and aesthetics. *Rope of Gold* charts the development of an intellectual woman into a committed journalist. It received some fine reviews, but languished in part because Herbst's publisher refused to reissue her two previous novels to form a trilogy, as she originally intended. *The Girl* follows the growing class and gender consciousness of a young waitress; it remained unpublished until the 1970s because publishers rejected it, saying it lacked authenticity. Thus, these significant female voices were barely heard amid the crashing tide of world war.

Although the Communist Party played a dominant role in the movement of literary radicalism during the 1930s, its control was not monolithic. Because of its small membership, its sectarianism toward other left-wing groups, and its alterations of political doctrine throughout the decade, the Communist Left remained a small subculture within the American social, political, and cultural milieux of the 1930s. Various factors—including the nature of artistic creation, the developing anti-Stalinist Left's influence among intellectuals, the diverging styles of revolutionary writing, and the reverberations of feminism—mitigated the presence of the Party in the lives and work of many revolutionary women writers. Nevertheless, literary radicalism provided a liberated zone for many women even though much of their work was criticized or ignored by their male counterparts in the movement. Perhaps this very exclusion was itself liberating, freeing women authors to experiment with genre, to outline a revolutionary literature that would speak with a feminine voice.

Thus, a contradictory relationship developed for the female authors who were engaged in the project of creating a revolutionary aesthetic. As women, they were separated from the sources that were to feed the revolutionary writer: if they were working class, it was unlikely that they had been industrial workers and therefore were not among the workers participating in the organization of militant industrial unions. Furthermore, their lack of education cut them off from dominant literary history. If they were intellectuals, their class position alienated them from the workers, even if their education better enabled them to create literature. In sum, neither literary radicalism nor literary history could fully accommodate radical female voices. Yet the variety of writings by women, a sampling of which is collected here, indicates that despite literary and political repression, women wrote in new forms that addressed class, gender, sexuality, and race as the complex background to the female experience in America.

NOTES

1. William Z. Foster, *Toward Soviet America* (New York: International Publishers, 1932).

2. Milton Meltzer, *Violins and Shovels: The WPA Arts Projects* (New York: Delacorte Press, 1976), photo caption following p. 20.

3. Meridel Le Sueur, "Women on the Breadlines," *New Masses* 7 (January 1932): 5–6.

4. Harvey Swados, ed., *The American Writer and The Great Depression* (Indianapolis: Bobbs-Merrill, 1966), includes four women authors out of a sampling of thirty-five. Jack Salzman and Barry Wallenstein, eds., *Years of Protest* (New York: Pegasus, 1967), includes nine women out of sixty. Joseph North, ed., *New Masses: An Anthology of the Rebel Thirties* (New York: International Publishers, 1969), includes selections by six women out of fifty-eight authors. Jack Conroy and Curt Johnson, eds., *Writers in Revolt: The Anvil Anthology* (New York and Westport, Conn.: Lawrence Hill, 1973), has selections by six women out of a total of fifty-one authors. Jack Salzman and Leo Zanderer, eds., *Social Poetry of the 1930s: A Selection* (New York: Burt Franklin and Co., 1978), has work by three women out of the twenty-four authors included. See Tillie Olsen, "One Out of Twelve: Writers Who Are Women in Our Century," *Silences* (New York: Delacorte Press, 1978), pp. 22–46.

5. Granville Hicks, et al., eds. *Proletarian Literature in the United States* (International Publishers, 1935).

6. Josephine Herbst, quoted in *Proletarian Writers of the Thirties,* ed. David Madden (Carbondale: Southern Illinois University Press, 1968), p. xxi.

7. An exception is Jean Bethke Elshtain, "The New Feminist Scholars," *Salmagundi* 70–71 (Spring–Summer 1986):3, who resists this categorization.

8. "The woman question" was the Party's shorthand for any issue relating to sexuality, feminism, women, or the family. See *The Woman Question* (New York: International Publishers, 1951).

9. See Cora Kaplan, "Pandora's Box: Subjectivity, Class and Sexuality in Socialist-Feminist Criticism," *Making a Difference: Feminist Literary Criticism,* ed. Gayle Greene and Coppélia Kahn (London: Methuen, 1985), pp. 146–176; Judith Newton and Deborah Rosenfelt, "Toward a Materialist-Feminist Criticism," *Feminist Criticism and Social Change* (New York and London: Methuen, 1985), pp. xx–xxxix; Lillian S. Robinson, *Sex, Class and Culture* (Bloomington: Indiana University Press, 1978), provided one of the first suggestions that class needed to be investigated alongside of gender if feminist criticism were to be effective. See also *All the Women Are White, All the Blacks Are Men, But Some of Us Are Brave,* ed. Gloria T. Hull, Patricia Bell Scott, and Barbara Smith (Old Westbury, N.Y.: The Feminist Press, 1982), pp. 43–44.

10. Michael Gold, "Go Left, Young Writers!" *New Masses* 4 (January 1929): 3–4.

11. V. F. Calverton, "Leftward Ho!" *Modern Quarterly* 6 (Summer 1932); 26–32.

12. Gold, "Go Left," p. 4.

13. Philip Rahv, "An Open Letter to Young Writers," *Rebel Poet* (September 1932): n.p.

14. Michael Gold, "Papa Anvil and Mother Partisan," *New Masses* 18 (February 18, 1936): 22.

15. Ibid., p. 3.

16. Agnes Smedley, *Daughter of Earth* (New York: Coward-McCann, 1929).

17. Walt Carmon, *"Daughter of Earth," New Masses* 6 (October 1930): 17–18.

18. Gold, "Go Left," p. 4.

19. *New Masses* 13 (October 2, 1934): 40.

20. Whittaker Chambers, "Editorial Note," *New Masses* 7 (January 1932): 7.

21. Josephine Johnson, *Jordanstown* (New York: Simon and Schuster, 1937), pp. 99–100.

22. Deborah Rosenfelt, "From the Thirties: Tillie Olsen and the Radical Tradition," *Feminist Studies* 7 (Fall 1981): 370–406.

23. Simon Eddy, "Ballad of a Slightly Addled Cultural Worker on the United Front," *New Masses* 23 (June 8, 1937): 19.

24. Meridel Le Sueur, "The Fetish of Being Outside," *New Masses* 14 (February 26, 1935): 22.

25. Quoted in Elinor Langer, *Josephine Herbst: The Story She Could Never Tell* (Boston: Little, Brown & Co., 1984), p. 120.

26. Quoted in Elaine Hedges, "Introduction" to Meridel Le Sueur, *Ripening* (Old Westbury, N.Y.: The Feminist Press, 1982), p. 14.

27. Peggy Dennis, *The Autobiography of an American Communist* (Westport, Conn.: Lawrence Hill, 1977), p. 294.

28. Quoted in Vivian Gornick, *The Romance of American Communism* (New York: Basic Books, 1977), p.134.

29. *Party Organizer* 1 (January 1932): 26–27.

30. "Sex class" was a term periodically used by socialist-feminists to connect a category understood by Marxists—class—to one understood by feminists—sex.

31. *Working Woman* 5 (November 1934): 34, 15.

32. Jane Benton and a Group of Workers, "Stockyard Stella," *Working Woman* 6 (January–April 1935): 4–5, 5–6, 45.

33. A section from the Soviet novel *Cement* appeared in *Working Woman* 4 (August 1933): 4–12. See Ann Barton, "Our Readers' Forum," *New Masses* 14 (January 1, 1935): 35.

34. Rebecca Pitts, "Women and Communism," *New Masses* 14 (February 19, 1935): 14–18.

35. *Working Woman* 5 (September 1934): 13.

36. Alan Calmer, "The Proletarian Short Story," *New Masses* 15 (July 2, 1935): 17–18; Ann Weedon, "Our Readers' Forum," *New Masses* 15 (July 16, 1935): 22.

37. Rebecca Pitts, "Women and the *New Masses*," *New Masses* 21 (December 1, 1936): 15.

38. Elsa Jane Dixler, "The Woman Question: Women and the American Communist Party, 1929–1941" (Ph.D. diss., Yale University, 1974).

39. Robert Shaffer, "Women and the Communist Party, U.S.A., 1930–1940," *Socialist Review* 9 (May–June 1979): 73–118.

40. Kenneth Burke, "Revolutionary Symbolism in America," in *American Writers' Congress,* ed. Henry Hart (New York: International Publishers, 1935), pp. 87–94.

41. See Tillie Olsen, *Silences* (New York: Delacorte Press/Seymour Lawrence, 1978), p. 143. Others would also include Henry Roth and, to some extent, Richard Wright.

42. Ella Winter, *Red Virtue: Human Relationships in the New Russia* (London: Gollacz, 1933), p. 148.

43. Mike Gold, "Notes on the Cultural Front," *New Masses* 25 (December 7, 1937): 2.

44. Don West, "Our Readers' Forum," *New Masses* 19 (May 19, 1936): 22.

45. Lauren Gilfillan, "Why Women Really Might As Well Be Communists As Not," *Modern Monthly* 8 (February 1935): 747.

46. Ruth McKenney, "Rehearsal for May Day," *New Masses* 31 (May 2, 1939): 9–10.

47. Meridel Le Sueur, "The Damned Crick's Rose," *New Masses* 38 (February 18, 1941): 38.

48. Gina Medem, "A Message from La Pasionaria," *New Masses* 24 (September 7, 1937): 20.

49. Mary Inman, *In Women's Defense* (Los Angeles: Committee to Organize the Advancement of Women, 1940), pp. 136, 48, 94, 95. Inman's piece was originally serialized in the *People's World*. Within a few months, Al Landry launched an attack in *Political Affairs* on the theory that housework was productive labor. Ruth McKenney took up his argument in the *New Masses,* rebutting Harrison George's assertion that housework was productive labor. See Dixler, "The Woman Question," for details of the debate. See also Jayne Loader, "Women in the Left, 1906–1941: A Bibliography of Primary Resources," The University of Michigan *Papers in Women's Studies* 2 (September 1975): 57–59.

50. See Dennis, *The Autobiography of an American Communist,* pp. 133–148, for one account of how a loyal Communist who was Jewish reconciled herself to the Stalin-Hitler pact.

I. FICTION

Writing Red: Women's Short Fiction of the 1930s

PAULA RABINOWITZ

When Michael Gold, editor of the *New Masses,* admonished young writers to "go Left!" he was calling for a new aesthetic as well as a new politics in literature. Gold asked his readers to "write . . . your life," re-creating the experiences of the "mine, mill and farm" in novels, poems, and plays.[1] This editorial was a more urgent call to put into practice Gold's prescriptives for "proletarian art" first outlined by him in the early 1920s.[2] Proletarian realism was to create "cinema in words" through "swift action" with "a social theme" that described the labor process "with technical precision." In as few words as possible, proletarian realism conveyed the "revolutionary élan," not the "drabness" of workers' lives, with "honesty" and without resorting to "melodrama."[3] However, debate raged throughout the pages of various left literary journals about the aesthetics and politics of "proletarian culture."

Critics and theorists of literary radicalism generally agreed the form most suitable to articulating a proletarian revolutionary culture was reportage. Capturing the immediacy of struggle and the consciousness of commitment for the reader, that curious form of engaged journalism best represented the aims of the movement. When it came to the other genres of writing, however, wide disparities emerged. E. A. Schachner argued that because of the oral traditions associated with each, poetry and drama best expressed the desires of a revolutionary culture.[4] Granville Hicks had implicitly argued for the primacy of the novel by outlining a typology of the revolutionary novel.[5] William Phillips and Philip Rahv tended to agree with him on this point. They argued that the novel was still a new and pliable form, unlike poetry and drama, both of which had a long history and tradition that, by the twentieth century, made them too elitist.[6] In any case, the short story, a genre of importance in American literary history during the nineteenth century (and reemerging today in significance) was rarely considered worthy of critical attention. Apparently if a short prose piece needed to be written, the dictates of literary radicalism pointed to reportage; otherwise the novel was needed to flesh out the contradictory character of Depression America. Still, the pages of the various journals devoted to the culture and politics of the Left were filled with short pieces of fiction, including some excerpts from the "collective novels" typical of 1930s radical fiction.[7] It is primarily from among those numerous, now utterly obscure, journals that the following selections were chosen.

Despite the overwhelming male dominance of the apparatus of literary radicalism—the editors of its journals, and the members of John Reed Clubs and the League of American Writers—a great many women published short pieces like the ones included in this volume. Short stories, poems, and reportage seemed unobtrusive within the pages of theory promulgated by male writers. When women were allowed to write theory, it was often about gender-related issues which relegated it to a secondary status. For instance, during its brief publication history, *Blast,* a magazine of proletarian fiction, edited for a time by William Carlos Williams, never printed a story by a woman. Presumably its editors took to heart Michael Gold's, Phillip Rahv's, and the other literary radicals' prescriptions for a masculine proletarian writing. On the other hand, in *Crisis,* the journal of the NAACP, edited by W. E. B. DuBois, most of the fiction and much of the poetry printed within its pages were written by women. The masthead flagged only male names, however, and the important theoretical and analytical pieces were reserved for male writers of stature. Again, women's creative writing seemed to hold a secondary place within the journal. A similar situation obtained at *Partisan Review* and *New Masses,* the two primary journals of Left politics and culture published under the auspices (for a time at least) of the CPUSA. Occasionally, a woman appeared on the masthead; toward the end of the 1930s Ruth McKenney and Joy Davidman were contributing editors of *New Masses,* and Mary McCarthy was theater reviewer and an editor at *Partisan Review.* (This is long after it had split from the CPUSA and was advocating an anti-Stalinist Left position.) However, Davidman reviewed books; McCarthy reviewed theater; and only McKenney achieved some status as labor reporter and theorist in addition to writing fiction.

Still, women's work could be found in the pages of these two journals, and a substantial number of the selections collected here are from those important journals. Surprisingly, in the journals published in cooperation with the John Reed Clubs from chapters outside New York—like the *New Force* from Detroit's John Reed Club—women were often editors and thus responsible for writing criticism and analysis, as well as publishing imaginative works. It is among these pages that we found a number of lost women's voices. These writers had been used by the John Reed Clubs as editors ostensibly to nurture the budding proletarian literary movement, but perhaps further to marginalize them as outsiders to proletarian culture.[8]

As late as 1968, Josephine Herbst declined an invitation to provide a contribution to David Madden's collection of critical essays, *Proletarian Writers of the Thirties*. Believing that the definitions of proletarian literature constricted the range of aesthetic and political issues important to 1930s writers, Herbst reminded Madden that the writing she called "vehicles for protest and engines for change" had addressed the "revolution in language, as in sex," as much as the politically volatile struggles by the working class for industrial unionism and against fascism.[9] For Herbst, as for many other women authors calling themselves literary radicals, the legacies of feminism, Freud, and modernist experimentation circulating within the culture of Greenwich Village during the 1920s supplemented their desire to write with the urgency that the issues of the 1930s demanded. These multiple influences sent women's revolutionary writing on a different path from the one blazed out by Michael Gold and the other theorists.

Actually, nobody could fulfill Gold's requirements for "proletarian realism." Even his own novel was criticized by E. A. Schachner, another Party literary critic, as too "romantic." But for the women authors, painting the portrait of the valiant male workers struggling against vampirish bosses meant repressing their own experiences in their writings. Women's literary voices had arisen into a full choir during the preceding two decades. The rise of modernism was as indebted to Virginia Woolf and Gertrude Stein, among many others, as it was to Ezra Pound and James Joyce. Yet women, too, were having their eyes refocused from internal struggles to those developing on the streets. In fact, the first truly proletarian novel, published in 1929, was Agnes Smedley's *Daughter of Earth*.

Women authors, along with their male colleagues, wanted to venture into the "mills, mines and farms" in search of the material out of which to fashion a new literature that would elaborate not only the psychological experiences of the individual but the social structures of class relations. But because authenticity of voice was valued so highly within the 1930s aesthetic of socially conscious literature, women's stories often did not penetrate the walls of the factory or descend to the depths of the mines. Women's writings—both fictional and nonfictional—often focused on the home life of the working class, taking apart the sexual division of labor in the family as it focused on the wives, mothers, and daughters of male workers. For example, Leane Zugsmith's "Room in the World" sensitively portrays the special pains that wives of unemployed workers took to shield their children from their husband's sometimes violent frustration. Meridel Le Sueur's "Sequel to Love" follows a young working-class woman's thoughts about her enforced sterilization resulting from an unwanted pregnancy. Lucille Boehm displays the ways poverty constricts the desires of a black teenaged girl so that she cannot escape a sense of guilt for her brief pleasure. Marita Bonner's powerful portrait of urban poverty in "The Whipping" focuses on the potential for tragedy locked within racial and class oppression and enacted, as in Le Sueur's story, by the state relief organizations.

Women were rarely employed in industrial or skilled trades work during the 1930s. With unemployment over 25 percent, many companies developed a policy of refusing to hire women (or of firing those already employed) on the grounds that they were taking jobs away from men. Women's labor power was restricted to the unorganized fields of domestic and service work or, if they were white and middle class, sales and office work, none of which held the ideological sway of the male-dominated jobs in steel, rubber, and automobiles. Thus, many of the stories by women focus on other sites of labor. Ramona Lowe's "The Woman in the Window" investigates the class, race, and gender divisions within a restaurant by delving into the degradations that Mrs. Jackson, a cook, must endure to keep her job; Tess Slesinger reveals the varying class and sexual strata within a small New York office in "The Mouse-Trap."

The shift in focus from interior to external reality sent writers across America and throughout the world recording the eruptions of class warfare. For women authors, in particular, this mobility expanded their literary horizons to include portraits of revolutions in China, Cuba, Germany, the Soviet Union, as well as every region of the United States. The selections in this section begin in China with a portrait of "Shan-fei, Communist," by Agnes Smedley and circle the globe to a hotel room in Havana in Josephine Herbst's "The Enemy." The rest of the stories track across the United States from New York to St. Paul to Chicago, detailing the devastation of the Depression on the lives of women and their families.

Stories that appeared in the *New Masses, Partisan Review, The Magazine, The Anvil, Crisis,* or any of the other numerous journals devoted to promoting the new aesthetic of revolutionary literature were often written as short didactic pieces. Many were based on true incidents, because the primacy of fact, the urge to document history, best exemplified by the exciting new form of reportage, informed fiction also. It is sometimes difficult to tell where the truth leaves off and the fiction begins. For instance, "Sequel to Love" represents Meridel Le Sueur's attempt to capture the speech patterns of working-class women whose stories she recorded while living in the Worker's Alliance in St. Paul. Similarly, Smedley lived and wrote in China between 1928 and 1941, traveling with the Red Army and producing some of the most influential reportage about the revolutionary struggle there. "Shan-fei, Communist" was one of Smedley's attempts to turn her knowledge of many Chinese women's lives into fiction. In the style of the great Chinese writer of the 1930s, Lu Hsun, she narrates, using an understated, reportorial tone, the history of social forces shaping the consciousness of a revolutionary. "The Enemy" by Josephine Herbst, a traditional, Western, well-crafted story, represents one of a number of fictional accounts of Herbst's own experience as a reporter for the *New Masses* on assignment in Cuba. It investigates the predicament of a middle-class journalist whose political sentiments are clearly aligned with the revolutionary movement in Cuba, but whose retrograde emotional ties to her estranged husband betray her political fervor. Emotional turmoil threatens to interfere with Mrs. Sidney's ability to react to the events taking place in Havana; yet her political commitment helps her overcome her personal pain.

If Mrs. Sidney in "The Enemy" is ambivalent about her dual position as committed leftist and rejected wife, and thus appears to be the extreme opposite of Shan-fei, the narrator of Eleanor Clark's "Hurry, Hurry" appears happily unaware of the impending social upheaval. "Hurry, Hurry" presents a parable of the decay of bourgeois culture in America. Through the eyes of its narrator, we see that the fall of middle-class culture destroys the wealth, but not the illusions, of the rich. Just as Elizabeth Thomas used the metaphor of the house in "Our House" to display the inequities of race relations in America, Clark presents the structure of capitalism as a house whose rafters, foundations, walls, and ceilings crumble slowly before the eyes of its owner. The festive atmosphere that develops as neighbors gather to watch the destruction hints at the myopia of the middle class, who, like Nero, will fiddle while Rome burns or, to use Josephine Herbst's metaphor, will "perish" in the "swamp" because they cannot see themselves for what they are—parasites whose fortunes depend upon the crippled lives of the workers.[10]

The form of the parable was fairly uncommon among 1930s writers, who were often overtly moralistic about bourgeois insensitivity. But a satiric approach to bourgeois hypocrisy made an acceptable counterpoint to the heroic portraits of working-class lives called for by Gold. The excerpt from Ruth McKenney's *Industrial Valley* juxtaposes the slow degradation of unemployment with the absurd folly of civic boosterism. Using the collage style pioneered by John Dos Passos in his classic proletarian trilogy, *U.S.A.*, McKenney sets in motion a dialectic between the two classes within the environs of Akron by writing the story of a place rather than a character. Akron's bourgeoisie manifest their quirky foibles through datelined "news items," while the workers are allowed a deeper humanity through realist narrative technique. This disparity reveals the class, social, and sexual divisions that underpin the community and burst out of the official pronouncements of the bourgeois press and elsewhere. This work again points to the blurred distinctions between factual and fictional writing within literary radicalism. The book is catalogued as nonfiction because its presentation—the portraits and clippings—appears to be a document of the Rubber Workers' Union sit-down strike of 1936 rather than a "true *story* of what happened to Akron, Ohio, from 1932–1936," as McKenney called the work.[11]

Black women authors were rarely concerned with industrial unionism since, for the most part, neither black men nor black women constituted more than a small minority of these workers. Instead, black women's stories deal with themes of racial prejudice, sexual inequality, and class differentials within the black community, and between blacks and whites. With the rise of pan-Africanism within the Marcus Garvey movement and the excitement generated by the Harlem renaissance during the 1920s, black nationalism had given a new sense of community to black artists. Traditional forms and themes from Afro-American literary history took on new meaning in the political context of the 1930s—for example, the theme of the tragic mulatto, prevalent in much Afro-American literature, now appears in a new dimension. In "Deepening Dusk," she is brought back into the black community through her love of her mother and desire for her lover, both of whom are dark-complected, and the consequent rejection of her white father. Because black women were so precariously positioned within the Depression economy, their imperative desire was to maintain their families. This concern becomes central to many of the stories by black women authors that appeared in the journals *Crisis* and *Opportunity,* the two leading black journals of politics and culture. In "The Woman in the Window," an ironic rewriting of Fannie Hurst's 1933 novel, *Imitation of Life,* a woman endures humiliation to keep her job, while teaching her children to fight for their self-respect. Another ironic treatment of the history of racial and class divisions appears in "Our House." The issues of racial stratification, economic privation, sexual desire, and women's relationships become intertwined in Lucille Boehm's story "Two-Bit Piece" and in Marita Bonner's "The Whipping."

The writings by women involved with 1930s literary radicalism often elaborated the complex relationship they felt between gender and class by connecting the expressions of female sexuality to women's political consciousness. The importance of sexuality to women's literature had clearly emerged during the first three decades of the twentieth century. Within the context of modernist investigations of interiority, Virginia Woolf, Gertrude Stein, and Nella Larsen, among others, explored the relationship of gender to perception and expression. Authors more concerned with social issues, such as Charlotte Teller, a socialist writer, equated women's sexual freedom with the end of bourgeois domination. While Walter Rideout— one of the few literary historians to recognize the importance of women's contribution to the genre of the "radical novel"—argues that by the 1930s women writers were not as concerned with expressing sexual identity, the selections that follow indicate that for a woman to "write red," she needed to focus her attention on sex and gender as well as on class and race.

Female sexuality, whether expressed as sexual relations, marital relations, maternity, love, or desire, marks many of the stories collected here. Because the family (or heterosexuality) came to stand for class relations in much fiction by women, the alienation women experienced from their sexual desire due to the sexual division of labor in the family often mirrored class relations within American society. Within the classic work of literary radicalism, the proletarian novel, some instance of extreme hardship at the work site—a mining disaster, an industrial accident, a plant closure—precedes the events leading to the strike. In the variations included here, the tensions that produce consciousness are often located within the spaces of the family or of heterosexuality. Thus, Shan-fei becomes a revolutionary leader in part as a reaction to her bondage under patriarchy. The narrator of "Sequel to Love" feels she is being denied the only source of power and pleasure by the relief agency that threatens to sterilize her. Vivvie's "deepening dusk," her growing consciousness of herself as a black woman, is precipitated by her sexual attraction to Tim. As she fantasizes about her estranged husband sleeping with his new lover, Mrs. Sidney's pain gives way to her desire to avenge the death of a strike leader. But, as "the enemy," women's retrograde emotional ties to men can stymie their revolutionary zeal. Thus, sexuality and political consciousness are linked in confusing, often contradictory, ways within many of the stories.

Perhaps the most fascinating example of the connection between bourgeois class ideology and its sexual consequences for women occurs in Tess Slesinger's "The Mouse-Trap." Here, Miss Betty Carlisle, an executive secretary in a small advertising firm, trades class solidarity for sexual privilege, only to discover that the two—class and sex—cannot be easily separated for women workers. Slesinger investigates office politics through each character's reaction to the "strike." Sexual desire, economic need, and political ideology interact in a complicated way that simultaneously unites the workers yet divides them from each other and from the boss. Betty Carlisle fails to judge accurately her class position within "the mouse-trap," the hierarchy of the office. Once she has succumbed to her boss's sexual advances, she is abruptly returned to her place among "the mice" by his offer of payment. Because of the intimacy that characterizes the boss/secretary relationship and the setting of the small business office in which men and women are stratified into rigidly gender-defined jobs, this story presents a different plot pattern than the classic proletarian narrative.

And Slesinger's audience is somewhat differently conceived than that of many of the other stories. "The Mouse-Trap" first appeared in the collection *Time: The Present,* which consisted of stories Slesinger had published in *Vanity Fair, Redbook, Scribner's Story,* and *American Mercury.* These journals appealed to the New York intellectual crowd rather than to the workers and farmers populating America who were supposed to be the mythical audience for the proletarian stories in other journals of the Left. The droll tone of the narrator stands in contrast to the narrative voice present in Leane Zugsmith's "Room in the World," which appeared in her collection of short stories published in 1938, *Home Is Where You Hang Your Childhood and Other Stories.* That volume included stories from both established literary journals, such as *The New Yorker,* and magazines devoted to literary radicalism, such as *The Magazine.* Here, the author uses the effects of privation on a young girl's fantasies to examine the impact of unemployment on a working-class family. It appears to be a classic example of proletarian fiction; yet the story drifts toward melodrama, offering little promise of change, perhaps conveying the despair that marked the final years of the decade.

In fact, many of the stories written toward the end of the decade reflect a weary pessimism about the possibilities for change. Marita Bonner's chilling story captures the growing frustrations among blacks in discovering that the northern cities were not necessarily the meccas they had appeared to be from the perspective of Southern racism. Bonner charts the effects of the Depression on the black community of Chicago with a keen eye. Her powerful stories, including "The Whipping," influenced other black writers, notably Richard Wright, to pursue the complex effects of urban disintegration and racial tensions on individual characters. Similarly, "Two-Bit Piece" and "The Woman in the Window," both published in *Opportunity,* belie the optimism of that journal's title. They, too, tend toward melodrama, as little room can be found for black women in either the white world or the black family. Likewise, despite Edward's realization that the Burden house is also his at the end of "Our House," there is not much expectation that the rigidly maintained divisions between the two sets of families will break down; racism and class divisions are as solid as the house that Edward built. Even when the house collapses, as in "Hurry, Hurry," the future remains grimly marked by death and futility.

This is a marked shift from the tone of early 1930s stories, like "Shan-fei" or "Deepening Dusk," which see a more positive future developing out of the suffering experienced, in these instances, by Shan-fei and Vivvie. The stories from the middle years are the most striking examples of a more complicated relationship among oppression, repression, and liberation. The possibilities of escaping the prison of working-class womanhood seem remote in both Slesinger's and Le Sueur's stories.

While the stories present a wide range of styles, forms, themes, and concerns, certain common elements link them. Although Smedley's piece is an anomaly, inscribing a foreignness in form and content, it paints the mother as a central figure in Shan-fei's developing feminist and revolutionary consciousness. The theme of the importance of motherhood to the development of class consciousness is reiterated in various ways throughout most of the stories included here. Whether mothers facilitate class or racial consciousness, as they do for Shan-fei and Mrs. Jackson's children, or merely smooth over tensions within the working-class family, as Pauline does in "Room in the World," they are an essential force in women's radical fiction of the 1930s. Maternity can be severely twisted under capitalism. The state may forcibly deny its possibility to women who are judged "unfit," as in "Sequel to Love," or may so corrupt a mother through bureaucratic red tape that she is made "unfit," as in "The Whipping." Motherhood may open women to pain and humiliation, as greedy bosses murder their children (as in "The Enemy") or cause them embarrassment (as in "The Woman in the Window"). Finally, bourgeois culture may so corrupt the family that the mother, as in "Hurry, Hurry," is more concerned with her furniture and her dog than with human life. However, for the bourgeois woman, like Mrs. Sidney, who can use her class position to aid her radical politics, maternity appears linked to revolutionary action; Mrs. Sidney overcomes her alienation by invoking the image of the suffering mother of the slain Cuban youth.

The thematic elaboration of maternity and motherhood is but one difference between men's and women's radical fiction of the 1930s. The concerns about class divisions, the alienating effect of capitalism, and the hypocrisy and corruption of the bourgeoisie were themes common among all literary radicals. However, the inclusion of gender consciousness and sexual expression as constitutive of the female experience for both working- and middle-class women was uniquely a result of women's somewhat attenuated relationship to literary radicalism. Thus, the shifts between interior consciousness and external reality within the stories points to the worldwide class-conscious struggle that was developing during the 1930s, but may also be a metaphor for female alienation from the Left. In their attention to women's speech, desire, and labor, women writers exposed and expressed the connections between language, class, gender, race, and sexuality as significant themes of the 1930s imagination. When they mapped out the landscape of revolutionary fiction, the "head-boys" had missed vital areas—the bedroom, the office, the restaurant or kitchen—where women lived and worked.[12]

Out of the hundreds of stories by women included in the dozens of magazines published by various factions of the literary Left throughout the 1930s, the twelve stories included here mirror the range of concerns that were important to women writing short fiction.[13] While they represent none of the most didactic examples of proletarian short fiction, such as "Stockyard Stella," these stories effectively convey the contradictory flavor of 1930s fiction: simultaneously innovative and reactionary in form and content.

Le Sueur, McKenney, and Zugsmith all wrote classic proletarian novels during the 1930s. Their stories follow Smedley's (who in many ways represents the mother of women's literary radicalism) as examples of stories that focus on working-class experience and consciousness through attention to speech and internal monologue as well as to the outward indications of working-class deprivations. The five stories by black authors all come from the two most important journals of the black Left, *Crisis* and *Opportunity*—whose names indicate the dual poles between which black women oscillated during the Depression. Finally, the last three stories point to the engagement between modernism and Marxism that characterized the anti-Stalinist Left centered on *Partisan Review:* Clark's and Herbst's stories appeared there (though Herbst was still affiliated loosely with the CPUSA, she was often a vocal critic of its literary and political positions), and Slesinger was connected politically and intellectually with its editors. These stories—longer, more complex, and more concerned with stylistic and formal experimentation than the more typically realist forms of the preceding stories—point to the variations within radical women's short fiction, confirming that the risky odyssey into the social world of class conflict necessitated a simultaneous disruption of literary conventions, even those unconventional conventions of 1930s literary radicalism.

Many of these authors were born at the beginning of the twentieth century, came of age during the bohemian 1920s, imbibing its modernist sensibilities, and matured both politically and artistically during the Great Depression. In a sense their writing and their lives reflect the political and literary currents of the years between the wars and, as such, stand as emblems for women's contradictory positions in American literary history and in American radicalism during the 1930s.

NOTES

1. Michael Gold, "Go Left, Young Writers!" *New Masses* 4 (January 1929): 3.
2. Irwin Granich [Michael Gold], "Towards Proletarian Art," *Liberator* 4 (February 1921): 20–24.
3. Michael Gold, "Editor's Notes," *New Masses* (1930). Reprinted in Michael Fulsom, ed., *Michael Gold: A Literary Anthology* (New York: International Publishers, 1972), pp. 203–206.
4. E. A. Schachner, "Revolutionary Literature in the United States Today," *Windsor Quarterly* 2 (Spring 1934): 27–64.
5. Granville Hicks, in a series of essays entitled "Revolution and the Novel"

New Masses 11 (April 3–May 22, 1934), outlined an elaborate typology of the new novel.

6. Philip Rahv and William Phillips [Wallace Phelps], "Recent Problems of Revolutionary Literature," in *Proletarian Literature in the United States,* ed. Granville Hicks et al. (New York: International Publishers, 1935), pp. 369–376.

7. The term is one designated by Granville Hicks in his series "Revolution and the Novel." Some examples include "The Iron Throat," which became the first chapter of Tillie Olsen's *Yonnondio* (originally published in *Partisan Review*); "Missis Flinders," which became the last chapter of Tess Slesinger's *The Unpossessed* (originally in her collection *Time: The Present*); and "They Follow Us Girls," which was slightly revised in Meridel Le Sueur's *The Girl* (and originally appeared in the *Anvil*).

8. Richard Wright believed race to be the reason the Chicago John Reed Club chose him to edit *Left Front*. See Richard Wright, *American Hunger* (New York: Harper & Row, 1977), p. 63.

9. Quoted in David Madden, ed., *Proletarian Writers of the Thirties* (Carbondale: Southern Illinois University Press, 1968), pp. xix–xx.

10. Josephine Herbst, "Author's Field Day," *New Masses* 12 (July 3, 1934): 22.

11. Quoted in Harvey Swados, ed., *The American Writer and the Great Depression* (Indianapolis: Bobbs-Merrill Company, 1966), p. 382 (emphasis mine).

12. While I did not undertake a detailed count of the ratio of women's stories to men's in the various radical literary journals, I would guess that Tillie Olsen's calculation of "one out of twelve" is too low. While these twelve stories represent about one out of twelve stories by women, they represent perhaps a third of all short stories written under the rubric of literary radicalism. Thus, work by Katharine Anne Porter, for instance, would not be included in this calculation since its form and content fall outside the parameters of *Writing Red*.

13. Josephine Herbst characterized the male literary radicals as such in a letter to David Madden, quoted by Madden in the anthology he edited, *Proletarian Writers of the Thirties*, p. xxi.

AGNES SMEDLEY

Shan-fei, Communist

This is the story of Shan-fei, daughter of a rich land-owner of Hunan, China. Once she went to school and wore silk dresses and had a fountain-pen. But then she became a Communist and married a peasant leader. In the years that followed she—but I will begin from the beginning—

Her mother is the beginning. A strange woman. She was old-fashioned, had bound feet, and appeared to bow her head to every wish of her husband who held by all that was old and feudal. Yet she must have been rebellious. She watched her sons grow up, go to school, and return with new ideas. Some of these ideas were about women—women with natural feet, who studied as did men, who married only when and whom they wished. When her sons talked, the mother would sit listening, her eyes on her little daughter, Shan-fei, kicking in her cradle. And long thoughts came to her. What those thoughts were we do not know—but we know that at least she died for the freedom of her daughter.

This battle was waged behind the high stone walls that surround many a rich Chinese landlord's home. The enemy was her husband and his brothers. And the mother's weapons were the ancient weapons of subjected women—tears, entreaties, intrigue, cunning. At first she won but one point—her husband consented to Shan-fei's education—provided the teacher was an old-fashioned man who came to the home and taught only the Chinese characters. But Shan-fei's feet must be bound in accordance with ancient custom, and she must be betrothed in marriage according to ancient custom. So the child's feet were bound, and she was betrothed to the weakling son of a rich neighbor, a corrupt old man with many concubines.

Until Shan-fei was eleven years of age, her father ruled as tyrants rule. But then he suddenly died. Perhaps it was a natural death, and perhaps Shan-fei's mother wept sincere tears. Yet the funeral was not finished before the bandages were taken off the feet of the little girl, and the earth on the grave was still damp when Shan-fei was put in a modern school one hundred *li* away.

But even though the bandages were removed, the little feet had already been crippled by five years of binding, and the half-dead, useless toes remained, bent under the feet like stones, to handicap the girl throughout her life.

Anyway, the bandages were gone, and with them the symbol of one form of enslavement. There remained the betrothal to the rich man's son. Such betrothals in China are legally binding, and parents who break them can be summoned to court and heavily punished just as if they had committed a dangerous crime. Shan-fei's mother, however, seemed to have tendencies that the feudal-minded ones called criminal. For she was suspected of plotting and intriguing to break the engagement. Worse still, it was rumored that she did not advise Shan-fei to be obedient as girls should be, but that she encouraged her to be free and rebellious. This rumor spread like fire when the news came that Shan-fei had led a students' strike against the corrupt administration of her school. She was nearing sixteen at the time, the proper age for marriage. Yet she was expelled in disgrace from the school, and returned home with her head high and proud. And her mother, instead of subduing her, whispered with her alone, and then merely transferred her to a larger and still more modern school in faraway Wuchang on the Yangtze, where rumor further had it that she was becoming notorious as a leader in the students' movements. Furthermore, men and women students studied together!

Things became so bad that at last the rich landlord filed a legal suit against Shan-fei's mother, and summoned her to court, charged with plotting to prevent the marriage. But the old lady defended herself most cunningly, and even convinced the court that all she desired was a postponement of the marriage for another two years. She convinced the judge—but not the landlord. And, as was the custom, he called to his aid the armed gentry of the countryside; and when Shan-fei returned home from her vacation that year, they made an attempt to capture her by force. They failed and Shan-fei escaped and remained in Wuchang for another year. When she returned home again, her capture was again attempted. With the aid of her mother, she again escaped, hid in the homes of peasants, and returned by devious ways to Wuchang, never to return again. When she reached Wuchang, however, the news of her mother's death had preceded her. Perhaps the death was also natural—perhaps not. Shan-fei says it was—that her mother died from the misery of the long-drawn-out struggle and family feud. "She died for my sake," she says, and in her manner is no trace of tearful sentimentality, but only a proud inspiration.

Shan-fei's school comrades tried to prevent her from returning home for the funeral. But this was more than the death of a mother—it was the death of a pioneer for woman's freedom. And Shan-fei, being young and unafraid and a bit proud that she had escaped the old forces twice, thought she could defeat them again. Lest anything did happen, she laid plans with her school comrades in the Students Union that they should look for her and help her escape if she did not return to Wuchang within a certain period.

The body of the old mother had scarcely been laid to rest when Shan-fei's ancestral home was surrounded by armed men and she was violently captured and taken to her father-in-law's home, where she was imprisoned in the bridal suite and left to come to her senses. She did not come to her senses, but instead, starved for one week. Her hunger strike was broken only by another woman rebel within this landlord's family. This woman was the first wife of the landlord, whom the Chinese call "Mother" to distinguish her from his concubines. This old lady watched and listened to this strange, rebellious, rich girl, around whom a battle had been waged for years, and also used the ancient wiles of a woman to gain the girl's freedom. This freedom, granted by the landlord, meant only the right to move about within the home and the compound, but did not extend beyond the high surrounding walls. In China, however, few or no secrets can be kept, and news travels on the wind. Perhaps that is how one girl and two men students from Wuchang happened to come to the neighborhood and bribed a servant to carry messages to Shan-fei. Anyway, one late evening Shan-fei mounted the wall by some means and disappeared into the dusk on the other side. That night she and her friends rode by starlight toward Wuchang.

This was the late summer of 1926, and China was swept by winds of revolution. Soon the southern armies lay siege to Wuchang. And Shan-fei gave up her studies and went to the masses. She became a member of the Communist Youth, and in this work she met a peasant leader whom she loved and who was loved by the peasants. She defied the old customs that bound her by law to the rich landlord's son, and announced her free marriage to the man she loved. And from that day down to the present moment, her life has been as deeply elemental as are the struggles of mother earth. She has lived the life of the poorest peasant worker, dressed as they dress, eaten as they eat, worked as they work, and has faced death with them on many a battlefront. Even while bearing her unborn child within her womb, she threw all her boundless energy into the revolution, and when her child was born, she took it on her back and continued her work. In those days, the Kuomintang and the Communist Parties still worked together, and as one of the most active woman revolutionaries, Shan-fei was sent back to her ancestral home as head of the Woman's Department of the Kuomintang. There she was further made a member of the Revolutionary Tribunal that tried the enemies of the revolution and that confiscated the lands of the rich landlords and distributed them among the poor peasants. She helped confiscate all the lands of her own family and the family of her former fiancé.

When the revolution became a social revolution, the Communists and the Kuomintang split, and the dread White Terror began, claiming tens of thousands of revolting peasants and workers. The militarists and the feudal landlords returned to power. Shan-fei's family and the family of her fiancé asked the Kuomintang for her arrest. And this order was issued. It meant death for herself and her child. Two women and three men who worked with her were captured, the women's breasts were cut off, and all five were beheaded in the streets. But the workers bored air-holes in a coffin, placed Shan-fei and her baby inside, and carried them through the heavily guarded gates of the city out into the graveyard beyond the walls. And from there she began her journey to Wuchang. Once she was captured because her short hair betrayed her as a revolutionary; but with her baby in her arms, she pleaded her innocence, and was released.

She reached the Wuhan cities only to be ordered by the Communist Party to return to the thick of the fight in western Hunan during the harvest struggle when the peasants armed themselves, refused to pay rent or taxes, and began the confiscation of the lands of the landlords. Shan-fei was with them during the days; at night she slept in the forests on the hills, about her the restless bodies of those who dared risk no night in their homes. Then troops were sent against them. The peasants were defeated, thousands slain, and the others disarmed. Again Shan-fei returned to Wuhan. But again she was sent back in the thick of the struggle. This time, however, she went, presumably as a Kuomintang member, to a city held by the militarists. Beyond the city walls were peasant armies. Inside, Shan-fei worked openly as the head of the Woman's Department of the Kuomintang; secretly, she carried on propaganda amongst the troops and the workers. Then in this city the chief of the Judicial Department met her and fell in love with her. He was a rich militarist, but she listened carefully to his love-making and did not forget to ask him about the plans to crush the peasants. He told her—and she sent the news to the peasant army beyond. And one of the leaders in this army beyond was her husband. At last the peasants attacked the city. And inside, so bold had Shan-fei become in her propaganda amongst the troops, that she was arrested, imprisoned, and condemned to death. She sent for the official who was in love with her. He listened to her denials, he believed them, released her, and enabled her to leave the city. But the peasant army was defeated and amongst those who emerged alive was her husband, who at last found her in Wuhan.

Shan-fei was next put in charge of technical work of the Party, setting type and printing. She would lay her child on the table by her side and croon to it as she worked. Then one day her home was raided by soldiers.

Her husband was away and she had stepped out for a few minutes only. From afar she saw the soldiers guarding her house. Hours later she crept back to find her child. The soldiers had thrown it in a pail of water and left it to die. Not all the tender care of herself and her husband could hold the little thing to life. Shan-fei's husband dried her bitter tears with his face—and Shan-fei turned to her work again.

Some things happen strangely. And one day this happened to Shan-fei: she went to visit the principal of the school where she had once been a student, and decided to remain for the night. With the early dawn the next morning, she was awakened by many shouting voices. She imagined she heard her husband's voice amongst them. She sat up and listened and heard distinctly the shouts: "We die for the sake of Communism! Long live the Revolution!" Her friend covered her ears with a pillow and exclaimed: "Each day they bring Communists here to shoot or behead them—they are using that big space as an execution ground!" A series of volleys rang out, and the shouting voices were silenced. Shan-fei arose and blindly made her way to the execution grounds. The soldiers were marching away and only a small crowd of onlookers stood staring stupidly at the long row of dead bodies. Shan-fei stumbled down the line—and turned. over the warm body of her dead husband.

The net of the White Terror closed in on Shan-fei until she was ordered to leave Wuhan. She went from city to city on the Yangtze, working in factories, organizing women and children. Never could she keep a position for long, because her crippled feet made it impossible for her to stand at a machine for twelve or fourteen hours a day. In the summer of 1929 she was again fighting with the peasants in Hunan. Sent into Changsha, one day, she was captured, together with the two men Communists, one a peasant leader. She sat in prison for six months, and was released then only because some new militarists overthrew the old, and in revenge freed many prisoners. But they did not free the peasant leader. Shan-fei bribed a prison guard and was permitted to see him before she left. About his neck, his waist, his ankles and his wrists, are iron bands, and these are connected with iron chains. The life of such prisoners in China is said to be two years. Shan-fei herself was not chained. But she emerged from prison with a skin disease, with stomach trouble, and with an abscess, and she was a pasty white from anemia. In this condition she returned to the peasantry and took up her fight. And in the spring of 1930 she was sent as a peasant delegate to the All-China Soviet Congress. Friends afterwards put her in a hospital and she was operated on for the abscess. During this period she kept the translation of Marxian studies under her pillow, and she once remarked: "Now I have time to study *theory*."

There are those who will ask: "Is Shan-fei young and beautiful?"

Shan-fei is twenty-five years of age. Her skin is dark and her face broad; her cheekbones are high. Her eyes are as black as midnight, but they glisten and seem to see through a darkness that is darker than the midnight in China. She is squarely built like a peasant and it seems that it would be very difficult to push her off the earth—so elemental is she, so firmly rooted to the earth. Beautiful? I do not know—is the earth beautiful?

MERIDEL Le SUEUR

Sequel to Love

I am in the place where they keep the feeble-minded at Faribault. This place is full of girls moanen' and moanen' all night so I can't get no sleep in to speak of.

They won't let me out of here if I don't get sterilized. I been cryin' for about three weeks. I'd rather stay here in this hole with the cracked ones than have that done to me that's a sin and a crime. I can't be sleepin' hardly ever any night yet I'd stay right here than have that sin done to me because then I won't be in any pleasure with a man and that's all the pleasure I ever had. Workers ain't supposed to have any pleasure and now they're takin' that away because it ain't supposed to be doin' anybody any good and they're afraid I'll have another baby.

I had one baby and I named her Margaret after myself because I was the only one had her. I had her at the Salvation Army home.

Pete and me had her but Pete never married me. He was always at the library after he lost his job.

Pete said he had a place on a farm. I guess he had a farm then and he said he would take me out there and give me red cheeks and we would have a cute kid.

I been workin' in the five and ten since I was twelve because I was big and full for my age. Before the New Deal we got eight dollars dependin' on if a girl was an old girl or a new one and extra girls got $6.25 a week for fifty-four hours work, but if you only worked fifty hours you got thirteen cents an hour. I hear from my girl friends it's different now and they cut down the girls a lot and a girl there now has got to do the work of two. That's what I hear. I ain't worked there now for a year and a half.

Peter used to meet me after work on Seventh there, and we used to go to a show or walkin' or to the park, and he used to tell me these things. He was a good talker and I guess he meant it. He never made the depression, although you'd think it the way people talk about him.

Gee, the baby Pete and me had was pretty! Red cheeks and kind of curly hair. I would like to of kept her right good. I hated havin' her and was sure

I was going to die off, but after I seen her I would have liked to of kept her good.

When I had her I was missen' all the shows in town and I was mad. They had to strap me down to nurse her and I had to stay there so long that I was even missen' them when they come to the fifteen centers and after that you have to go a long ways out to see them.

But where I got mixed up with the charities was about havin' this baby. One month I missed and got nervous and went to a doctor and he wouldn't do nothin' because I didn't have no money. I went to three like that, and then one give me some pills and I took one and it made my ears ring so I was afraid to take any more. I cried for about two days but I didn't take no more pills.

I went to another doctor and he told me I was goin' to have a baby and I come out and went up to a corner of the hall and began to cry right there with everybody goin' by and a crowd come around. I thought you got to be quiet or you'll get arrested now so I was quiet and went on downstairs but I was shakin' and the sweat was comin' off me.

My girl friend tooken me home with her and told me I better go on and have it because to get rid of it would cost about one hundred dollars.

My father is a garbage collector and he wouldn't be ever makin' that much.

I swan that summer I don't know where I was goin' all the time. I kept lookin' in all the parks for him because I thought he was goin' to skip town and when I see him he hollered at me that he didn't have no money to skip.

I went to the clinic and they told me to eat lots of oranges and milk for my baby. My girl friend didn't have no work and her and me went out lookin' for food all the time because she kept tellin' me I had to eat for two now.

I kept lookin' and lookin' for Pete and lookin' for somethin' to eat. When I could see Pete seems like I could rest. I would follow him to the library and sit in the park until he come out and I would feel alright.

We kept lookin' for food. We walked miles and miles askin' at restaurants for food. I got an awful hankerin' for spice cakes. Seems like I would putnear die without spice cakes. Sometimes we would walk clean over town lookin' and lookin' for spice cakes.

I thought I was goin' to die when I had my baby . . . I was took to the Salvation Home and had it there but I didn't like it none there and they had to strap me down to make me nurse the baby. Seems like there is a law a mother's got to nurse her baby.

I wanted to keep the baby but they wouldn't let me. My dad wanted to keep it, even, and my sister's got twelve kids and she wanted it. Even then it was such a cute kid. Kind of curly hair. But they rented it out to a woman and now they got me here.

My dad spent about fifty dollars with lawyers to keep me out but it ain't no good. They got me here until I have that operation.

I got a letter from Pete and he says you got no business to be there; you ain't dumb. Miss Smith that comes here to talk me into havin' an operation says I like men too much, that they can't let me get out at all.

I like men. I ain't got any other pleasure but with men. I never had none. I got to lay here every night, listenin' to the moanen' and thinkin' are they crazy, and my dad keeps saying to have it done it will be alright, that I won't get old or anything too soon. It ain't a natural thing that it should be done to a young girl.

I might know a man sometime with a job and getting along pretty, and why shouldn't I have a baby if it was alright so the Salvation Army wouldn't take care of me or anything and I wouldn't bother them? Like before, which wasn't our fault because I believe what Pete said to me about the farm and all.

We had a cute kid, an awful bright kid, Miss Smith says it sure is a cute kid, an awful bright kid alright.

They keep sayin' I like men but why shouldn't I like men, why shouldn't a girl like a man? But for us girls that work for our livin' we ain't got no right to it and I was gettin' seven dollars at the five and ten and that seems to be all I got a right to, my measly seven dollars, and they're firin' girls all the time now so I wouldn't get that back, even.

They don't want us to have nothin'.

Now they want to sterilize us so we won't have that.

They do it all the time and the police follow a girl around and the police women follow you around to see if you're doin' anything and then they nab you up and give you a lot of tests and send you here and do this to you.

They don't want us to have nothin', alright.

Pete and me sure had a cute kid, but we'll never see it any more.

Now I'm locked up here with the feeble-minded.

RUTH McKENNEY

From *Industrial Valley*

PARADE

January 2, 1932

The unemployed of Akron paraded today. Early Saturday morning a rumor swept the crowded streets of East and South Akron. The story spread from one soot-blackened frame house to another: The Mayor will be handing out jobs at City Hall today for his new work relief program.

Job Hendrick still lay in heavy sleep when his wife brought him the news. His gaunt face with the high cheekbones was collapsed and empty on the naked mattress. There were no pillows on the bed. Missus Hendrick had sold the pillows three weeks ago.

"Job," Missus Hendrick roared. "Hey, Job, get up."

Job Hendrick let go of his sleep reluctantly. He groaned.

Missus Hendrick repeated gently, "Get up, old man. The Mayor is handin' out jobs."

Now he heard. He sat up yawning. His cotton underwear stretched across his broad chest as he sucked in the air and stretched.

"Gimme that overcoat," Missus Hendrick began briskly. "I'll try and give it a press, so's you'll look halfway decent—not like a bum."

Mister Hendrick scooped up the overcoat from the bed. Missus Hendrick had sold the blankets two months ago.

"How do you know?" he said, holding the overcoat in his arms and looking up at his strong big wife.

"Missus Gettling said Missus Howry told her."

Mister Hendrick got on his feet. He grinned at his wife, and as she reached out for the coat, he swatted her one across the buttocks. She laughed.

Mister Hendrick's own grin wore off slowly. His face was still contorted with the smile while his mind went back to its familiar treadmill: the rubber shops laying off, and the kids needing food, and what had a man come to when he didn't have a pillow for his head or a blanket to cover him at night?

Missus Hendrick was ironing furiously when her old man came down the creaky steps. Clouds of steam rose from the ironing board and Missus Hendrick's face was red with heat and excitement. The two Hendrick kids sat solemnly watching.

Liz junior spotted her father first. She squealed and ran to the doorway, catching him by his big solid thighs. "Pa, will you buy me a sled like what I didn't get for Christmas if the Mayor gives you a job?"

"Will you shut up about that sled!" Missus Hendrick said furiously. "The answer is 'No,' we got more important things to buy if your Pa gets that job."

Mister Hendrick rubbed his hand over his daughter's reddish-blond hair.

"I made you a cup of coffee, Job," Missus Hendrick said in a soft tone, as though she were ashamed.

"Where'd you get that?" Mister Hendrick asked heavily.

"Where'd you think? I borrowed it." Irritation played in Missus Hendrick's voice again. Her husband trod carefully as he went to the kitchen stove for the coffeepot. Liz was a good wife, he reflected, but lately she was always flying off the handle, enough to drive a man crazy.

When Missus Hendrick got her husband into his freshly pressed overcoat, she went to the door with him. The kids stood around to have their Pa kiss them and pinch their cheeks, rather thin just now for pinching purposes. Then Missus Hendrick laughed and gave Mister Hendrick a hug.

"Good luck, old man," she said.

"Yeah."

Job Hendrick and Tom Gettling tramped up the street together. They told each other that probably this whole thing was just some crazy idea of the womenfolks.

Tom skirted two kids dragging a spindly old Christmas tree to the curb for the garbage collection. "But I guess," he mumbled, "it was in the paper."

Job gulped. Mister Gettling carefully examined the gray sky, overcast with streaks of black rubber smoke. It made him feel funny in the stomach to see tears in the eyes of Job Hendrick, who was the sweetest second baseman he knew, even after years in the shops, and about the best Number 12 tirebuilder in the business. Number 12 is a medium tire, but a mean one to get together.

"Jesus," Mister Gettling offered, "the smell is somethin' awful today."

Job was grateful. He sniffed with a great show of interest.

"Ain't no worse than usual."

Tom did not argue. The rubber smell was never any worse and never any better. Mister Gettling and Mister Hendrick were veterans of the rubber smell. For ten years they had eaten, and slept, and made love with the acrid rubber stench high in the nostril and deep in the throat. Still, after ten years, Mister Gettling and Mister Hendrick gagged in the mornings when they first awoke and started smelling rubber as they put on their pants. Nobody ever got used to the smell.

"Anyway, it won't stink in heaven." Mister Gettling hoped Mister Hendrick would smile at the ancient pleasantry.

Mister Hendrick did not smile. He shuffled past the rows of boxlike frame houses in silence. Tom tramped at his side, afraid to speak. They turned into Main Street.

Job Hendrick faced the main plant of The B. F. Goodrich Company. He knew the shape of every huge black iron gate. He knew the thickness of every thick brick wall. He could walk blindfolded among the smoke-blackened buildings and say which shop made Number 12 tires and which bleak six-story pile housed raw rubber. He knew how tall the three brick smokestacks stood to dominate the great expanse of dark brick and steel. He could pick his way like a careful cat among the maze of railroad tracks that ran among the buildings. Out of this solid square mile of gates and tracks and powerhouses, he could select the precise spot where the brown paper to cover the finished tires was cut to size. Job Hendrick had grown from a gawky mountain boy to a heavy solid man within those thick brick walls.

Job Hendrick knew the rubber shop. He knew it, and he hated it. The powerful black bulk, stretching up and down the street, and as far back as the eye could see, still, after all these years, made his heart heavy. He was afraid of it, really.

"Goddamned joint," Mister Hendrick muttered. "Looks like the West Virginia State Prison, only bigger."

Tom kicked at a cigar butt oozing out of the sidewalk slush. "Don't look like they're doin' much."

Job ran his practiced eye over the acres of dirty windows. He jerked his angular chin toward the three rows near the street which showed lights. "The truck tire is still up."

Mister Gettling sighed. "I heard they were only operatin' two shifts for a special order."

Job shuffled slowly up Main Street. He glanced into Joe's Hamburg Place, but he didn't see the two dicehounds shooting crap in the half dark, he didn't see Joe himself wiping shot glasses and passing the time of day with a former customer, now insolvent. He passed Dixie's Lunchroom, but he didn't spot Alec Browning, a Number 12 department man, trying to hit Miss Dixie up for some credit on a hamburg. Mister Hendrick was too sad to see anything but the black pile of buildings across the street.

"Rubber ain't the only business that's gone sour," Mister Gettling muttered.

Job eyed a pale dirty-faced whore who stood shivering in the narrow entrance of Pete's Hostelry, Men Only, Fifty Cents a Night, Private Room, $1.00. "Yeah."

Mister Hendrick and Mister Gettling tramped by Sunshine Drug Store noting through the mud-specked plateglass window that Old Doc was still doing a little business in tickets for the numbers game. The cold made him walk a little faster past a sign swinging in the wind, "Doctor for Men, Free Examination," past a thirty-cent lunchroom where a solitary customer was buying a bottle of under-the-counter needle beer.

When they could see the marble entrance to City Hall, Mister Gettling and Mister Hendrick hung back. They idled along staring at the bleak stone armory across the street, watching lawyers bustle up the sidewalk to the County Courthouse. They mounted the two shallow steps to City Hall. Mister Gettling swung open a heavy bronze-and-glass door and they stepped shyly into the dirty marble lobby.

Job spotted Joe Rummel standing in a little clump of men near the elevator doors. He brightened. "What's doin'?" He spoke as though he were in church.

"Dunno," Joe whispered. "I just got here. We're waitin'."

Mister Hendrick stood very quietly. Every few seconds the big bronze-and-glass door swung open and more men shuffled across the marble floor. After their first murmured questions they waited, also silent, their hands limp and meek in their pockets.

Mister Hendrick elbowed his way right to the elevator door. He needed to be first when the Mayor called for job applicants. The crowd kept pressing him. They, too, needed to be first when the Mayor started taking down names. Mister Hendrick felt the warmth of Mister Gettling's body. He could feel Joe Rummel's apologetic breath on his neck.

Mister Hendrick was nearly knocked down by the rush of air and the bang of bronze hitting steel when the elevator doors suddenly opened before him. Behind Job, three hundred men crowded forward wordlessly.

"Lay off the pushing," Mister Hendrick mumbled. He looked straight into the eyes of a tall pot-bellied police captain. The police captain ran a finger under his collar, where it squeezed against his Adam's apple. He swallowed. He felt like wetting his lips but he tried not to, because he wanted to seem easy and careless, as though he met mobs of hungry unemployed storming City Hall every day of his life.

Mister Hendrick believed that the police captain was going to select the first men from the crowd and take them up to the Mayor. Mister Hendrick opened his mouth. He tried to speak. He meant to say, "Take me. Pick me out, for the love of God. I'm a good man and I need the work. I got kids. Oh, Jesus Christ, take me."

But Mister Hendrick was so scared no sound came from his mouth. He heard the captain's heavy voice only faintly. He heard something dim and far away about registration Monday. A phrase rang in his ears, but it had a ghostly sound like the roar from an ocean shell, "The Mayor hereby orders you guys to clear out and to dis-perse."

Mister Hendrick heard, but at first he did not understand. Mister Gettling pulled at his sleeve. "Job, Job come on. We got to get out of here." Mister Gettling grabbed Mister Hendrick's arm. "Job." Mister Hendrick heard the shuffling sound of men's feet moving slowly and patiently across marble floors. He followed Mister Gettling out the bronze-and-glass door.

The heavy gray mass of men dissolved slowly. In murmuring groups, the unemployed plodded away from City Hall, shrunk into their coats against the cold and the shame. Mister Hendrick took his place in this parade.

LETHE

January 3, 1932

People who had forty cents for a ticket filed into Loew's, downtown on Main Street, the whole day Sunday to see Greta Garbo suffer all, even death, for love in a film called *Mata Hari*.

Under a ceiling featuring stars and the Milky Way, surrounded by Moorish minarets, real oil paintings, and plaster oversized Roman statues, the audience sat impassive, watching Miss Garbo, in the role of a European lady spy, find regeneration through the Grand Passion.

NEWS ITEMS

January 4, 1932

Ed S. Rose, a Goodyear company policeman, was elected President of City Council. He opened the first session with a hearty prayer.

The Summit County commissioners, in an extra session of the Board meeting at the County Courthouse, cut the budget again and wiped out the post of the County Humane Officer. The County Humane Officer had charge of orphans, old people, the blind, and the insane.

Mayor C. Nelson Sparks announced that after Wednesday all racketeers and bootleggers in town would be arrested.

William O'Neil, President of the General Tire and Rubber Company, one of the largest of the junior-sized rubber shops in Akron, made a speech to the Akron Real Estate Board.

"Come out of the gloom of the Depression," Mr. O'Neil said, "and bask in the sunlight for a change. It's time we did more boosting and boasting." He reminded his audience that Akron had long ago been officially dubbed the "City of Opportunity" by the Chamber of Commerce.

Building permits in Akron last year totaled $2,076,667, a drop from $9,000,000 reported at the end of 1931.

The *Beacon Journal* congratulated Summit County for its falling marriage license record. The annual report showed that during 1931 the number of marriage licenses dropped to the lowest level in the past fifteen years.

"There are altogether too many people in the world now to subsist upon the opportunities it affords," the *Beacon Journal* wrote firmly, "and the ignorant and the unfit, having scarcely any other interests in life, will multiply and replenish the earth until we shall not know what to do with them."

Akron pastors made plans today at the luncheon meeting of the Ministerial Association to share in the city-wide campaign against Depression gossip. After a good lunch of creamed hardboiled eggs on toast, ice cream, and homemade cake, the ministers, representing both the polite Congregational and Episcopalian churches and the workers' churches, like the free Methodists and the unorthodox Baptists, listened to Dr. Roy Sanborn of the Akron Rotary Club make a speech.

Dr. Sanborn explained that the Rotary Club believed a great deal of the current trouble around town was caused by idle and vicious rumors. He said he thought the ministers could help a great deal by joining the "war" against gossip.

After his speech, it was moved and seconded and carried unanimously to set aside a special anti-gossip Sunday in Akron churches. All the ministers went home turning over in their minds texts from the Bible that might be used to encourage men to stop talking about the Depression.

DEATH BY HIS OWN HAND

January 15, 1932

Gilbert Edgar, until yesterday a Vice-President of The First-Central Trust Company, Akron's only big bank, blew out his brains early this morning.

Mr. Edgar's death was an unexpected sacrifice to the cause of holding the big bank together through the dark days of the Depression. The men who had voted Mr. Edgar out of his job as Vice-President at the big marble bank got a nasty shock when they heard that poor old Gilbert had driven his car into a back road on the lonely hills of suburban Fairlawn and put a gun to his head. They hoped fervently that the suicide of an ex-Vice-President would not make depositors "lose confidence." First-Central could scarcely stand a run on the bank.

But the modest headlines in the papers did not disturb the 100,000 innocent rank-and-file depositors. The public could hardly know that First-Central, which represented a long series of bank mergers over the years, was now the classic house of cards, propped up by a huge R.F.C. loan and the grudging good will of the rubber companies.

Mr. Edgar, one of the many Vice-Presidents left over from the series of mergers, was thrown to the wolves to cut down operating costs at First-Central. The rest of the directors, Akron's leading businessmen, crossed their fingers and hoped that strict economy and a rise in real estate values would save the bank.

Mr. Edgar was Akron's first banker suicide.

THE SILVER BEAVER

January 15, 1932

Paul Litchfield, President of The Goodyear Tire and Rubber Company, the largest rubber company in the world, was made a Silver Beaver today at a special ceremony held by Akron Boy Scout troops. This honor came to Mr. Litchfield after fifteen years of devoted service to scouting.

LEANE ZUGSMITH

Room in the World

When she heard Ab's footsteps approaching the door, she knew, without having to see or to hear him, that it had been the same as yesterday and all the days before, since he had been fired from the job he had held as watchman for the office building. He couldn't do anything but talk about it all night long, and every day he went back trying to get to some one higher up who would tell the new superintendent: "Ab's been with us nine years, there ain't no reason to let him go." If she was him, Pauline thought, she'd give it up and if, like he said, there wasn't no job for him no place, she'd go on Relief. With a five-months-old baby and a three-year-old boy growing so fast that the Lord only knew how she was going to make this suit of his any bigger, and a girl of eight, already in the second grade, she'd give it up. But Ab was bullheaded, always had been, and maybe he'd get back, like he said.

As Ab came in, she hastened to close the door leading off the kitchen into the room where Jappy was taking his nap. Even when Ab raised his voice, it wouldn't wake the baby in the market basket near the stove. She was a dandy sleeper, better than Jappy, much better than Frances ever had been.

She thrust the needle into the material, waiting to see if Ab was going to speak first. If he kept on staring at her, it was up to her and it meant he was good and sore. After a while, she knew it was up to her.

"Either the clock's fast," she said in the casual, conversational tone she had lately learned to use, "or Frances must of been kept in."

Gloomily he stared at her.

"She done her homework, I know." Pauline turned Jappy's drawers inside out and studied the problem of enlarging them.

"I tried every God-damned one of them," he said between his teeth. "I seen all their chippy secretaries. They're all too God-damned busy to see me. I'm only working there *nine* years. Maybe that ain't long enough."

"No one can say you ain't tried," she said.

"Tried? I done everything but crawl along the corridors on my belly. It's 'see the super. It's up to the super.' Nuts!"

"Them real-estate people are over the super," she said sympathetically, and she thought: He won't give it up yet. No use telling him about the gas or how they wouldn't give her credit at the other grocery store she tried out.

"They won't even see me. You seen what they written me."

"It was a sin the old super had to die," she said.

"The new one will take me back," he said ominously. "I ain't saying how but I'm gonta get back on the job."

Hooding her anxious eyes as she watched him to read what was in his mind, she heard Frances at the door. She hurried to open it, her mind still on her husband's words. The kid was all excited about something, the way she got sometimes, dancing around the room. She sure was high-strung; good thing the baby didn't seem to take after her. Pauline was afraid she'd begin to bother her pa, but he didn't seem to take notice, banging his hand down on the kitchen table, crying out:

"I ain't going back crawling to them, neither, to get it!"

She cast a swift look at the baby to see if she had been disturbed by the noise. "Maybe—" Pauline began.

"Maybe, nothing! I'll be back on the job, wait and see."

Frances kept tugging at her arm. "*Ma,* I been telling you."

Ab glared at his daughter.

"We're talking now, Pa and me," Pauline said quickly.

"Only, Ma, let me tell about the new little girl, she come today. She's got curls just like Shirley Temple." Frances's voice went up high.

"Shut up!" said Ab.

"The new little girl, she looks just like Shirley Temple."

"Play in the other room." Her mother pinched her cheek. "Jappy's asleep in yours and his."

"No, I don't wanta. I wanta tell you about the new little girl, Ma, she's got red paint on her fingernails. Can't I have—"

Her mother interrupted her. "You're getting your Pa worked up, not minding." She reached for a tin pail. "Go on down and get me five cents' worth of milk, hear me. Tell him your Ma said she'd stop in and pay up tomorrow."

Ab breathed heavily after the little girl had left the room. Without looking up from her sewing, his wife said calmly: "She's only eight." And she thought: In a while, when we can't get no credit no place, there won't be that much spirit in any of them.

"I'm trying to think out what do do, and she comes in babbling till she gets me all mixed up."

"Try to think what you was thinking before."

"What do you think I'm trying to do?"

The tick of the clock sounded loud now. The baby's occasional soft snores could be heard. Pauline kept her head bent over her sewing until Ab spoke up.

"You know how they do when a lot of them go out on strike," he said.

"Well?"

"Like I read once in a newspaper, see, a fellow and his whole family, they go out with signs, asking for his job back."

Her face became thoughtful. "Like them pickets is what you mean?"

"You got me."

She ceased to sew. "I couldn't leave Frances take care of the baby."

"No. She'd let it smother or something." He looked down at his hands for a while. Presently he said: "I could take the two kids, see, all of us wearing signs asking for my job back."

"I could make the signs OK, if we had some kind of stiff paper," she said. "You wouldn't walk Jappy too long, would you, Ab? He don't stand much walking."

Ab stood up, his face lighted. "That would get them, all right, you bet! Maybe them newspaper guys will come around and take our pictures." He pulled a pencil from his vest pocket and smoothed the wrinkles from a brown paper bag.

"Maybe down at the corner, they'd give you some stiff paper," said Pauline.

He wet the pencil, leaning over the kitchen table, too elated to sit down. "Now, we'll say—" He wet the pencil once more. "What'll we say?"

"If the sign's for the kids it had oughta say something about 'my Pa' and so on."

"You got brains, Pauline," he said. " 'Please get my Pa back his job.' How's that?"

"OK."

"We'll make Jappy's and Frances's alike. Now mine." He wet the pencil. "What would you say?"

" 'Get me back my job at the Stark Building,' how about that?"

"No," he said. He started to print letters. "How's this? 'Fired for no reason after nine years being watchman at the Stark Building.' "

"That's OK," she said.

"OK? It's the nuts!" he cried out gleefully. "Wait till I see the faces of them birds who thinks they ain't gonta take me back!"

It was getting past the baby's feeding time; Pauline thanked her stars that she was so good she wouldn't start bawling right off. She couldn't pick her up with Jappy goose-stepping around, already dressed to go out, the sign flapping as he thrust each leg straight out before him, Frances trying to see how the sign looked on her before the little mirror over the dresser, and Ab yelling: "Let's go to town. Come on, you kids."

Jappy couldn't be held down. He kept singing: "I'm a picket, I'm a picket, I'm a picket," until they couldn't help laughing.

"Them signs are going to blow all around on them," Pauline said.

"Don't worry about them signs," Ab cried out. "Come on, you kids."

"I'm a picket," shouted Jappy. In a fit of wildness, he dug his forefinger into the top of his cap and began whirling around.

"You'll get dizzy. Stop it!" his mother called out.

Frances ran in. "I can't see what I look like, Ma," she complained.

Jappy started going round too fast and fell down.

"You bent the sign," his father said crossly, picking him up.

Jappy smiled when he saw that he didn't have to cry.

"It'll only take a minute." Pauline threaded a needle and began to sew the bottom corners of the sign on to Jappy's little coat. "I'll sew on yours, too," she told Frances.

"Lift me up, Pa, in by the looking-glass, so's I can see," Frances begged.

As Ab took her into the other room, Pauline said to her son with exasperation: "Keep still, will you!"

"I'm gonta be a picket," he screamed joyfully. "I'm gonta go up to them dopes—"

"Where did you learn that?" She bit off the thread.

"I'm gonta be a dope, I'm gonta be a picket."

Frances came back, saying sulkily: "I can't read what it says in the looking-glass."

"You know what it says. I told her." Ab followed her.

"What's mine say?" cried Jappy.

"It says 'Give my Pa back his job,'" said Frances, holding still while her mother sewed the bottom corners of her sign on to her jacket.

"Give my Pa back his job," Jappy chanted, starting once more to goose-step.

Ab grabbed his hand. "Come on. I ain't gonta wait another minute."

Picking up the baby, Pauline followed them to the door. As soon as she had closed it, she heard sounds of bawling outside. It was Jappy, all right. She opened the door. Ab called angrily to her from the stairs. "He wantsta take his Popeye doll along with him. He ain't gonta."

Jappy's cries were louder now that he knew his mother was listening. "Let him," she said. "It won't do no harm." Might do good, she thought, them seeing a little kid with a doll.

"I'll get it."

"Make it snappy," Ab called back.

She found the wooden figure from which all the paint had streaked.

Jappy was back at the door with Frances just behind. The little boy smirked. "Popeye the Sailor's gonta be a picket," he said.

"Hurry up!" Ab called out.

"Popeye wants a sign." Jappy held the doll up to his mother. "Make him a sign." His chin was beginning to tremble.

She snatched a fragment of paper from the table, scribbled on it and attached it precariously to the doll. "Hurry." She gave both children little pushes and then stood with her ear to the crack of the door where she could hear them talking as they went toward the stairs.

"Popeye's sign says 'Give my Pa back his job,'" said Jappy.

"It don't say nothing," said Frances. "It's only scribble."

"It do, too," he said.

Then their voices became fainter. She wished she could see the street from their windows to watch them walking away. Hope Ab don't forget he shouldn't keep them out too long. The baby began to whimper, and she patted its back as she unbuttoned her blouse. It don't do no good for me to skimp on eating, she thought, or I'll only take it away from the baby.

When they came back, Ab couldn't talk of anything but the expression on the new super's face and how people had stopped them and they almost had their pictures taken. As Pauline ripped the stitches off Jappy's sign, she noticed that he was almost asleep on his feet. When she started to rip the stitches off Frances's sign, she saw that her skinny legs were trembling. She looked up into the little girl's miserable face. "Why, what's the matter, honey?"

Before Frances could get out a word, she began to bawl. She bawled just like she did when she was a baby.

"What happened to her?" Pauline turned to Ab.

"I don't know." He was beginning to be gloomy again.

Pauline put her arms around Frances. "Tell Ma," she said.

Her breath catching, the tears streaming down the monkey face she was making, Frances said: "The new little girl seen me."

"A lot of people seen you," said Pauline. "That don't make no difference." She was trying to keep her voice steady.

Frances struggled out of her mother's reach. "The new little girl seen me," she got out between sobs and ran from the room.

"I try to get back my job," said Ab heavily, "and that's the thanks I get."

Before she spoke, she looked around for Jappy and, finding him asleep on the floor, she said, trying to pick her words:

"She got a crush on some little girl at school she says looks like Shirley Temple."

"That ain't gonta get my job back." Ab bent his head over the table where his sign and Jappy's lay.

Both of them could hear, through the closed door, Frances's frenzy of weeping.

Pauline swallowed. "Other people seeing her don't make no difference, on account of she's at the age, see what I mean?"

"No," he said, but his lowered voice had in it a curious strain.

"She's high-strung, Ab. To some other kid it mightn't mean nothing, only with her it might set her back, you know how kids are."

She waited for him to reply, watching him make marks on the back of his sign with his pencil. It was the truth, he might as well admit it. Other people didn't have to take out their kids with signs on them begging for their Pa's job. The weeping in the next room had subsided into long sighs and occasional hiccups.

Presently, without looking up, he said: "I shouldn't oughta take her tomorrow."

"Jappy likes it," Pauline said hopefully.

He made more marks on the back of the sign. Still without looking up, he said: "We could change the words tomorrow." He pushed the lettering toward her, keeping his eyes averted. The crooked printing read:

"Ain't there room in the world for us?"

Now it's gonta bust out, she thought. Only you can't let it go, not with the kid bawling in the other room and him so down in the mouth. She swallowed the thing in her throat. And, searching for it, she found the tone she had lately learned to use.

"It don't seem like 'ain't' is the right word there," she said in a casual, conversational voice.

EDITH MANUEL DURHAM

Deepening Dusk

If you were very bright, with silky hair instead of wool, pomaded and hot-combed dead straight, you had to be careful. You must never dare to laugh at the amusing fancies, bobbing so deliciously into your brain, else the grinning, frisking black girls, who found so much to giggle over, would freeze you out of the fun. They would get mad and accuse "Stuck on your color. Trying to be white." They would say you were laughing because they were black; they might even call you "White folk's nigger." Vivvie Benson had learned to be careful. She knew all this and thought it silly. White was nothing to be stuck on. Black wasn't funny.

Ma was black and wooly headed but didn't Vivvie love her? Love her? Why Ma was all the world! No one would dare to laugh at Ma. Out of nothing Ma made the prettiest clothes for Vivvie and twisted her hair into perfect curls; Ma kept the neatest house, had the earliest garden, hung out the whitest wash. Vivvie was proud of Ma, the strongest, smartest, best woman in the world. Vivvie loved her black.

There was Tim, so slick they called him "Shine." Vivvie never used that name though she loved it. "Shine" fitted Tim, fitted pat to his satin polished skin. Everything gleamed about Tim; his hair was not plastered like the rest of the boys', it was crisp live crinkles of blackness; his straight teeth flashed with glistening whiteness; he had eyes that sparkled, that danced when they looked at Vivvie, and changed to rolling fiery balls in a sea of white when other eyes danced at Vivvie.

No other girl so fair as Vivvie, no other boy so dark as Tim, yet Vivvie loved him, next to Ma. Girls younger than she had steady fellows but Ma said seventeen was much too early. Tim could not be her beau. He might only come now and again to sit and look at Vivvie while she chattered. Always Ma was close at hand. Kate Benson's eyes were keen for this only child. Tim often felt them, cutting under his skin.

This summer afternoon, in the spotless dining-room, Tim looked across the checkered cloth of the table, at the fragile blossom that was Vivvie, a creamy, tender bud in her cool green frock, tissue thin, still dainty and fresh after many launderings; Vivvie looked back at Tim, wholesome and strong, not minding his faded overalls and the tear in his chambray sleeves. She knew he would leave her for the heat of the foundry where he would sweat all night. For six years he had done the labor of a man. Vivvie was proud of the brawn of Tim.

Vivvie was retelling stories, the kind she delighted to read (the boy delighted in any tale that had her voice for the telling) of beautiful damsels, lovely princesses in distress and of gallant knights to the rescue. "Oh, Tim," she sighed, but happily, "if I might have lived back then and been a lovely damsel."

The boy answered the wish in a voice that had grown deep early and rumbled:

"If any fellow ever bothers you I'll knock the guts—" Tim bit the offending tongue into confusion for daring to spit out rough talk before Vivvie, "I mean the stuffin' out of him!" How else could he tell his princess he would die to be her knight? He had no words to speak his heart.

The girl flushed, in no other way would she let him know her ears had caught the ugly lapse, that she wanted him to knock the stuffings out of anyone who came between them. Vivvie loved the sparkles in his eyes, the glossed skin of his muscular arm, showing through the torn chambray sleeve, satin casing steel. It looked touchable, only girls did not touch boys, nor let boys touch them. Ma said so. That was what made dancing wicked, touching. A girl might get bad, and there would be a baby, the most wicked thing that could happen, unless you were married. Tim's mother was not married. Vivvie could not believe it wicked for Tim to be born. Not Tim. The soft cheeks grew warm and dark with color.

Fascinated by the unusual play of color in the girl's face, the boy watched, breathless, till the questioning dark fire of his eyes drew the dreaming gray of Vivvie's; one growing second Tim held her gaze, then long lashes curled downward, veiling the glory in. Once only, in a lifetime, has man a right to such a vision.

Her hand lay on the table against the red ground of the checked cloth, tiny, blossomlike. Tim stretched his calloused, great, dark hand beside it, marveled at the contrast. Vivvie forgot what Ma had taught. Her hand crept over the little space between them. "Tim," she whispered, shy, sweet.

"Tim."

Slowly his palm closed over her fingers, tightened.

"Vivvie, oh Vivvie!" Shoulders inclined forward, chins tilted, over the table their lips met.

"Vivvie!" Another voice was calling. Like guilty sinners they started, grew rigid in their chairs. "Time this boy was leaving if he means to hold his job." Ma followed the voice into the room. She glanced from one to the other casually, then keenly as she saw something new in the two faces. Tim had grown ashy, Vivvie deeply pink.

Slowly Vivvie recovered her voice, "Yes, Ma," she answered, and rose to get his cap. She did not look up as she placed it in his hand, but Vivvie felt Tim looking at her, caressing her with his smile. She was glad he was going, she wanted to tell Ma all about it, that she loved him. Next to Ma!

Kate Benson stood, watching, waiting. "I want to talk to Tim a bit. You go in the kitchen, Vivvie, and see if the kettle's boiling." An excuse to be rid of her, the door closed between them by Ma's firm hand. Vivvie pushed her curls far back behind her ears. She had to hear. When she heard she could not see. Impatiently she alternated eye and ear at the keyhole. This was her affair, not even Ma could shut her out of it.

Tim was twisting from toe to toe, awkward beneath Kate Benson's determined gaze.

"I couldn't speak before the child," Ma was saying, "but you are near grown and will understand. You like my baby, Tim?" The voice was soft and kind, but some undertone left Vivvie afraid. Her heart stopped for the boy's reply.

"Awf'ly," proud and ashamed was Tim, "worse than likin'," he added boldly.

"I thought as much, and I'm sorry, but you will get over it before you die, boy. I'm asking you now, don't come here any more." What ailed Ma, was she crazy? Why Tim had to come there, how else were they to see each other. "I want you and Vivvie not to see each other."

The applied eye saw Tim, writhing in wordless confusion. Vivvie longed to help him talk up to Ma, Ma who was spoiling every thing. "Why, Mis' Benson, why, I been coming'." No use looking, she had to hear.

"When Vivvie was a little girl; but things seem to be changing. I've been watching you cast sheepeyes at my little girl lately. I ain't going to have you fooling with her."

Tim stuttered miserably, "What you mean, Mis' Benson?"

"You old enough, twenty, ain't you? You understand me well enough. There's to be no fooling with my Vivvie!"

Tim was not stuttering now. Vivvie's heart leaped, he was angry, had found his voice at this sacrilege. He understood Ma now. "That's awful, Mis' Benson. Why Vivvie is good. She's good, I tell you. I wouldn't try. I want her always good. It's not fair, what you're thinkin'. Not Vivvie." Tim was talking up.

"And you don't get a chance. I ought to know my girl is good without your telling. I mean her to stay that way till she finds some man fitting to marry her. You never could."

"Why?" he dared. No answer, so he found his own. "You mean on account of Ma."

Vivvie saw the ashy agony in Tim's young face. Her heart was wrenched for him, and strangely for his mother. Terrible to have her son ashamed of her. Never, never, vowed the peeking Vivvie, shall a child of mine be shamed for me. But listen, Tim had something to say for her.

"Ma ain't really bad, folks are just down on her because she got the worst of it. Do you s'pose I could treat Vivvie like that—, I can't call him the right name before you, Mis' Benson, like that thing treated Ma?" That was it, it was his father he was ashamed of. Vivvie was glad; it was unthinkable to be ashamed of one's mother.

"I guess Vivvie is safer with me, on account of that, than some fellows with fathers. I wouldn't treat the worst girl like that. I couldn't fool Vivvie. She's good. She—, she's a queen to me." Oh, never could Vivvie have resisted that pleading voice, "please, Mis' Benson, let me come see her like always. I won't talk no love to her. I won't make up to her, till you say she's old enough. I—I won't even touch her hand. I gotta come, Mis' Benson, I gotta."

Ma could deny him. "No, Tim."

"But, Mis' Benson, you gotta be fair. How could I help my father? I ain't blamin' my mother none, not for nobody. I ain't bad."

Ma's voice was kindlier, though still there was rock behind it. "I am sorry, Tim. I'm not thinking you worse than the others. You may be better. Only I got higher plans for Vivvie. None of them are going to hang around her. There's lots think she is easy falling, but I mean to show all these folks how to raise a lady, even though her daddy was a white man."

Vivvie saw and heard no more. That last sentence had left her sick and sore with a great disgust. She did not hear when Tim was eased onto the porch and the door shut firmly behind him, alone in the dusk, but not in his misery. Vivvie was suffering, a pain she had never known before— shame! Shame. Her father a white man! She knew now why the black girls had shut her out, they thought she was trying to be white. Only the trashiest white men and the trashiest colored women—she tried to stop the trembling of her hands. They were hot, her face was burning with shame. Ma couldn't be wrong. She never had been. She stood there, burning and shaking, waiting for Ma, for Ma who must set things right.

Kate Benson started in surprise at the stern-eyed Vivvie waiting in the little kitchen for her, pouncing on her accusingly:

"I heard you, Ma, I heard you. I must know why you did it. I must."

The mother stared, never before had the child been rude. A good thing she had dismissed that boy, her baby was getting serious about him. They ripen so early, these children of the sun. Kate Benson hoped she had not waited overlong. Her attempt at amused laughter was shaky, "Why? Because you are only a baby, honey, just Ma's baby yet, sweethearting is for women, Vivvie. Ma has to guard you from the beaus yet awhile."

"Oh, that!" Vivvie waved Kate's words aside, "I am not talking about

Tim. It's you I am asking about, about you and my father. You have to tell, Ma."

What under heaven ailed the child? "Tell you what, girl?" What was she bawling about? "What is there to tell about your Pa? What is wrong? Answer me, Vivvie." But Vivvie was crying, crying. The mother's heart was shot with fear, the big fear that dims all others for the mothers of girls. If she had not watched close enough? If she had not been in time? Nothing like that could happen to her baby! "Tell me what ails you, girl," she bade, her voice made sharp with pain. "Answer, you hear me, mind your Ma."

"You never told me my father was a—a" (whisper) "a white man."

Relief, perplexity, it was not the great fear any longer. "What need? You ought to remember your Pa, and there hangs his picture in the room," her eyes rested on Vivvie, unbelievingly, "you mean you thought all this time your Pa was colored?"

"I thought he was light complected like I am."

The dark woman gazed at the creamy, crimson flushed face before her, and her own eyes filled with determined light, "He was, like you; but he was a white man, and you are white, too, if your Ma is black."

"I am not! I won't have him for a father; I won't have you for—" the child stopped, frightened by her own vehemence. Almost she had disowned Ma. She still loved Ma. Tim loved his mother, bad as she was.

"Now listen, girl. You are not old enough yet awhile to call your Ma to account, and it strikes me you're a bit behind hand choosing your Pa and Ma. Everybody always knew who your Pa was, and as much as folks enjoy minding my business for me, with all the gabblers in the world, ain't you never heard remarks?"

So that was why the girls stopped talking, the kind ones, and the mean ones said things about "white trash" when she came on them suddenly. Only now, did she know, why those things concerned her. All her life they had taunted her, about her shameful parents, and she had been too dumb to see. She spoke slowly, her tears dry.

"They say about colored with white—, they say all the colored ones must know her too well is why she had to mix with trash. They say it's an accident when that kind gets married. They said it to me and I never knew they meant you. I never knew what they meant."

"I should think you wouldn't understand them, the hussies."

Timidly, Vivvie put her question, "Were you married?"

"I was married, tight enough, and I'll have pay of anyone, white, black, grizzly or gray that says I wasn't. I should think you'd be ashamed, asking your Ma such a thing?"

"I am not, I'm only ashamed of that."

"Well, you can stop having tantrums, if you are, my miss. Many a girl would be proud she had a white Pa to give her a bright skin and good hair."

"I am not. I am ashamed that I had to be born. I had rather be black, like Tim."

"Hush up girl. You are as glad of your good looks as the next one." This was a hardness she had never dreamed to face. Who would have thought the child could take on so? "You know, baby, white and colored have always mixed, since slave days. You mustn't carry on so."

"Slavery times were different. They couldn't help themselves. You don't have to do such things now. No one made you—"

Kate's sharp angry voice cut her off. "Vivvie! Stop that talk this minute! You hear me! A child of mine to be so bold. That comes of letting you talk with that Tim, putting the devil in your mind."

"He never, he never," Vivvie defended. "Tim wouldn't say a word to me that an angel couldn't hear." Oh, it was terrible for them both, standing hard-eyed and angry, they who loved each other so.

It was time to end the scene. The child would be falling out next thing. "Be that as it may," Ma's voice rang with the old firmness, "You march yourself up the stairs, and wash your face in some good cold water, see if that will calm you down. Having tantrums all over the place like a five-year-old. March! before I turn you across my apron like you was one."

Left alone, the woman dropped on a kitchen chair, rocking her gaunt shoulders backward and forward, moaning, weeping. "My one little baby, my baby, I lost her now, I lost her, Lordy, Lordy, my baby. Oh mercy, mercy." Presently she rose, they must eat. Setting the kettle on the stove, she poked the fire viciously beneath it. "Did I know who said such things to her I could twist their neck with a grin."

In the trim little chamber above, a girl writhed on the bed, twisting her face in hard, dry, sobbing, a fit of shame, and rage and utter wretchedness. Having tantrums. Her slim body, wearied with its angry twitchings, grew still, out of the welter of unaccustomed emotions two thoughts stood out clearly; Ma, who had forced "trash" on her for a father, had dared to despise Tim, Tim who loved her. The other thought? She was going to get up and walk straight out to Tim, he was black enough for both of them.

Sliding from the bed, she stood looking down at the crumpled pillow, at the bright counterpane, wrinkled and soiled where her heels had dug in. Automatically she patted and smoothed them. Vivvie had her mother's taste for tidiness. Something of softness crept into her eyes, as her fingers touched one bright square, and then another, scraps from gay blossom-colored frocks made for Vivvie, only here and there a sober blue or gray bit from Ma's work dresses. Ma had given Vivvie the best, always. Too bad she must be hurt. Turning from the bed Vivvie's sober gaze was caught by the fluttering whiteness of the frilled curtains. Ma preferred stiffly starched Nottingham, but it was Vivvie's choice that framed the window. It was

Kate Benson's hand that kept them snowy and fresh. Vivvie need never touch a washboard. She held her hands idly before her, soft, creamy, flawless, and thought of Ma's, roughened and black, of Tim's big strong wrists, beside her own on the redchecked table. Too bad they both loved her. She could love only Tim.

At the washstand she lifted the pitcher and poured cool water into the big bowl. The baby Vivvie had been bathed in that bowl. Often had Ma told her so. Too bad, she supposed Ma would be hurt. Vivvie patted her face dry, rehung the towel neatly on its rack.

Beside the bed was Ma's deep chair, a towel pinned to its back protected the new cretonne covering; the covering had changed many times but the chair and its mission had been the same since first Vivvie could remember. It was there every night that Vivvie would snuggle into Ma's arms and tell her all the story of her day; every night she would kneel before it, with Ma's hand upon her head, "Bless Ma, make me a good girl," she would pray, then "Bless my baby, keep her a good girl," that was Ma. This night there would be no story and no prayer.

Afterward there would be goodnight. Vivvie could sleep so calmly knowing Ma was there beside her, to cuddle and warm next when nights were cool, to waken for comfort when Vivvie dreamed of scary things. It had all been so sweet, not to last.

Vivvie gulped, but couldn't cry, there was work to do. In a corner was Vivvie's desk. Ma had placed it where she need not be disturbed in her study by the noise or sudsy smells from the kitchen. From its nooks the girl drew paper and pen. The note took but a minute.

"Ma, I have gone to Tim."

It was bald. What else was there to say? Nothing. The note slipped under the inkwell. Ma would find it when she dusted in the morning. After Vivvie had gone to Tim tonight, Ma wouldn't dare to stop her in the morning.

Down the narrow stairs, calling, "Ma, oh, Ma!" She must act like nothing had happened. She would tell her that she must see Rosie Kauffman next door about her algebra. That would give her an hour to locate Tim before Ma got uneasy. She called again, funny Ma did not answer. As she stepped down into the kitchen, Vivvie crinkled her nose. Not like Ma to let her kettle burn, she must be upset. Vivvie lifted the smelly thing from the fire. If Ma was in the backyard Vivvie would walk out the front; save questions.

Halfway across the dining-room, she stopped short, hands fluttering to her breast. Something was wrong. Why was Ma lying on the floor, her head under the table?

"Ma," shrilled Vivvie, "Ma!" Never had Kate Benson failed that cry. Vivvie dropped on the faded carpet beside her, shaking the huddled form, calling without answer. Ma must be deaf, or—dead. Her shrieks pierced the air,

"Dead! I killed her! Ma! Ma! Ma!"

Pushing through the narrow door they came, plump Mrs. Jacobs, slim Mrs. Harris, anxious to aid. The Jewish woman's white hands were stained pink from the berries she had been hulling, the dark woman's brown hands were dusty, straight from the biscuit pan; busy women, both of them, dropping everything for a child's cry of terror.

Vivvie did not look up, intent only on making Ma answer. Jane Harris pulled her away, straightened the crumpled figure. Vivvie screamed again.

"Quit that noise, girl," the woman gave sharp command, "Screechin' can't help your Ma. Go to my house and 'phone the doctor."

The girl stood there, silenced by this briskness, but with no power of motion.

"The child is useless," Mrs. Harris complained, chafing Ma's wrists. Mrs. Jacobs was bringing water. Behind her mother's broad shoulders, Rosie Jacobs appeared.

"Rosie, you go," Jane Harris directed, "tell Doctor Talbert to come right off. Vivvie here is nothing but a stick."

With only time for a pitying glance at Vivvie, Rosie sped on her errand. Vivvie was seeing only Ma. She was trying to ask these women a question. Funny how loud she was screaming till Mis' Harris hushed her, now her throat wouldn't work at all. Still she had to know. Had she murdered Ma with the terrible things she had said, and the worse things she had thought and had not dared to say? There was a question she must have answered. Haltingly the syllables came,

"Is she—is Ma—dead?" Vivvie had spoken so low she was surprised when Mrs. Jacobs answered,

"The poor maidala," plump hands patted the girl's rigid shoulders, comfortingly, "the mama you have still by you."

Then she was not dead. Tears came. A soothing voice, "So, so, you should not cry."

Through the unchecked tears Vivvie questioned further, "Will she die?"

The crisp Harris voice answered, "If she looks to you for help she will." The brisk cruelty of the sentence, as the brown woman meant it to, dried the tears and checked the hysteria she had seen rising.

"Go you up and get your Ma's gown ready, and turn down the bed."

Climbing the stairs like a freshly wound mechanical toy, the words followed her, "A thin woman, but long and heavy, can we manage her Mis' Jacobs? Here's Rosie back, better let her. Here, you Rosie, you're young and strong, we can carry Mis' Benson up."

Vivvie had a gown unbuttoned and spread on the chair-back, a best one Ma had laid away for sickness, she who had not needed a doctor since

Vivvie was born in this bed whose covers were turned so neatly back. Vivvie stood watching while they laid Ma on the sheet, but put her hand out for a bar when they reached for the gown.

"No, I will do that, I can fix her," she told them. Mrs. Harris eyed her keenly. "Well," she agreed. Understandingly they left her alone with Ma. It was the first personal service the daughter had ever rendered. Somehow she undressed Kate, she could see plainly now that Ma still breathed. Like someone asleep, somehow Vivvie got the nightgown smooth under her, and pulled the sheet up under her chin. Some of Vivvie's terror was gone though she was still afraid.

"Overwork, the heart weakened, evidently she has had a shock," that was the doctor's verdict. Perfect rest, quiet, to be guarded from unpleasantness, was all Kate Benson needed, he did not wish to be alarming, but another shock might prove fatal. He and his little black bag were gone. Jane Harris had followed him down the stairs, Vivvie was alone with Ma, who was breathing easily, and sleeping. Vivvie sat there, her hands light on the pillow, her eyes waiting, intent on Ma's face. Oh, she had so very nearly killed her! If only Ma would get well, Vivvie would never, never hurt her again; she would learn to work so Ma might rest; she would even give up Tim; everything Ma wanted of her Vivvie would do, if only she would get well.

Ma opened her eyes, smiling into Vivvie's anxious face. Oh, it was heaven to see Ma smile again! Nothing should ever come between them! Not a dozen white fathers should separate them!

"Well, Vivvie, have you forgiven your Ma for not making you black?" surprising how natural Ma sounded, "for letting you be born?"

"Oh, Ma! Nothing matters if you will get right again. I love you, Ma, if I am a wicked little fool."

"Don't say such words, Vivvie, they ain't lady like. You're not ashamed to be my baby?" Kate caught both the child's hands.

"Oh, Ma!"

"Well, then, that's good, because I have to talk to you about these things, I thought you always knew." Kate tightened her clasp on Vivvie's fingers. "Hard on you finding out like that. Ma's going to tell you all about it."

Something warned Vivvie, she did not want to hear, "Not now, dear, the doctor says you must be still."

"What's that doctor know about my business," it was the old Ma speaking, "you listen to me. More room out than in and I want to tell you all about it now. About me, and your Pa."

Vivvie didn't wish to listen, but she must.

"Your Pa's people were quality, well off. He was a youngun' still when he came here and stopped at the Brittney House, on his first job, just a kid, though he was twenty-five or some; I was young too, not twenty yet, but I felt lots older, because I had made my livin' so many years then. I was doin' chamber work at the Brittney House. You can't know about such things, baby, so, I'll slur it over much as I can. I was makin' his room one day when he came in. Well, he wanted me, bad."

Vivvie turned her head away, it wasn't fitting to hear these things about Ma. It didn't sound like Ma, and she wasn't speaking right. Ma who was so proud of her schooling.

"You needn't flinch away, baby, Ma isn't going to shame you." Kate had sensed Vivvie's uneasiness. "I pulled away from him and gave him some sass, but I didn't report him. The manager expected us girls to take care of ourselves. He would only have blamed me and maybe I'd lose my job. Well, to make a long story short, he wouldn't let me rest. I was a good girl, raised decent, so I made him see he couldn't have me, not the way he wanted me. Well, he hadn't ever been denied anything in reach of his hand, and he thought he had to have me. So we got married. You see it pays a girl to be good, Vivvie!"

It paid, yes, and here was Vivvie paying, because Ma had been "good"!

"Well, it raised a stink. Colored folks like to talk their heads off. I quit the Brittney House and your Pa's boss fired him soon as he heard what he'd done. That wasn't good for him. He never had done any laboring work and that was all there was for him after he married colored in a small place like this, where everybody minds your business. He never got hardened, it killed him earlier than he was due to die.

"Well, if either of us was ever sorry we never let on. He wrote his folks he had married a servant, without saying I was colored. The servant part was bitter enough to them. They forgave him after a while, but never came near him. He used to visit them when we could scrape up enough to dress him fitting. He was proud and scared when you came, Vivvie. Tiny and red, but we could see then you were to be bright, and I was tickled."

Vivvie interrupted, choking over the words, "You loved me because I was fair?" Kate Benson drew her child's averted head down to her breast and held her close, so the girl could not see the tears rising, holding back.

"As if I wouldn't love my baby just the same, white as milk or black as coal, ma like or pa like. It was only we felt it would make things easier for you. Your Pa said then, 'If the dusk doesn't deepen, Kate, we can send her home and make a lady of her.' He loved you, Vivvie. He took you with him once, but you were too little to remember. Your Grandma was crazy after you. He said it again when he was passin', and I promised him. And almost I waited too long. Your Grandma wrote me for you. Time I sent you away. You can pass."

This was shameful, abasing; Vivvie's cheeks burned. She wasn't going to try any such thing. It was foolish, wicked, mean. It would divide her from

Tim. She nipped the hot protest on her tongue. Opposition would excite Ma. She asked, calmly as she could, "Is it right, Ma?"

"Think your Ma would tell you wrong?" Ma demanded. "Go look in that glass." Obediently Vivvie crossed to the tall old dresser, looked long and despairingly into the mirror. She had no need to look. Vivvie knew what it reflected, and now that Ma had spoken she knew what she had not thought of before: it was the face, the hair, and the eyes of a white girl looking back at her, and Vivvie did not want to see it, now.

"Come back now, babe." Ma's eyes were on her, ruling her, beseeching her. "Now tell me what's wrong with our plan? Don't that glass say you are more white than black?"

The mirror said it, though Vivvie knew it lied. Lied, because it could not reflect her heart, her heart full of love for the black mother she used to have (this was not really Ma, saying such terrible things, only someone she had to be careful not to shock), full of Tim, Tim, Tim! Yes, her face was the dawn, but in her heart! What had Ma said? Deepening dusk? Too bad the mirror could not reveal the soft, brown dusk in her heart. She could never pass, if that should show.

Ma was speaking again, waiting for an answer. "Well, Vivvie?" The answer wouldn't come. Ma's eyes grew keen. "You aren't bothered over Tim, a baby like you. Wasn't anything serious?" she queried. Vivvie could not trust her voice, words might come with a violence that would shock Ma and kill her. Vivvie had promised obedience if Ma lived, and Ma was living, demanding. "You don't think you're in love with that black boy?"

Slowly Vivvie shook her head. Ma pulled Vivvie down to her again. "Well I'm glad. Nothing stands in our way. Not for nothing have I slaved to keep you a lady, babe, your hands white and soft. You never will have to come the hard way your Ma did. You needn't marry a poor man that can give you only a livin'. You can choose from the finest."

The finest? Tim. "I will never marry, Ma." Vivvie broke her silence to say. Never marry Tim, never to have chubby brown babies with dancing eyes!

"Glad that is settled. Vivvie, I will rise from here in the morning. Doctor or no. You go down now and tell Sis' Harris she can go home to her men folks. You and me will be all right. I mean to nap a bit. Kiss me, babe."

Vivvie put her lips to Kate's and went from the room on her errand. Ma did not sleep, she lay there with eyes closed, wondering, fighting, aching. She shouldn't have asked the child to kiss her, the caress had said too much, had near shattered the plans of a lifetime. Vivvie's lips had been hard and cold, the kiss of one already slain for sacrifice; it lay heavy on her lips, too lifeless to strike in. She had never counted on the child turning from her like that.

After all it was babe's happiness they had planned for, Pa and she. Ma would have to decide alone, her pale kin or the dusky. How could she tell? Babe must be happy.

Down in the kitchen, Vivvie delivered her message. Mis' Harris was reinforced, by three other neighbor women, all crooning songs; they hushed when Vivvie came in. Jane Harris was the first to speak, as one with authority.

"You can tell Kate Benson I stay right here. Who she thinks is going to see after her? Not you. It's a disgrace, sisters, and I say it right to Vivvie, here, that a woman with a grown daughter falls out from overwork. You ought to be ashamed, child, and mend your ways, the way your Ma has slaved for you."

Vivvie said nothing, what they said mattered little. "Sis Harris," one of the other women remonstrated, "you oughtn't be so hard on the girl. It's her Ma's fault for not teachin' her, lettin' her loll around fine lady like with her Ma in the tub. I never had any too fine to put their hands in suds, but I started them early. It's a shame how this child's been raised."

Vivvie turned on them all, furious, drowning their chorused approval.

"You stop blaming her. Ma knew what she was doing. She was minding her own business like you busybodies better do."

"Well, sassy, too."

"Youngun's don't have respect."

"Mine better have."

"A girl of mine talk like that—"

"I'll talk worse than that if you blame Ma anymore," Vivvie shamed and hurt, struck back, she wanted some one else to suffer, as she did, and Ma, as Tim would suffer when she turned away from him. She had to hurt them. Slowly she said:

"Ma was shocked, you heard the doctor say it, Mrs. Harris. You wish to know how? I told her the talk that your fine daughters have been doing, because my father was white; their nasty hints and slurs. Of course the daughters repeated what they had heard their mothers say. It hurt and angered her. That is why Ma is ill up there alone."

Before the women recovered breath, the girl had turned her back upon them. Their comment followed her up the stairs.

"If it was one of my girls I'll whale the sin out of her, talking about Mis' Benson where the girl could hear."

Jane Harris spoke soberly, "It wasn't just the girls, that talked. The Lord forgive us all for a bunch of gabbing fools. Making the child's way still harder with our scoldings, and her heart sick about her Ma."

Vivvie closed the bedroom door behind her. Ma's eyes were tight shut, she crossed the floor and stared out the window into the growing twilight, gazing across the field behind the house as darkness gathered over it. She could not see, but beyond that marshy field was the river. Tim had taken her there, to teach her to swim, oh long ago, before she knew that Tim was a boy and she a girl, that Tim was black and she was white; when she was only Vivvie and Tim was only Tim. They had whipped Tim for leading her off to drown, as if Tim would ever let her be hurt!

But she was hurt, now, and Tim could not help her. She was hurting, hurting all over, with the ice that lay on her heart. No one could help her. She had even lost Ma. Thinking, thinking, of the hard bare road before her, Vivvie threw out her hands in a vague appeal to the dark, the warm, kind dark, in a wordless prayer for the laugh and song of her own kind, for Ma to come back like Ma again, for Tim, Tim, Tim, and the round brown babies she would never see. Only lies, and fear, and more lies, with the ice growing around her heart. Oh the warm sunshine of her own kind, that could be felt even in the darkness, and she had to leave. She couldn't kill Ma. Her hands fell in helpless surrender, her head bowed with the weight of it.

"Vivvie," the voice, faint so low she scarcely heard it, "come here to Ma, babe."

It was difficult crossing the floor, Vivvie did not want to talk, she wanted only to stay by the window, staring into the growing dark, mourning. She stood by the bedside looking down at this stranger, an alien demanding obedience.

"I thought you were sleeping."

"No, child, I've been waking up. Kneel by the bed so I can see you better. Your face is all over shadow."

"It is nearly dark."

"Kiss me again, Vivvie." Wondering, the girl bent her clouded face to Kate. It was not like Ma to sue for caresses. Another frozen kiss lay on Ma's lips. With both hands Ma pushed the girl's head up again.

"Look at me, Vivvie, straight at me! You've been lying!"

"Ma!" rather feeble, the protest.

"Lying," Ma repeated, accusing, "you are grieving your heart out."

"No," Vivvie denied dully, "no."

Kate Benson's voice rose in an exalted chant, "Yes, oh, yes, glory be! You've been lying to your Ma."

"No."

"The truth, Vivvie," Ma charged her sternly, "I was primin' you to lie, but not to me, babe, not to me. You're lovin' Tim."

Vivvie pulled away from Kate and drew herself erect, tall with a new dignity as she stood above her mother, "Yes, I always will. He is worth loving. I will not be ashamed."

"You had rather wash and scrub and sweat? rather be poor and fretted with a swarm of black and brown and yellow little darkies than do what I tell you? rather than be white and rich with your path easy? Answer, Vivvie."

Her path easy? Vivvie saw nothing but thorns. Must she cling to her lie? She had promised, Ma was not to be hurt again, whatever happened. "No," she said steadily, "no."

"Vivvie, I'm askin' once more. The truth, child, if it kills us both."

Moments passed in silence, then, "Vivvie, mind your Ma."

The sobs came, dry and hard, "Yes, Ma. I lied, I tried to lie! The more I think white the better I love black. Oh Ma, I had rather a thousand times! How can I leave my own? How stop being what I know I am?" Dropping to the floor she buried her face in the quilts. "Oh Ma, Ma, let me stay, those others aren't my kind, not my people, they don't want me, I don't want them. I only want, Tim, and you, and my own, only want to stay where I belong. Let me stay, let me stay!"

Ma's long arms tightened round the trembling shoulders. "Sure, honey, you're stayin' right here."

Tears came, warm tears. Ma mingled hers with Vivvie's. They washed away the glacier that had risen in Vivvie's heart, that divided her from Ma. "Guess," Ma said slowly, "I haven't broke that promise to your Pa. That dusk seems deepenin' down where it can't be seen."

Vivvie was pressing kisses, soft and fragrant against Ma's cheeks. Forgotten doctor's orders, the growing darkness. She could no longer see Ma. It was enough to know Ma, the real Ma, was there. That she could tell her everything, how she loved Tim and the sparkle of his eye.

The door opened noiselessly. Behind Mrs. Harris and the lighted lamp she carried came the sound of singing, hymning voices from downstairs. Kate Benson greeted her neighbor with a broad grin. "Thought I ordered you all home." Vivvie gained her feet, stood dewy faced in the soft lamplight.

"We decided we could stay with you a spell. You sure are getting well in a hurry. Declare you don't look sick a bit."

"Who said I was? That Doctor? What's he know about black folks insides? Just soldierin' on you Mis' Harris. Pull that shade, and set a chair for Mis' Harris," Kate commanded, complaining fondly. "This girl don't know the first thing about a house, Mis' Harris. Soon as I rise from here she's going through a course of sprouts. She thinks she wants to marry Tim when she's out of school. Babe is goin' back home."

Jane Harris looked puzzled, "Back home?" she echoed.

"I chose outside the lines, but Vivvie here, wants to bring the color back."

Mrs. Harris fidgeted in her chair, then blurted, "See here, Kate, that youngun' of yours let out something, said you was upset by gossip over that choosin' of yours."

"Go long, Harris. Ain't I been colored too long to let colored talk worry me? Vivvie, go down, tell those sisters they needn't be selfish with their tunes; bring that meetin' sound up here."

Jane Harris wondered why Ma whispered, "Glory, glory. My babe's come home to stay."

LUCILLE BOEHM

Two-Bit Piece

The red sun was sweating in a humid sky. It died fiercely, shedding blood-colored heat over the crowded block. The narrow sidewalks were alive with people, rocking on the peg-legged chairs they had dragged out early that morning, playing cards at rickety tables, squatting on the stoops and fanning themselves with soggy handkerchiefs. Even the boarded-up houses, bleached and rotting in the sun all day, had come to life. Kids swarmed through them, chased each other, screaming; flailed the old woodwork with their pocket-knives. Men going home from work dangled foamy cans of beer.

'Liz was playing Old Maid with Patsy Crews and Bea Sutherland on the front steps of her house. The three of them shrieked as Patsy picked the Queen from Bea's hand. 'Liz's wide, laughing lips drew back, stripping brilliant teeth and wet bluish gums. When her name was shouted through the hallways she trumpeted all the louder, pretending not to hear.

"'Liz! Hey, 'Liz!" It was her big sister, Louise, standing outside the kitchen in the rear flat. "Got some change on you, 'Liz?"

'Liz dealt the cards without looking up. Louise pushed her wide body through the dark, dingy hall and planted herself in the doorway.

"'Liz!" she bellowed, "ain't you still got that two-bit piece I gave you?"

'Liz squirmed around on her step and looked at her sister quickly.

"Two-bit piece!" Her lips exploded into a noise that was half a giggle, half a poop. "What you think I am? Brenda Frazier?"

"Don't be so fresh!" warned Louise, "what become of that two bits anyhow?"

'Liz gave an exasperated shrug. "I dunno."

"Ain't you got even a dime, huh, 'Liz?"

The girl shook her head until her hair flew in her eyes, Louise clicked her tongue and sighed. She turned, tramped back through the hallway muttering, "O.K. Don't pay *me* no mind. All you get tonight is boiled potatoes, an' if you don't like it—" she slammed shut the kitchen door—*"lump it!"*

The baby in the bedroom woke with a start and began to bawl. He was almost swallowed up in the wide sagging bed that four people shared at night. He wailed piercingly, wriggled like a tiny black bug pinned to the lumpy sheet.

"Shut your face!" snorted Louise. She dumped a few peeled potatoes into the water-filled pot on the stove. The baby yowled in the next room. He sounded like he would tear his guts out. Louise popped the cork off the gasoline flagon and poured some of its contents carefully into the stove tank. She screwed on the cap, pumped the tank, and turned up a low flame.

Then she shoved through two red rags of curtains into the bedroom and grabbed the baby. "You gonna shut up?" she yelled into his sniveling face. She carried him back to the kitchen on one arm, gave him a piece of cold toast to keep him quiet. With her free hand she took a fork and poked at the potatoes. . . .

There were six for supper that night. But Gloria, when she got there, said she couldn't eat. Sullenly she shoved her plate aside and got up from the table. Shuffled over to the bed, her knees rubbery under the burden of her expected child. The others ate the lukewarm potatoes in silence. No one but Boodgy dared to speak. He banged his fork down on the plate when he had finished his meager portion. "Is this all?" he asked.

The volcano that had smoldered in Louise's chest all day erupted. She rose to her full height and breadth, pushed away the table with spread hands. A bit more force and she would have shoved it clear out the window. Its thin legs quavered, the plates chattered nervously.

"Sure, that's all!" she exploded at her husband, "Maybe there'd be more if you didn't have enough in you already to smell the place up like a brewery! I been sweatin' in this kitchen all day! But I can't make sumpin' outa nothin'!"

'Liz ducked under the range of fire. She reached down quickly, jerked something out of her shoe. Then she scraped back her chair and bolted out of the room.

"Where you goin'?" screamed Louise, but 'Liz was already halfway down the hall. She scooted into the street, raced across the gutter like a fleeing thief, her damp fist tightly clenched around a coin. A gang of kids had already gathered in front of the candy store opposite her house. They were whistling, clapping, hopping to their own music when she bounced among them.

Two bits on a Saturday night, the gang, and the piccolo! It would be worth six sacrificed suppers.

"Look what I got!" 'Liz held high the birthday money she had saved. there were cries of "Geez!" . . . "Where'd you get it, 'Liz?" . . . "Solid!" A dozen hands pawed her raised arm. "Let's have a tune on the piccolo, hey!"

Proudly 'Liz mounted the candy store steps at the head of the group. "I want change of a quarter," she announced grandly, "an' I want *Panassie Stomp* on the piccolo with the Count."

The music throbbed out of the lit machine, groaning with the full undertone of the running bass. The kids jammed themselves into the little store and began to dance. 'Liz was at the hub of the excitement. The boys took her on in turns, sending her swiftly over the rough boards. Their dancing was agitated, quick with the restless rhythm of hunger. One by one the nickels plunked into the machine. *Wolverine Blues, Twilight in Turkey, Doggin' Around.*

Wearying, 'Liz and her partner broke into off-time. Slow, rocking, searching movement, at once hollow and full with the weight of hunger. Another partner broke in, on time. Again the world sped 'round, 'Liz flung out her body like they do at the Savoy. Routine. Break. Jig walk. Close together, far apart, together again. Teasing. Almost having and then not having. Her empty stomach was rumbling, beating wildly against the belt of her dress. A knot was tying itself around her heart, tighter, tighter. Together, apart, together. The street spun in all directions.

'Liz stumbled forward. She fell on her face. "Aw, 'Liz!" . . . "Cut it out, 'Liz!" . . . "You gon' get your dress all dirty!" They thought she was kidding. Prodded her with their knees, poked her with the tips of their shoes. She lay still.

One or two of the girls tittered uncomfortably. The others stood around gawking, foolish. Rooster left a poker game nearby to investigate the trouble. He bent over 'Liz, chafed her wrists. Then he called to the man behind the counter, "Hey Joe, give us a shot of King Kong for the kid!"

He lifted her over to the doorway. Joe had poured out a jigger of the watery, yellowish liquid from a musty bottle stuffed with orange peels and kimmel seed. Rooster tilted the glass to 'Liz's lips. Whiskey dribbled down each side of her chin. She gulped, shuddered. Her eyes blinked open and she spat the stuff all over her dress. The first thing she thought of was Louise. If *she* ever found out what had happened tonight! 'Liz shut her mind against that awful possibility. Louise musn't know!

"Say, you won't tell Louise about this, will you?" she begged. "Please, don't tell Louise!"

"No no," . . . "It's O.K." . . . "We won't rat," they all assured her.

She got up, unsteady, shivering. Started slowly across the street toward her stoop, shaking like a scared puppy.

Suddenly someone found a nickel that hadn't been used. Plunk, it was fed into the slot of the piccolo. *Fortune Tellin' Man* blared out. And in the darkness they moved again—thin shadows of hungry kids and their hungry dancing.

MARITA BONNER

The Whipping

The matron picked up her coat. It was a good coat made of heavy men's wear wool and lined with fur. She always liked to let her hands trail fondly over it whenever she was going to put it on (the way women do who are used to nothing).

She shook it out and shrugged her shoulders into it.

"I'll be back home again in time for dinner!" She smiled at the warden as she talked. "Helga will have 'peasant-girl,' for dessert, too!"

The hard lines that creased around the man's eyes softened a little. "Peasant-girl-with-a-veil! Ah, my mother could make that! Real homemade jam, yellow cream!—good! Nothing here ever tastes as good as it did back in the old country, I tell you!"

The woman balanced her weight on the balls of her feet and drew on one of her leather driving gloves. Through the window she saw her car, nicely trimmed and compactly modern, awaiting her. Beyond the car was a November sky, dismal, darkening, and melancholy as the walls that bounded the surrounding acres of land which belonged to the Women's Reformatory.

At the end of her drive of thirty-five miles back to the city again, she would go to the apartment that—through warmth of color and all the right uses of the best comforts—seemed to be full of sunshine on the darkest days. She looked down, now, as she stood near the warden and saw her right hand freshly manicured.

Her mother's hands back in the stone kitchen with the open hearth found in every peasant home in Denmark had always been gray and chapped with blackened nails this time of year. No woman who has to carry wood and coal from a frozen yard can have soft clean hands.

The thought made the matron shrug again. "I like things as they are here—but it would be good to go home some day to visit!"

She hurried a little toward the door now. Nobody lingers in the impersonal grayness of an institution whose very air is heavy with fierce anger and anguish and sorrow, buried and dulled under an angry restraint just as fierce and sorrowful.

She had nearly reached the door before she remembered the colored woman sitting alone on the edge of the bench beside the window. The matron had just driven up from the city to bring the woman on the bench to stay at the Reformatory as long as she should live.

She had killed her little boy.

The judge and the social worker said she had killed him.

But she had told the matron over and over again that she did not do it.

You could never tell, though. It is best to leave these things alone.

"Good bye, 'Lizabeth!" the matron called in a loud voice. She meant to leave a cheerful note but she only spoke overloud. "Be a good girl!"

"Yes'm!" Lizabeth answered softly. "Yas'm!"

And the women separated. One went out to the light. The other looked at the gray walls—dark—and growing darker in the winter sunset.

Everything had been gray around Lizabeth most all of her life. The two-room hut with a ragged lean-to down on Mr. Davey's place in Mississippi where she had lived before she came North—had been gray.

She and Pa and Ma and Bella and John used to get up when the morning was still gray and work the cotton until the grayness of evening stopped them.

"God knows I'm sick of this!" Pa had cursed suddenly one day.

Ma did not say anything. She was glad that they had sugar once in a while from the commissary and not just molasses like they said you got over at McLaren's place.

Pa cursed a lot that day and kept muttering to himself. One morning when they got up to go to work the cotton, Pa was not there.

"He say he goin' North to work!" Ma explained when she could stop her crying.

Mr. Davey said Pa had left a big bill at the commissary and that Ma and the children would have to work twice as hard to pay it up.

There were not any more hours in any one day than those from sun-up to sun-down, no way you could figure it.

The Christmas after Pa left, Mr. Davey said Ma owed three times as much and that she could not have any flannel for John's chest to cover the place where the misery stayed each winter.

That was the day Ma decided to go North and see if she could find Pa.

They had to plan it all carefully. There was no money to go from Mississippi northward on the train.

John had to get an awful attack of the misery first. Then Bella had to stay home to take care of him.

The day Mr. Davey's man came to find out why Bella and Jim were not in the field, Bella had her hand tied up in a blood-soaked rag and she was crying.

The axe had slipped and cut her hand, she told them.

That meant Ma would have to wait on Bella and John.

Lizabeth worked the cotton by herself and the Saturday after Ma laid off, Mr. Davey would not let them have any fat back.

"Y'all can make it on meal and molasses until you work off your debts!" he told Lizabeth.

Ma had said nothing when Lizabeth had told her about the fat back. She had sat still a long time. Then she got up and mixed up some meal.

"What you makin' so much bread to oncet?" Bella asked Ma.

"Gainst our gittin' hungry!"

"Can't eat all that bread one time!" John blared forth. "Better save some 'cause you might not git no meal next time! We owe so much!"

"Heish, boy!!" Ma screamed so you could hear her half across the field. "I ain't owe nobody nothin!"

Lizabeth's jaw dropped. "Mr. Davey, he say—!"

"Heish gal!" Ma screamed again. "I ain't owe nuthin, I say! Been right here workin' nigh on forty years!"

She turned the last scrap of meal into a pan. Then she stood up and looked around the table at three pairs of wide-stretched eyes.

"I'm fixin' this 'gainst we git hungry! We goin North to find Pa tonight!"

You would not believe that three women and a half-grown boy could get to Federal Street, Chicago, from Mississippi without a cent of money to start with.

They walked—they begged rides—they stopped in towns, worked a little, and they rode as far as they could on the train for what they earned. It took months, but they found Federal Street.

But they never found Pa.

They found colored people who had worked the cotton just like they themselves had done, but these others were from Alabama and Georgia and parts of Mississippi that they had never seen.

They found the houses on Federal Street were just as gray, just as bare of color and comfort as the hut they had left in Mississippi.

But you could get jobs and earn real money and buy all sorts of things for a little down and a little a week! You could eat what you could afford to buy—and if you could not pay cash, the grocer would put you on the book.

Ma was dazed.

John forgot the misery.

Bella and Lizabeth were looping wider and wider in new circles of joy.

Ma could forget Pa, who was lost, and the hard trip up from the South when she screamed and shouted and got happy in robust leather-lunged style in her store-front church run in the "down-home" tempo.

John spent every cent that he could lay a hand on on a swell outfit, thirty dollars from skin out and from shoes to hat!

Bella's circles of joy spread wider and wider until she took to hanging out with girls who lived "out South" in kitchenettes.

She straightened her hair at first.

Then she curled her hair. After that she "sassed" Ma. Said she was going to get a job in a tavern and stay "out South" too!

They heard she was married.

They heard she was not.

Anyway, she did not come back to 31st and Federal.

John's swell outfit wasn't thick enough to keep the lake winds from his misery. He began to have chills and night sweats. The Sunday he coughed blood, Lizabeth got a doctor from State Street.

The doctor made Ma send John to the hospital.

"He be all right soon?" Ma asked after the ambulance had gone.

The doctor looked grim. "I doubt if they can arrest it!"

"Arrest it! Arrest what? John's a good boy! He ain't done nothing to git arrested!"

The doctor looked grimmer. "I mean that maybe they can't stop this blood from coming!"

Ma looked a little afraid. "Well, if they jes' gives him a tablespoon of salt that will stop any bleeding! My mother always —"

The doctor put his hat on and went out. He did not listen to hear any more.

The second fall that they were on Federal Street, Lizabeth met Benny, a soft-voiced boy from Georgia.

Benny said he was lonely for a girl who did not want him to spend all his money on liquor and things for her every time he took her out. That is what these city girls all seemed to want.

They wanted men to buy things for them that no decent girl down home would accept from men.

Lizabeth was glad for just a ten-cent movie and a bottle of pop or a nickel bag of peanuts.

They were married at Christmas. The next year, in October, baby Benny came.

In November John died.

In February of the second year Benny—who had begun to go "out South" in the evening with the boys—suddenly stayed away all night.

Ma had hysterics in the police station and told the police to find him.

"He may be dead and run over somewhere!" she kept crying.

The policemen took their time. Ma went every day to find out if there were any news. Lizabeth went too!

She stopped going after she saw the policeman at the desk wink at another when he told her: "Sure! Sure! We are looking for him every day!"

Mrs. Rhone who kept the corner store asked Lizabeth one morning, "Where's your man? Left you?"

Lizabeth bridled: "He was none of these men! He was my husband!"

The other woman probed deeper: "Who married you? That feller 'round to the store-front church? Say! Hee-hee! They tell me he ain't no reglar preacher! Any feller what'll slip him a couple of dollars can get 'married'— even if he's got a wife and ten kids "out South," they tell me —!"

Lizabeth shrank back. Benny had been truly married to her!!

This woman just did not have any shame!

But after that Lizabeth grew sensitive if she went on the street and saw the women standing together in gossiping groups.

"They talkin' about me! They saying I weren't married!" she would tell herself.

She and Ma moved away.

The place where they moved was worse than Federal Street. Folks fought and cursed and cut and killed down in the Twenties in those days.

But rent was cheap.

Elizabeth only got twelve dollars a week scrubbing all night in a theater.

Ma kept little Benny and took care of the house.

There was not much money, but Lizabeth would go without enough to eat and to wear so that little Benny could have good clothes and toys that she really could not afford.

"Every time you pass the store you 'bout buy this boy somethin'!" the grandmother complained once.

"Aw I'd a liked pretty clothes and all that stuff when I was a kid!" Lizabeth answered.

"How she buy so much stuff and just *she* workin'!" the neighbors argued among themselves.

"She must be livin' wrong!" declared those who could understand all the fruits of wrong living in all its multiple forms.

Little Benny grew to expect all the best of things for himself. He learned to whine and cry for things and Lizabeth would manage them somehow.

He was six years old in 1929.

That was the year when Lizabeth could find no more theaters to scrub in and there were no more day's work jobs nor factory jobs. Folks said the rich people had tied up all the money so all the poor people had to go to the relief station.

Lizabeth walked fifteen blocks one winter day to a relief station. She told the worker that there was no coal, no food, the water was frozen, and the pipes had bursted.

"We'll send an investigator," the worker promised.

"When'll that come?" Lizabeth demanded vaguely.

"*She* will come shortly! In a few days, I hope!"

"I got nothin' for Ma and Benny to eat today!" Lizabeth began to explain all over again.

"I'm sorry! That is all we can do now!" the woman behind the desk began to get red as she spoke this time.

"But Benny ain't had no dinner and —"

"Next!" The woman was crimson as she called the next client.

The client—a stout colored woman—elbowed Lizabeth out of the way.

Already dazed with hunger and bone-weary from her freezing walk, Lizabeth stumbled.

"She's drunk!" the client muttered apologetically to the woman behind the desk.

Lizabeth had had enough. She brought her left hand up in a good old-fashioned back-hand wallop.

Everybody screamed. "They're fighting!"

"Look out for a knife!" yelled the woman behind the desk.

Her books had all told her that colored women carried knives.

A policeman came and took Lizabeth away.

They kept Lizabeth all night that night. The next day they said she could go home but it was the third day that they finally set her on the sidewalk and told her to go home.

Home was thirty blocks away this time.

"Where you been, gal!" Ma screamed as soon as the door opened. "You the las' chile I got and now you start actin' like that Bella! Ain't no food in this house! Ain't a God's bit of fire 'cept one box I busted up—!"

"She busted up my boat! She busted up the box what I play boat in!" Benny added his scream to the confusion. "She make me stay in bed all the time! My stomach hurts me!"

Lizabeth was dizzy. "Ain't nobody been here?" She wanted to wait a little before she tole Ma that she had been in the lock-up.

"Nobody been here? For what?"

"Get us some somepin' to eat! That's what the woman said!"

"No, ain't nobody been here!"

Lizabeth put on her hat again.

"Where you goin' now?" Ma shouted.

"I got to go back."

"You got to go back where?"

"See 'bout some somethin' to eat, Ma!"

Benny began to scream and jumped out of the bed. "You stay with me!" he cried as he ran to his mother. "I want my dinner! I —"

"Heish!" Lizabeth out-screamed everyone else in the room.

Frightened, Benny cowed away a little. Then he began again. "I want to eat! The lady downstairs, she say my mother ought to get me somethin' 'stead of stayin' out all night with men!"

Lizabeth stared wildly at her mother.

Hostile accusation bristled in her eyes, too.

"That's what the lady say. She say—" Benny repeated.

And Lizabeth, who had never struck Benny in her life, stood up and slapped him to the floor.

As he fell, the child's head struck the iron bedstead.

His grandmother picked him up, still whimpering.

Lizabeth went out without looking back.

Fifteen blocks put a stitch in her left side. Anger made her eyes red.

The woman behind the desk at the relief station paled when she saw Elizabeth this time. "You will have to wait!" she chattered nervously before Lizabeth had even spoken.

"Wait for what? Been waitin! Nobody been there!"

"We are over-crowded now! It will take ten days to two weeks before our relief workers can get there!"

"What's Ma and little Benny going to do all that time? They gotta eat!"

The other woman grew eloquent. "There are hundreds and hundreds of people just like you waiting—!"

"Well I stop waiting'! Bennie got to eat!"

Fifteen blocks had put a stitch in her side. Worry and hunger made her head swim. Lizabeth put one hand to her side and wavered against the desk.

This time the woman behind the desk *knew* that Lizabeth had a knife— for her alone! Her chair turned over as she shot up from the desk. Her cries brought the policeman from the next corner.

"We better keep you for thirty days," the police court told Lizabeth when they saw her again.

"But little Benny—!" Lizabeth began crying aloud.

There was a bustle and commotion. A thin pale woman pushed her way up to the desk.

Lizabeth had to draw back. She stood panting, glaring at the judge.

He had been looking at her at first in tolerant amusement. But while this pale woman talked to him across his desk, cold, dreadful anger surged into his eyes.

"What's that you're saying about little Benny?" he demanded suddenly of Lizabeth. "He's dead!"

Lizabeth could not speak nor move at first. Then she cried out. "What happen to him? What happen to my baby?"

"You killed him." The judge was harsh.

A bailiff had to pick Lizabeth up off of the floor and stand her up again so the judge could finish. "You whipped him to death!"

"I ain't never whip him! I ain't never whip little Benny!" Lizabeth cried over and over.

They took her away and kept her.

They kept her all the time that they were burying Benny, even. Said she was not fit to see him again.

Later—in court—Ma said that Lizabeth had "whipped Benny's head" the last time she was at home.

"I ain't hit him but once!" Lizabeth tried to cry it to the judge's ears. "He didn't have nuthin' to eat for a long time! That was the trouble."

"There was a deep gash on his head," testified the relief worker. "She was brutal!"

"She brought knives to the relief station and tried to start a fight every time she came there!"

"She's been arrested twice!"

"Bad character! Keep her!" the court decided.

That was why the matron had had to drive Lizabeth to the Woman's Reformatory.

She had gone out now to her car. Lizabeth watched her climb into it and whirl around once before she drove away.

"Won't see her no more! She's kinder nice, too," Lizabeth thought.

"It is time for supper! Come this way!" the warden spoke suddenly.

Lizabeth stumbled to her feet and followed him down a long narrow hall lit with one small light.

That relief worker had said she would see that Ma got something to eat.

That seemed to settle itself as soon as they had decided they would send her to this place.

"You will work from dawn to sun-down," the matron had said as they were driving up from the city.

She had always done that in Mississippi.

It did not matter here. But she asked one question. "They got a commissary there?"

"A commissary!" The matron was struck breathless when Lizabeth asked this. She had decided that Lizabeth was not normal. She had seemed too stupid to defend herself in court. "She must be interested in food!" the matron had decided to herself.

A slight sneer was on her face when she answered, "Of course they have a commissary! You get your food there!"

Lizabeth had drawn back into her corner and said nothing more.

A commissary. She understood a commissary. The same gray hopeless drudge—the same long unending row to hoe—lay before her.

The same debt, year in, year out.

How long had they said she had to stay?

As long as she lived. And she was only thirty now.

But she understood a commissary and a debt that grew and grew while you worked to pay it off. And she would never be able to pay for little Benny.

RAMONA LOWE

The Woman in the Window

The employment agency sent her to a place that wanted a cook. Fifteen a week, they paid. Twelve hours a day, but after all fifteen's good wages.

When the proprietor, Mr. Parsons, saw her he was delighted. He rubbed his hands and showed her the kitchen. There was no need for a prolonged interview. He could see that she was just the thing. And the rest of the establishment was invited to take a peep to see what a treasure had been found.

Mrs. Jackson went right to work frying chicken with a lofty unconcern for the curious faces peeping in at the door and the proprietor's nervously evident pleasure. The tenth time the proprietor appeared in the kitchen he was accompanied by a stout man with an appraising eye, apparently a partner in the restaurant.

"Mr. Kraft," Parsons said loudly by way of introduction, "this is our new cook."

Mrs. Jackson turned her broad back indifferently on the two men. This was not the expected reaction. Parsons cleared his throat for attention. "I didn't get your name."

"You never asked it," Mrs. Jackson corrected him brusquely. "My name's Mrs. Jackson."

"What's your first name?" asked Kraft, surveying her with the brazen air of a master.

"Where I works," Mrs. Jackson replied with finality, "I'm known as Mrs. Jackson."

Kraft, trying to overlook this show of dignity, simply remarked, "She'll be a beaut in the window, Mike. A beaut!"

The proprietor rubbed his hands and addressed Mrs. Jackson. "You look straight from the South," he said.

Mrs. Jackson, suspicious of the compliment, was noncommittal.

"I'll bet your home's in Georgia," continued Parsons chaffingly. Without waiting for this conjecture to be confirmed, he turned to his partner. "How soon can you get the equipment up?"

"Couple of weeks for everything," Kraft replied.

"Good. Good. Mrs. Jackson, we're going to make a few alterations, but business will go on just the same. When the alterations are complete, you will be cooking in the window!"

Shock ran through Mrs. Jackson. Her mind had not followed the trend of their remarks to this conclusion.

"Yes, ma'am," Kraft rocked on his heels. You'll be displayed just like the pancakes and the waffles."

Mrs. Jackson was verbally not quite equal to the unexpected. She knew where she stood, but she didn't know how to express it. "The 'ployment agency jus' tol' me cookin'," she floundered.

"That's all it is," said Kraft. "Cookin'."

"What you talkin' 'bout a winda?" she wanted to know.

"We're gonna let you do your cookin' in the winda," Kraft explained.

"I doan like nobody watchin' me cook," she protested.

The proprietor sensed the need of tact. "It should be a privilege," he assured her, clipping his words and using his hands for emphasis.

"Humph!" was Mrs. Jackson's wordless comment. Signs of anger were becoming evident.

Kraft selected a piece of chicken from the freshly cooked pile.

"I ain' one for a show, Mr. Parsons," Mrs. Jackson explained; "so if it's a show you want I reckon you'll have t' get somebody else."

But the proprietor's zeal could not recognize lack of enthusiasm in anyone else. "We're gonna have all new equipment," he announced. "Everything new. You can see everything that's going on in the street. Our customers will see how clean and tempting everything is. We'll run the frauds that advertise Southern cooking out of business."

Mrs. Jackson was not interested.

But Kraft, eating his piece of chicken, knew a formula for compulsion to his will. "We'll make it eighteen a week—give you a vegetable preparer and a dishwasher," he offered.

Mrs. Jackson did not take long to consider. A family that had to be supported, when jobs were scarce and poor-paying, made duty triumph over pride.

Parsons beamed. "Then it's eighteen a week. All settled."

Kraft wiped his greasy fingers on a dish towel with the satisfied and confident air of a man who always knows how to settle all things. "Anybody who can cook chicken like that is worth a million," he said.

When the alterations were complete, Mrs. Jackson was moved into the window. She was wearing her neat blue cover-all apron. But she hadn't reckoned with enterprise.

Parsons hovered about, rubbing his hands.

"Mrs. Jackson, that's fine. Now. I wonder if you have a skirt. Green or purple. And a big white apron. Then we'll have to have a bandanna."

Mrs. Jackson was appalled. She drew herself up indignantly. "No, sir!" she said. "I ain' got none of them things."

Parsons was not discouraged. "Well, we'll have to get them, Mrs. Jackson. We'll have to get them."

And he did. . . . He got a voluminous dark purple skirt, a big white apron, a loose snowy blouse, a green shaw and a red bandanna. "Now," he cautioned, "no corsets, Mrs. Jackson, and we're made."

Mrs. Jackson, who had always minimized her bulk with the soberest of colors, was stubborn. "I'm cookin' in this here winda, but I ain' gonna look like no circus freak."

"This is Southern," said Parsons brightly.

"The South ain' never had nothin' looked like that," averred Mrs. Jackson.

Parsons, convinced of his infallibility, was heedless of criticism. "Now I'm just going to make you a present of this," he said.

But Mrs. Jackson would have none of his generosity. "What I want with that stuff?" she snapped.

Parsons, baffled by this ingratitude, was reduced to one word, "Please."

"Why, folks'd laugh," argued the offended woman.

Parsons was exultant again. "That's just it! That's just what we want! We want people to laugh."

Mrs. Jackson put down her cooking fork with a look that predicted resignation from a distasteful occupation.

"Twenty dollars a week," offered the resolute Parsons, remembering how Kraft had achieved his success.

Mrs. Jackson had a conscience quickened by four little children who had to be clothed and fed and who belonged to her. She grumbled, "Ain' *nobody* ever wore no such foolishness!" But she accepted.

Parsons was jubilant. There was his bright spot to attract, his mass of color to display, his invitation to new volumes of business. He arranged the bandanna-ends to stand up like two-impudent ears. His caricature lacked but one detail.

"Now if you could just smile, Mrs. Jackson."

But Mrs. Jackson couldn't. "I spose you think smiles is put on like cloes," she said. "I ain' no actress, Mr. Parsons."

So she set to work in the window. Children trooped past, just out of school. One of the white youngsters, sighting her, cried out gleefully, "Oooh lookee, Aunt Jemima!"

"That Aunt Jemima?" queried another.

"Sure that's Aunt Jemima. Hey, you, Aunt Jemima!"

One of the colored youngsters, flattening his dusky face against the pane, saw his mother.

The blood ran molten from her throat to the pit of her stomach.

"Oh black mammy! Oh Aunt Jemima!" shouted the white children. And one broke out in song.

"Nigger, nigger in the pot.
Stew him till his bones all rot."

The dark youngster ran on, his companions following with their tormenting ditty.

Mrs. Jackson wondered if her other children would pass by. The perspiration stood out on her forehead. She had no strength to wipe it away. She leaned against the table and looked out, and the world looked in curiously at the embodiment of a fiction it had created. But then three round, dark faces appeared at the pane who had never imagined this fantasy before them. They gazed with wonder. With an almost imperceptible movement of her head, she ordered them away. They started to run, but the youngest looked back and asked, "What's Mama doing there?"

Coming out of the alley-way, her day's work done, Mrs. Jackson was confronted by a huge new neon sign in front of the restaurant. It bore the legend: *Mammy's.*

What could she say to the children? Should she take advantage of her superior position and force them to an unquestioning subservience to the indignities of human life, or should she make them comrades in her battle for a livelihood? When she reached the door of her flat, she paused. She was so ashamed. Four pairs of eyes were wide open as she tiptoed into the room. "You wake?" she asked.

"Yes'm," replied the eldest.

Mrs. Jackson took off her coat and hat busily, wishing vaguely that they had been asleep and she might defer explanation till morning at least. But her young son allowed her no leeway. "Mama, that wasn't you in the winda, was it?" He asked the question with a downward inflection, as though convinced that it couldn't have been she.

"Yes, honey, that was me. Why ain' you children sleep?" There was silence for a moment. Then another question.

"What you in the winda for?"

"I got t' work. Tha's my job."

"I thought you did cookin', Mama," remarked one of the girls.

"Tha's cookin'."

Her son thought. Then he spoke. "I don't like that kind of cookin'."

"Now you children jus lissen t' me. There's some things you got t' unnerstan'. Some work's dignified 'n' some ain' so dignified. But it all got t' be done. My work's cookin' 'n' there ain' nothin' wrong with that. If I didn' cook you wouldn' have no shoes 'n' I wouldn' have no shoes 'n' we wouldn' have nothin' t' eat 'n' I 'speck we'd jus' lay up here 'n' die." She paused for breath, then went on:

"The owner man where I works thinks he gonna dress me up t' look like a ol' Southern mammy 'n' get a lotta business—"

"What's a ol' Southern mammy, Mama?"

"A Southern mammy's a ol' colored woman who had the nursin' of all the little white children t' do in the South doin slavery times. Sometimes you hears folks talkin' big 'bout their ol' mammy 'n' how powerful much they loved her 'n' all."

"Is that good, Mama?" asked her son, doubting that a mammy was to be approved."

"Well, when you hears such talk you jus' say 'uh, huh,' 'n' let whoever's talkin' talk on."

"Then what happened after you was a Southern mammy, Mama?" The little girls were impatient.

"Then I had t' do my cookin' in the winda. 'N' when you go pas', you can speak, but doan you linger. 'N' if your little fren's asks questions, you tell'm that's your mama all right. She's got t' work for a livin'." She paused. *"'N' son, doan you never let me see you run no more when a body say nigger. You turn roun' 'n' give'm such a thrashin' they woan never forget. Unnerstan'?"*

The youngster remonstrated. "They said in Sunday school we wasn't to fight—"

"You got t' use a little horse sense bout some things, son," his mother replied tersely. "Now you all go t' sleep."

The little boy went back to his cot and the little girls snuggled against each other under the thin blanket. Mrs. Jackson was about to lift her weary self from the edge of the bed when the smallest girl, as if divining the trouble stirring in her mother's soul, crept up to her and whispered, "Mama, I thought you looked pretty in the winda. Real pretty."

ELIZABETH THOMAS

Our House

"Yes, built by Edward. Of course I planned it. A good many years ago . . . been with us a long time. . . ."

"I don't know; Negroes live forever."

As Dorcas went in and came out, the door let the diners' voices through to Edward who stood beside the pantry table. Mr. and Mrs. Burden were going away this evening for their usual autumn holiday and he had been told to be at hand for any last instructions. Waiting, he listened absently as they answered their guest's remarks about the panels, the fireplace, and the moldings of the dining room.

"In all Cumberland county you won't find a better house, if I do say so. My plan of course."

"Edward had his brothers to help him, you must remember, dear," Mrs. Burden's voice said. "They were all young fellows then, quick and obliging. Cephas married first, didn't he? Or did Amser? They took other places with their wives. Ungrateful after we'd given them work. But we'd have had to let them go later, so it was just as well. Then Edward married and his wife came to cook for us. She was an excellent cook, for years . . . but she died."

Yes, Lulie had died; first she had lived though, that gentle smiling brown girl Edward had found and brought here long ago. In the cabin beyond the orchard she had raised their brown smiling babies; here in the big house she had worked for the white folks and pleased them. In that cabin and this kitchen she had lived all of her gentle life; as he stood and watched his granddaughter in her trim apron and skimpy black dress pass through the pantry carrying the dishes of succotash, tomatoes, hot rolls which his cousin Tilly had cooked, the memory of Lulie was a pleasant scent to him.

"Jelly?" Mrs. Burden's voice urged, "a little with your meat? I put up more than a hundred glasses of jellies this summer . . . to my friends at Christmas . . . of course I don't do the preserving myself."

Edward heard without giving much thought to what was being said. Mr. and Mrs. Burden had been talking for a good many years: to their son grown and gone now, to their guests, to each other, to him and his kin. Sometimes they spoke crossly, sometimes they complained or called in a hurry, but mostly they just talked. The sound was as much a part of Edward's working life as was the sound of the animals breathing in their stalls, the whispering of the brush harrow he dragged over the garden, the creaking of winter boughs in the orchard. Like the other creatures and objects they, too, said their own words over and over.

Yet this evening they were saying something he had not heard before or hearing had not heeded. "Edward growing old"—yes he supposed he was, with his occasional miseries, though he had no exact record of his age. After this house was built Mr. Burden had given him charge of the land. Cornfields, calves, peach trees and apple trees, he had raised up the land as carefully as he had raised up the house. For awhile his children had helped him—white teeth shining, bare toes shoving the dust—but they had grown up and gone out to their own work, and he was still in charge, still worked the land. When the Burdens gave up the horses he had learned to drive a car. And only this afternoon he had carried out on his shoulders the trunk packed for a month's visit; a heavy trunk, but he had black man's shoulders—

His proud reflections were broken into by the tinkle of the bell.

"Well, Edward, trunk off?"

"Yes, sir." He handed the check to Mr. Burden.

"Edward, this is Mr. Doby who is going with us tonight. He has been admiring the house. I told him I never could have built it without you."

The guest set down his wine glass and looked up at Edward.

"Did you make these fireplace columns, too? And that corner cupboard?"

Edward glanced at the two flat pillars which held up the mantel protecting the drowsing red fire; he glanced toward the corner where china was ranged on carved shelves; he smiled down at the guest.

"Yes, sir," he said.

"Wonderful. And that great door and those windows?"

"Yes, sir, Mr. Burden he chose the wood, I worked it for him."

"You did some fine work in this room. Such dignity, so tranquil—that's one of the handsomest doors I've ever seen."

Edward's brothers stepped into his heart. . . . Those days when all of them worked together, big strong fellows, prising the ox-huge foundation stones, swinging the long boards over their shoulders, black boys' shoulders. . . . Sometimes they sang or shouted for pleasure in the feel of their strength as they worked.

"Thank you, sir," Edward said. "It's a long time ago."

"It is indeed," said Mr. Burden. "I couldn't build a house like this today, Doby. Eh, Edward?"

"No sir, not like this."

"Well, come now, we must get that 7:45. Bring the car around. We'll leave it at Romer's to be overhauled while we're away. But no—you can't get back then."

"I'll get back, Mr. Burden."

"Any last orders to Edward, my dear?"

"No. I don't think so. I've talked over everything with Tilly. She and Dorcas will get the canning finished and clean the house. You're going to help them with the windows and rugs, Edward. Take good care of the house. It will be a vacation for all of you."

"Yes'm, thank you."

Edward helped Mr. Burden up from his chair, the guest helped Mrs. Burden up from hers, and they went out of the dining room by the big door. Edward went out by the pantry door, through the back entry, and brought the car around.

It was late when he got back from the station. Tasting crisp autumn air, he hoped Tilly was saving him some supper. But though the kitchen waited in warmth with a spicy smell from the stove, no one was there. The table was crowded with glass jars and with the baskets of beans, onions, cucumbers, and corn he had carried in that afternoon. "Two–three days' work for Tilly to find the top of that table," he said to himself, going on through the entry into the large square hall.

From the library came the glow of the lamp and the sound of swing on the radio. Edward looked in. Dorcas in a blue silk frock stood at the telephone snapping the fingers of her free hand and swaying her thin little body to the music while she giggled and chatted with a friend.

"Who's gonna fetch you to the shindy? Stan an' the others is comin' for me. Uh, huh." . . .

"Who told you, come into Mr. Burden's library without a dustcloth in your hand?" he began. "Who told you, call on his telephone? For all the world like this house belongs to you"—

"Edward," came Tilly's voice, "supper; come eat now."

He went back across the hall. The radio stopped and Dorcas scurried past him to the dining room. There his cousin Tilly stood by the table, a tall black woman in a cotton dress, her hair braided in three tight little braids close to her head. She held a pot of coffee in her hand.

"In here," she said.

The doilies, the wine and water glasses still marked the family places.

They sat down and helped themselves from the warm dishes Tilly put back on the table.

Presently from the kitchen came a soft low whistle. When Dorcas answered, it came again. Then there was the sound of footsteps and murmured words. The pantry door was pushed open and one by one they edged slowly in, the colored boys and girls on their way to the shindy. Edward knew them all. Here came Stan, here came Amser's grandchildren who worked in white folks' houses too, here came Cephas' two youngest boys, mechanics in a garage, and a cousin driver for a truck gardener. Tonight they had scrubbed off their work and wore their finery. Their sleek brown faces were glistening with pleasure. "Evenin' Uncle, evenin' Tilly. 'Scuse us," they said respectfully, "we've come by for Dorcas." They stood around the table or backed themselves shuffling against the wall. The younger ones rolled their eyes.

But when Dorcas invited them to draw up they became easier and soon drew chairs to the table. "You got any for us, Tilly?" they asked, and sat down and ate. Seeing a little wine left in the decanter, "Let's taste that," they cried and poured it into a glass and passed it around. They talked and laughed; they made a warm gay circle around the table. Slowly, wonder filled Edward looking at them. It wasn't only the supper and so many eating. There had always been plenty on Lulie's stove and she could make it seem like more than it was and serve it round to everybody who came. No, it was . . . my folks, he thought, my folks sitting here around this table; and wondered if he had spoken out loud, or if it seemed as strange to them as to him.

Here was the same room he had stood in a few hours ago. He had been praised for it; his moldings, his windows, his mantel shelf—see those old red woodcoals blinking to sleep in the ashes—his house. "My plan of course," Mr. Burden had said. Edward and his brothers had built long and four-square with large square rooms, and their kin had taken care of the house ever since: kept it warm, kept it clean, fed it, dressed it—and the white folks inside it. White folks. . . . He hadn't built it for himself, none of his kin had worked in it for themselves, yet now they were sitting here like it belonged to them.

Edward's working day had been long, he was tired. He pushed aside his plate of uneaten supper, went to the kitchen and, putting his hand into the back of the oven, brought out some sweet potatoes which he put on a plate. Taking his bowl from the kitchen dresser he went back to the dining room. Here he sat down again, filled his bowl with milk and coffee, and ate his sweet potatoes, breaking them with his hands. He pushed his chair a little sideways from the table toward the fire. The young people were making ready to leave. Dimly he heard them telling their thanks to Tilly and Goodnight, Uncle; but he made no reply, though what he was studying about as he looked at the coals and ate slowly in silence, he could not have told.

He was engrossed in watching a crowd of colored folks who appeared to be coming and going around a house. They walked in groups, in friendly twos and threes. The men wore over-alls, the women aprons, and they carried things in their hands: a broom or a saw, a hoe, a mop or a hammer or shovel. Some carried heavy boards and stones, some guided animals. Edward grew dreamy watching the vision of them. Who were they and what house was it? He couldn't rightly make it out. Looks like it's this house, looks like it's their house. . . .

The telephone rang and Tilly being busy with the dishes Edward answered the call.

"No sir, Mr. Burden he's not here.

"This his house, you ask?"

The question seemed part of his dream by the fire and out of his dream he answered.

"Somehow I don't rightly know, his house or mine. Looks like it must be our house. . . ."

ELEANOR CLARK

Hurry, Hurry

No one was there when the house began to fall. It was a beautiful June day, warmer than it had been. I remember that people had been particularly expansive that morning as after a thunderstorm. They had gathered on the porch steps at the store at mail-time, exclaiming on the warmth of the sun and the color of the tiger-lilies that had just sprung out all over town. One of the ladies, receiving a long-awaited letter from her nephew, had suddenly become very witty and had kissed everyone in the store, and this could never have happened on an ordinary day. Naturally it occurred to no one that a disaster was about to take place.

The only creature that might have given some warning was the French poodle, de Maupassant, who had been locked in the house and should have sensed that everything was not quite right, but he gave no sign of life until the end. Probably my mother had spoiled him too much by that time. Certainly she loved the dog, especially since the accident that paralyzed one of his paws, so that it was hard for her to deny him anything. People laughed at her for this, and she laughed at herself, but she could always find something in him to excuse her behavior. She loved the aristocracy of him, the way he tossed his luxurious black mane—Louis Quatorze she called it—or drew his shoulders a little together and pointed up his slender glossy snout. In the evening he snuggled at her feet, and then, though in the daytime her profile was too sharp and her green-flecked eyes leapt too quickly to the defense, there was something almost of a madonna in my mother's face. But she had spoiled the dog. In the end he was incapable of serious thought and must have played or slept through the whole catastrophe. The servant spent most of his time writing love letters to the village saxophonist.

I too was of no use, partly because I was walking on the hill about half a mile from the house. The other reason is simply that I was not interested. Later when I saw all my mother's property tumbling to ruin I did try to concentrate on the tragedy of it: shook myself, rubbed my arms and legs, even kicked my shins and jumped up and down as if my feet were asleep, but with no effect. I spent the entire time—two or three hours it must have been—under a maple tree, and rescued nothing but one silver-backed hand mirror which fell out of an upper window and happened to land in my lap. I think that I was also the last person in the village to be aware that the house, where I was born and spent most of my childhood, was beginning to collapse. I noticed it quite by accident from the hill. The house was swaying very gently, the top of the cobblestone chimney with a graceful and independent motion, rather like the tail of a fish, and the foundations with a more irregular ebb and swell as if the stones were offering a futile resistance to their downfall. The kitchen ell and the woodshed had already gone down, tearing an ugly wound in the north wall and leaving the servants' quarters exposed.

Naturally I made my way back as quickly as possible, but the lane had become so overgrown with sumach and brambles that it was almost half an hour before I reached the road. By that time the whole town was present and the lawn was already clotted with little groups of people (in one place the ladies of the Altar Guild, in another the three families that lived off the town, and so on) debating the causes of the collapse and the possibilities of doing something about it. My mother was running from one group to another, shaking hands with everyone, receiving advice and expressions of sympathy. She had been at a cocktail party and cut an especially charming figure, with her white picture hat and her flowered print. So much so that for some time—until the front wall actually began to bulge out over the lawn, like a paper bag slowly surcharged with water—most of the people were unable to keep their minds on the disaster and acted as if they were attending an ordinary funeral or tea.

Now and then my mother paused in her rounds as hostess, tucking the minister's arm under hers, and while appearing to cast down her eyes, with one of her green calculating upward Victorian glances managed to caress his face. "Ah Padre," she sighed, plucking at the black cloth under her fingers, "what a good friend you are," and added, turning to the church ladies. "He's the best Democrat any of us has ever seen." The minister, who had also been at the cocktail party and whose cheeks were somewhat flushed, gazed with sly benevolence over his flock, laughed his deep-bellied indifferent laugh, and kissed my mother's hand. "Ha ha ha," rattled the church ladies, and with one motion, as from a released spring, began to run in tiny circles around him, pointing delightedly at his full chest and the rather uncouth vigor of his jaw. "Always joking," said the minister, "here her house is on the verge of collapse and she talks about democracy! What a woman!" At this the church ladies could no longer control themselves, they rolled and pivoted with laughter, poking each other's corsets and smacking their lips enviously toward my mother. "It's true, upon my word it's true!" she cried, one arm to the sky. "He treats us all the same, rich and poor alike! Here's to Padre!" and she raised her empty hand still higher in a toast. "The best friend this community has ever had!"

In the meantime the disintegration of the house was becoming more and more apparent. From the upstairs bedrooms, and even in the pantry and dining room, beams could be heard falling, and already a wide crack was beginning to open diagonally across the front living room wall, exposing the dust-covered leaves of books, first the historical works and later the vellum-bound editions of Dante, Baudelaire, and Racine. It was this, I think, that first awoke my mother to a real awareness of what was happening. It was not only that the books were threatened with destruction; it was also obvious to everyone that their pages had not been cut. Even the town servants noticed it, even Myrtle who was hired for the lowest and heaviest form of cleaning, but Myrtle was a poor half-deformed creature and she would not have dared to smile behind her fingers as the others did.

One by one the books fell among the barberry bushes, raising a cloud of grayish powder so stifling that the people nearest were forced to stumble back over the flower beds, holding handkerchiefs to their mouths. "Oh good Lord! the books! the books!" my mother gasped. She ran up under the crack in the wall, and holding her white hat with one hand, with the other attempted to catch the volumes as they toppled from their shelves. But they were coming too fast. Many of them, too, fell apart immediately against the outer air, leaving only something like silica dust midway to the ground, so that my mother was soon taken with a violent fit of coughing. At last, reeling and choking under the rain of classics that were now striking her head and breast and shoulders, she was obliged to stagger back toward the road. "A wonderful woman," the ladies said, and they began to scamper to and fro, picking little bunches of sweet william, wild roses, and delphinium for my mother's hair. Gratefully she closed her eyes and was nestling her gray curls more warmly against the Padre's ample lap, when the cobblestone chimney tore itself loose from the main beams of the house and crashed through the lower branches of the elms and across the lawn.

Immediately my mother sprang up.

"George! Burt! Albert!" she called. "Somebody's got to save my things! Where's the Fire Department? Fire Department!" The Fire Department was not really a department at all, but a group of farmers who no longer farmed, so they had nothing better to do than to jump on the fire engine as it went by. They were now lying on the grass passing around a bottle of beer and laughing at some story or joke. "George!" my mother wheedled. "Albert! Burt!" and she ran from one to another, prodding and kicking them with her white pointed toe. The firemen looked up slowly at the waving roof and the colonial columns which were beginning to bend like wax candles in the sun, then hoisting their quids all together to the other side of their faces they announced, "It ain't a fire," and lay down again, covering their necks against the afternoon sun. "But the highboy!" my mother cried. "The highboy! It belonged to my grandfather, it's been in my family for two hundred years, my little old Aunt Mary left it to me in her will. She was so weak she could hardly hold up her head, and she whispered to me"—here my mother's voice broke—"she said, 'I want you to have it, because it's the loveliest thing I have, and you're the only one that's stood by me all these years.' "

This recital so moved my mother that for a full minute she stood with her face in her hands, sobbing, but perceiving that she had still had no effect on the Fire Department she whipped away the last traces of her grief and turned to hunt out Cedric the servant. Cedric, however, was in no condition to be called upon. The collapse of the kitchen ell, taking with it the entire outer wall of his room, had revealed him stark naked playing pinochle with one of the summer residents, an incident that he was now trying to explain to the saxophonist. "Cedric!" my mother shouted. "Come here at once!" But just then a shutter fell on Cedric from the attic window and with a moan he dropped to the ground, followed by his friend. Fortunately my mother was spared this scene. She had just remembered de Maupassant and was threatening to run into the house for him when she was assured that someone had seen someone taking him away.

In the end it was Myrtle who went in for the highboy. She was not at all anxious to go, even cried a little when it was first suggested, which was rather a surprise because everyone knew that her life was not worth anything. She had lost four fingers in a meat chopper, so perhaps it was the pain she was afraid of, or the noise: it was hard to tell. At any rate, as soon as she heard that the Selectmen had chosen her for the job she began to whimper and for several minutes stood twisting her fingers in her apron, made out of an old pair of bloomers my mother had given her, and chewing her hair. "Oh no," she muttered to herself, "you don't see *me* going in there"—she had the habit of talking to herself while she worked, even told herself long stories sometimes as she cleaned out the toilets—"Not me, nossir! They come up to me all together and they says, 'Now Myrtle,' they says, 'you just run along in there and bring out that hairloom. 'Tain't as heavy as it looks,' they says, kind of coaxing-like, 'and mind you don't smash it on the way out.' I like that! Mind you don't smash it, they says, on the way out! And there was the whole house rolling around and a crack in the front big enough to drive a Ford through. Why you could watch the ceiling come down in the parlor, and all the upstairs furniture coming down too, bang! bang! bang! Mind you don't smash it, they says, on the way out! And do you want to know what I said?" Myrtle placed her crippled hands on her hips and with her eyes fiercely lit up she went on, raising her voice to a scream in order to hear herself above the splintering and crashing of the house. "I says to them, 'No!' I stood right up to them and I says, 'I ain't going into that house, not if you give me a million dollars I ain't! And as for what I think of you' . . . Yes," her lower lip began to twitch and her voice dropped suddenly, "as for what I think of you. . . ." But she was now surrounded by all the important people in town, including my mother, the minister, and the schoolteacher—a tiny knifish man with a cone-shaped head and glasses—and realizing that she had been overheard she was taken by a fit of trembling and was unable to go on. "I just got the habit of talking to myself," she apologized, letting out a choked laugh, and then she began to cry again, with her head hanging and her red stubs pressed into the hair over her eyes.

"I have no sympathy with any of them," said the schoolteacher. "They ought to be horsewhipped, they don't want to work." He strode through the crowd, receiving with a wrinkling of his beagle's nose their murmurs of agreement, tore off a stout black cherry switch and with little nasal shouts, like a cheerleader, began to slash at Myrtle's ankles. "Oh mercy," said Cedric. He giggled a little, then with a sob turned back to hide his face. "Oh darling," he moaned, waving his fingers in the direction of Myrtle who was now hobbling toward the doorway, "It has such dreadful feet!"

My mother was not wholly in sympathy with the schoolteacher's tactics. She pushed her arm under Myrtle's, and half dragging, half comforting her, pressed a dollar bill between her thumb and what was left of her forefinger. "I want you to take this, my dear, and get yourself something pretty." Without raising her eyes Myrtle took the money and poked it in her shoe.

In the doorway a new difficulty arose, the columns and the doorframe itself having already collapsed, leaving only an irregular space no bigger than the entrance to a small kennel for Myrtle to pass through. However several white-flanneled husbands now sprang into action, lifted Myrtle over the debris on the stoop, and twisted and heaved her headfirst into the hall. In less than a minute there was nothing to be seen of her but one soleless shoe with the crisp corner of a dollar bill sticking out at the side. "It seems rather a pity," the minister murmured, looking at my mother. "Yes," she hesitated. "Poor dear Myrtle, she's such a pitiful litle creature really and she has so little. . . . but of course I can make it up to her." She smiled, grabbed the dollar, and with a hidden ladylike gesture forced it into the Padre's reluctant hand. "For the new altar cloths," she whispered. "I have so little these days, but this much I *can* do for the community."

For almost half an hour Myrtle fought her way through the wreckage inside the house, trying to reach the highboy in the downstairs guest room. From time to time we could see her face in an upstairs window, perspiration dropping from her hair, or her arm through one of the cracks that were now widening on every wall. "Hurry!" my mother shouted, with increasing anger as one by one her treasures—a Russian ikon, the Dresden china coffee cups, the Renaissance desk brought so tenderly from Florence—fell and were crushed. "Hurry up, Myrtle! Hurry up! Hurry up!" And every time a part of Myrtle came into view the schoolteacher's eyes brightened and he danced back and forth cracking the black cherry whip above his head. "She's a good worker but terribly slow," the ladies agreed, twisting their handkerchiefs and criticizing Myrtle's progress through the house. Some of them, the old New England stock, filled the time more usefully: dusted the grass and bushes where the books had fallen and arranged those that had remained intact in neat piles along the flagstone walk.

During this time the front of the house had been bellying more and more out toward the lawn so that it was no longer possible to see into the guest room. "It's gone!" my mother cried. "Ah, Padre!" and she leaned against the minister. But a moment later Myrtle appeared again, this time on all fours, crawling up the circular staircase with the highboy on her back. "Bring it down! *Down,* Myrtle!" All the downstairs exits, however, were blocked; the lower half of the staircase too was caving in, leaving Myrtle hanging by two fingers while with the other hand she struggled to keep the massive piece of furniture from slipping back into the pit. Now and then over the sounds of falling timber we could hear her groaning and crying out, "Oh Holy Virgin, help. . . . Oh blessed mother of God. . . ." Then the whole front of the house squeezed down slowly, and we heard nothing more but the breaking of beams and an underground commotion of water as heavy objects fell through to the cellar.

The next and last time that we saw Myrtle she was trying to reach one of the attic windows, still struggling under what must have been a part of the highboy, though it was bashed to a skeleton. Her face was dreadfully distorted, as if she had been pinned under some heavy weight and in freeing herself had pulled her features half off. Of her nose there was nothing left but a bloody splinter of bone, and her chin, which had been rather underhung, now stuck out in sharp diagonal, forcing her mouth into an enormous grin. Yet in spite of this it seemed as if she were trying to smile, perhaps out of pride in having salvaged as much as she had. She kept pointing at the mahogany ruin on her back, nodding continually and working her mangled features in an effort at communication. "I can't bear it," Cedric said, "they oughtn't to allow such things," and he turned yellow and vomited in a patch of lilies. Everyone else was shouting at Myrtle—"Don't throw it!" "Wrap it in a blanket!" "Let it down here!"— but she had suddenly let go her load. Even from the ground one could see the wild look that came into her eyes, a brilliant hatred aimed down at the crowd. Yet perhaps there was some confusion in it too, for before the wall crashed her face changed again—for a moment she resembled a small wounded animal crying for its life—and she fell with her torn-off wrists lifted up in prayer.

The rest of what happened was so sudden that I have no clear recollection of it. I remember that shortly after Myrtle's death the ladies set to gathering flowers again and made a kind of tiny monument of them on the grass, with POOR MYRTLE written in English daisies across the top. The schoolteacher scoffed at this, saying there might have been some sense to it if she had done what she was sent for, but the general opinion was that the ladies had been very kind to think of such a thing. "She was very bitter," the minister said, "but a good soul too," and he took the carnation from his buttonhole and tossed it on the mound.

I think it was at about that time that the French poodle suddenly clawed its way up to the window of my mother's bedroom, the only part of the house that was still standing. Yapping and rolling his eyes he perched on the swaying sill, his bandaged paw held up and a large drop of yellow liquid rolling down his aristocratic nose. "Moppy! Moppy!" my mother cried, running up under the wall. "Did you think your mummy had forgotten you? Oh Moppy you did, you're crying! he's crying," she repeated, almost crying herself. "He thought I was going to leave him there all by himself. Come to me, my darling, come to your mummy, jump!"

I remember the two of them that way: the dog afraid to jump, tossing his ruff and his long silken ears, and my mother in a new flowered print and a picture hat, holding up her arms, with an expression of love, almost—I thought at that moment but I am not sure now—almost a look of fulfillment in her face, which at times made one think of a madonna though the profile was too sharp. And then the last of the house fell and buried them.

JOSEPHINE HERBST

The Enemy

The roar of the explosion came in the middle half of the picture. It was an American film with inserts tagged on in Spanish and the American voices coming steadily from empty smiling faces not now distinctly heard were a long way off. A harsh smell of smoke stung the lazy cigarette-bogged air. Several men in the back rows bolted up the dark aisle. Two from the front fumbling with pocket flashlights stumbled against one another and brushed by Mrs. Sidney as she started from the aisle seat.

"Senora, sit down," said a man rapidly thrusting his flashlight toward the American lady. She sat down. The picture went on in the dark house. American college kids played a ukelele and a big car bulging with boys in white pants and blazers and girls in fluffy dresses rolled before her eyes as incredible in the sudden tenseness of the picture house as Fiji Islanders dancing around a mess of cannibal flesh. She sat strained to the noises of the street, on edge, alert and waiting. A machine gun splattered into the boom of a second explosion and then the iron shutter at the entrance of the theater rang down with a loud chatter. People sat back in their seats stiffly as if an order had come for "Hands up." No one spoke. A single thin scream pierced the iron shutter and the frail building and then it was dead quiet.

"What'll you gimme," said the American voice.

"What you got?"

"Got nothin' but luv," crooned the voice with ukeleles whanging a chorus.

A man got up and walked out rapidly holding his hat over his belly. Mrs. Sidney rose deliberately and went to the back of the theater. In the vestibule a dozen men stood quietly. They were smoking and looked at her curiously, at her American clothes and her eyes very blue in her tanned face. One of the men without smiling broke the intentness of his fixed gaze. She spoke to him. "What happened?"

"A bus blew up. Right outside. You can't go now."

"How?" said Mrs. Sidney taking a cigarette slowly from her pocketbook. The Cuban looked with admiration at the coldblooded American.

"A bomb," he said shrugging.

She put the cigarette in her mouth. "Allow me," he said graciously as if at a party. He flourished a nice nickle-plated lighter. Mrs. Sidney moved her head politely and held it steadily.

"And the machine gun?"

"Police," he said suddenly sucking back the smile that had appeared faintly. "People killed?" she went on, looking at him. He nodded, staring hard, and she moved off carelessly as if humming a catchy tune. She did not dare ask who was in the bus, had strikers been killed by gun fire or were the scabs dead. She waited instead, walking aimlessly feeling the eyes envious and contemptuous of American tourists. Wheeling suddenly she caught them looking, brazenly friendly and wary. Inside the theater the American voices were again coming unmolested and banal from the screen. The heavy iron shutter rolled up. Creaking it rose and stuck half way above the now opened doorway. Mrs. Sidney went to the edge and looked out between the shoulders of two men. The street was completely empty. A little rain must have fallen. In other doorways iron curtains were raised or were raising and a very few people stood staring into the naked street. She did not see it at first and then she saw it. A pool of blood gummed the pavement in front of the theater. The wreck from the bus had been cleared away. Little pieces like bedraggled confetti clotted the gutters.

Mrs. Sidney looked at her watch. Ten forty-five. In a few minutes she must leave to be back at the hotel by 11:00. "The man" might come. She thought of him as "the man" with the detachment of distrust just as she thought of those Cubans whom she had seen every day before her trip down the island as friends. The friends were now in jail or in hiding. She had no way to reach them or to learn what was going on anymore except through the man. To keep herself free and above suspicion she must continue to walk, to look aimless, to buy foolish souvenirs, stare at the capitol like a tourist and be indifferent to death.

The awaited moment had come. For two months she had been waiting. There had been time for doubt of her to wear thin. Both sides had been suspicious. The American officials had concluded she was O.K. A little sentimental about the poor and oppressed but then she was a woman with a woman's heart and the administration had no wish to antagonize such people. There were plenty of stinks on the island and the best way to act was to be open and frank and show the best side up. Her credentials were first rate, first rate papers. And her manners, perfectly respectable, clothes smart, really it was a pleasure to pass her on to the sugar crowd who liked to pretend their affairs were an open book.

The other side of the fence had not swallowed her so easily. Where was her money coming from? Still three penciled lines drawn swiftly from the lining of her pocketbook quieted their doubts. Their proud doubting eyes had softened. Even if they were taking a chance, they must take it or die with their story untold. They thought of the great American cities, the United States gorged with fat, so near yet so far, the high buildings, millions of cars, swell clothes and factories. Useless to tell them that poverty numbed millions there, that factories idled. At evening along the sea wall, they sat, dozens of Cubans, feeling the narrow island press cruel as a cage upon their backs. As the boats glided through the narrow pass, they watched the gulls enviously, straining their eyes toward the mainland, the light on the waves dazzling them. To be away, to be free, to breathe without fear. If only the world rightly knew of their sorrows. They suffered the illusion that their griefs were unique, that no one had borne such trouble, that if the world knew, the end would come and a new day truly begin. They had a terrible respect for print and understood the lies of the island well. As for those papers that dared speak, they were soon silenced. Castor oil and guns worked here as in Italy. In dreams those Cubans saw their story liberated with all the elaborate Spanish turns of phrase, the indirectness that was oratory wasted, and they fancied that such long passionate pieces would appear in headlines in New York papers, that citizens riding in subways and great smoothly running cars would read, would freeze with horror, would immediately quit everything to telegraph, Stop, stop.

And underneath this phantasy that was widespread among Cubans who longed for liberation from their troubles, the hard heads that counted cynically on organization only to achieve their purpose allowed themselves to hoard a tiny hope that she might really stir up sympathy for their cause. They had suspicion of her respectability and respect for her credentials and they agreed, the realists, that she should be trusted and watched.

They had let her go down the island that had been turned into a long lush wasteland of pale green sugar cane, both crowds passing her from hand to hand. Managers from sugar plants had waited with cars to take her in the front door and show her around the elaborate factory where the sickly sweet pulp changed its hue from vat to vat. In the hot sweet air they smiled and bowed and she looked past their plump whitecoated shoulders through slits of windows to the green waving sea where the lumbering bull carts waited for the bent backs to load them.

She sat with them at luncheon in the dim cool dining room, the ice tinkling, the melons fragrant, the fish browned and delicate, and the wine poured into colored goblets. Politely and skillfully they fenced back and forth, sizing each other up. At last truculent, impatient, the American spoke. "Listen here, Mrs. Sidney, with all due respect to our manager who is a Cuban, a lot of these people don't want things better. He'll tell you, isn't that so? Try to do things and see what thanks you get. I admit they live like pigs but my God what would they do if we weren't here to help them out? This island ain't the one sore spot in the world either. It's practically universal. Look at what you got at home. Why pick on us. What about the farmer in the states? Say, there's a problem, he's whining around and on his back. Want me to tell you why? For the same reason these babies are flat. Speculation. Why there's no bigger gambler in the world than the farmer. Makes Wall Street look like a piker. They were riding high right after the war, same as here. Then what did they do. They speculated. Bought land. Greedy and anxious to clean up and now they can't take it. Well we have to take it. We can't whine and crawl out of it. We have to stay right here, Johnny on the spot and keep going. If this New Deal keeps up with the strange hold it's got on business, I don't know where I'll be. I actually envy the man on relief, he hasn't got my troubles and he knows where he stands."

Mrs. Sidney looked at her plate, stirring her coffee. The Cuban manager now put in his oar. "We can't answer your questions. We're not seers, you know. The past is gone and who knows the future. Wages are, as I told you, set by law. Anything you want to know about sugar now," he smiled brightly, "Let's discuss sugar as sugar. Then we'll get somewhere."

Mrs. Sidney couldn't help herself, her hand shot out angrily and then caught her napkin and the thrust changed to a diplomatic gesture. She patted the napkin gently and forced the words to come mildly, "Sugar as sugar. A process. I'm afraid I haven't got a technical mind. I'm interested in what happens in making sugar and where it goes when it is made. The people who make it and eat it you know." The set faces glaring unfriendly and alien warned her. She put a smiling face on like a mask, turning soft and feminine. "I like people," she confessed in a little voice. "It's sometimes a limitation, don't you think?" At that the American allowed himself to smile broadly, he eased back in his chair, and the two managers looked at one another in a relieved and condescending manner.

Alone in the small bare hotel of the hot baked town she waited for evening. Her notebook filled with scraps of their conversation flatteringly interpreted in case someone should search her papers in her absence. She wrote with her head down, her eyes digging into the page, fiercely intent, not daring to give herself any thoughts but these. When night came, she followed the directions that had been given her in Havana by word of mouth, repeating them to herself as she hurried down the back street, past the gasoline station, turn to the right to the tobacco store, walk two doors further and enter a long hallway, knock on the door with the card tacked over the bell. The door opened and the circle of dark eyes, wary, suspicious, softened. She stepped in. Did she know Castello? What was he doing? What had he said? What were things like in the states? Then as each man took self-consciously the offered American cigarettes, a door to a court opened and two men in white wrinkled workpants and no shirts came in, looking hard as if to discover whether or not this woman could help them, turning at last with backs bare and across the backs great broad flaming scars, the wounds of the machete.

All the way down the island managers of hotels obsequiously jerked out her chair from the best table but alone with waiters, as the fish was served, a scabby story of resented wrongs poured like a sauce over the food. At night after dinner the American lady tripped down the front steps as the lights went on under the palms of the little square, and strolling idly, suddenly disappeared down a steep street to one block south, two west, the archway with the iron grill, where young boys from the high school waited in their white suits. Their dark faces melting in the darkness, their white suits came towards her touchingly headless, and she followed them to the home of the dead boy's mother. His bloody oncewhite suit sprawled empty and useless with the dried accusing stains upon his narrow bed. In the dim whitewashed room of the dead boy she had stared at the collapsed clothes. On the walls above the bed hung a crucifix and a picture cut from an illustrated paper of a young Russian girl laughing, holding in one arm a sheaf of wheat. She turned from the picture catching a quick flash in the eyes of the boy nearest her. Her knees felt shaky but she answered their eyes, the dead boy's mother and his alive companions, looking at them one by one, promising, reassuring their steady asking gaze with a promise, her lips dry, her eyes as burning as theirs.

Back in the big hotel the stink from the open sewers wafted up with the breath of the sea. Shots had begun in the night. When day came little school children marched through the filthy streets carrying placards scrawled in chalk. "We want pencils. We want water. We want books." Swiftly the strike had crawled over the back of the evil island, coiling in the deathly green of the ripening sickly sugar cane.

She had got to Havana just before the big buses quit running. At night "the man" had come with news of her friends. She looked at her watch again, stepped firmly under the edge of the iron shutter that hung like a blade above her. No one else moved. They were watching her now with speculative indifferent eyes. In the greenish reflection of a light a few doors away, faces were suety pale. Shots began somewhere in different points of the city. The rattle of a machine gun sounded in a nearby street. She stepped out and began walking, erect and leisurely, close to the houses that leaned together in the night away from her. Hugging the dark side of the street, she crossed the now empty streetcar tracks, in shadow reached the Cuban hotel. A little group cluttered the doorway.

"Senora," said the clerk pushing forward. "You shouldn't be out. Didn't you read the proclamations? It's dangerous. They're shooting."

The faces of the Cuban guests that had become familiar at mealtimes now appeared changed and distant. "Is it as bad as that?" said Mrs. Sidney in an unseemly gay voice feeling the disapproving eyes of the fat woman who sang in the vaudeville house on Sundays. Going up in the elevator the boy pointed to women gabbling together on the landings. "They afraid," he said using his bad student English proudly. "Won't go downstairs. You not afraid?" He arched his brows pleased with himself and anxious to identify his own braggadocio, the cover of his alarm, with her recklessness.

For the first time she realized that she was not really afraid and her lack of fear set her apart as if she had been a victim of leprosy. She took no pride in it. A sense of nerves crippled by personal disaster humbled her. The deadly blow had already fallen and she continued to live. The thoughts that were terrible as hopeless disease pounced down on her as she entered her own room. She stood with her back to the door, looking at the snapshot of her husband tucked in the mirror over the dresser. A sudden burst of firing in the street lit up the towers of a nearby hotel as if fireworks were going off on some holiday celebration. She began to change her clothes, hastening, the need to do something racing as with some impending disaster. The shots came rapidly from beneath her window but no one screamed. Explosions far off scattered into deadly quiet. The streetcars had stopped except for an occasional one run crazily by a frightened scab with guns of guards at his back. Her hands were shaking as she fumbled with the dresses in the wardrobe. The green silk Tom had bought her on their last time in New York together stuck to her fingers. There it hung mournfully like a headless woman. When a knock came, she stared stupidly. The little game she sometimes played with herself that Tom had come back to her reminded her only of her incompleteness. She said quietly, "Just a moment," and dressed.

The man came in jauntily dressed in a white suit that since he had known her was washed and pressed frequently. His homely face with the brush of moustache beamed with a too familiar intention. She tried to smile cordially, disliking him for reasons that she was ashamed of, his stiff hair and small eyes. She tried to tell herself that he was to be trusted, that the friends now in jail had trusted him, were trusting him, but a memory of an afternoon in the office of the paper now guarded by police diluted her tolerance. They had smiled with impatience at his impractical enthusiasm.

On his part, distrust of her was coated with a fine appearance of amiability. He entered the room now as if she had been a mistress and a rather humble one.

Mrs. Sidney bore it quietly moving lightly away from him. The homely bed jutted out between them in the narrow room. He walked up and down bursting with importance and a pure impersonal joy that the strike was moving rapidly. His heedless optimism struck her as dangerous but she held her tongue. "Didn't I tell you?" he began. "What do you think now? No, you believe the embassy crowd. They knew better. Pretty good."

"I only said that they didn't believe a general strike could or would be pulled."

"Well this will show them. Did you see Murphy? Is he going to get you an interview with Bertolli?"

"Yes," said Mrs. Sidney. "Tomorrow. Today Bertolli is too tired. 'Poor Bertolli,' he said, 'he was up till four this morning.'"

"He knows that. You see, they are working hand in glove."

"At first he wouldn't hear of it. Said the most important people couldn't see Bertolli. I said, look here I've got to get off this island and I can't go without an interview with Bertolli. I pretended I was getting nervous and wanted to get off the island. He almost shouted at me. 'You getting nervous,' he said. 'What about me? If I didn't hold to myself just like that, I'd go to pieces.'"

"He said that?" The man was looking at her delightedly now and began to walk toward her. She backed away from him and picking up a brush off the dresser began brushing her short hair. Coming close to the mirror she took down the kodak picture and hid it under the dressercloth. "Oh yes," she went on talking fast. "He said he was nervous and he looked it. He was wearing a checked suit like a race track man and he had the nervous air of a man who thinks maybe he had put a big bet on the wrong horse and can't afford to lose. He asked how'd I like an interview with Mendoza? I said it was too late for Mendoza who had moreover been nothing but president and a tool. Also a fool. Murphy grinned and said 'fool and tool, quite a rhyme there,' and then he said that Mendoza was an honest man and that meant something in a place like Cuba. He seemed to be mulling over something in his mind and as I just kept on saying, a fool and a tool, he broke out with the fact that he was sore at Mendoza too, he was too slow and dumb and had I any idea what that man had wanted to do today of all days. He had wanted to go out to his chicken farm, mind you. I laughed and said looking straight at him, 'Well of course Mr. Murphy, there are only two people of any importance on this island, yourself and Bertolli.' He swelled up a little, then looked modest and said he guessed maybe I was right. I said that with a military dictator like Bertolli around there was naturally no place for a weakling like Mendoza. He caught me up on that.

'Don't call Bertolli that. And when you see him don't put such ideas into his head, he's got too many like that already.' Murphy didn't want any American putting ideas into Bertolli that might get him, Murphy, into a jam."

"The son of a bitch," said the man working his small moustache and walking nervously up and down. Mrs. Sidney had been sitting quietly on the edge of the bed. Her own narrative had steadied her again. With her contempt for Murphy the air in the room seemed to become purer. Where she was sitting she could see her own reflection in the mirror of the wardrobe and the wild idea that she could put on her hat, pack a bag, take an airplane and in twelve hours find Tom made her for the moment deaf and dumb.

"I said," the man was saying, "but you aren't listening, that you did a good job." He walked over to her and pinched her cheek. "What are you mooning about?"

"Nothing," said Mrs. Sidney.

"Well get a piece of paper and let's get the questions down that you're to ask Bertolli. I memorized them at the headquarters this afternoon when they asked me to come here. Can't trust anything in writing on me, I might get picked up."

She opened the drawer of the little desk and as if there was no escaping, the two cablegrams and Tom's letter in the well-worn envelope stared at her. Mrs. Kate Sidney, Havana. When he had made trips away from her he used always to write Mrs. Thomas Sidney.

"Can't you find any paper?"

"Here's some," said Mrs. Sidney. She sat quietly watching his fingers trace the important words, trying to focus on the little strokes he was making so that she wouldn't have to listen to the hum of the letter she knew by heart. Shut in the drawer though it was, in its envelope, it had a body and life. It was an enemy, behind her and around her. "There's no need to see me. Amy and I love each other deeply. Don't try to rake over the dead ashes." It was useless to resurrect that other message, cabled two months earlier, I love you darling always will Tom. The tenderness of the one made the other all the more mysteriously inexplicable. Some terrible darkness had come over her own little world and there was no time even to understand it. She couldn't get on a train or take an airplane or run. She wasn't just a woman anymore. At that moment it seemed the most important thing in the world to be and she drooped in all her muscles with bewilderment at what seemed her fate. The old silly words to explain life were no good, and she seemed to be waiting in darkness.

"Here you are," he said. "Now try to find out something concrete about how he means to try to break the strike."

"I already told you. Force. Murphy kept saying that they would stop at nothing. Why you know yourself that they've got lousy barracks all over this island. The kids can't have schools but they've got barracks. There's no food but look at the soldiers in their brand new rain capes and yellow shoes. Then the United States gunboats. They aren't on deck now but what's to prevent them from quietly slithering into the harbor. It's been done you know. Remember the banana strike at Columbia? Jesus Christ, I think it's clear." She broke off, striking a match and puffing at a cigarette furiously. Walking over to the desk she slammed shut the drawer that was open a crack and stood looking down at it.

"Listen," said the man in a patronizing voice. "This strike has the island behind it. The strikers are prepared too. This is a strike of a high political order. A crisis. Trouble is, you're a bourgeois pessimist."

The word was too much. "Don't throw that word at me. Don't. I can't stand it. A goddamned label. When am I going to get rid of it? What must I do?" She had her hands over her ears, looking at him furiously.

He backed away from her. "Don't get hysterical," he said. "What's come over you?" She pulled herself up and to keep from crying turned her back to him. When had she ever had any ease? All her life she had made her own way and making her own way had taken her from Tom. She had lost him, wasn't that enough? It wasn't his fault; even now, she was defending him as she always had, remembering the long rides in the country together, the meetings and then afterwards the winter nights, the reading and studying into sometimes morning until a light that was more than day seemed breaking. She and Tom had gone the same way together but some rotten link somewhere had broken. She hung her head and he came over toward her and patted her arm.

"O.K. I guess I'm tired," she said getting to her feet as she saw his intention to come closer to her dampen the smooth red skin of his forehead. The sharp little nose jutted out shiny from the determined cheeks. He reached toward her and she stifled the longing to push him rudely, smiled at him instead pitying his lonely desire. "Tomorrow then," she said gently.

"Tomorrow," he said, excited and tense. His longing for some small human gift kept him lingering. She tried to lean toward him but stiffened miserably and dug some cold cream out of the jar instead automatically rubbing it over her cheeks and lips. "Goodnight," she said, "And be careful of yourself."

Grateful at her concern he waved happily and went out. Alone she turned out the lights and gave in to exhaustion. She lay down in the darkness and tried hard to focus on the questions for the next day.

Tom was alive somewhere but he was not Tom anymore. All the clues to understanding him seemed lost and broken. Something that he called love had changed him so that the little baby picture she carried with her showing him with chubby hands staring solemnly at her was more like Tom than this new being who pushed her away without any need of her anymore. Her uselessness broke in sudden crying, she grasped frantically at the memory of the questions trying to focus on what she must say, the probable answers. The Spanish words slid away from her as if she were no longer to be trusted. Her plans for the next day deserted her as aloneness settled upon her like some doom.

The shooting had stopped and the early morning light came over the building opposite with a chilly freshness. Tom would be asleep now, his arms around this other woman as they used to lie listening to the early birds. The cardinal had been ruby red against the snow. In the morning they went out hand in hand to look at the garden. The peas grew an inch in the night. The tiger lily was opening with an orange heart. And sadly the eyes of the mother of the dead boy looked at her reproachfully. She kept her inner sight on those eyes, quieting gradually, lying still, her eyes looking down steadily at the mangled clothes of the dead boy. He had walked around and had laughed and it was he who had led the little band of high school boys on strike for more books, for water, for freedom and *more light*. Now she quit sobbing, ashamed of her tears and tried to think only of the dead boy who suddenly seemed to her alive and fresh and strangely familiar. Holding tightly to his young bruised hand, she clung to him desperately, as the sick and the injured cling to the well and the strong, and at last her breath came evenly as she shut her eyes and went to sleep.

TESS SLESINGER

The Mouse-Trap

Miss Betty Carlisle, Mr Peter Bender's secretary-receptionist, came
through the outer office with a sheaf of Mr Bender's letters for his signature—remembering, of course, to switch off the light over her typewriter
as an example to the "human mice" as Mr Bender humorously called
them. She was gracefully conscious of herself, as though she were still
home in Kansas watching a smart New York secretary in the movies
floating, brisk and yet charming (just as her clothes were both tailored and
soft), through the maze of desks and telephones and tables, while the mice
turned up faces friendly but a little respectful, a little envious, wholly
admiring; she liked to smile poignantly, the letters at her breast, at Fred
Dickinson—one of the "super-mice"—who always eyed her sheepishly
over the waist-high partition around his desk. The outer office, Mr Bender
had told Miss Carlisle, resembled a miniature city-room. The mice, who
went scrabbling on all day behind Miss Carlisle's back where she sat facing
the entrance with her Fifth Avenue tailleur and her Main Street, Topeka,
smile, consisted of the three stenographers, the two young checking boys
(who were better at finding scandal in the papers than Bender, Inc.,
Advertisements), Gracie the telephone girl, and Willy and Jasper, the little
errand-boys who looked as though they'd forged their working-papers.
With the super-mice, lined round the edge of the room at semi-partitioned
desks, were Joe Murphy, the copy chief (an Irish smart Aleck who thought
he was the brains of the agency, reflected Miss Carlisle, and yet let anyone
down to the colored office-sweeper call him Joe)—and his fellow-copy-
writers: Nicholls, who wrote up office supplies; and an old maid who
covered household furnishings and had published two poems somewhere;
Fred Dickinson, who managed production; the art man, Mr Furniss; the
two slick salesmen—"account executors"—who were never at their
desks; and old Mr Partridge the book-keeper, whom they all called The
Monitor because he kept tabs on everybody. Miss Betty Carlisle, remembering how Mr Bender said of the lot of them that some people were just
born to be mice, smiled kindly as she passed, guiding her tailleur gently

between the switchboard and a filing-cabinet, and always holding Mr Bender's letters as though they were a bouquet that she was bringing him. It was only when she emerged from behind the switchboard and started down the aisle of tables which led to Mr Bender's door—Peter T. Bender, PRESIDENT, *Private*—that she noticed, or rather *sensed,* sort of, that something was wrong today in the Mouse-Trap.

For they all, except Fred Dickinson, who dropped his eyes at once to his illustrated folder, were not greeting Betty Carlisle so much as they were staring at her. All of them, from the art man down to Willy and Jasper; especially Joe Murphy with a cigar in his mouth; especially Mildred Curtis, the stenographer Mr Bender didn't quite "trust"; especially Gracie, with her wreath of telephone wires quivering on her head; especially Sandusky the Polish checker—in short all of them (except The Monitor, who went on clicking righteously at his adding-machine) behaved as if Betty Carlisle's switching off the light over her typewriter and passing down the room among them interrupted something that might have been going on all the afternoon behind her back.

It made Betty feel uncomfortable, sort of. She was really on the friendliest terms with them all, and before Mr Bender and some of the "accounts" had started taking her to lunch she had gone along with any of them to the cafeterias and the cheaper restaurants. Were they speculating on her relations with Mr Bender, she wondered? But they had had plenty of time for conjecture on that score; in fact the girls had laughingly congratulated her on her conquest, and seemed, the prettiest of them, curiously indifferent to Mr Bender's charm. "Hello there," Betty said nervously to Mildred Curtis who was screwing up her eyes like an artist measuring the landscape: "How's every little thing?"

"Oh, just *fine,*" said Mildred Curtis, grinning; and for some reason Joe Murphy seemed to regard Mildred Curtis's answer as something by way of a joke. Mr Partridge looked up at their laughter and fell to clicking again with irritated passion—while over in his corner Sandusky broke a rule and lighted a cigarette before the open files. Betty heard one of the little errand-boys delivering himself of a Bronx cheer behind her back as she opened Mr Bender's door at last and shut it on the human mice to breathe in the pleasant cool penthouse atmosphere with some reverent relief.

"Hy-a, Baby, done already?" Mr Bender was probably the handsomest and pleasantest boss any secretary-receptionist from Kansas ever had. However well-dressed and aristocratic Betty Carlisle might feel in the outer office, with the underlings, she always felt a little shabby in Peter Bender's presence. There was a certain tacit richness of air that he wore, in his clothing, his nostrils, his elegant carriage, which no amount of Fifth Avenue tailleuring could supply to Betty. She never had the feeling, not even in her smartest suits, that she could relax (like the horsey young matrons in the cigarette endorsements)—she always thought of herself as she had looked trying the suit on, or standing before the mirror that morning: remember to hold the stomach in, one hip a little raised, left foot drawn to the right so that her legs (still rich with the basketball muscles from home) resembled an advertisement for hosiery; there was no "at-ease" stance in her repertory, not in Peter Bender's presence. But back of the discomfort there was a slight and curious thrill: as though it were really rather exciting to remain a slave to Peter, to be shabbier than he was, to wear out her manicure doing his work on the typewriter—while he sat taking his whiskey "snifters" and phoning for news of the stock-market or the tennis courts.

She liked his friendly arrogance (as though he felt the thrill himself, from *his* side of the desk) as he held out a lazy hand for the letters. She liked seeing how the white pages that she had taken such pains with were made to look instantly casual and ten times more potent—each sheet came out resembling him, careless, a little rumpled, but expensively tailored to begin with. Betty was proud of having been tailor to those handsome pages.

She watched him blot each one as though he stamped it with the royal seal, and then he set them in a disordered pile upon his desk. Betty took them up reluctantly; she didn't want to leave—she did want him to ask her to dinner again. "Oh say," she began breathlessly, "I put up that sign you told me, you know, in the Ladies' Room—and every time I think of it I go in and switch off the light."

"The sign? oh yes. Do any go-o-od?" Peter Bender was yawning absently.

"Well, not much. I was thinking, Mr Bender—" she couldn't bring herself to call him Peter, not in office hours—"I could take out the electric bulb altogether, they can see well enough by the lights from across the court, and *I* wouldn't mind—"

"Oh hell no, don't bother," said Peter Bender pleasantly. "It doesn't come to anything, really, even if they leave it on all day. It's just a kind of symbol, I mean, always let 'em know we keep our eyes open, that's all."

"And how about the light over *my* desk?" said Miss Betty Carlisle, flirting bravely with the boss but wishing she could let her stomach out, for just a minute. Oh *please* ask me to dinner, she prayed, thinking of her windowless kitchenette; I'm so homesick, sort of.

"Oh, you!" said Peter Bender lightly. "You've got attention-value, baby, you're the 'hook'—we need you in the limelight. . . ."

But no dinner invitation, thought Betty sadly. She turned to go, feeling still trim but dejected, as if for no reason in the world her tailleur had suddenly begun to droop—and found she hated to face the Mouse-Trap without a happy assurance in her smile. And then she remembered the hostility, or whatever it was, in the outer office as she had come through.

"They looked so funny out there this afternoon, sort of," she said—humbly, for her motive was only to stay a little longer and give him another chance to ask her to spend the evening.

"The mice?" said Peter Bender, yawning. "They always look funny, they eat too many hamburgers. But especially today?"

"Oh, they looked, I don't know exactly, but I *sensed* something—"

"You *sensed* something?" Peter Bender was at once a different man, rather like his signature, firm and keen, very upright and aware, a glorified photograph of the rising young business executive. "I cut that little Gracie this morning—still she wouldn't have the spirit exactly—"

"I think Mildred Curtis," said Betty on a hunch, "Mildred and that Polish checker, and Joe Murphy—"

Peter Bender sat for a minute, tapping his teeth with a pencil, the way he did when he was rebating a commission to hatch a new account. "Murphy's a racketeer," he said, contemplative; "I'm not afraid of Murphy. But those other two, I'd just as soon be rid of them. Sandy's a foreigner, and I don't quite like the way Curtis does her hair, I hate that type." He walked to the wall which held a little shutter giving upon the outer office. "Hmm, look at that," he said to Betty.

The copy-writers had left their partitioned desks and were standing in a tentative group about the switchboard, behind which Gracie looked very small and frightened, wearing her telephone wreath like a crown of electric thorns. Mildred Curtis and Joe were doing all the talking, while young Sandusky stood by flexing his muscles as if they were all he had to talk with. The art man hovered on the edge with his hands in his pockets, and Mr Partridge, at home in his glass cage, did his accounts furiously. The desks and the typewriters abandoned by the stenographers looked surprisingly blank and ominous—but everything was canceled out for Betty by the fact that the boss, standing shoulder to shoulder with her at the little window, had lightly put his arm around her waist.

"Tell you what, baby," said Peter Bender, shutting the window on the Mouse-Trap and growing tall and strong and curiously gay, "we'll catch the mice in their own trap, see, we'll spring it while they're setting it for us. Stick around, Betty, I'm going to put on one swell show—and then we'll make whoopee tonight in celebration."

"My, I think you're wonderful, Peter—" Betty Carlisle's heart was singing at the prospect of sticking around and making whoopee with Peter Bender; and she felt so elated by his touch that she called him easily by his first name now, even though it was still an hour short of closing time. "You don't seem upset or anything!"

But Peter Bender was extracting his whiskey bottle from a built-in cellar and whistling merrily. "Take it in my stride, baby," he said, grinning. "No, I get rather a kick out of it, to tell you the truth; I like having something to buck. Reminds me of the good old days at college when we went out strike-breaking and had the time of our lives with the scabs' daughters . . . some of the boys took the other side, after all, strikers have daughters too. Here you are, baby, have a snifter with me." He held his glass towards her. "To the best-laid plans of mice and men!" he said. "And how about a little kiss—for luck?"

Feeling naughty but terribly gay, Betty leaned over the desk to kiss the boss. She was somehow afraid to let herself enjoy the kiss, it didn't seem suave—so all she really liked was the idea, the idea that Mr Bender wanted to kiss her. She had never known a man whose first kiss was so prolonged, like any Kansas fellow's third or fourth—and the end was as abrupt as the beginning. No, not abrupt either, he wound things up like an artist, a caress here, a murmur there, a polite renunciation in the way his hand finally left her brow—but while Betty was still recovering, still flushed from not letting herself enjoy the kiss, Mr Peter Bender was finished and putting away the whiskey, and looking like a business executive again. "Thank you, honey!" he said merrily, "you've got the softest touch system of any secretary I ever had, that prize committee didn't lie about you, back there in Topeka. Topeka, Topeka," he said, patting her lightly, "sounds like a port in Japan or something. . . . But business before pleasure, Bender! Let's go, honey!"

Betty Carlisle was terribly excited as Peter Bender stepped ahead and opened the door for her (the outer office was a bedlam!) exactly as though she were one of his lady accounts or his fiancée. She had never felt prouder in her life, not the day when the high-school principal back in Topeka had announced that she had won the stenography contest, not when the girls in her class presented her with a fitted suitcase for coming to New York. She walked out of Peter Bender's office at Peter Bender's side, thinking, "Betty Bender, Betty Carlisle Bender, Betty dear you were wonderful this afternoon, it gave me ideas about how we could be partners for life, how about it, baby?" She could not resist giving her head a little toss as Peter Bender's sudden appearance startled the mice into frightened silence, and she hoped, standing at his side before them all, that she looked, as she felt, like his bride.

"Well, well, well," said Peter Bender, and his voice rolled like a smooth ball into his employees' midst, "what have we here, a football huddle or a family picnic?" There was an embarrassed silence, while Mr Bender allowed his eyes to rest coolly on each mouse in turn (Dickinson scraped an uneasy foot up the leg of his pants; Joe Murphy screwed up his face in a "clever" way—but more, Betty thought, to show that he was *equal* with the boss than really to go against him—while Mr Partridge, still bottled in his glass office, stared indignantly over the top of his comptometer). "Or is it a guessing game, do you think, Miss Carlisle?" he said, and stood and waited for the laughter which didn't come.

"We've been doing some guessing ourselves," said Mildred Curtis; and the mice stood awkwardly, glancing from their leader to their boss. "Listen, Carlisle," said Mildred Curtis bluntly—and Betty drew in her stomach and her chin and moved a little closer to the boss, "there's just one thing we want to know—are you with us or against us? Did Mr Bender raise your salary just to put out lights behind our backs, or also to spy on us?"

"Certainly not, Mildred," said Betty, flushing at the brusque "Carlisle" in Peter Bender's presence. "Naturally I noticed, I *sensed,* that you-all were acting funny all day, and naturally, we all work together after all, so I spoke to Mr Bender." Her heart almost skipped, it felt so good to say "I spoke to Mr Bender," really as if she were already *Mrs* Bender! "And both of us wondered what it was all about."

"It's 'about' wages," said Mildred Curtis—and Betty flinched at "wages," it sounded so like a chambermaid. "And you'd better think twice yourself—how much does Carlisle make, Sandy? twenty-five, and has to dress like a million. How do you do it, Carlisle?"

Betty thought of the sales she attended at 8:00 on business mornings, sometimes standing on the pavement with other receptionists in search of sample bargains from 7:00 until the doors opened; also of how she got on without breakfasts to pay for having her hair done. "I know how to buy," she said coldly.

"Gracie knows how to buy too," said Mildred with a short laugh; "only she doesn't know what to do it with since this morning." There was a ripple of laughter over the office, as though Mildred had given the mice a bit of her nerve. Gracie blushed at her switchboard till her cheeks were almost as red as her eyes.

"Why Gracie!" said Peter Bender pleasantly. "Are you with grievance, my dear?" There was a burst of timid laughter, on the other side now—shot through with reluctance, and here and there (you couldn't put your finger on it) a stir of indignation. "I *thought* you looked a little pale," said Peter Bender, as Gracie turned almost purple under her trembling telephone wires. Betty Carlisle shook with laughter, Fred Dickinson caught her eye and grinned meekly, Miss Pierce, the pretty stenographer, stuffed her handkerchief into her mouth like a school-girl. But there was a wave of restlessness from somewhere, Sandy flexing his muscles and Joe Murphy murmuring something like "let 'em eat cake"—and Peter Bender, *sensing* it, grew lightly grave. "But seriously, Miss White, Gracie, do you think this is quite fair play? Now if you have a complaint to make, my dear girl, why don't you come to me directly? instead of whining behind my back—" Gracie covered her face with her hands.

"That's not fair play, either, Mr Bender," said Mildred Curtis. "We've *all* got complaints—this isn't Gracie's fight, it's all our fight." Sandy and his fellow-checker nodded.

"Fight?" said Peter Bender, underlining the word incredulously. He stood there with his hands in his pockets, very boyish and puzzled, glancing from one face to another. The faces remained blank and hard, set against him. Peter Bender stepped forward to become one of them, and Betty saw how his hand rested in a friendly way on the shoulder of Jasper, the littlest errand-boy. "Look, my good people, this is so much nonsense. To hell with the happy family racket, you all know I've never pulled anything like that, that's factory stuff—if you people have any complaints to make, I'm sorry and surprised as hell to hear it, I think you're a pretty swell bunch of people and I always thought we got along like nobody's business." He shook his head, rather hurt. "But, good Lord! I want everybody to be satisfied! There's no question of any fight! Now look," he concluded, brisk and kind, "we'll get much farther if you all come into my office, one at a time like gentlemen—and let's have a drink and talk things over privately—"

"And get the can privately too," said Sandusky insolently, "like a gentleman, with a drink—no, thanks."

"Be quiet, Sandy," said Mildred Curtis. "It's too late for that, Mr Bender. We've got a lot of complaints in common and we're all going to stick together—either you meet our terms or we quit in a body."

"Quit? Terms?" said Peter Bender, brushing his hand over his brow as though he couldn't have heard correctly.

"Cold," said Sandusky, grinning.

"The curtain rises," said Joe Murphy with relish.

"It's all too much for me," said Peter Bender, weary and sad. "All right then, sneak out like servants, give notice like a bunch of servants, and I'll treat you all the same way. Two weeks' wages, and of course I can't conscientiously recommend you as loyal—"

"We're not sneaking out like servants, Mr Bender," said Mildred Curtis dryly. "We're *walking* out—we're giving you the works this time: a strike."

"Heh, heh, heh," said Joe Murphy, with a humorless laugh like a poor comedian.

There was silence then, all over the office, and you could hear Sandusky lighting a cigarette and Dickinson scraping his shoe on his pants. The air in the Mouse-Trap, thought Betty, was charged with something odd and sultry. For a moment terror landed in her heart, she didn't know what to expect—but a glance at Peter Bender, standing lazy and composed, assured her: he was taking it in his stride.

"Strike," said Peter Bender, dilating his handsome nostrils as though he had come across a hair in his soup. "Strike!" he said, turning it gracefully into a rather graceless joke. "Strike!" he said, almost baby-talking it, kidding it, turning it round in his mouth like a teething-ring and sticking it between his teeth to show he didn't fear it.

"Egad, you got it!" said Joe Murphy, "Strike's the word." "With all the fixin's," said Sandusky, grinning. The younger checker unwrapped a bundle of cuts and sent them spinning across the floor. The little errand-boy freed himself from Peter Bender's stroking hand and ran giggling to his partner—and one or the other of them made a noise like an aborted Bronx cheer. There was a strange tension now, Betty felt, as though the silence were made of suppressed sounds—not sounds of battle exactly, but a hushed and hurried cleaning-up of weapons. You could hear Gracie White sobbing quietly with her head on the horizontal switchboard keys.

"Of course you all realize," began Peter Bender slowly—when suddenly Mr Partridge slammed shut his desk and came wheeling his old book-keeper's body righteously toward the boss, his briefcase in his arms like a baby. The striking mice drew back and made an aisle for him, as though a leper passed too close.

"Mr Bender, Mr Bender, I just want you to know sir, I am totally dissociated from these unfortunate events in the office, I have grieved for you sir, since I learned the facts. I have been helpless to offset the general Bolshevik spirit—"

"That's all right, Partridge old man, I appreciate your attitude," said Peter Bender a bit hastily, for The Monitor was an incorrigible old windbag.

"And I just want you to know, Mr Bender," said Mr Partridge, trembling, "that I cannot brook this scene, I beg to be permitted to go home, as you know I have never left before till after closing time. And you may count on me, Mr Bender, if there is anything I can do, through thick and thin, come what may—"

"Sissy!" breathed the younger checking-boy. "Why don't you marry the boss, scab?"

"I understand perfectly, Mr Partridge," said Peter Bender quietly. "And thanks, thanks." ("Tableau," breathed Joe Murphy, "ole Black Joe and young Marse Henry reaching across social chasm to wring each other's hands.") "And there is one thing you can do for me, Mr Partridge—take these youngsters home, get them out of this nightmare." He pointed, stern and kind, to Willy and Jasper, who stopped chewing their gum in united horror. "Go home, Willy, go on home, Jasper," said Peter Bender; "think of your parents, you two kids—Jasper, your dad is living on city relief, I think? and your mother is having another baby, Willy? Well, now, don't act like a couple of spoiled kids playing hookey, there aren't many offices in town that'll take on a pair of young monkeys with no training at all, you don't want to break your parents' hearts, do you?"

There was a cry from Sandusky: "He's bribing you, kids, don't fall for that stuff, stick to your guns." But the youngest checking-boy, Sandusky's partner, looked scared, he was not so old himself, and this was the first job he had ever had.

"Let's try and keep our voices down, Sandusky," said Peter Bender quietly; "and don't shout the whole night-school vocabulary at a couple of innocent little kids." ("Women and children first," murmured Joe Murphy around his cigar.) "Go on along with Mr Partridge, you kids," Peter Bender was advancing on the frightened little boys and patting their bottoms in the direction of the elevator. "Let me know when that new baby's about due, Willy old boy, we'll see if we can't give it some kind of welcome party. . . . See that you buy 'em each a soda, Partridge, and charge it to wear and tear. . . . Run along, son, if you want to keep your job. . . ." Mr Partridge went trembling on his way, the little boys, with a backward glance at Mildred, followed sheepishly.

"Now that the kindergarten has retired," said Peter Bender, "do you people realize that you're trying to do something that will absolutely brand you? This—this—what do you call it, Sandy? this *strike* of yours," he said, pronouncing it like something in a very poor nursery rhyme, "of all the uncivilized performances! No, listen," he said, sad and grave, and addressing particularly the super-mice, "we're all experts here, professionals. You. Nicholls, a writer! Miss Heald, I think you've published poetry. Dickinson, Furniss, an artist—and you, Murphy, have you thought of your wife?" Everyone glanced briefly at Joe, for it was commonly known that he had married above his class, a fine girl who demanded the best of everything. "And all the rest of you," said Peter Bender, shaking his head as though they had all become demented, "all the rest of you—haven't I given bonuses to the entire staff for slogans? My God," he said, becoming more and more deeply alive to their tragedy, "why, you people are behaving like a bunch of, of *factory* hands!"

"Why not?" cried Mildred Curtis. "We get paid like factory hands, don't we?"

"And cut like them!" shouted Sandusky—Gracie at the switchboard sniffed.

"There's been some misunderstanding, Mr Bender," Dickinson's unhappy murmur started down the aisle and died.

"Scene two," said Joe Murphy.

"Let's not shout at each other, Sandy, please," said Peter Bender. "How can you, Dickinson, and you, Nicholls, and the rest of you, align your-selves with such rot? And you, Miss Pierce, a pretty girl like you—how would you like your boyfriend to find you, Miss Pierce, down on the sidewalk carrying placards on your shoulders like a sandwich man? Why my God, my dear, you're too charming to go in for such stuff as that! Joe, you *can't* have thought this thing through, why your wife would be fear-fully upset, and I can't blame her. . . . Gee, listen, these are damn tough times, friends, for all of us, no one knows it better than I—do you think I *enjoy* cutting salaries? I cut them so I can afford to run this office, so you can all keep your jobs. . . . Well, say, it's a free country, I'm the last guy in the world to try and coerce you into staying against your will. I'd hate like hell to see any of you leave, but you know I can fill your places easily, I can get college professors to write copy and débutantes to sell it—while you people will have a hard time finding work anywhere else. But that's not the point." Here Peter Bender plunged his hands into his pockets and faced them honestly. "The point is it's still a free country, you're free, every one of you, to stay and keep your jobs, or free to go and jeopardize your families' safety—and perfectly free to go and make damn fools of your-selves on the street. But gee, listen, folks," he swept his hand, boyishly earnest, through his hair, "I guess I'm just a dumb guy, just a sentimental fool, I thought you all were happy here, and now—*organizing* against me! behind my back! well, gosh! I couldn't feel worse if my own sisters and brothers hired a lawyer instead of coming simply to me. . . ." (You could hear Miss Pierce, still blushing from her compliments, gently blow her nose, and Betty Carlisle herself was swallowing hard.) "And what do you think of yourself, Mildred Curtis, don't you feel you've undertaken a pretty grave responsibility, playing upon people's sympathies and getting them to risk their jobs?"

"I sure do," said Mildred Curtis, steely-eyed. "And I'll tear up our list of demands any time they ask me to."

"No, No, No!" shouted a number of voices in the office, but definitely, thought Betty, standing by, her senses as keen as though she were count-ing votes, definitely not more than half. The top staff of the super-mice looked as though it felt itself rather foolish, Dickinson was pawing the ground like an embarrassed pony, and Joe Murphy was scowling with his cigar gone dead in his mouth.

"No, listen, folks," said Peter Bender, talking in the voice he had used with the little errand-boys, at once stern and very kind, "remember this is the fifth year A.D.—After Depression. There are 400,000 families in New York City alone living on relief, figure five to a family it comes to about two million—and where is this strike or whateveryoucallit going to land you, except out on the streets with the rest of the unemployed? . . . No, seriously, friends, I'm shocked, and hurt, and really surprised—but most of all I'm concerned as hell for all of you. I'd hate like the devil to see any of you become officers in the army of the unemployed." (The art man suddenly departed for the Men's Room, and although he had left his hat on his desk he did not reappear that afternoon.)

"There's another point I'd like to make," continued Peter Bender, sad and urbane, "if you'll permit me to grow a little sentimental—a point about good sportsmanship. Probably the most decent thing that ever happened in this country is the show-down made by the depression. Some of us, at the first hint of bum luck, bumped ourselves off. Couldn't take it. A lot of others suddenly showed they had guts; met with reverses and took it in their stride.

"Well, I consider that we're having a show-down right now in this office." Peter Bender looked about him, so noble himself, thought Betty, that he raised them all for one minute, to his level. "I think I can spot the quitters from the stickers already, the ones that can take it. . . . Why my God, Miss White, Gracie!" he cried, turning to her so swiftly that she started, "aren't you ashamed of making so much of one little tough break? Why my God, my dear girl, last week I got socked as hell in the stock market, but you don't see me picketing Wall Street, do you? Do you advise me to picket the Stock Exchange, Gracie, tell me? How about it, Miss Pierce, will you pose as my starving child? Why, my God!" Peter Bender laughed easily, and then harder, and then allowed himself to shake with his laughter as though he couldn't control it. Betty Carlisle joined in, as heartily as refinement would permit, pretty soon Miss Pierce was laughing too, and Dickinson started coughing till you couldn't tell whether he was laughing or clearing his throat. Nicholls was giving Miss Pierce excited little glances as though he wanted to date her up, and one or two of the others were hiding their laughing faces from Mildred Curtis. Betty Carlisle was almost drunk with admiration for handsome Peter Bender; he really is a leader, a leader of men, she said to herself, while her shoulders shook with laughter and her legs shivered with a sort of thrill.

"Now as for you, Gracie," said Peter Bender, pulling himself out of his laughter, "as for you, my dear, I think you've been misled. You don't want all your friends to lose their jobs on account of you, do you, Gracie?"

"No, Mr Bender," said Gracie weakly.

"And you don't want to lose your own job, Gracie, do you? I think you've got a little sister partly dependent on you, well, you don't want to let her down like that, do you, my dear?"

"That's not fair," shouted Mildred Curtis. "Don't let him bully a weakling like that, you ought to be ashamed, Mr Bender—"

"And here's your good friend calling you a weakling, Gracie," said Peter Bender gently. "Now look, I don't know a darn thing about this communism, but I do know a thing or two about plain old-fashioned friendship.

How good a friend do you think Mildred here can be to you, Gracie, wouldn't a good friend rather lend you some of her own salary than get you to risk all of your own?" Peter Bender put his hand on Gracie's shoulder.

"Swine," muttered Joe Murphy in admiration.

"I don't know, Mr Bender," sobbed Gracie, "I didn't know it would be like this, I didn't mean to start any trouble—she started it, Mildred did, she said, she promised me—"

"Gracie! pull yourself together!" Mildred Curtis swept to the switchboard with Sandusky, mute and passionate, close behind her. "Gracie! You know you said you couldn't live on what you make, twelve dollars a week, my God! and two sisters! And we're all in practically the same boat. Gracie, don't you see, most of us have been cut already and the rest of us will be—if we don't stand together and protest right now. Don't give in, Gracie, remember all you said this morning, you don't want to let your fellow-workers down, do you, Gracie? We've all sworn to fight for you."

"I don't want to f-f-fight," sobbed Gracie.

"And nobody will make you fight, Gracie," said Peter Bender kindly. "Come now, my dear, you're all unstrung for nothing. Look up, Gracie, there's a good girl. Now look, I didn't know you were in such a spot with all those sisters and everything, suppose we promise you a nice Christmas present, a bonus, will that be all right, Gracie?"

The whole office went up in arms at that, Sandusky leading the storm. "Don't give in to that, Gracie! For God's sake where's your pride? Are you going to let us down, Gracie, for a lousy little bonus, it won't be more than twenty-five dollars, Gracie, Gracie, Gracie!"

"I—I promised Mildred," muttered Gracie. Then she lifted her head from her hands and saw the whole office staring at her. Terror and a kind of hysterical joy seemed to dawn in her at once. So many people staring at her! Betty saw her weak, red eyes float from face to face, waver between Mildred's and the boss's, and then she gathered strength enough to speak. "I promised her," said Gracie, urging her telephone-girl voice out in a kind of high-pitched nasal defiance, "I did promise her, but she never told me there'd be all this fuss, and anyway like you said, what kind of a friend can she be to go and let me lose my job and all?"

"Gracie!" The whole office seemed to breathe her name, typewriters, filing-cabinets—the very walls, as though a member of the staff were dead before their eyes.

"I can't help it," cried Gracie, sobbing again, "everybody tells me what to say, and all I want . . . oh, I want to go home, Mr Bender, I don't want to fight, please Mr Bender, let me go home. . . ."

"Certainly, Gracie, that's the wisest thing you can do," said Peter Bender. "Poor girl, you've had a bad day of it—look, Miss Carlisle, help her find her things. . . ." Gracie tried to rise, and Mildred Curtis fastened her hands about her wrists. (Betty Carlisle leaped forward at the boss's order but Sandusky blocked her way.) "Let go of her, Mildred, she's sick," said Peter Bender reproachfully.

"Gracie, you're not really quitting?" said Mildred in a low, harsh voice.

And Gracie, trembling, sobbing, fidgeting, crying out that she didn't want to lose her job, suddenly freed one hand and in a frenzy of helplessness, like a baby in a tantrum, reached up and struck Mildred Curtis a blow full across the mouth. Mildred fell back, stunned, while Gracie, more frightened than ever, put her erring hand behind her back. Sandusky let go of Betty and ran to Mildred, and Betty, righteous and brave, led the trembling telephone-girl to the elevator. The door clanged after her with a curious air of finality.

"All right, ladies and gents, break it up for God's sake—" Peter Bender was speaking briskly, "quit standing around looking like Amateur Night at the local movies, we've got fifteen minutes to closing time and anybody that hasn't checked in at my office by then is out cold, this is no Union Square." (He was moving quietly toward the private office.) "How about it, friends? A snifter or a bowl of soup on some nice breadline?" He clapped his arm around Dickinson and gave him a hearty boost toward his private door. "Come on there, Miss Carlisle will shake up drinks for anyone that's got the sense to admit he just woke up with dyspepsia this morning . . . this way, folks, I'd hate to think I was never going to see you people again. . . . Remember, it's 1934 . . . step on it, Dickinson, come on there, Nicholls, Miss Pierce, Murphy, all of you—there's thirteen minutes to go, all aboard that's staying aboard. . . ."

There were murmured shouts of "Scab!" "White-collar slave!" "Rat!" as Dickinson went as far as the impetus of the boss's push could carry him. Then he turned, hiding his head behind one shoulder and looked mutely at his fellow-mice, at his boss, and at last, very humbly, at Betty Carlisle, who smiled kindly back to him (he really did look, she thought, more like a rat than a mouse) and then proceeded, like a rat in reins, to work his way to the private office. "Come on, folks!" cried Peter Bender, genial and grim; "twelve minutes to go—"

"Comrades!" The strong, inarticulate Sandusky had found his voice. "Don't let him bully you, it doesn't matter about Gracie, it's better if we get rid of the scabs in the first place. I propose we knock out all mention of Gracie and go on with the strike as planned. As Mildred said before—"

"Eleven minutes," said Peter Bender, baring his wristwatch. (Miss Pierce slid a step or two toward Dickinson.)

"As Mildred said before," Sandusky's voice had grown thick with emotion, "we're all in the same boat, either now or tomorrow, as Gracie—only some of us have got guts!" He turned to look at Mildred, but Mildred was standing with her hand to her mouth where Gracie had struck her, looking like a blind girl. "Stand by, Comrades—"

"Ten minutes," said Peter Bender.

"Don't listen to him," shouted Sandusky hoarsely, "he can't do anything if we all stick together and hold out against him. Nicholls, come back, Mister Nicholls, Mister Dickinson—*you'll* stick by us, won't you, Joe?"

But Joe Murphy, with that dead cigar in his mouth, was reaching for his hat. "Nope—show's over, Sandy, far as I'm concerned. Count me out, I'm like Gracie, I've got no guts; I want my job, my filthy, God damned, bootlicking job. I don't sneak through the can like our artist, I go out like an advertising man." He pulled his hat theatrically over one eye. "Your martyr has quietly folded her tents and gone home—and now exit your advertising man." He started for the door. "Never trust an advertising man, Mildred, they can write a good list of demands for you, but they've all got million-dollar wives and grand pianos to support. . . ."

"Drink, Murphy?" said Peter Bender cordially.

"No thanks, Bender, I can buy my own poison," Joe Murphy bit on his cigar. "My congratulations, by the way, you're as lousy as I am, Bender. . . . So long, all of you that've got guts—the rest of you I'll see tomorrow and the next day and the day after, at half-past nine." He clicked his heels and saluted bitterly. "Partridge and Murphy, the Monitor Boys." The door slammed after him and they could hear him whistling "Onward Christian Soldiers" as he waited for the elevator to take him the way Gracie had gone.

"Nine minutes," said Peter Bender. "Come on, Miss Carlisle, you're wanted to make drinks."

Betty Carlisle's head was high as she stepped through the aisle of workers at Peter Bender's side. If anything, the glances full of hate that she received from the dwindling mice made her drunker, prouder, recklessly gay. They're all so jealous they're about to pop, she thought drunkenly—even that Mildred. "There's a pretty nasty name for female scabs, Miss Betty Carlisle," the youngest checker called out after her, and Betty let her nostrils quiver a little, like Peter's, and felt more aristocratic than ever. And then Peter Bender led her into the private office.

Dickinson was standing by the window with his back to them when they came in, and his whole body looked weak and dejected, as if it had slipped inside his suit. Miss Pierce was wandering on the terrace admiring the fine city view, and Nicholls was standing, a little embarrassed, pretending to examine Peter Bender's lithographs. "Where's all the gaiety song and dance?" cried Peter Bender, shutting the door smartly on the Mouse-Trap. "Come on, Dickinson, snap out of it, round up the glasses and ice, Miss Carlisle, Miss Pierce stand by and look pretty—"

"It's certainly mighty lovely in here, Mr Bender," said Miss Pierce shyly. "I didn't ever really have a chance to take my time and look around before."

"I agree it's pleasanter than the inside of a cell," said Peter Bender, pouring highballs all round. "Which is where you *might* be headed for—"

"Oh, you wouldn't have sent us all to jail, Mr Bender, would you really?" cried Miss Pierce gayly. "Oh Mr Nicholls, do you believe him, do you really?"

"To jail, Mr Bender!" cried Dickinson, trembling bravely as though he had just realized what a brave thing he had done in escaping it.

"Sure thing," said Peter Bender cheerfully. "Well, bottoms up!" The door opened shyly, and two more stenographers stood shyly in the frame. "Oh Mr Bender, we'd like to explain, it wasn't altogether clear to us, I was just tellng Julie—" "To hell with it," cried Peter Bender, "have a drink instead—we've six more minutes."

There they were drinking with the boss and you could see *they* weren't used to it, thought Betty Carlisle warmly. To show them all, and Peter Bender, and herself too, that *she* was, Betty hoisted herself upon Peter Bender's desk and sat there swinging her handsome legs, in their long, fine chiffon hose. Over the top of her glass she gave Mr Bender excited little looks, and she felt the intimacy between them growing, till she was proud and happy enough to sing.

"I dunno, I dunno, Mr Bender," said Dickinson, who could hardly swallow his drink, "I dunno just how I feel about it, Mr Bender, I didn't feel quite right then, not loyal to you or anything, and I don't feel quite right now—I guess I must be soft, Mr Bender," said Fred Dickinson, sighing deeply.

"Soft!" cried Peter Bender. "Why, my God, I'm soft as hell myself! I'm a hell of a sentimental chap when it comes to personalities, personal troubles and all that kind of thing—but causes! heaven preserve me from causes and fanatics, they leave me ab-so-lutely cold! Now take that little Mildred Curtis, does she give a tinker's damn for Gracie? No, certainly not, she was *using* Gracie for her own ends—and playing on your sympathies for her own ends too—"

"She don't come of a good family at all," said Miss Pierce, wiping her mouth very nicely.

The door opened again, and they heard Fleetman, the cosmetics copy man, with one hand on the knob—"can't help it, Mildred, two kids, you know—" and then he stood inside: "I—" began Mr Fleetman, "I don't quite know what to say, Mr Bender—"

"All right, all right, don't bother saying it," said Peter Bender, "the drinks are on the house." The clock jumped and everybody saw that it was three minutes to five, a nearby church-clock began to chime ahead of time. The two recruits from the stenographers' contingent glanced nervously at the door as though they feared that Mildred Curtis might burst in. "I just want to tell you all," said Peter Bender, rising, glass in hand, "now that we're all here together, how deeply and sincerely I appreciate your loyalty.

I won't forget it either." It was two minutes to five and Peter Bender spoke more rapidly. "Honestly, on the whole I'm glad this thing happened, it's a show-down sure enough." Again the door opened, and this time the younger checking-boy slunk through; one of his eyes was newly blacked, and it was clear that he had been crying. He stood there sullen, in an agony of embarrassment; he was there, but he was not going to admit it in so many words. Peter Bender hurried on, one hand on the checking-boy's shoulder. "From now on there will be perfect harmony in the office, because everybody that's staying on has learnt a lesson, and has proved himself—" The churches were chiming 5:00 all up and down Fifth Avenue, the office clock recognized the time at last, the hand jumped and stood still. "I think you people had better run along now," Peter Bender said.

"Do we, do we have to go through *there?*" said Dickinson, pointing to the outer office.

"No, no, go out my private door, you won't be seen," said Peter Bender impatiently. He shook hands gravely with each one of them, only the youngest checker slinking out with his right hand over Sandusky's black eye. "Christmas is coming, and so is prosperity," he promised them quickly, as voices rose in the outer office, "and you will find that I won't forget the people who stood by me in a crisis."

Dickinson's frightened tail had scarcely trembled through the private exit when the door of the Mouse-Trap, on the last stroke of five, burst open. Three stood there, Mildred Curtis, Sandusky, and Mr Partridge's part-time boy.

"Am I to understand," began Peter Bender, smiling tentative but grim, his sleeve rolled up above his wristwatch.

"There are just a few things we feel like telling you, Mr Bender," said Mildred Curtis, giving Betty Carlisle a look that Betty said afterwards gave her the creeps, sort of, it was so funny. "We feel like telling you what we think of your—"

"I've had enough of your feelings," said Peter Bender, preparing to shut the door. Sandusky, inarticulate again with anything but his muscles, lunged forward with his fists raised, Mr Partridge's part-time boy and Mildred Curtis held him back, and Peter Bender, smiling, poked him out and slammed and locked his door. Then he and Betty Carlisle stood still and looked at each other warmly in the locked room, and Betty thought that everyone in the world was leaving them together, her breath came and went with excitement as the voices (was Mildred Curtis sobbing? no, it sounded rather like Sandusky) died in the Mouse-Trap, the final steps were heard, the elevator outside rose again, and carried the last people in the world away.

"Oh my dear, my dear!" cried Peter Bender, "I hope you know how swell it was. Oh my God, I haven't had such a good time since the War!

And did we rout them, baby! and did we scare them! and did we get rid of just the ones we wanted to get rid of! I feel swell, baby swell! Come and kiss papa, honey, quick!"

He grew before her eyes into a giant of a man, his virility somehow enhanced, as a general's must be returning home after victory. She felt he could do anything in the world he wanted, have anything in the world he looked at, and when he caught her in his arms and began dancing with her about the empty office, Betty Carlisle felt that she would give him anything he asked for. "You were marvelous," she whispered, "I admired you so— and slamming the door in their faces at the end, I nearly died!"

"And how you stuck by, baby, you were wonderful too, you can take it in your stride yourself." He kissed her with a new and violent passion. "Let's have music and drinks."

He turned on a little radio in the wall and poured them both highballs, which he set with a pitcher of cracked ice and a bottle of whiskey on a little modernistic table beside the divan. She had a vision of him standing there and looking at her for a moment before he switched off the lights and threw open the door to the terrace, so that the fading light of city afternoon cast a dull yellow shadow on their faces. He led her to the couch and sat beside her, kissing her and drinking, laughing, holding her highball to her lips.

"I got such a thrill, baby," he whispered, "seeing you there beside me all afternoon, like a swell little partner." Such heady happiness leapt in Betty's heart that she wanted to tell him that she loved him. "You're a swell-looking gal, kid, and you've got brains as well as legs," he whispered. "You know how to live, you know what it's all about—don't you, Betty? don't you?" She lay quiet, feeling in her bones that her life was about to be settled. "It doesn't happen often, Betty, does it, that two people are so able to think alike, and enjoy things together, like we do." He pressed closer, and she caught the scent of his expensive shaving-lotion mingling with his country-club tweeds. "I'm just nuts about you, baby," he whispered gayly.

They lay there kissing each other for a long, slow time. "You've got such a soft beautiful mouth," he said, "you sure learned how to kiss back there in Topeka, how were the Kansas boyfriends, not so slow, eh?" "Oh no, I—" she murmured but he stopped her by kissing her again. "We could have such a swell time together, baby, I knew it the first time I saw you, such a swell old time together, if only you—God damn that orchestra! I hate those twangy Negro blues, wouldn't you think they'd learn something new!" He left her to change the radio station, and Betty lay there still and frightened.

"Turn it off altogether, Peter," she said shyly. "Oh no, I like a little music," he said crossly, fiddling in the dark with the knobs and the buttons. "There, there we are, I've got the real thing now, to hell with Harlem! This is the Biltmore, honey, now we can relax and imagine we're in a suite upstairs."

He came back and lay beside her, taking her in his arms. "Oh Peter, don't, oh please don't!" whispered Betty Carlisle, all her Kansas training—and something else besides, some unnamed fear—sending the tears to her eyes.

"Why not, baby, I'm nuts about you, honestly. . . ."

She lay there paralyzed, Betty Carlisle did, unhappily acquiescent as though she were taking dictation from the boss. A funny kind of gloomy cold wind blew in from the city through the penthouse door—they were so terribly high up! thought Betty, thinking of the nineteen floors and the elevator rising and falling and carrying the city's mice to and from their work, above the city's roof-tops.

"The wind," she said faintly, struggling for time, "won't you please shut the door?" "Are you cold, baby, with *me* here?" he whispered tenderly, and gathered her more closely in his arms. "No, I'm not cold, it scares me, the wind does—it makes me nervous, sort of." "My God," he said, "what's the matter with you anyway—turn off the music, close the door—can't you take a bit of wind in your stride, Betty? Kiss me, honey," he said irritably.

"No, no, no," sobbed Betty Carlisle—but Peter Bender was the boss, and soon he was kissing her till she couldn't talk—Peter Bender was the boss, and he could take everything in his stride, music, wind, other people's fear—and love; and it was not at all long before Betty Carlisle, who had never let the Kansas boys take liberties, had let the boss take the final liberty with her, on the evening of the day they had settled the strike together.

"You won't be sorry, baby," he was whispering, soft as air, "you'll never be sorry, honey, I'll help you out, I heard what the little Curtis said this afternoon, and I hadn't realized it before, I'll see to it you have plenty of nice clothes, baby, honestly I will—"

She lay there paralyzed, Betty Carlisle did, not exactly taking in his words but hearing the meaning just the same. All at once there was a terrific gust tearing up from the street nineteen floors below; the terrible volume banged against the penthouse door and sent it leaping and shuddering inside the room. "Please shut the door, please, please," said Betty Carlisle, almost sobbing now, for the wind seemed to threaten something, her own peace of mind maybe, coming as it probably did all the way from home in Kansas, blowing across prairies (like all the young stenographer-receptionists who were too pretty to stay home, who fled with their fitted suitcases year after year—and what became of them all, she wondered! scattered in offices and penthouses above Fifth Avenue and God only knew what happened in their heads and hearts as those fitted suitcases, those gifts from home, wore out!) blowing across prairies and coming through the narrow city streets and rising to the nineteenth floor. . . .

"God damn it!" cried Peter Bender—and jumped from the couch with his shirttails flying to buck that Kansas wind. He set his shoulders against the door and pushed and shoved and cursed, and he would get it just so far when the wind from home would develop a sense of humor and fling it back in his face. Betty Carlisle sat up on the couch and felt the wind cool on her cheeks, and she began to laugh a little at Peter Bender's antics. "God damn this thing!" he shouted like a puny giant above the gale, his expensive voice breaking with anger; but for all his bank-accounts and tennis muscles, thought Betty Carlisle, struggling into the jacket of her tailleur, for all he had been able to slam the door in the faces of the striking mice, he couldn't do a thing against the wind. . . .

"Where are you going?" he shouted to her as the wind roared between them. "Wait a minute, where are you going?"

"Home," Betty Carlisle cried back in a defiant nasal Kansas twang— and not caring any more that her tailleur was mussed or her silk stockings wrinkled, or even if she looked more like a stenographer than a receptionist.

"You little fool," he shouted back, pushing against the door, "don't be such a little fool, if you're going to take it this way, how in hell are we going to have any fun, how are we even going to get along in the same office, one of us will have to look for another job—" and he abandoned the door and gripped her by the shoulders.

But Betty Carlisle had grown desperate, and kicking and struggling, she pitted her good basketball muscles against his tennis-and-golf-and-whiskey wrists and gave him a kind of half-Nelson that her brothers had taught her in Topeka, before she realized she had lost her job and crept out and down the stairs like a mouse to catch the elevator from the eighteenth floor.

II. POETRY

Worlds Moving: Women, Poetry, and the Literary Politics of the 1930s

CHARLOTTE NEKOLA

The poetry of radical women in the United States in the 1930s may surprise contemporary readers. The dominance of formalist literary tradition has made it easy to forget that poetry can ask difficult political questions. In the 1930s, an entire generation of poets regularly addressed such issues as power and money in the United States, the dangers of aestheticism, the politics of hunger, and the growth of fascism. Women were prolific producers of poetry, although their works have been largely ignored in the anthologies and critical works available today. In these poems also appear the antecedents of feminist poetry today. Poems that celebrate womanhood, for example, may be found in the works of radical women writers of the 1930s.

In determining which poetry to select for this volume, we looked for work that could tell us about the unique political debates of the 1930s and women's participation in such debates, as they focused on class, race, gender, and international politics. We included work that typifies the poetic innovations of politically minded poets of the 1930s and at the same time contributes something new to our understanding of women's poetry and the history of women; we selected work that was also strong, formally. The works appeared in publications ranging from the Yale Series of Younger Poets, to now out-of-print volumes from large and small publishing houses, to anthologies of radical literature now available only in archives, to such political periodicals as *New Masses* and *Opportunity*.

How well known these poets are depends on the audience approaching their work. Margaret Walker and Muriel Rukeyser were young writers in the 1930s whose reputations grew in the decades that followed. Genevieve Taggard and Lucia Trent, less familiar to readers now, were older and had established prolific poetic careers by the 1930s. Some of the writers enjoyed a certain amount of recognition within 1930s radical circles—for example, Joy Davidman and Ruth Lechlitner, who have mostly escaped literary memory since then. All of the poets published volumes of poems in the 1930s or thereafter, with the exception of Gladys Casely Hayford, Kathleen Tankersley Young, Susan McMillan Shepherd, and Mary LeDuc Gibbons, who were occasional contributors to the journal *Opportunity,* and Florence Reece and Aunt Molly Jackson, lyricists whose songs became known in union and leftist circles. Three of the poets—Rukeyser, Davidman, and Walker—won the nationally prestigious Yale Younger Poets Award for collections of their poetry.

A surprising number of these writers worked in more than one genre: Walker and Davidman later wrote novels; Rukeyser wrote plays and screenplays as well as biography and criticism; Taggard, Rukeyser, and Davidman contributed reportage, reviews, and essays to *New Masses* and many other journals. Josephine Johnson's first major work was her Pulitzer Prize-winning novel *Now in November* (1934). Taggard and Trent both edited collections of radical poetry in the 1920s.

The better-known poets had ties with both established and less well-known publishers. Taggard, by 1938, had published extensively, including a volume of her collected poetry. Harper & Row published her poems, and she was reviewed by such now-well-known contemporaries as Allen Tate and Edmund Wilson, but she also contributed to radical journals such as *New Masses* and published other works with smaller publishers. Rukeyser won the Yale Younger Poets Award with *Theory of Flight. U.S. 1,* her almost journalistic, collage-like poetic investigation of silicosis in West Virginia coal mines, appeared by a less well-known publisher. Davidman won the Yale Younger Poets Award, wrote for *New Masses* during the 1930s, and appeared in a collection of political poetry in 1944 published by a small house. Others, such as Trent and Lechlitner, published only with smaller houses and in periodicals. Trent's activities as a writer were quite varied: she published her own work, published collections of poems, and edited anthologies with her husband, the poet Ralph Cheyney. Together, their publishing credits ranged from the *New York Herald Tribune* to *Birth Control Review* to *World Tomorrow.* With Cheyney, she also published a volume of literary essays called *More Power to Poets!,* an investigation of the conflict between proletarian and modernist poetics and a call for a democratization of the aesthetics of poetry. Walker, though at the beginning of her career as a poet, would have been familiar to readers of *Opportunity* in the last years of the decade.

Leftist women poets of the 1930s found themselves in a perplexing position. Theoretically, they were encouraged, like all revolutionary writers, to speak of the world and to speak directly. Women, then, could write "big" poems with a voice of authority. For American women poets whose tradition was largely private, often domestic, these were liberating propositions. Yet the particularly masculine rhetoric of revolutionary literary ideology also alienated the woman writer since it made her female concerns invisible. Despite such contradictions, politically minded women poets in the 1930s challenged traditional American poetry with experiments of both form and content.

Poetry was a weapon of class struggle: this was the main message of literary radicalism. Its focus was to be social, public, and mass—not private. Bourgeois poetry, radical critics said, suffered from an excess of private despair and hid in language too highly wrought and too obscure for a mass audience. It led readers to mere escapism, wandering in a subjective wasteland. Revolutionary poetry should speak directly, address experience, and incite collective social action.

It would have been difficult for women in that era to miss the image that the poetry-as-weapon metaphor provoked: weapon as gun or knife, knife or gun as phallus. Stanley Burnshaw reminded the radical poet that the weapon must not be a "thin, shadowy, over-delicate instrument but a clear, keen-edged, deep-cutting tool."[1] Did the woman revolutionary, then, have the right tools? Whether specifically sexual or simply macho, depictions of the revolutionary poet were difficult to apply to women. Polarized ideas of male and female qualities clearly contributed to difficulty in describing that anomaly, the female revolutionary poet. For male poets, gender and the revolutionary "weapon" were completely compatible, organically fit. Shaemus O'Sheel says that Maxwell Bodenheim's verse "crashes forward with the threat of an angry man"; Joy Davidman's lines, however, have a "hushed compassionate quality . . . but steel-strong courage too." And he comments that "searing irony is one of Norman Rosten's weapons" but that Martha Millet's poetry has a "feminine power of suggestion, and a masculine command of irony."[2] O'Sheel's 1944 attempt to associate such qualities as irony or anger with the idea of a female poet was not even approached by Mike Gold's dismissive declaration in 1926: "Send a strong poet," he said, "a man of the street . . . a man fit to stand up to skyscrapers . . . send a man."[3]

According to revolutionary rhetoric, men were the fit creators and the fit subjects of revolutionary poetry. Joseph Freeman reported that Soviet critics "observed that the poet . . . describes people who make friends and enemies, love women and are loved by them."[4] Presumably, then, the "people" whom the poet described would have been heterosexual males. All revolutionary poetry was to avoid the merely private, but it seems that the female interior, in particular, was a suspect subject for the radical poet. Bodenheim's poem "To a Revolutionary Girl" views its subject as a repository of bourgeois sentiment, lost in her own subjectivity. The poet warns her against the "softer regions of your heart,/The shut-off, personal, illogical/Disturbance of your mind," and concludes that she is, after all, "a girl."[5]

Accounts of revolutionary literary history did not find a place for the female revolutionary either. Joseph Freeman's list of important predecessors of radical writers, prepared for an introduction to a collection of proletarian literature of the 1930s, was exclusively male. He calls up such names from the 1920s as Jack London, Upton Sinclair, John Reed, and Floyd Dell, and omits important women writers from the same era: Lola Ridge, Anzia Yezierska, and Genevieve Taggard, for example.[6] Similarly, in a 1934 article in *New Masses,* Burnshaw named practicing revolutionary poets in 1934: "Fearing, Bodenheim, Kreymbourg, Freeman, Schneider, Gold, Kalar, Louis, West, Gregory, Funaroff, Rolfe, Spector, Hayes, Maddow"[7]—all male, all white. By 1934, women poets had regularly published revolutionary poetry in *New Masses,* in other radical journals, and in book-length collections. But no women poets appear in Freeman's or Burnshaw's canons of praiseworthy revolutionary writers. Their absence created a serious problem for aspiring women revolutionary poets: they could not find each other on the family tree.

Women poets were hidden within revolutionary literary poetics, as were issues of special interest to all women. Gender, unlike class, did not constitute a worthy political or literary subject. According to Freeman, for example, a writer is "conditioned by the political state in which he lives, by the knowledge of his time, by the attitudes of his class, and by the revolution which he loves, hates, or seeks to ignore."[8] Sex and race do not figure in Freeman's analysis. The invisibility of gender as a literary issue perhaps only points to the relative absence of women's issues on revolutionary agenda. Poets Lucia Trent and Ralph Cheyney insisted, in an essay called "A Poet's Utopia," on relationships among sexism, racism, and the writing of poetry. They called for "comradeship on a free, equal, and unself-conscious footing between those of both sexes and all races."[9] Outside such a Utopia, women might have had difficulty in finding their language, their heritage, and their issues recognized as part of the literary revolution. Yet, though women's position in revolutionary literary history remained marginal, and though revolutionary literary theory had a clearly masculine rhetoric, women poets frequently wrote the same kinds of political poems as their male colleagues. And they also wrote poems that specifically spoke to women. In all events, their work is unusual in the history of women's poetry and the history of 1930s literature.

Sometimes, the subject matter of their poetry is typical of the era—work, international politics, or the American condition, for example. The scrutiny of the workplace in Rukeyser's poem "Absalom" or the call for unionization in the songs of Florence Reece or Aunt Molly Jackson took women writers into the arena of work and the politics of work, which were more often chronicled by men. The concern for foreign political upheavals voiced in Taggard's "Silence in Mallorca" is characteristic of the international perspective cultivated by radical groups in this era, but it is unusual for women poets to cast so far abroad for the subject of their poetry. Rukeyser's "Fifth Elegy: A Turning Wind" and Davidman's "Twentieth-Century Americanism" take panoramic views of the American continent and condition in the popular style of 1930s documentary, in the kind of epic sweep more often practiced by Walt Whitman and his predominantly male heirs. Walker's poetry addressed the history of racism and the roots of black history across the American landscape. Some poems by white women also focused on race, as in Taggard's "Proud Day." And, boldly, some women poets summed up the general upheaval of the times, as in Taggard's "Ode in Time of Crisis," Josephine Johnson's "Ice Winter," or Katherine Tankersley Young's "All Things Insensible." Such poems encompass the mood of an entire decade. Margaret Fuller, speaking of herself as an artist in the middle of the nineteenth century, complained that "womanhood at present is too straightly bounded to give me scope."[10] The aesthetics of revolutionary poetry in the 1930s called for works on a large and searching scale, with the kind of "scope" that Whitman assumed and Fuller felt to be beyond her reach. Cultural and political gains made by such movements as early-twentieth-century feminism and the Harlem renaissance joined with radical vision to open up possibilities of "big" poems with "scope" for women—the kind of poems called for in a decade of economic and political crisis.

Poetry by women in the 1930s matched leftist arguments against ironic despair, aestheticism, and meaningless or elitist erudition in the works of such modernist poets as T. S. Eliot and Ezra Pound. In "Turn to the East" Genevieve Taggard attacks Pound's appropriation of Chinese culture for his poetry; she also portrays El Greco and D. H. Lawrence as paralyzed with despair in "Called Divine." Lucia Trent's "Parade the Narrow Turrets" takes on academics as well as sad young men who embody the ironic pose. The speakers in these poems of protest are set against a male representative of the modernist stance. Such men—professors, famous artists and writers, wise men, and despairing young men—belonged to a tradition that was largely elite and concerned with problems of individual ego. That these poems were written by female poets addressing a predominantly male tradition adds the element of gender to their refusal of modernism and aestheticism: perhaps they were also protesting the male heirship to that tradition. None of these writers, for example, attacked the cultural borrowings of H. D. or the formal experiments of Gertrude Stein.

Politically minded male writers seldom wrote poems that dealt with issues of gender or celebrated specifically female traditions. Radical thinkers generally thought the problems of women would be resolved by class struggle. Gender itself was a relatively quiet issue. Yet poems survive from this era that seem to be precursors of the radical feminism of the

1960s, when gender became the foremost topic. Such poems are rare in the body of poetry by politically minded women of the 1930s, but they do surface often enough to make a body of work. Some offer a persistent image of the strength of woman, through generations of mothers and grandmothers—as in Taggard's "To My Mother," Walker's "Lineage," Davidman's "This Woman," and Gibbons's "Mothers." Reproductive themes seldom found in poetry emerge as the subjects of Ruth Lechlitner's "On the Wall to Your Left" and of Trent's "Breed, Women, Breed." The political potential of women's voices emerges in Rukeyser's "Ann Burlak" and Taggard's "At Last the Women Are Moving." Unusual within this body of poetry on womanhood are poems that analyze gender and class, or gender and race, at the same time. A sentiment that recurs among radical women poets of the 1930s is the insularity of middle-class or upper-class women in the face of hunger and unemployment, as in Rukeyser's "More of a Corpse Than a Woman" and Trent's "Lady in a Limousine." In Trent's "Breed, Women, Breed" working-class women are seen as "breeders" of workers for the ruling class. Divisions between women of different races and social classes are sharply portrayed in Hayford's "The Palm Wine Seller," Gibbons's "Mothers," and, indirectly, in Shepherd's "White Man's Blues."

The ideals of proletarian poetry embraced work and the workplace as central subjects, yet relatively few poems by women on work appeared in the 1930s. Poetry by men in this decade is full of worker-heroes, complaints of displaced workers, political-organizer heroes, and of accounts of strikes and of the physical facts of coal mines and steel mills. The "brotherhood" of "workmen" found a noisy outlet in such lines as Joseph Kalar's "Once I rubbed shoulders with sweaty men/pulled when they pulled, strained, cursed."[11] Though women fiction writers and journalists wrote about the mechanics and politics of the workplace, the female equivalent of the male work poem is hard to find. Tillie Olsen's "I Want You Women Up North to Know," about Mexican needle workers, is unusual in that it not only details the conditions of work itself but also outlines the relationship of third-world workers to a capitalist economy. The most expressive female lyrics on work—those of songwriters like Aunt Molly Jackson and Sarah Ogan Gunning—have their roots in the anonymous songs of women textile workers from the late nineteenth century.[12] Absent, too, is poetry that depicts the double day of women workers—at the mill and at home, at the factory and at home, for example. Whether work in the home could be considered productive labor was a debatable issue within radical circles, and it would seem that work at home was as yet largely unrecognized as work. So it is not surprising that few poems of domestic labor emerge from this era.

A note on other kinds of poems that readers who are familiar with feminist poetry from the 1960s and 1970s might have expected to find: we did not find works that analyze women in their power relationships with men, as in Sylvia Plath's "Daddy" or Adrienne Rich's "Snapshots of a Daughter-in-law." Two aspects of 1930s literary and political culture would have made the climate inhospitable to such work: the general dismissal of "the personal" as subject matter (except that journalism was full of first-person worker narratives, for example, which were thought to translate to larger principles); and the absence of sexism as a major topic of political debate. We did not find poetry that discussed a women's community, or love relationships between women. But we occasionally found poems in which a female speaker specifically addressed a female reader—as in Davidman's "Letter to a Comrade," too lengthy for inclusion here—suggesting the importance of political kinship based on gender.

The poetry of politically involved women of the 1930s asks its readers to become engaged in, not detached from, the social and economic problems of the world, as it warns against indifference, hunger, or fascism. Women poets had a double stake in refusing aesthetic detachment: they could speak outside of an inherited literary tradition, and they could speak for their own route to liberation as they spoke for others. Like their male colleagues, revolutionary women poets were encouraged to think big and to speak directly. For women especially, these were expansive ideas. "Comrade," says a Joy Davidman poem, "Possess understanding." The fusion of personal with social vision in their poetry claims for the women poets of this decade a unique place in the history of American women's writing. They leave us a sense of our own possibilities as political thinkers to work out the complex relationships among gender, class, and race. These poets ask us not only to envision new worlds but to proclaim them—like Rukeyser's Ann Burlak, to "speak the desire of the worlds moving unmade."

NOTES

1. Stanley Burnshaw, "Notes on Revolutionary Poetry," *New Masses* 10 (February 20, 1934), p. 22.

2. Shaemus O'Sheel, "Introductory Note," in *Seven Poets in Search of an Answer: A Poetic Symposium,* ed. Thomas Yoselhoff (New York: Bernard Ackerman, Inc., 1944), pp. 9–10.

3. Michael Gold, "America Needs a Critic," *New Masses* (1926), reprinted in *Mike Gold: A Literary Anthology,* ed. Michael Folsom (New York: International Publishers, 1972), p. 139.

4. Joseph Freeman, Introduction to *Proletarian Literature in the United States: An Anthology,* ed. Granville Hicks et al. (New York: International Publishers, 1935), p. 11.

5. Maxwell Bodenheim, "To a Revolutionary Girl," reprinted in *Proletarian Literature in the United States,* ed. Hicks, p. 147.

6. Freeman, in *Proletarian Literature in the United States,* ed. Hicks, p. 27.

7. Burnshaw, "Notes on Revolutionary Poetry," p. 22.

8. Ibid., p. 14.

9. Lucia Trent and Ralph Cheyney, "A Poet's Utopia," in Trent and Cheyney, *More Power to Poets!: A Plea for More Poetry in Life, More Life in Poetry* (New York: Henry Harrison, 1934), p. 72.

10. Margaret Fuller, *Memoirs,* vol. 1, p. 279, quoted in *The Woman and the Myth: Margaret Fuller's Life and Writings,* ed. Belle Gale Chevigny (Old Westbury, N.Y.: The Feminist Press, 1976), p. 63.

11. Joseph Kalar, "Worker Uprooted," reprinted in *Proletarian Literature in the United States,* ed. Hicks, p. 170.

12. See Louise Bernikow, *The World Split Open: Four Centuries of Women Poets in England and America, 1552–1950* (New York: Random House, 1974), p. 300.

MURIEL RUKEYSER

Ann Burlak

Let her be seen, a voice on a platform, heard
as a city is heard in its prophetic sleep when
one shadow hangs over one side of a total wall
of houses, factories, stacks, and on the faces
around her tallies, shadow from one form.

An open square shields the voice, reflecting it
to faces who receive its reflections of light as
change on their features. She stands alone, sending
her voice out to the edges, seeing approach people
to make the ring ragged, to fill in blacker
answers.
           This is an open square of the lit world
whose dark sky over hills rimmed white with evening
squares lofts where sunset lies in dirty patterns
and rivers of mill-towns beating their broken bridges
as under another country full of air.
Dark offices evening reaches where letters take the light
even from palest faces over script.
Many abandon machines, shut off the looms,
hurry on glooming cobbles to the square. And many
are absent, as in the sky about her face, the birds
retreat from charcoal rivers and fly far.

The words cluster about the superstition mountains.
The sky breaks back over the torn and timid
her early city whose stacks along the river
flourished darkness over all, whose mottled sky
shielded the faces of those asleep in doorways
spread dark on narrow fields through which the father
comes home without meat, the forest in the ground
whose trees are coal, the lurching roads of autumn

where the flesh of the eager hangs, heavier by
its thirty bullets, barbed on wire. Truckdrivers
swing ungrazed trailers past, the woman in the fog
can never speak her poems of unemployment,
the brakeman slows the last freight round the curve.
And riveters in their hardshell fling short fiery
steel, and the servant groans in his narrow room,
and the girl limps away from the door of the shady doctor.
Or the child new-born into a company town
whose life can be seen at birth as child, woman, widow.

The neighbor called in to nurse the baby of a spy,
the schoolboy washing off the painted word
"scab" on the front stoop, his mother watering flowers
pouring the milk-bottle of water from the ledge,
who stops in horror, seeing. The grandmother going
down to her cellar with a full clothes-basket,
turns at the shot, sees men running past brick,
smoke-spurt and fallen face.
            She speaks of these:
the chase down through the canal, the filling-station,
stones through the windshield. The woman in the bank
who topples, the premature birth brought on by tear-gas,
the charge leaving its gun slow-motion, finding those
who sit at windows knowing what they see;
who look up at the door, the brutalized face appraising
strangers and holsters; little blackened boys
with ther animal grins, quick hands salvaging coal
among the slag of patriotic hills.

She knows the field of faces at her feet,
remembrances of childhood, likenesses of parents,
a system of looms in constellation whirled,
disasters dancing.
            And behind her head
the world of the unpossessed, steel mills in snow flaming,
nine o'clock towns whose deputies' overnight power
hurls waste into killed eyes, whose guns predict
mirages of order, an empty coat before the blind.
Doorways within which nobody is at home.
The spies who wait for the spy at the deserted crossing,
a little dead since they are going to kill.
Those women who stitch their lives to their machines
and daughters at the symmetry of looms.

She speaks to the ten greatest American women:
The anonymous farmer's wife, the anonymous clubbed picket,
the anonymous Negro woman who held off the guns,
the anonymous prisoner, anonymous cotton-picker
trailing her robe of sack in a proud train,
anonymous writer of these and mill-hand, anonymous city walker,
anonymous organizer, anonymous binder of the illegally wounded,
anonymous feeder and speaker to anonymous squares.

She knows their faces, their impatient songs
of passionate grief risen, the desperate music
poverty makes, she knows women cut down
by poverty, by stupid obscure days,
their moments over the dishes, speaks them now,
wrecks with the whole necessity of the past
behind the debris, behind the ordinary
smell of coffee, the ravelling clean wash,
the turning to bed, undone among savage night
planning and unplanning seasons of happiness
broken in dreams or in the jaundiced morning
over a tub or over a loom or over
the tired face of death.
          She knows
the songs: *Hope to die, Mo I try, I comes out,*
Owin boss mo, I comes out, Lawd, Owin boss mo
food, money and life.
          Praise breakers,
praise the unpraised who cannot speak their name.
Their asking what they need as unbelieved
as a statue talking to a skeleton.
They are the animals who devour their mother
from need, and they know in their bodies other places,
their minds are cities whose avenues are named
each after a foreign city. They fall when cities fall.

They have the cruelty and sympathy of those
whose texture is the stress of existence woven
into revenge, the crime we all must claim.
They hold the old world in their new world's arms.
And they are the victims, all the splinters of war
run through their eyes, their black escaping face
and runaway eyes are the Negro in the subway
whose shadowy detective brings his stick
down on the naked head as the express pulls in,

swinging in locomotive roars on skull.
They are the question to the ambassador
long-jawed and grim, they stand on marble, waiting
to ask how the terms of the strike have affected him.
Answer: "I've never seen snow before. It's marvellous."
They stand with Ann Burlak in the rotunda, knowing
her insistent promise of life, remembering
the letter of the tear-gas salesman: "I hope
"this strike develops and a damn bad one too.
"We need the money."
        This is the boundary
behind a speaker: Main Street and railroad tracks,
post office, furniture store. The soft moment before storm.
Since there are many years.
And the first years were the years of need,
the bleeding, the dragged foot, the wilderness,
and the second years were the years of bread
fat cow, square house, favorite work,
and the third years are the years of death.
The glittering eye all golden. Full of tears.
Years when the enemy is in our street,
and liberty, safe in the people's hands,
is never safe and peace is never safe.

Insults of attack arrive, insults
of mutilation. She knows the prophetic past,
many have marched behind her, and she knows
Rosa whose face drifts in the black canal,
the superstitions of a tragic winter
when children, their heads together, put on tears.
The tears fall at their throats, their chains are made
of tears, and as bullets melted and as bombs let down
upon the ominous cities where she stands
fluid and conscious. Suddenly perceives
the world will never daily prove her words,
but her words live, they issue from this life.
She scatters clews. She speaks from all these faces
and from the center of a system of lives
who speak the desire of worlds moving unmade
saying, "Who owns the world?" and waiting for the cry.

Absalom

I first discovered what was killing these men.
I had three sons who worked with their father in the tunnel:
Cecil, aged 23, Owen, aged 21, Shirley, aged 17.
They used to work in a coal mine, not steady work
for the mines were not going much of the time.
A power Co. foreman learned that we made home brew,
he formed a habit of dropping in evenings to drink,
persuading the boys and my husband—
give up their jobs and take this other work.
It would pay them better.
Shirley was my youngest son; the boy.
He went into the tunnel.

My heart   my mother   my heart   my mother
My heart   my coming into being.

My husband is not able to work.
He has it, according to the doctor.
We have been having a very hard time making a living since this trouble
came to us.
I saw the dust in the bottom of the tub.
The boy worked there about eighteen months,
came home one evening with a shortness of breath.
He said, "Mother, I cannot get my breath."
Shirley was sick about three months.
I would carry him from his bed to the table,
from his bed to the porch, in my arms.

My heart is mine in the place of hearts,
They gave me back my heart, it lies in me.

When they took sick, right at the start, I saw a doctor.
I tried to get Dr. Harless to X-ray the boys.
He was the only man I had any confidence in,
the company doctor in the Kopper's mine,
but he would not see Shirley.

He did not know where his money was coming from.
I promised him half if he'd work to get compensation,
but even then he would not do anything.
I went on the road and begged the X-ray money,
the Charleston hospital made the lung pictures,
he took the case after the pictures were made.
And two or three doctors said the same thing.
The youngest boy did not get to go down there with me,
he lay and said, "Mother, when I die,
"I want you to have them open me up and
"see if that dust killed me.
"Try to get compensation,
"you will not have any way of making your living
"when we are gone,
"and the rest are going too."

    I have gained mastery over my heart
    I have gained mastery over my two hands
    I have gained mastery over the waters
    I have gained mastery over the river.

The case of my son was the first of the line of lawsuits.
They sent the lawyers down and the doctors down;
they closed the electric sockets in the camps.
There was Shirley, and Cecil, Jeffrey, and Oren,
Raymond Johnson, Clev and Oscar Anders,
Frank Lynch, Henry Palf, Mr. Pitch, a foreman;
a slim fellow who carried steel with my boys,
his name was Darnell, I believe. There were many others,
the towns of Glen Ferris, Alloy, where the white rock lies,
six miles away; Vanetta, Gauley Bridge,
Gamoca, Lockwood, the gullies,
the whole valley is witness.
I hitchhike eighteen miles, they make checks out.
They asked me how I keep the cow on $2.
I said one week, feed for the cow, one week, the children's flour.
The oldest son was twenty-three.
The next son was twenty-one.
The youngest son was eighteen.
They called it pneumonia at first.
They would pronounce it fever.
Shirley asked that we try to find out.
That's how they learned what the trouble was.

I open out a way, they have covered my sky with crystal
I come forth by day, I am born a second time,
I force a way through, and I know the gate
I shall journey over the earth among the living.

He shall not be diminished, never;
I shall give a mouth to my son.

More of a Corpse Than
a Woman

Give them my regards when you go to the school reunion;
and at the marriage-supper, say that I'm thinking about them.
They'll remember my name; I went to the movies with that one,
feeling the weight of their death where she sat at my elbow;
        she never said a word,
        but all of them were heard.

all of them alike, expensive girls, the leaden friends:
one used to play the piano, one of them once wrote a sonnet,
one even seemed awakened enough to photograph wheat-fields—
the dull girls with the educated minds and technical passions—
        pure love was their employment,
        they tried it for enjoyment.

Meet them at the boat: they've brought the souvenirs of boredom,
a seashell from the faltering monarchy;
the nose of a marble saint; and from the battlefield,
an empty shell divulged from a flower-bed.
        The lady's wealthy breath
        perfumes the air with death.

The leaden lady faces the fine, voluptuous woman,
faces a rising world bearing its gifts in its hands.
Kisses her casual dreams upon the lips she kisses,
risen, she moves away; takes others; moves away.
        Inadequate to love,
        supposes she's enough.

Give my regards to the well-protected woman,
I knew the ice-cream girl, we went to school together.
There's something to bury, people, when you begin to bury.
When your women are ready and rich in their wish for the world.
        destroy the leaden heart,
        we've a new race to start.

Fifth Elegy: A Turning Wind

Knowing the shape of the country. Knowing the midway to
migrant fanatics, living that life, up with the dawn and
moving as long as the light lasts, and when the sun is falling
      to wait, still standing;

and when the black has come, at last lie down, too tired to
turn to each other, feeling only the land's demand under them
Shape that exists not as permanent quality, but varies with
      even the movement of bone.

Even in skeletons, it depends on the choices of action.
A definite plan is visible. We are either free-moving or
fixed to some ground. The shape has no meaning
      outside of the function.

Fixed to Europe, the distant, adjacent, we lived, with the land—
promise of life of our own. Course down the East—frontiers
meet you at every turn—the headlights find them, the plain's,
      and the solar cities'

recurrent centers. And at the middle of the great world the wind
answers the shape of the country, a turning traveller
follows the hinge-line of coast, the first indefinite
      axis of symmetry

torn off from sympathy with the past and planted,
a primitive streak prefiguring the west, an ideal
which had to be modified for stability,
      to make it work

Architecture is fixed not only by present needs but
also by ancestors. The actual structure means a plan determined
by the nature of ancestors; its details are determined by
      function and interference.

There are these major divisions: for those attached to the seafloor,
a fan at freedom, flexible, wavering, designed to catch food
from all directions. For the sedentary, for those who crouch and look,
      radial symmetry,

spokes to all margins for support. For those who want movement,
this is achieved through bilateral symmetry only,
a spine and straight attack, all muscles working,
      up and alive.

———————————

And there are years of roads, and centuries of need,
of walking along the shadow of a wall, of visiting houses,
hearing the birds trapped in the wall, the framework trembling
      with struggles of birds,

years of nightwalking in stranger cities, relost and unnamed,
recurrent familiar rooms, furnished only with nightmare,
recurrent loves, the glass eye of unreal ambition,
      years of initiation,

of dishallucination on the diamond meadows,
seeing the distances of false capes ahead,
feeling the tide-following and turning wind,
      travelling farther

under abrasive weather, to the bronzy river,
the rust, the brown, the terrible dead swamps,
the hanging moss the color of all the hanged,
      cities whose heels

ring out their news of hell upon all streets
churches where you betray yourself, pray ended desire,
white wooden houses of village squares. Always one gesture:
      rejecting of backdrops.

These are the ritual years, whose lore is names of shapes,
Grabtown, Cockade Alley, Skid Row where jobless live,
their emblem a hitch-hiker with lips basted together,
      and marvel rivers,

the flooded James, a double rainbow standing over Richmond,
the remnant sky above the Cape Fear River, blue stain on red water,
the Waccamaw with its bone-trees, Piscataqua's rich mouth,
      red Sound and flesh of sand.

—A nation of refugees that will not learn its name;
still shows these mothers enduring, their hidden faces,
the cry of the hurt child at a high night-window,
      hand-to-hand warfare,

the young sitting in libraries at their only rest

or making love in the hallway under an orange bulb,
the boy playing baseball at Hungry Mother State Park,
        bestiaries of cities

and this shape, this meaning that promises seasonal joy.
Whose form is unquietness and yet the seeker of rest,
whose travelling hunger has range enough, its root
        grips through the world.

The austere fire-world of night: Gary or Bethlehem,
in sacred stacks of flame—or stainless morning,
anti-sunlight of lakes' reflection, matchlight on face,
        the thorny light of fireworks

lighting a way for the shape, this country of celebrations
deep in a passage of rebirth. Adventures of countries,
adventures of travellers, visions, or Christ's adventures
        forever following him

lit by the night-light of history, persevering
into the incredible washed morning air.
The luisarne swamp is our guide and the glare ice,
        the glow of tracklights,

the lights winding themselves into a single beacon,
big whooping riders of night, a wind that whirls
all of our motives into a single stroke,
        shows us a country

of which the birds know mountains that we have not dreamed,
climbing these unsuspected slopes they fade. Butte and pavilion
vanish into a larger scape, morning vaults all those hills
        rising on ranges

that stand gigantic on the roots of the world,
where points expand in pleasure of raw sweeping
gestures of joy, whose winds sweep down like stairs,
        and the felled forests

on hurricane ridges show a second growth. The dances
of turkeys near storm, a pouring light, tornado
umbilical to earth, fountains of rain, a development
        controlled by centers,

until the organs of this anatomy are fleshed away at last
of gross, and determining self, develop a final structure
in isolation. Masterpieces of happiness arrive,
        alive again in another land,

remembering pain, faces of suffering, but they know growth,
go through the world, hunger and rest desiring life.
Mountains are spines to their conquest, these wrecked houses
        (vines spiral the pillars)

are leaning their splintered sides on tornadoes, lifted careening
in wheels, in whirlwind, in a spool of power
drawing a spiral on the sun, drawing a sign of
        strength on the mountains,

the fusing stars lighting initiated cities.
The thin poor whiteness raining on the ground
forgotten in fickle eclipses, thunderbirds of dream
        following omens,

following charts of the moving constellations.
Charts of the country of all visions, imperishable
stars of our old dream: process, which having neither
        sorrow nor joy

remains as promised, the embryo in the fire.
The tilted cities of America, fields of metal,
the seamless wheatfields, the current of cities running
        below our wings

promise that knowledge of systems which may bless.
May permit knowledge of self, a lover's wish of conversion
until the time when the dead lake rises in light,
the shape is organized in travelling space,
this hope of travel, to find the place again,
rest in the triumph of the reconceived,
lie down again together face to face.

GENEVIEVE TAGGARD

Try Tropic

(For a Sick Generation)

Try tropic for your balm
Try storm,
And after storm, calm.
Try snow of heaven, heavy, soft and slow,
Brilliant and warm.
Nothing will help, and nothing do much harm.

Drink iron from rare springs; follow the sun;
Go far
To get the beam of some medicinal star;
Or in your anguish run
The gauntlet of all zones to an ultimate one.
Fever and chill
Punish you still,
Earth has no zone to work against your ill.

Burn in the jewelled desert with the toad.
Catch lace
Of evening mist across your haunted face;
Or walk in upper air, the slanted road.
It will not lift that load;
Nor will large seas undo your subtle ill.
Nothing can cure and nothing kill
What ails your eyes, what cuts your pulse in two
And not kill you.

Return of the Native

Now, after years serving demonic excess,
Exalting those whose god-passions send them mad,
I am stranded on a simpler shore, much less
Sumptuous,—a land permanently sad,

Bearing a sombre harvest—an old island,
With cactus and asphodel and olive on
The rock itself. This oddly, is my land.
Here a moderate joy yellows the sky each dawn.

We toil—here toil has lost its hectic haste.
The outrageous wrongs men do, lessen, diminish.
We are frugal, we share, we despise waste.
The work I have is good. It is not mine to finish.

To My Mother

The long delight and early
I heard in my small years clearly;
The morning song, bed-making, bustle for new undertaking,
With dish-washing and hay-raking,

This vanished or seemed diminished,
Was lost, in trouble finished.
I did nervous work, unsteady, captive work and heady.
Nothing well-done and ready.

And heard in other places
Than home, and from foreign faces
The dauntless gay and breezy communal song of the busy,
I—idle and uneasy.

I said, my work is silly,
Lonely and willy-nilly.
See this hand with nicotined habits, this useless hand that edits
A chronicle of debits.

Join, if I can, the makers,
And the tillers of difficult acres;
And get somehow this dearly lost, this re-discovered rarely
Habit of rising early.

Silence in Mallorca

I

Our stony island, Spain's laconic child
Quiet. Nada. Cover the glowing spark.
Hush all the hótas and hush hush the wild

Arabian cries. Now in Europe's dark
Whisper weep secretly plot but never sing.
On cliffs against the sky moves the new mark

Shape of the plane, the loathed imperial thing
The hawk from Italy, the spy of black.
Ground where we labor darkens with its wing.

A few shot first. Then nothing. Then the attack.
Terror of the invader. Puff of shells,
And Juan our best man ambushed in the back.

Hide hide in the caves; listen in the dry wells. . . .
Clang—the obedient treachery of church bells.

II

They shot the mayor of Inca. They jailed
The poor the free the poor the free the brave.
Out of the puerto when the felucca sailed

Planes roared and swooped and shot them on the wave.
Our people serve the invader and his gun.
Our people, Spain. Slow tempo of the slave.

We are cut off. Africa's blazing sun
Knew these same hawks that now around us prey.
And Barcelona suffers. Is there no one

To save us but ourselves? From far away
After victorious battle. . . . Cry, we cry
Brothers, Comrades help us. Where are they?

Our island lying open to the sky.
Mallorca, the first to fall, the last to die.

III

O wild west wind. . . . Liberty's open roar,
Blow on this island, blow the ocean clean,
Drown out tormentors, blow equinox, blow war

Away from the world. Drive to us the unseen
Battalions, clouds of planes by workers flown,
Give us our land again, quiet and green,

Our children singing and our land, our own
Ways, our wives, our delegates. Blow here.
The indifferent sea washes the beach of stone,

And Mediterranean silence, primitive fear
Steps in the foot of Tomàs, the new slave.
Moves in the hovering hawk, spiraling near.

We bend, we work,—this island inferno and grave.
Come with the wind of your wings. And save.

Proud Day

(Marian Anderson on the steps of the Lincoln Memorial)

Our sister sang on the Lincoln steps. Proud day.
We came to hear our sister sing. Proud day.
Voice out of depths, poise with memory,
What goodness, what splendor lay long under foot!
Our sister with a lasso of sorrow and triumph
Caught America, made it listen. Proud day.

The peaceful Lincoln sat so still. Proud day.
Waiting the Republic to be born again. Proud day.
Never, never forget how the dark people rewarded us
Giving out of their want and their little freedom
This blazing star. This blazing star.
Something spoke in my patriot heart. Proud day.

Autumn Song for Guitar

Lost in the shuttffle—wheat fields cut,
Wheat's on the train.
Autumn rain
Shuts off the farm, sweeps down the road,
Blows men to town, blows men
Lost in the shuffle.

Chaff off the hay-field; where to now?
Back to the town.
Let's go, we're going down
For winter pavements and the rainy snow.
Cards in a rented room, nothing to do.
Lost in the shuffle.

Too many of us. Walk the street and get
Jobs in the line.
(Another stiff got mine.)
Move on all night, all winter. (All my life?)
Move on, get going, you're
Lost in the shuffle.

Creative Effort

Have you a theme?
                Starvation.
In this country?
                Yes, starvation. In this country.
Do you mean, nothing to eat?
                Yes, to begin with.
Unpleasant theme and very hard to handle.
This is a rich country. . . . Why not drop the theme?
Who will enjoy it? You sound a little odd.
Why make it worse than it is? I agree it ought to be helped.
Have you some other theme?
                The mouth then smiled.
Some better theme?
                Yes, said the poet:
Blood on the moon, a face to starve your smile.

Ode in Time of Crisis

Now in the fright of change when bombed towns vanish
In fountains of debris
We say to the stranger coming across the sea
Not here, not here, go elsewhere!
Here we keep
Bars up. Wall out the danger, tightly seal
The ports, the intake from the alien world we fear.

It is a time of many errors now.
And this the error of children when they feel
But cannot say their terror. To shut off the stream
In which we moved and still move, if we move.
The alien is the nation, nothing more or less.
How set ourselves at variance to prove
The alien is not the nation. And so end the dream.
Forbid our deep resource from whence we came,
And the very seed of greatness.

This is to do
Something like suicide; to choose
Sterility—forget the secret of our past
Which like a magnet drew
A wealth of men and women hopeward. And now to lose
In ignorant blindness what we might hold fast.
The fright of change, not readiness. Instead
Inside our wall we will today pursue
The man we call the alien, take his print,
Give him a taste of the thing from which he fled,
Suspicion him. And again we fail.
How shall we release his virtue, his good-will
If by such pressure we hold his life in jail?
The alien is the nation. Nothing else.
And so we fail and so we jail ourselves.
Landlocked, the stagnant stream.
So ends the dream.

O country-men, are we working to undo
Our lusty strength, our once proud victory?
Yes, if by this fright we break our strength in two.
If we make of every man we jail the enemy.
If we make ourselves the jailer locked in jail.
Our laboring wills, our brave, too brave to fail
Remember this nation by millions believed to be
Great and of mighty forces born; and resolve to be free,
To continue and renew.

JOSEPHINE W. JOHNSON

Under the Sound of Voices

—Returning as they have always returned,
Descending the shafts again. Re-entering the tunneled darkness,
The violence over. The strikers and talkers,
All the yeast, the maggots, the uneasy fermenting over,
The loud leaders shot. The stubborn walled,
—Stone-circled above instead of below earth—
The mayors and the sheriffs and the lies,
The sourceless shots, the night-riding, over.
Crows on the ditched food. Conditions altered.
The dead voiceless. The living doled.
All things adjusted.

. . . *All things adjusted.*
—But down in the darkness,
Under the sound of voices, under the lawful clanging,
Under the drills and the shafts, and the steel moving again,
Grow the invisible tunnels, the caves hollowed and cracking,
The shale crumbled, the ancient rocks gnawed under,
The sound, loud and unheard, of subterranean waters
Rising nearer, breaking the iron dikes and ore,
The once impregnable layers of diorite. . . .
And unseen, unheard, this invisible mining
Tunnels the stratum of an ancient stronghold,
Shatters the granite of a world.

He Who Shall Turn—

In the hour when we too become sick and infected,
White with the scale, and tissue dissolving,
Cry out astonished for cause of our suffering;
There is one answer alone to be given,
Hard in our ears and bitter with justice:

He who shall turn from the leper and leave him,
Has taken that leper into his household;
Eats with him, sleeps with him, wears his foul clothing,
Drinks from one glass with that unseen companion,
Goes with the leper down into his darkness,
Dies of the leper's disease.

Ice Winter

Now it is winter, and the agate snow
Lies frozen southward on the palace walls.
The arctic owls drift down along the wind
Above the marshlands and the brittle grass.

O white and marble wind,
I who was young in suffering am grown old.

The night is shattered with the frozen stars,
The hours move
Slow as the wheeling of this cold and northern cross
Turning its arc above the bitter earth.

Here in my heart the nails of frost are driven.
From their high towers the pigeons fall
Frozen to earth, ice-chiseled in the cold.

.   .   .

It was in the autumn he went forth.
—Let me remember the autumn!
The lost fire and the fallen flames . . .
The oak trees' brazen death, the molten fields.
It was in the autumn he went forth,
Following the war's blood-river to its source . . .

Now is the shape of all things darkness.
A river of ice lies on my heart.

I have gathered together the wise men of the kingdom,
The seers and prophets and the men of wisdom,
Crying to them in my intolerable grief;
And they have not answered me.
The wise men of the kingdom have stared into their hands
And looked beyond me.
They have lied wearily, saying in tired voices,
"As the stars are without will, and the storms destroy,
So men go out to war."
They have said unto me,
"Thou art not alone in thy suffering.

For thy one grief are those ten thousand who have suffered likewise,
Who have known also
The caverned loneliness, the tombs of dolomite, the darkness . . .
Therefore make of thy life a high white pillar rising
Austere above thy grief."

These are the words of wise men, O my beloved,
—Old men who have outgrown mortality and fear.

I shall remember your love
Written in ice upon my heart, and without pain.
I shall grow still.
.   .   .
The granite lilies chiseled on the wall
Lie rimmed with everlasting snow.

Stone lilies of the palace wall,
I too am stone.

MARGARET WALKER

For My People

For my people everywhere singing their slave songs repeatedly: their dirges and
their ditties and their blues and jubilees, praying their prayers nightly to an
unknown god, bending their knees humbly to an unseen power;

For my people lending their strength to the years, to the gone years and
the now years and the maybe years, washing ironing cooking scrubbing
sewing mending hoeing plowing digging planting pruning patching dragging along never gaining never reaping never knowing and never understanding;

For my playmates in the clay and dust and sand of Alabama backyards playing
baptizing and preaching and doctor and jail and soldier and school and mama
and cooking and playhouse and concert and store and hair and Miss
Choomby and company;

For the cramped bewildered years we went to school to learn to know the
reasons why and the answers to and the people who and the places where
and the days when, in memory of the bitter hours when we discovered we
were black and poor and small and different and nobody cared and nobody
wondered and nobody understood;

For the boys and girls who grew in spite of these things to be man and woman,
to laugh and dance and sing and play and drink their wine and religion and
success, to marry their playmates and bear children and then die of consumption and anemia and lynching;

For my people thronging 47th Street in Chicago and Lenox Avenue in New
York and Rampart Street in New Orleans, lost disinherited dispossessed and
happy people filling the cabarets and taverns and other people's pockets
needing bread and shoes and milk and land and money and something—
something all our own;

For my people walking blindly spreading joy, losing time being lazy, sleeping
when hungry, shouting when burdened, drinking when hopeless, tied and

shackled and tangled among ourselves by the unseen creatures who tower over us omnisciently and laugh;

For my people blundering and groping and floundering in the dark of churches and schools and clubs and societies, associations and councils and committees and conventions, distressed and disturbed and deceived and devoured by money-hungry glory-craving leeches, preyed on by facile force of state and fad and novelty, by false prophet and holy believer;

For my people standing staring trying to fashion a better way from confusion, from hypocrisy and misunderstanding, trying to fashion a world that will hold all the people, all the faces, all the adams and eves and their countless generations;

Let a new earth rise. Let another world be born. Let a bloody peace be written in the sky. Let a second generation full of courage issue forth; let a people loving freedom come to growth. Let a beauty full of healing and strength of final clenching be the pulsing in our spirits and our blood. Let the martial songs be written, let the dirges disappear. Let a race of men now rise and take control.

Dark Blood

There were bizarre beginnings in old lands for the making of me. There were sugar sands and islands of fern and pearl, palm jungles and stretches of a never-ending sea.

There were the wooing nights of tropical lands and the cool discretion of flowering plains between two stalwart hills. They nurtured my coming with wanderlust. I sucked fevers of adventure through my veins with my mother's milk.

Someday I shall go to the tropical lands of my birth, to the coasts of continents and the tiny wharves of island shores. I shall roam the Balkans and the hot lanes of Africa and Asia. I shall stand on mountain tops and gaze on fertile homes below.

And when I return to Mobile I shall go by the way of Panama and Bocas del Toro to the littered streets and the one-room shacks of my old poverty, and blazing suns of other lands may struggle then to reconcile the pride and pain in me.

Lineage

My grandmothers were strong.
They followed plows and bent to toil.
They moved through fields sowing seed.
They touched earth and grain grew.
They were full of sturdiness and singing.
My grandmothers were strong.

My grandmothers are full of memories
Smelling of soap and onions and wet clay
With veins rolling roughly over quick hands
They have many clean words to say.
My grandmothers were strong.
Why am I not as they?

GLADYS CASELY HAYFORD

The Palm Wine Seller

Akosua selling palm wine,
In the broiling heat;
Akosua selling palm wine
Down our street.

Frothing calabashes
Filled unto the brim,
Boatmen quaffing palm wine
In toil's interim.

Tossing off their palm wine,
Boatmen deem her fair;
Through the haze of palm wine,
Note her jet black hair.

Roundness of her bosom,
Brilliance of her eyes
Lips that form a cupid's bow,
Whereon love's dew lies.

Velvet gleam of shoulder
Arch of bare black feet;
Soft caressing hands,
These her charms complete.

Thus illusioned boatmen
Dwell on 'Kosua's charms.
Blind to fallen bosom,
Knotted thin black arms.

Lips creased in by wrinkles,
Eyes dimmed with the years,
Feet whose arch was altered
Treading vales of tears.

Hair whose roots life's madness
Knotted and turned wild.
On her heart a load of care;
On her back a child.

Akosua selling palm wine
In the broiling heat.
Akosua selling palm wine
Down our street.

KATHLEEN TANKERSLEY YOUNG

All Things Insensible

I envy the sleep
Of each cold stone
Where yellow moss
Is overgrown;

I envy flowers
That fall
Their last dark
Burial;

Insensible things
That do not hunger:
Roots that have died
And can not stir:

All things: as stones
And moss and water:
All things that
Do not hunger.

LUCIA TRENT

Breed, Women, Breed

Breed, little mothers,
With tired backs and tired hands,
Breed for the owners of mills and the owners of mines,
Breed a race of danger-haunted men,
A race of toiling, sweating, miserable men,
Breed, little mothers,
Breed for the owners of mills and the owners of mines,
Breed, breed, breed!

Breed, little mothers,
With the sunken eyes and the sagging cheeks,
Breed for the bankers, the crafty and terrible masters of men,
Breed a race of machines,
A race of aenemic, round-shouldered, subway-herded machines!

Breed, little mothers,
With a faith patient and stupid as cattle,
Breed for the war lords,
Offer your woman flesh for incredible torment,
Wrack your frail bodies with the pangs of birth
For the war lords who slaughter your sons!

Breed, little mothers,
Breed for the owners of mills and the owners of mines,
Breed for the bankers, the crafty and terrible masters of men,
Breed for the war lords, the devouring war lords,
Breed, women, breed!

Lady in a Limousine

Through her lorgnette's disdainful glass
She looks upon earth's naked, patient grief.
Life's puppet tragedies emerge and pass
Like any aimless cloud or casual leaf.

She sits, a woman in an opera box,
Transparent china on a lofty shelf,
And does not know that this poor world she mocks
Contains no sadder object than herself.

Parade the Narrow Turrets

Thumb over your well-worn classics with clammy and accurate eyes,
Teach Freshmen to scan Homer and Horace and look wise.
Dress in your new Tuxedo as gauchely as you please.
And at official dinners kowtow to fat trustees.
Wince at the Evening Graphic, whose bold pink pages shriek,
Frown on the drooping shopgirl, rouging her lip and cheek.
Lecture to gray-haired ladies on ruins of ancient Rome,
And preach across a tea-cup on the sanctity of home.
What do you care if miner's brats shudder and starve and die,
What do you care if blacks are lynched beneath a withering sky?
What do you care if two men burn to death in a great steel chair
While the world shouts their innocence and honest men despair?
Go live in your Ivory Tower. Build it as high as you can,
And parade the narrow turrets as a cultivated man!

RUTH LECHLITNER

On the Wall to Your Left

Named in no catalogue, Madam, hung
In no paid exhibition, this painting (why
Are you shocked and bewildered, Madam?)—
                         Among
The twisted sheets in copulation lie
The victim and his bride: masked Murder's
                         knife
Enters their flesh. In the near shadow sits
Modern fertility, the gaunt mid-wife
With psychoanalytic herbs: she knits
Loin-cloths for ghosts. And what are these
Steel lutes and smoky throats?—the wedding
                         song
Industrial, Madam. Notice please
Law the gay organ-grinder with his long-
Tailed monkey chained: see how the monkey
                         prances!
Companion to his lean and nimble feet
A skeleton eugenically dances
Pale in the sun-gold opulence of wheat.
This is the painting, Madam. Sorry to hear
You find the technique crude, possibly
                         worth
Less than the wall space. But the meaning's
                         clear:
The artist is unknown; the title, "Birth."

SUSAN McMILLAN SHEPHERD

White Man's Blues

I want to be softly free
And moan the Negro blues.
I want to be softly free
To moan the Negro blues,
But being white I sit
And read the evening's news.

I want to feel like the colored man
Who makes his poems sing.
I want to feel like the colored man
Whose poems always sing
In my red heart like the flutter
Of the tanager's black wing.

But in my chair I sit and hear
The alley black man laugh.
I sit and strain my ear to catch
The alley black man's laugh,
Sad to think that I should live
A life that's only half.

MARY LeDUC GIBBONS

Mothers

Colored mothers have watched the moon from their cabin windows,
And have wondered how many moon-turnings and cotton pickings would
pass,
Before the small dark heads huddled at their feet
Would have their turn at watching and at wondering.

I sit here tonight and watch the moon through a window,
And wonder how many moon-wanings and heartbreakings will pass,
Before you, small golden head
Will have your turn at watching and at wondering.

After all, at night we are the same outline against the moon, aren't we?
Except your kerchief silhouettes prettier than my hair, dark mother.

JOY DAVIDMAN

This Woman

Now do not put a ribbon in your hair;
Abjure the spangled insult of design,
The filigree sterility, nor twine
A flower with your strength; go bare, go bare.

The elements foregathered at your birth
Gave your hard throat an armor for despair,
Burned you and bathed you, nourished you with air,
And carved your body like a tree of earth.

This is the symbol that I shape of you;
Branching from the broad column of your flesh
Into the obdurate and fibrous mesh
Stubborn to break apart and stiff to hew;
Lost at your core a living skeleton
Like sharp roots pointing downward from the sun.

Twentieth-Century Americanism

Lies have been told about this American blood
making it seem like laughter or like some animal
couched with a golden throat in the desert. Our roots
push apart the bones of an Indian's skull. Arrowheads
strike fire and flint sparks out of us. These lies,
these Indian rivers, these arrowroot sweet waters
seething in the blue flag. We have not drunk these rivers,
we have not chewed and eaten this earth. These ghosts
do not walk in our veins with painted feet.

Come now all Americans
kiss and accept your city, the harsh mother,
New York, the clamor, the sweat, the heart of brown land,
the gold heart and the stone heart, the beast of American blood,
the cat stretching out before a borrowed fire
beside the steam heat, in apartment houses.

We are not the dark cheekbone of the Indian
and there are no painted feathers for our killing
which happens grimly, beside clapboard and raw steel.
We are not the stone ribs underneath Manhattan
but we come and go swiftly in the sick lights of subways;
men with narrow shoulders, children and women,
Italians, Jews, Greeks, Poles, and even Anglo-Saxons
all worn down to the thin common coin of the city.
And our minds are made after new electric models
and we have no proud ancestors.

                      (Lost, lost
the deerskin heritage, the pioneer musket,
barn dance, corn harvest, breakers of new soil.
Lost the great night and thin assertive song
up from the campfire, lynxes drinking the Hudson,
bobcat in Westchester. What fish swim Manhattan,
what clean and naked rivers? lost and lost
the homespun and the patchwork quilt, the bread

risen in the home oven and smelling new.
Do not claim this for us. We have the radio.
We have the cat and the tame fire.)

                              Beside
  the bedroom window long trains ride,
  the harsh lights come and go outside.

And our minds
and the minds of our children. Give us the World Series,
the ballplayer with thick nostrils and the loose jaw
hanging heavily from a piece of chewing gum,
and when the baseball is over give us no time;
fill our mind with the Rose Bowl and Yale and Notre Dame
leaving no time for thought between the baseball and football seasons.
Feed us music to rot the nerves, make us twitch with music,
burrow with music beneath the comfortless brain and beneath
the aching heart and the worn heart and beneath
the honest gut and rot the gut with music
in the snake of nerve that sits in the knee reflexes,
wriggle in the dust with the snake's belly. All night
delight us with the yellow screaming of sound.

And give us
the smile, the glitter of rich houses, the glitter,
porcelain teeth and skin smoothed by diffused lighting,
(skin-cream, face-food, oil of Peruvian turtles
bright and grinning out of all the subway advertisements)
the dark movie house and old cigarette smoke
and the knee of the stranger sitting in the next chair.
If you close our burlesque houses, we will reopen them
and watch twelve hours long the one crude smile
and the same silk uncover the same thigh.
And from the film
borne home to bed with the familiar wife
weary and good, and burrowing into night
into her breast with the blind face of a child;
out from the bed to the familiar daylight
the invoice the slick glass desktop the worn counter
and madam these goods guaranteed not to stretch.
Borne from the bed to sewing machines, taxis, and the building trades,
and if you wear a pencil behind your ear long enough you don't even feel it,
just like eyeglasses. And we go home at night
bearing in two hands like the image of god

the dear shelter, the clothing, the bright fine food.
And daily, daily, we expend our blood.

> Give us this day our daily bread.
> Give the pillow the aching head,
> give Harlem midnight the hot bed.

> Let not the trespass keep us from
> the clean new streets of kingdom come.
> Forgive the sin, forgive the slum.

But when summer comes
we will bathe in the city waters, pronounced free of sewage
only the doctors who swam there came down with a rash.
And in winter we will go skating in Central Park
being sorry for the animals who live in cages,
and the trees will be blue. And the towers will look blue on the snow,
the wet fine street will shine like a salmon's back.
And we shall see spring bloom upon the tops of skyscrapers.
We shall be happy. We shall buy silk and new ties
walking in the sun past bright stone. This is New York,

our city; a kind place to live in; bountiful; our city
envied by the world and by the young in lonely places.
We have the bright-lights, the bridges, the Yankee Stadium
and if we are not contented then we should be
and if we are discontented we do not know it,
and anyhow it always has been this way.

Prayer Against Indifference

When wars and ruined men shall cease
To vex my body's house of peace,
And bloody children lying dead
Let me lie softly in my bed
To nurse a whole and sacred skin,
Break roof and let the bomb come in.

Knock music at the templed skull
And say the world is beautiful,
But never let the dweller lock
Its house against another knock;
Never shut out the gun, the scream,
Never lie blind within a dream.

Within these walls the brain shall sit
And chew on life surrounding it;
Eat the soft sunlight hour and then
The bitter taste of bleeding men;
But never underneath the sun
Shall it forget the scream, the gun.

Let me have eyes I need not shut;
Let me have truth at my tongue's root;
Let courage and the brain command
The honest fingers of my hand;
And when I wait to save my skin
Break roof and let my death come in.

TILLIE OLSEN

I Want You Women Up North to Know

(Based on a Letter by Felipe Ibarro in *New Masses,* Jan. 9th, 1934.)

i want you women up north to know
how those dainty children's dresses you buy
   at macy's, wanamakers, gimbels, marshall fields,
are dyed in blood, are stitched in wasting flesh,
down in San Antonio, "where sunshine spends the winter."

I want you women up north to see
the obsequious smile, the salesladies trill
   "exquisite work, madame, exquisite pleats"
vanish into a bloated face, ordering more dresses,
   gouging the wages down,
dissolve into maria, ambrosa, catalina,
   stitching these dresses from dawn to night,
   in blood, in wasting flesh.

Catalina Rodriguez, 24,
   body shrivelled to a child's at twelve,
catalina rodriguez, last stages of consumption,
   works for three dollars a week from dawn to midnight.
A fog of pain thickens over her skull, the parching heat
   breaks over her body.
and the bright red blood embroiders the floor of her room.
   White rain stitching the night, the bourgeois poet would say,
   white gulls of hands, darting, veering,
   white lightning, threading the clouds,
this is the exquisite dance of her hands over the cloth,
and her cough, gay, quick, staccato,
   like skeleton's bones clattering,
is appropriate accompaniment for the esthetic dance
   of her fingers,

and the tremolo, tremolo when the hands tremble with pain.
Three dollars a week,
two fifty-five,
seventy cents a week,
no wonder two thousands eight hundred ladies of joy
are spending the winter with the sun after he goes down—
for five cents (who said this was a rich man's world?) you can
    get all the lovin you want
"clap and syph aint much worse than sore fingers, blind eyes, and
    t.m."

Maria Vasquez, spinster,
    for fifteen cents a dozen stitches garments for children she has never
    had,
Catalina Torres, mother of four,
    to keep the starved body starving, embroiders from dawn to
    night.
Mother of four, what does she think of,
    as the needle pocked fingers shift over the silk—
    of the stubble-coarse rags that stretch on her own brood,
    and jut with the bony ridge that marks hunger's landscape
    of fat little prairie-roll bodies that will bulge in the
    silk she needles?
(Be not envious, Catalina Torres, look!
    on your own children's clothing, embroidery,
    more intricate than any a thousand hands could fashion,
    there where the cloth is ravelled, or darned,
    designs, multitudinous, complex and handmade by Poverty
    herself.)

Ambrosa Espinoza trusts in god,
    "Todos es de dios, everything is from god,"
    through the dwindling night, the waxing day, she bolsters herself up with
    it—
but the pennies to keep god incarnate, from ambrosa,
and the pennies to keep the priest in wine, from ambrosa,
ambrosa clothes god and priest with hand-made children's dresses.

Her brother lies on an iron cot, all day and watches,
on a mattress of rags he lies.
For twenty-five years he worked for the railroad, then they laid him off.
    (racked days, searching for work; rebuffs; suspicious eyes of policemen.)
    goodbye ambrosa, mebbe in dallas I find work; desperate swing for a
        freight,

surprised hands, clutching air, and the wheel goes over a
leg,
the railroad cuts it off, as it cut off twenty-five years of his life.)
She says that he prays and dreams of another world, as he lies there, a
heaven (which he does not know was brought to earth in 1917 in Russia,
by workers like him).

Women up north, I want you to know
when you finger the exquisite hand made dresses
what it means, this working from dawn to midnight,
on what strange feet the feverish dawn must come
    to maria, catalina, ambrosa,
how the malignant fingers twitching over the pallid faces jerk them to work,
and the sun and the fever mounts with the day—
    long plodding hours, the eyes burn like coals, heat jellies the flying fingers,
down comes the night like blindness.
    long hours more with the dim eye of the lamp, the breaking back,
    weariness crawls in the flesh like worms, gigantic like earth's in winter.
And for Catalina Rodriguez comes the night sweat and the blood
    embroidering the darkness.
    for Catalina Torres the pinched faces of four huddled
    children,
    the naked bodies of four bony children,
    the chant of their chorale of hunger.
And for twenty eight hundred ladies of joy the grotesque act gone over—
    the wink—the grimace—the "feeling like it baby?"
And for Maria Vasquez, spinster, emptiness, emptiness.
    flaming with dresses for children she can never fondle.
And for Ambrosa Espinoza—the skeleton body of her brother on his mattress
of rags, boring twin holes in the dark with his eyes to the image of christ
remembering a leg, and twenty-five years cut off from his life by the railroad.

Women up north, I want you to know,
I tell you this can't last forever.

I swear it won't.

FLORENCE REECE

Which Side Are You On?

Come all you poor workers,
Good news to you I'll tell,
How the good old union
Has come in here to dwell.

Which side are you on?
Which side are you on?

We're starting our good battle,
We know we're sure to win,
Because we've got the gun thugs
A-lookin' very thin.

Which side are you on?
Which side are you on?

If you go to Harlan County,
There is no neutral there,
You'll either be a union man
Or a thug for J. H. Blair.

Which side are you on?
Which side are you on?

They say they have to guard us
To educate their child,
Their children live in luxury,
Our children almost wild.

Which side are you on?
Which side are you on?

With pistols and with rifles
They take away our bread,

And if you miners hinted it
They'll sock you on the head.

Which side are you on?
Which side are you on?

Gentlemen, can you stand it?
Oh, tell me how you can?
Will you be a gun thug
Or will you be a man?

Which side are you on?
Which side are you on?

My daddy was a miner,
He's now in the air and sun,*
He'll be with you fellow workers
Till every battle's won.

Which side are you on?
Which side are you on?

---

*Blacklisted and without a job.

AUNT MOLLY JACKSON

I Am a Union Woman

I am a union woman,
As brave as I can be;
I do not like the bosses,
And the bosses don't like me.

   Refrain:

Join the NMU,
Come join the NMU

I was raised in old Kentucky,
In Kentucky borned and bred;
And when I joined the union
They called me a Rooshian Red.

When my husband asked the boss for a job
These is the words he said:
"Bill Jackson, I can't work you sir,
Your wife's a Rooshian Red."

This is the worst time on earth
That I have ever saw;
To get shot down by gun thugs
And framed up by the law.

If you want to join a union
As strong as one can be,
Join the dear old NMU
And come along with me.

We are many thousand strong
And I am glad to say,
We are getting stronger
And stronger every day.

The Hungry Blues

I am sad and wearied, I have got the hungry ragged blues.
Not a penny in my pocket to buy one thing I need to use.
I was up this morning with the worst blues I ever had in my life
Not a bite to cook for breakfast, or for a coal miner's wife.

When my husband works in the coal mines he loads a car on every trip,
Then he goes to the office that evenin' and gits denied of scrip
Just because it took all he had made that day to pay his mine expenses,
Just because it took all he had made that day to pay his mine expenses
A man that will just work for coal light and carbide, he ain't got a speck of
sense.

All the women in this coal camp are a-sittin' with bowed down heads
Ragged and barefooted and their children a-cryin' for bread.
No food, no clothes for our children.
I am sure this aint no lie.
If we caint get no more for our labor, we will starve to death and die.

Please dont go under those mountains, with the slate a-hangin' over your head.
Please dont go under those mountains, with the slate a-hangin' over your head.
And work for just coal light and carbide, and your children a-cryin' for bread.
I pray you take my counsel, please take a friend's advice,
Dont load no more, dont put out no more till you can get a livin price.

This minin' town I live in is a sad and a lonely place;
This minin' town I live in is a sad and a lonely place;
For pity and starvation is pictured on every face.
Everybody hungry and ragged, no slippers on their feet,
Everybody hungry and ragged, no slippers on their feet
All a-goin round from place to place bummin for a little food to eat.
Listen my friends and comrades, please take a friend's advice,
Dont put out no more of your labor till you get a livin price.

Please dont go under those mountains, with the slate a-hangin' over your head.
Please dont go under those mountains, with the slate a-hangin' over your head.
And work for just coal light and carbide, and your children a-cryin' for bread.
I pray you take my counsel, please take a friend's advice,
Dont load no more, dont put out no more till you can get a livin price.

III. REPORTAGE, THEORY, AND ANALYSIS

Worlds Unseen: Political Women Journalists and the 1930s

CHARLOTTE NEKOLA

Women reporters in the 1930s rode mules through revolutionary Cuba, shared trenches with troops in the Spanish Civil War, and interviewed sea captains in the Soviet Arctic. Within the United States, their work ranged from first-person accounts of strikes, to discussion of the relationship between black women and the steel industry, to accounts of work conditions in mills and department stores, to analysis of the politics of lynching in the South. The depth and range of their work far exceeds the parameters of what historian Marion Marzolf describes as the usual range of women's work in journalism in the first decade of the twentieth century: "women's pages, feature writing, magazine writing and editing stunts, columns, and sob-sister reporting," with some women assigned to hard news.[1]

Yet the history of radical women journalists is almost totally absent from accounts of documentary of that era and from recent accounts of women in journalism. William Stott's *Documentary Expression and Thirties America* mentions Josephine Herbst, Mary Heaton Vorse, and Meridel Le Sueur as part of the number of journalists who covered strikes, radical movements, the unemployed, and Midwest farmers, but offers no further analysis or detail of their work.[2] In the "Reportage" section of Joseph North's anthology of writings from the radical journal *New Masses,* only two of the eleven writers featured are women.[3] Daniel Aaron's literary history of the period, *Writers on the Left,* makes passing reference to Herbst, Anna Louise Strong, Vorse, Le Sueur, and Ella Winter, mainly along the lines of who ran into whom in what foreign country or who attended what writer's congress, and discusses the theoretical content of one of Le Sueur's essays briefly.[4] His coverage, however, of such better- and lesser-known male writers as Malcolm Cowley, Floyd Dell, Max Eastman, Joseph Freeman, Mike Gold, and Granville Hicks is extensive. None of the writers included in this volume appear in Schilpp and Murphy's *Great Women of the Press,* Beasley and Silver's

Women in Media: A Documentary Source Book, Marzolf's *Up from the Footnote: A History of Women Journalists,* or Belford's *Brilliant Bylines: A Biographical Anthology of Notable Newspaperwomen in America.*[5] To judge from the texts available, women journalists at present occupy a marginal position in the history of radical journalism, and radical journalists occupy a marginal position in the history of women journalists.

This part begins with international reportage—Josephine Herbst in Cuba, Agnes Smedley in China, Anna Louise Strong in China and Spain, and Ruth Gruber and Ella Winter in the Soviet Union—that asks questions about revolutionary political and social orders of the 1930s abroad, and especially about the position of women within these societies. The focus then shifts to the domestic upheaval of the United States in the 1930s—its economic crisis and political turbulence. Tillie Olsen, Mary Heaton Vorse, Vivian Dahl, Mary Guimes Lear, and Ella Ford document working conditions, unemployment, and women's participation in strikes. Meridel Le Sueur's essay takes on an issue much discussed in radical circles: the relationship between the middle class, the intellectual literary Left, and a proletarian political movement. Dorothy Day's, Thyra J. Edwards's, and Myra Page's essays demonstrate the effect of unemployment on individual lives. The anonymous worker narratives offer the immediate, concrete experience of a working woman. Elaine Ellis and Mollie V. Lewis focus on the particular problems of black women workers. Vorse's "Hard-Boiled" discusses race relations in an issue central to leftists in the 1930s—the trial of the Scottsboro boys. And the final group of essays presents more theoretical works that analyze both class and gender—Mary Inman on domestic labor as the "pivot" of capitalism, Grace Hutchins's description of the double day of women workers, and Rebecca Pitts's and Hutchins's analyses of the position of women under capitalism.

The more well-known women journalists from this era who wrote for large daily newspapers include Ishbel Ross of the *New York Herald Tribune;* Doris Fleeson, a New Deal Democrat close to Eleanor Roosevelt who wrote for the *New York Daily News;* and Dorothy Thompson, controversial columnist for the *New York Herald Tribune* and wife of Sinclair Lewis. The authors in this volume, however, usually wrote for smaller leftist journals that welcomed their focus on class, gender, and/or race issues. We sifted these pieces from periodicals that spanned the many variations of radical thinking: *New Masses, The Partisan Review, Modern Monthly, Modern Quarterly, The Daily Worker, Clipper, The Anvil, Working Woman, Crisis, The People's World, Opportunity, The Catholic Worker, The New Republic,* and the regional journals of John Reed clubs.

Readers of these journals in the 1930s would have found reviews and advertisements for such book-length works of reportage and analysis on political subjects as Ruth Gruber's *I Went to the Soviet Arctic* and Grace

Hutchins's *Women and Capitalism.* In general, Hutchins, Pitts, Strong, Gruber, and Winter were optimistic about the possibility that Communism could offer lasting improvements in the social, economic, and intellectual status of women. Their analysis required a sharp examination of the status of women under capitalism. And the economic crisis of capitalism in the United States forced a harder look at the conditions of working women. Worker narratives and strike reportage appeared frequently in these publications, and the building of unions was often presented as a solution for both black and white women. Hardest to locate among these published works were those that specifically addressed the intersections of class and gender, and even harder, the intersections of class, gender, and race. What we have chosen to include are uniquely important early discussions of questions that largely went underground during the 1940s and 1950s.

Politically and socially minded women journalists in the 1930s frequently reported on the same issues as their male colleagues—revolutions, strikes, labor conditions—but they also wrote about issues of special interest to women, for example, women's status in the Soviet Union and China and the working conditions of women in female-dominated occupations. Where did a woman journalist with political interests publish in the 1930s? A feminist writer had no particular home. Mari Jo Buhle comments in a recent book that the erosion of the women's movement in the 1930s caused a sharp decline in the feminist radical press, and that the Communist Party was mainly interested in feminist journalism that "met specific tactical purposes." Radical women writers and editors went to the official cultural/literary journal of the U.S. Communist Party (CPUSA), *New Masses,* and more generally to the mainstream press.[6]

New Masses published reportage by women writers on the same subject matter as male writers, including Josephine Herbst on the Cuban Revolution and Ella Ford on the Gastonia strike. But *New Masses* seldom featured articles whose main focus was the status of women, unless the analysis of the article eventually led to the Party's position on the primacy of class struggle. For example, Rebecca Pitts's "Women and Communism" takes on questions familiar to contemporary feminists—the biology-as-destiny debate, the position of women under capitalism—but eventually turns the discussion to the solution of these feminist issues as implied in the new social and economic structure of the Soviet Union. When Pitts wrote an article on "Women and the *New Masses,*" it was not a discussion of women's special place within the pages or among the editorial staff of that journal, or within Left literary movements. Rather, it was a testimonial to women's identification with class struggle.[7]

Similarly, *Working Woman* magazine, the woman's journal of CPUSA, centered at first on class struggle. As the Party moved into the Popular Front, *Working Woman* focused on anti-fascism. At the same time it regularly featured coverage of women's participation in strikes and in Party-sponsored organizations, discussed reproductive issues, and, later, offered household hints and beauty tips.[8] Thus, though radical publications did include articles by women writers and some discussion of women's issues, they seem to have been chosen primarily because their authors wrote about political issues important to the Left, not because they discussed gender or issues of special importance to women, or included an analysis of sexism along with class bias or racism. Ultimately, however, leftist publications provided an unusual forum for women writers, one that allowed unique theoretical arguments to emerge, especially when issues of gender and class coincided, as in Inman's analysis of women's invisible work in the home as "the pivot" of the capitalist system, Pitts's analysis of women's sexuality under capitalism, and Hutchins's delineation of the double workday for women workers. Radical journals also published voices of completely unknown working women, as in the narratives of Ella Ford from the *New Masses* and the anonymous domestic workers in *Working Woman.*

Despite the inclusion of race issues on the radical political agenda of the period, the greatest diversity of journalism by and about black women can be found not in leftist journals of the 1930s but in such black cultural and literary journals as *Opportunity* and *Crisis.* Robert Shaffer points out that while articles about women in *The Communist,* the Communist Party's theoretical journal, and the *Party Organizer,* an internal newspaper, usually included a section on black workers, few articles on blacks extended their analysis to black women.[9] While race was the important issue in *Opportunity* and *Crisis,* women writers contributed articles through the decade that explored the triple oppression of race, gender, and class. The editorial staffs of *Opportunity* and *Crisis* as listed on their mastheads were made up solely of men. Regular features on race, unemployment, labor, work, politics, and foreign relations were overwhelmingly written by men. Women writers appeared occasionally as the authors of short stories, arts and theater reviews, portraits of outstanding women, or social issue articles on education, housing, unmarried mothers, or the status of women workers. It would seem that women authors were assigned to somewhat traditionally "female" areas—the sentiment of poetry, the fiction of fiction, the problems of education and "women's questions"—rather than to analyses of work and the world. Yet articles that broke this pattern did occasionally appear. Elaine Ellis's "Women of the Cotton Fields" delineates conditions of black women workers, discusses the relationship of enforced sterilization to labor supply, and ends on a hopeful note about unionism. "Negro Women in Steel," by Mollie V. Lewis, highlights black women's role in working against racial obstacles in the labor movement.

Thyra J. Edwards's "Chicago in the Rain" joins a large tradition of in-the-streets social worker documentary of the 1930s.

Investigative journalists such as Ida Tarbell and foreign correspondents such as Peggy Hull had worked for major publications in the 1920s, but resistance to the idea of women as journalists was far from unheard of in the following decade. Emma Bugbee, the only female hard-news reporter for the *New York Tribune,* and a feminist, evaluated the newspaper industry in 1928 as "essentially fairminded," though she thought that women were probably less likely than men to get the best reporting assignments. [10] In her 1938 survey of 881 women who worked in journalism and other media-related jobs, Iona Robertson Logie stated in her introduction that "it is generally acknowledged that in spite of many economic and social advantages, women have still to cope with diverse forms of discrimination, sometimes in salaries, sometimes in advancement—sometimes both." The majority of women straight-news reporters were employed in small cities and towns, not major metropolitan centers. [11] In 1922, Ella Winter began working for European newspapers, and observed that newspaper-women were still a "rarity" in England. Back in the United States, she was told by a radical editor of the *Daily Herald* that she might write on fashion. [12]

Josephine Herbst was asked by both Farm Research, a research and information bureau, and *New Masses* to examine the results of Roosevelt's farm policies and to evaluate rural protest in 1934. But according to Herbst's biographer, the Farm Research employee assigned to go with her, Webster Powell, viewed Herbst as a secretary. When Herbst traveled to Cuba to investigate the revolutionary Realengo, her biographer comments that her sex was an obstacle in winning the confidence of inner political circles: "she was a good comrade, but she was, after all, a woman." [13] Thus, however daring a woman reporter might be, however far she went to investigate less traditional journalistic subjects like revolutions or strikes, she still had to face the problem of being taken seriously as a political thinker. In 1923, Leon Trotsky agreed to let Max Eastman write a biographical portrait of him, although Anna Louise Strong had previously made the same proposal. In 1935, the League of American Writers' Congress sent a fifteen-man delegation to Cuba, led by Clifford Odets, to visit prisons and Realengo 18, the revolutionary outpost that had already been covered in the *New Masses* by Josephine Herbst. [14] These incidents suggest that more than once in the literary history of this period men wound up finishing "serious" jobs begun by women reporters.

At the same time, it is possible that their sex enriched women journalists as reporters of revolutionary times. When Herbst traveled to Cuba to investigate Realengo 18, her biographer comments that it was "useful to be a woman" since she was apt to be perceived "less as a radical and more as a bleeding heart."[15] When Anna Louise Strong reported on the Russian revolution in the 1920s, she was interested in how the revolution actually changed the everyday workings of industry, agriculture, education, and especially the roles of women and children. Other reporters, such as John Reed, were more theoretical; Strong's biographer comments that "Most foreign journalists . . . tended not to take seriously or ignore the efforts being made to transform the fabric of ordinary existence and productivity. . . . John Reed . . . stressed the new political structure, the military, the leadership."[16] Strong maintained this emphasis in her later works, such as "Fighters for Women's Rights," and it is also reflected in the contents of Ruth Gruber's "Finding Women" and in Ella Winter's "Woman Freed." Women's experience in social work in the 1930s gave them material for firsthand observation of the conditions that prompted what Stott calls social-worker documentary, such as Dorothy Day's "A Good Landlord" and Thyra J. Edwards's "Chicago in the Rain."

Like their male colleagues, female journalists in the 1930s practiced varieties of documentary journalism often termed "reportage." The basic technique of documentary reportage during that decade was to describe an individual who was representative of a larger group, and thereby draw larger conclusions from the particular facts of the individual.[17] It was the ideal form of writing for revolutionary and proletarian aesthetic: it was "true," without the distortions or excess of bourgeois individualistic fiction; it used the individual in the service of the mass; it raised political consciousness by linking one person with larger political movements; it replaced private despair with mass action.

Tess Slesinger reported that the 1939 meeting of the League of American Writers defined the writer's task as "the job of *seeing* the mess in which the plain people had been trapped, of interpreting it for them, of reflecting their own image so clearly and correctly that the plain people themselves would feel a part of life with a voice and a weapon and an ally, and cease to think of themselves as helpless victims and alone."[18] Other genres of writing borrowed heavily from the conventions of reportage, as in the documentary style of proletarian novels and short fiction, the interjection of news headlines and statistics into lines of poetry, and the mixture of documentary collage with fictional vignettes, as in Ruth McKenney's *Industrial Valley*.

Georg Lukács said that "genuine reportage is in no way content simply to depict the facts: its descriptions always present a connection, disclose causes and propose consequences."[19] Thus, journalists were asked to move from the realm of fact to the realm of larger political thought. This in itself was perhaps a liberating possibility for women writers conventionally consigned to the more trivial emotional landscape of journalism—sob-sister reporting, gossip columns, fashion and society reporting, for example. At the same time that reportage allowed for an expansion of ideas beyond the self, it also encouraged women to speak about themselves, and to speak about the female self as subject. Stott describes the role of the writer in the most common forms of documentary reportage as a "participant observer"; the author could use "vicarious persuasion: the writer partook of the events he reported and bared his feelings and attitudes to influence the reader's own."[20] For example, Mary Guimes Lear's own story as a striking garment worker, as well as the story of the strike's heroine and the story of striking garment workers in general, builds authority for the female self in "Bessie: A Garment Strike Story."

For women still emerging from a popular ideology of female selflessness and domestic virtue in America, the possibility of using an "I" as a reporter in the world was in itself intoxicating, as the somewhat euphoric titles of book-length reportage by three writers of the era suggest: Anna Louise Strong's *I Change Worlds,* Ruth Gruber's *I Went to the Soviet Arctic,* and Ella Winter's *I Saw the Russian People.* "I was there," these pieces say over and over, while they do the business of documentary reportage. These women journalists seem to have taken a certain amount of pleasure in pointing out their presence in world events. Josephine Herbst's account of herself in "A Passport from Realengo 18" suggests a sense of awe at finding herself in an amazing position: "I am a stranger in a pair of overalls and a blue workshirt sitting astride a very bony and mangy horse." Despite the title of Agnes Smedley's report on war conditions in China, "The People in China," her article starts with a graphic statement of her own presence: "I rode from the village and town through the Fanchang district." Her status as participant observer allows much room for statements demonstrating the weight and scope of her own observations: "I saw many thousands of children growing to manhood and womanhood during this war, in mental darkness," and for her own views: "I must pay high tribute to the character of the common people of China." She is also able to tell the tale of her own participation, living under artillery fire with guerrillas, lecturing in training camps, or sick with malaria. The participant "I" eventually turns into the collective "we" when Smedley says, "We ate bitterness."

Similarly, Herbst's narrator in "Realengo 18" eventually merges into the voice of universal protest. In these pieces, female self is able to make statements for both self and other, and eventually to join a larger political mass. As in all participant-observer pieces, there are really two stories: the writer's story of her own participation, and the story of what she observes. Thus, these pieces document not only events but the fact that American women writers immersed themselves in political struggles far removed from personal and domestic realms.

The convention of informant narratives—reportage composed completely of quotations from the subject—offered the opportunity for disenfranchised individuals, male and female, to speak in their own voices. Stott says that the informant narrative was a widespread convention in the 1930s, used frequently for both worker and bourgeois narrators in both radical and mainstream publications.[21] In the case of some of the most marginal women workers, the popularity of worker narratives provided an audience for stories that probably would have remained untold. *Working Woman* magazine published pieces such as "My Life: A True Story of a Negro Worker of the South" and "And Mine: A True Story of a Negro Worker of the North"; their authors tell their own tales and also analyze relationships among race, sex, and class in the workplace. Ella Ford's "We Are Mill People" recounts her work experience and simultaneously reports on the shift from agrarian to industrial economy, the intimidation of labor by management, the movement of black workers into organized labor. These first-person narratives gave weight to the female subject at the same time that they recorded the history of labor.

Generally absent from these accounts are descriptions of domestic work as part of the working day of women. Ella Ford, for example, does not tell her readers what she did at home before she came to the mill, or what work she had waiting for her when she got home. But Grace Hutchins's *Women Who Work* does include a chapter on "The Double Burden," which makes it clear that "workplace" for women meant both home and factory. The era's most radical analysis of women's domestic labor was Mary Inman's "The Pivot of the System," which named women's domestic work as productive labor, the "pivot" of capitalism. The national leadership of CPUSA resisted Inman's theory so vehemently that she eventually left the Party.[22] The Inman debate, and the general absence of women's narratives that fused description of both domestic and workplace labor, suggests that there was not yet adequate language for or analysis of the double workday experienced in the daily lives of working women.

American women wrote in the midst of world-changing revolutions. The political and social writings of American women in the 1930s give us a rich chapter in the history of women's political thinking. Their essays on early experiments in Communism in the Soviet Union and China provide an unusual insight into what women from a tradition of individualism saw as liberating in the collective ideal. Strike coverage offered firsthand documentation of women's role in the growth of unionism in a decisive decade in labor history. Worker documentaries illuminated the conditions of women's labor and also women's awareness of the politics of the workplace. The Depression as seen in streets and tenements is recorded in social-worker documentary. In theoretical essays, women added gender as another element of political analysis and explored the complex relationships among sex, work, and class. These works also show us how women prevailed over the reigning ideologies of their time. Some women began to view work in the home as productive labor, despite resistance from other theorists who claimed to know the politics of work. Many women writers managed to publish "serious" journalism despite generally acknowledged discrimination in the profession. They addressed issues of gender when such problems, if articulated at all, were thought to be subsumed in the process of class struggle. In radical circles, discussion of self was shadowed and even eclipsed by discussion of class, yet these women did write about the female self and the relation of that self to the world. And they offer us views of that world, in the midst of political turbulence, at some of its most difficult and promising moments.

NOTES

1. Marion Marzolf, *Up from the Footnote: A History of Women Journalists* (New York: Hastings House, 1977), p. 33.

2. William Stott, *Documentary Expression and Thirties America* (New York: Oxford University Press, 1973), p. 180.

3. Joseph North, ed., *New Masses: An Anthology of the Rebel Thirties* (New York: International Publishers, 1969), p. 18.

4. Daniel Aaron, *Writers on the Left: Episodes in American Literary Communism* (New York: Harcourt, Brace, and World, 1961), pp. 158, 278–279.

5. See Madelon Golden Schilpp and Sharon M. Murphy, *Great Women of the Press* (Carbondale and Edwardsville: Southern Illinois University Press, 1983); Maurine Beasley and Sheila Silver, *Women in Media: A Documentary Source Book* (Washington Women's Institute for Freedom of the Press, 1977); Marzolf, *Up from the Footnote;* and Barbara Belford, *Brilliant Bylines: A Biographical Anthology of Notable Newspaperwomen in America* (New York: Columbia University Press, 1986).

6. Mari Jo Buhle, *Women and the American Left: A Guide to Sources* (Boston: G. K. Hall, 1983), p. 169.

7. Rebecca Pitts, "Women and the *New Masses,*" *New Masses* 21 (December 1, 1936), p. 15.

8. Buhle, *Women and the American Left,* p. 169.

9. Robert Shaffer, "Women and the Communist Party, USA, 1930–1940," *Socialist Review* 9, no. 3 (May–June 1979): 78–79.

10. Bugbee quoted in Marzolf, *Up from the Footnote,* p. 50.

11. Iona Robertson Logie, *Careers for Women in Journalism: A Composite Picture of 881 Salaried Women Writers at Work in Journalism, Advertising, Publicity, and Promotion* (Scranton: International Textbook Co., 1938), pp. 7, 36.

12. Ella Winter, *And Not to Yield: An Autobiography* (New York: Harcourt, Brace, and World, Inc., 1963), pp. 79, 80.

13. Elinor Langer, *Josephine Herbst* (Boston: Little, Brown, 1984), pp. 159, 172.

14. Aaron, *Writers on the Left*, pp. 124, 303.

15. Langer, *Josephine Herbst*, p. 164.

16. Tracy B. Strong and Helene Keyssar, *Right in Her Soul: The Life of Anna Louise Strong* (New York: Random House, 1983), pp. 88, 89.

17. Stott, *Documentary Expression and Thirties America*, p. 172.

18. Tess Slesinger, "Writers on the Volcano," *Clipper: A Western Review* 2, no. 4 (June 1941): 5.

19. Georg Lukács, "Reportage or Portrayal?" (1932), reprinted in *Essays on Realism*, ed. Rodney Livingston and trans. David Feunback (Cambridge: MIT Press, 1981), p. 49.

20. Stott, *Documentary Expression and Thirties America*, p. 179.

21. Ibid., pp. 191, 193.

22. Shaffer, "Women and the Communist Party, USA," p. 87.

JOSEPHINE HERBST

A Passport from Realengo 18

On the earthen floor of the house of the poet of Realengo 18, one of the Realengo men draws with a stick a map of Cuba. The hardbaked earth swept clean with a broom makes a good blackboard. He shapes the island and we stare at its smallness that is now being related to the world. Outlines of the United States take shape roughly. There is an ocean, Europe and a sudden great bulge of the stick moved by an inspired curve makes the Soviet Union. Everyone in the room smiles. Jaime, the actor, turned Realengo farmer these ten years, says excitely that in my pocketbook I carry a passport that has a visa from the Soviet Union upon it. Two little girls sitting together on a narrow bench keep their seats, everyone else crowds forward. The passport goes from hand to hand.

Through the doorway is a view down the valley. We are very high on top of the world in Realengo. We are in the midst of steep cultivated mountains with banana and tobacco growing in regular rows. Around these cultivated patches virgin forest bristles in tough areas. Realengo 18 feels somewhat protected by its location, by its difficult trails too narrow for the artillery of an army. Last August airplanes whirled overhead looking for places to drop bombs. Now four men of Realengo are gravely studying the map of Cuba on the floor and they are looking at my visa from the Soviet Union.

They stare slowly at the visa and pass it from hand to hand. Someone picks out the tiny hammer and sickle on the seal. Jaime says that there ought to be a visa from the Soviet of Realengo 18. He says there are plenty of blank pages and I should certainly have a visa from the first Soviet on the North American continent. The visa has changed the atmosphere of the room in a moment. Realengo 18 is a small spot on a small island and we have been discussing the problems of this island, its relation to the world. Every person in the room has been weighed down with the great bulk of the United States pressing from above on that map drawn upon the floor. We have been looking at the map and feeling the powers that are against this small island in its battle for freedom. The visa is a kind of magic that restores everyone.

The wife of the poet gets up briskly and makes some coffee. She serves it in tiny cups with sugar-cane juice. Though this island is devoted to sugar, there is no sugar here, only the juice of the cane pressed out with a rude handmade machine of logs. Sugar sells, is not eaten, is not made in Realengo. Jaime, who has traveled in his day and knows the ports of South America, loves my passport. He keeps looking at it and insisting that I get a visa from Realengo. They are now discussing it gravely and the question is to be taken up with the secretary. After that it will be taken up with the president, Lino Alvarez. A stir and bustle of business and the relation of this tiny spot to the great one-sixth of the world where the Soviet Union flourishes changes the entire mood of the party. We get on horseback again and start out over the trails.

In Realengo 18 it is not possible just to travel. In every hut is a Realengo man who wants the news. I am a stranger in a pair of overalls and a blue workshirt sitting astride a very bony and mangy horse. This only lasts a moment. The next moment I am in the house, we are smiling and talking. The man of the house may be very ill of malaria. This sickness is a terrific scourge in Realengo where the outside world seems never to have come except for plunder. Agents from the big sugar mills below penetrate Realengo 18 on horseback wearing very white starched clothes, riding haughtily with whips in their hands and guns on their hips. Realengo men passing on their own humble horses never speak to these emissaries. The silent procession goes past the rider whose spying eyes look sharply. Contempt is thick in the air as the invader disappears. Realengo men exchange glances; someone spits loudly and with fury. Not a word may be spoken until we are in the house of the sick man whose bright feverish eyes want all the news. From what deep source does this talk about politics and history come? Their own struggle to hold the land to which they have given so much labor is the answer.

There isn't a hut that must not have a look at the visa. It is taken out, passed shyly, delightedly; again the question of putting a Realengo visa in the book is seriously pondered. An old woman cannot stop her tirade against the spies sent in by the sugar companies long enough to look but her son thrusts it under her nose. She cannot read, few can, yet those who do read talk much. They explain, going over and over the situation in the world, relating it to this little world of Realengo 18. They are practical people, not romanticists, not Rousseaueans. They know that they need more than the fighting men of Realengo to keep their land and be free, they need more than Cuba.

Doves strut around cooing. The little pigs hunt frantically for bits of food, nuzzle each other's hide searching for crumbs. A lean and hungry look is in this fertile land. A fire is made on the pile of stones that makes a hearth and the very sight of the crude fire makes fierce talk bubble up about the day that will some day come when they will have electricity, radios, and their children will not need to pause on the long toil up the hill from the stream with the heavy water jug. So much tiredness in children, so many thin bodies, yet the little girl in the house where I spend a night hunts for a tiny bit of a broken comb to comb out lovely hair. She takes a morsel of soap from its place behind a splinter on the wall, delicately washes her hands in a tin basin, laughing. "Some day we will have lots of water, lots of soap."

They believe in that *some day* and they believe in their *today* and are proud of their struggle. They should take their place beside the great of the world, they have fought well. Everyone agrees on the necessity of the visa. So it is no surprise that night, very late, with the darkness heavy with the scent of many flowering herbs, to hear footsteps coming along the banana path. Under the banana leaves they are carrying a typewriter and Lino Alvarez their leader is coming with many papers to show me. We go through these papers first, with a tiny oil lamp flickering and the owner of the house sitting upright in a hammock very excited and happy at all the company that has suddenly filled the room. The wife has made a wonderful drink out of oranges yanked hastily from a tree by the children and she has brought out a treasure, a tiny round tin box the size of a silver dollar, with a white powder in it. It turns out to be nothing more extraordinary than soda, a pinch of which makes the drink foam up in a way to delight everyone. Lino Alvarez, with his white clothes and blue shirt and the sword of the Spanish general that he wears since his days as a soldier in the Spanish-American war, wants the entire background of the struggle in Realengo understood. His stubborn integrity makes the trickery of the companies who have tried to defraud these people seem even more shameful. We are going over the papers and it is only toward the finish that the matter of the visa is again brought up. The question has been threshed out long before the trip to this house was made, it seems, because the visa is now ready. Lino Alvarez did not think a visa should be placed in the book but he thought a paper of some kind was fitting. The paper was already in an envelope and as it is laid down the whole scheme of these mountain lives resolves itself more clearly. Not only miles but steep mountains apart, they must have been busy all that day hurrying up and down, consulting, carrying messages, by some secret telegraphy of the mountains transmitting news.

They are very proud as I read the visa. The secretary and one of the vice presidents sign. Lino Alvarez, the president, signs slowly. He is only learning to write now. Little pigs grunt for food and in the excitement of signing, a huge pan of corn that had been painfully shelled that day by the entire family so that on the next day it could be ground up for Realengo bread, a thick corn mush, fell to the floor. All the children scrambled to save it from the assault of the greedy pigs. The mother pig outside with a brood of very thin tiny young screams for her share. A horse sensing food whinnies. Doves begin chortling and bristling around one's very legs. The whole room is humming and what kernels are not saved are scooped up and guzzled by the noisy pigs. Hunger is here, it was here all during the evening meal of ñame and malanga but no one is paying attention to it. Bright eyes are looking at the paper as I put it in my pocketbook they take seats again gravely.

This is a small hut. The district of Realengo is small in comparison to Cuba and Cuba is only a tiny island but no one in Realengo feels alone in the fight for freedom. They talk too much of what is going on in the world. They know too much to be alone.

I am writing this many weeks later than the visit yet it is impossible not to write of it as if it were in a continuous present. This is Pennsylvania farming land. On May Day the farmers of this community had May Day in Doylestown. A woman told of the effort to evict her family of eight children. It took many hours to get her off the land. They had to pay her a dollar apiece for five pigeons before she would go and the little humble triumph sounded good to every farmer. The meeting on the courthouse lawn closed with singing the *Internationale* and I remembered one Sunday afternoon in Realengo 18 where it rained hard on the palm roof all day and little boys played a game with beans on the earthen floor. The calf stepped inside out of the rain and a parrot screamed on its hoop swung from the roof. After a while it got dark. We had been talking about the problems of Realengo and some of the men had again drawn maps to show the relation of this district to Santiago and Havana where workers had gone on strike in sympathy with Realengo last August. Soon it was too dark to make maps and we began singing, first the *Marseillaise* and then the *Internationale*.

Everyone knows that since that time much blood has been shed in Cuba; the iron military rule has tried to crush strikes, stifle protests. Neither jail nor guns can completely silence such singing.

AGNES SMEDLEY

The People in China

IN THE YANGTZE RIVER VALLEY REGION, WEST OF WUHU

I rode from village to village and town to town through Fanchang district, making a special study of the civilian refugee problem. After Mujiatien I passed on through one endless line of human suffering. There was no temple without masses of refugees sleeping on the stone floor, with bits of straw under them. In one large village near Bufachen I found 1,000 refugees living in three or four temples and abandoned buildings.

It is difficult to describe the living conditions and health of the refugees, for there seem to be no appropriate words in any language. There is absolutely no medical relief at all. Most temples are indescribably dirty and in a dangerous, unsanitary condition. The refugees sleep on the floors in their old patched padded quilts, or on boards, benches, tables, or altars wherever there is an inch of space. The courtyards of the temples are piles of straw, old rags, fragments of decayed vegetables, mingled with green stagnant pools of water.

Everywhere I found sick men, women, and children lying in bundles of rags. There was no sense in trying to learn the nature of their disease, for I had no medical supplies with me, nor am I a doctor. They suffered from every kind of ailment; from what the refugees and the sick men told me, some cases were clearly typhoid, others pneumonia and dysentery. In my mind remains a general picture of scabies in every form, from the initial stages to scabies infections, with people lying sick in bed, unable to move, covered with open sores. I saw countless children with great open gashes of scabies on their necks, feet, and hands. Everywhere babies were covered with scabies, many with red bleeding sores all over their faces that might be due to malnutrition. To my unutterable misery, mothers with diseased babies in their arms fell on their knees before me, crying and asking for medical care, pointing to their babies and to sick members of their families lying in their padded rags with high fevers. There was practically no family but had lost one or more members from sickness and disease since December. There are no statistics of death. It was clear that in summer cholera and typhoid can take root in the entire district, wipe out the refugees and other civilians, and dangerously affect the army as well.

The only doctor in the Fanchang district government is an old-fashioned Chinese doctor who deals in herbal medicine. He does not know the use of modern drugs. The only other medical forces are the sanitary units of the New Fourth Army companies and regiments. The New Fourth Army base hospital and field hospital are two days of hard marching (as an army marches) over hills and mountains.

WITH THE NEW FOURTH ARMY

Talks with the Japanese wounded and captives show that they were picked off fishing vessels, off miserable farms, out of taxis or factories and sent off, filled with lies—if anything—to China to kill.

They always think I am a Russian—they have been told, evidently, that Japan is fighting the USSR. Before long they mingle with the Army as do the Chinese. No guards watch them. In fact, they refuse to go back to Japan or to their own Army for they know they would be killed by their officers. They have also had enough of war. They are afraid to step out into the country for fear the civilians would kill them, but two of them teach Japanese in the Training Camp, and all of them work in the Enemy Work Department putting out handbills and such things for distribution among the Japanese troops.

SOUTH OF THE YANGTZE: KINGHSIEN

A regular system of refugee relief was introduced by the Government in the past, of using a certain proportion of public rice stored in the public granaries for food for the refugees. Japanese occupation of many places brought much of this relief to an end, for the Japanese looted the granaries and rice shops, fed themselves, and transported vast quantities to Wuhu, Nanking and other Yangtze cities.

Not all refugees—but the vast majority of farmers and most of the artisans and students, primary school teachers, and such intellectuals—are totally destitute. Some find work: the school teachers sometimes found schools and run them on monthly collections from the public. Men and women alike cut fuel from the mountainsides and sell it. Some find a little day work as farm laborers or as carriers. Many able-bodied young men volunteer or are conscripted into the various armies or guerrilla bands. Countless numbers have died of hunger and disease, no statistics being kept. Thousands wander over the land, begging from door to door or from the armies.

Despite all the misery here, I was impressed by a number of other facts. The refugees, particularly the women, try to keep their clothing clean—and succeed where the conditions are not too impossible. The refugees are patient and have kept their humanity toward others in most cases. I have found few or no records of criminality. While many refugees have sold their children that they might get food for them and something for those unsold, still they keep their children with them wherever possible. I have found no criminal children of the type who became a problem following upheavals in Western countries or in countries of widespread unemployment. On the whole, I must pay high tribute to the character of the common people of China, who ask only for the means of making a living. In every region we visited I heard of refugees who would not register with the Refugee Relief Committee because they were ashamed. In only a few places did any refugees approach me personally as beggars. Above all I was impressed by the helpless refugee children.

In one of the Kinghsien refugee stations we found a man who told us his story, which is perhaps typical of thousands: "We left Wantze, near which we cultivated six mow of land, just as the Japanese approached. We had no time to take anything with us. We had six sons. One I sold for fourteen dollars; one I gave to a farmer who agreed to feed and care for him; one son died of smallpox this winter; we have these three little sons left."

On the road we halted at a poor tea shop to get some water. The servant was a little boy perhaps twelve years of age. The old woman who owned the shop told us that this child had stood before her shop the day before, weeping. His father had been killed by the Japanese near Wantze, his mother had wandered off, and he had no home. He was wandering the roads, looking for his mother. The old woman took him in, but she did not know what to do with him, for she earned too little to keep him.

In Kinghsien, the physical condition of the refugees may be said to be typical of all in the three districts studied. A physical examination showed that fully 95 to 99 percent were sick or diseased. Nearly all had scabies, often infected; only three or four in each station were without trachoma; some were blind from trachoma and others would later go blind. Even little babies had trachoma. Here are the afflictions we found: scabies, trachoma, tuberculosis, malaria, beri beri, anemia, rheumatism, syphilis, dysentery, various intestinal disorders, including worms, goiter, chronic ulcers—and practically all had lice.

There is absolutely no medical relief for the refugees, nor are there any doctors or nurses about Kinghsien.

I saw many thousands of children growing to manhood and womanhood during this war, in mental darkness, without any plans, any disciplined study or work, almost all of them sick or diseased. This is the future generation of China and these children, coming from the toiling people, will constitute the basis of future China. What kind of men and women will they be?

SUNJIAPU

I could find no person here who had lived under the Japanese occupation, for all eighty who had been in the town were slaughtered as the Japanese were driven out. When the Chinese recaptured the town, they found the brothel only partly burned, with the corpses of the bayonetted women still unburned. They found the bodies of the men: some of these bodies, decapitated, were still on their knees, their hands tied behind them. At a mass meeting in the town, at which I spoke, everyone attended. The children were half naked, ragged, barefooted little things, their eyes inflamed with trachoma.

How can mere words comfort people in such conditions, with the gaunt ruins of their homes forming a background before me? Yet I carried nothing beyond words. I only wish that the foreign friends of China who give money, medical supplies, and other relief could have heard their names shouted from thousands of throats.

I tried to give the people courage by telling them, among other things, of their countless friends and sympathizers among the peoples of democratic countries and in the Soviet Union. It seems almost deception to speak of such aid, because not one copper of it or one ounce of medical supplies has ever come into these regions though foreign funds have been used to erect refugee zones in cities under Japanese occupation. Yet in many such zones, the men have merely constituted a reservoir of forced labor for the Japanese army.

Throughout my trip, also, my mind was filled with the knowledge that thousands of Chinese doctors and nurses still remain in port cities or even in Japanese-occupied cities and regions, and do not leave their comfort to come into Chinese territory, care for their harassed people, or help the wounded of their armies struggling for the country's liberation. It seems to me essential that all Chinese who remain in Japanese-occupied regions, and all doctors and nurses in particular, shall free their minds of every illusion about the Japanese and about the future of themselves and their country if the Japanese should be victorious.

Chinese and foreigners may be shocked when Japanese frankly say: "We do not want to help the wounded Chinese. We want them to die." Of course the Japanese want the Chinese to die! That is why they are in China. The reason they have not killed more than they have killed up to now is only that they do not have the technical facilities for killing them. They have not killed, outraged, and debased many medical workers in port and other cities because they have not had the time or opportunity; first they must try to destroy the Chinese government and the Chinese armies. After that—should such a thing be possible—they will turn their attention to the detailed job of mopping up every Chinese everywhere who entertains a shred of illusion in his brain that he is a man with the rights of a man.

Foreigners who also still foolishly believe that they and their womenfolk will, at the worst, be in Japanese concentration camps are also living in a daydream. The Japanese will do to these foreigners, and their women, exactly what they have done to Chinese women everywhere, and to Russian women in Manchuria. China and the Chinese are today the great barricade between civilization, on the one hand, and the ruthless barbarism of the Japanese military machine, on the other. If we permit the Chinese barrier to be broken down, we cannot expect any other treatment than that meted out to the Chinese.

NORTH ANHWEI

I crossed the Yangtze with a unit of the New Fourth army. At midnight we passed between two Japanese garrison points on the river, each one about 1½ miles distant. But the Japanese hug their walled defense points at night, and are in effect prisoners within them. The nights belong to the Chinese. Had the ancient walls around Chinese towns and cities been destroyed long ago—as they are being reluctantly destroyed today—the Japanese could not hold most of the points they hold now. When we crossed the Yangtze the only traitors were the moon, and the dogs that yelped from enemy-occupied towns when they heard the distant thud of our soft-soled feet.

It would be a fine journalistic stunt to boast that I had passed through "darkest Africa," through great danger and hardship, and that I was the first "white man" ever to set foot there. Instead I found an American business man starting an egg factory in North Anhwei, while Honan and Hupeh are one great American "bible belt" in which missionaries are industriously harvesting souls, some of them preaching that the war, like the countless sicknesses that are rife among the people, is due to sin. But I found also some missionary doctors conducting modern hospitals, and none of them seemed to regard the malaria mosquito, the relapsing fever louse, or the dysentery germ as messengers of the Almighty to punish the "heathen" for their sins. They were ministering to the sick and wounded in a true Christian spirit.

So far I have passed through few hardships other than those incidental to such a long and hard trip through a country at war, where one must ride or walk over vast regions in which all roads have been torn up. The Chinese are the ones to suffer real hardship. As for danger from the

Japanese, the safest place in China is the "enemy rear." The only Japanese you see are those brought in by guerrillas, and those captives all begin to lecture in mass meetings telling the people that they were conscripted and forced to come to China; they did not want to come and would be only too glad to go home.

Anhwei, for instance, is a region of great landlord estates, often of many thousands of acres. Many owners fled to the port cities or to the rear, leaving agents to collect the usual rent, which is 50 percent of the crop. Some landlords remain, a few work for the Japanese, and some sit on the fence, waiting to see which side will win. The peasants cultivate their land; their sons are conscripted to fight the Japanese, the older men and young boys are conscripted as carriers for the Army and for the wounded and for destruction or repair of the roads. And they must bear the full burden of repairing the enormous damage done to their homes by the Japanese. Without rights of citizens they must still shoulder the full burden of the war while the landlords with their sons and daughters sit in the far rear or in port cities waiting for victory, when they can return to their old feudal luxury. The sons of some have gone to America or England to study—and to escape the war.

Few people except the peasants see anything wrong with this. But I have met many Army commanders who face this problem clearly and are sunk in depression because they have no power to change it. For the armies are ordered to fight only and to leave administrative power in the hands of politicians. Many politicians are interested only in preserving social conditions as they were in the past.

However, in the enemy rear, Chinese administrative organs continue to function right up to within the shadows of occupied towns along the railways and rivers. In Anhwei these administrative organs are being reformed to some extent according to the "Kwangsi System." Many old officials, none too honest, and always inefficient and socially backward, have been replaced by younger men and a few women. These younger officials have been trained for three months in the provisional provincial capital, Lihwang. Sometimes, however, the change is but a change in personnel, for often in the new officials are sons or relatives of the old. Not always though. An honest administration will indeed give the Government more revenues. Beyond this no basic social changes are being undertaken and until these changes come, the misery and suffering of the common people cannot be lightened.

HONAN

This province does not share the reform activity of Anhwei. One special commissioner over eight districts in eastern Honan expressed himself in this way: "We do not have the same system as Anhwei. By this we do not gain anything, but at the same time we do not lose anything. We keep things as they are."

"Things as they are" in eastern Honan are indescribably bitter. This region was formerly Soviet; over it poor peasants fought for years, holding the territory as their own. No human beings have ever lived on a lower level of existence than do the common people here. The Communist uprising in this region in the past was the uprising of serfs against a feudal landlord and merchant class. By "keeping things as they are" officials do not change any of the causes that led to the first Communist revolt.

I have never seen more hunger and more sickness. In the north the poverty is deepest, intensified by Japanese depredations. There is resistance to the Japanese in Honan, but it is bitter resistance rooted in racial consciousness and self-preservation only, unrelieved by enlightened political thought and change. It is based on conscription, the obedience of the "lower classes" to their rulers. Here and there one can find an enlightened magistrate who wishes his people to be educated and organized, but he is restrained by orders from above. In the province the Japanese are confined to a few points along the Lunghai railway in the north, and to Sinyang, their farthest point on the Peiping-Hankow railway, in the extreme south. From Sinyang northward the railway has been totally destroyed, and I found a big machine-shop, worked by hand, in which railway workers were hammering rails into big swords and selling them at $3.20 (Chinese) each to the local armed forces. Sinyang in the south has been under attack by the Chinese armies and local guerrillas.

As I approached North Hupeh the war began to make itself felt once more, for we neared one of the main fronts of the country. The Japanese rear is peacefully in Chinese hands, but near the front the days and nights are tense with air raids and with alarms. The terror that sweeps through a Chinese town when an air alarm sounds at night must be lived through to be understood. Doors slam, voices cry, the streets are filled with running feet, children cry for their mothers, mothers scream for their children, and there is a confusion of voices in mortal terror. I heard here once more—for the tenth time—a story, this time from foreigners, that the Japanese burn their severely wounded, when in retreat. It is said they think this demoralizes their army less than if they left their wounded to be captured by the Chinese.

ON THE HUPEH FRONT

The greatest of luck has enabled me to work for a number of months on one of the main fronts of the country, with some of the great national armies. Reaching the headquarters of the Fifth War Zone, I was given permission to turn back to the east in North Hupeh, and later to go to Central Hupeh, and be with big regular armies during one of the periodic Chinese offensives against the enemy. Later still I crossed the Da Hung mountain range that runs through the province, passed through Japanese garrison points, and got into the rear of the Japanese with the guerrilla forces that operate north and west of Hankow. I spent two months alone with these guerrillas and it was really a difference "between the quick and the dead."

So, for months, I have lived under artillery fire, with our buildings trembling always from fighting. Often we were so near the front that we could listen to the machine-guns and rifles and trench mortars of the Chinese hammering away, and we lay down to uneasy sleep in huts well within range of Japanese guns. The wounded came in endless lines, on stretchers carried by the special stretcher-bearer battalions of the Army Medical Service of the Ministry of War. Many bearers were peasant volunteers, and some of the wounded were local peasants who had acted as auxiliaries and guides of the regular troops.

I suppose the happiest moment I have spent since Hankow fell was when I was with an artillery unit on the North Hupeh front, and was allowed to go right up with them to watch them open the offensive against the enemy. Our guns were mounted on a high plateau and through glasses we could see enemy defense positions on surrounding mountain tops. The joke of it was this: our guns had a range of thirty or more miles, while the Japanese guns had a range of only fifteen miles. They did not know the Chinese had new artillery pieces. So, when our field pieces opened up, we sat out on the plateau and watched, and in five or ten minutes we could watch our shells bursting in Japanese defense positions. This may be a perverted kind of joy, but if it is, then I am glad to admit it. It was perhaps the first time since the war began that Chinese guns could give the Japanese something of their own medicine. An amusing sidelight to this was our Divisional General, who was one of General Feng Yu-hsiang's Christian Generals. This Divisional General carried a big black hymn book with him and when he had time and felt a bit lonely in this lonely, unhappy world, he would ask a guard to bring his hymn book. He would then sing hymns in Chinese, and he had a deep bass voice that literally shook the rafters of the peasant huts. I kept thinking of the Metropolitan Opera and thinking what a loss this man was to music.

For months I have lectured in various regimental training camps. Each regiment has such a camp to train lower officers or "political soldiers," and there I lectured on a variety of subjects connected with my observations during the war on various fronts, on China's international position, on democracy, on the necessity of internal reforms before China can gain the final victory. Most military men at the front are very progressive.

Unlike so many politicians, they have stood under the shadow of death for all these years, have seen their units wiped out repeatedly, have reformed and retrained new units, and gone on fighting. They long for any social or political changes that can strengthen China and enable her to take her place as one of the most progressive and democratic nations of the world. Chen Yi, the general of one division with which I worked for a number of weeks, killed himself when surrounded by the Japanese. He faced capture or death, and he chose death. His division covered the retreat of other Chinese armies and it stood its ground and was almost totally annihilated.

The medical service is a thing that deserves a special treatment and I cannot deal with it here, in a few lines, save to say that in one Army within three weeks alone, we had 2,600 wounded, and of these only 1,000 men lived to reach the field hospital in the rear. It takes two weeks for stretcher bearers, walking twenty miles a day, to reach that field hospital. Nor can the hospital be moved nearer the front, for the region is a vast plain over which the Japanese could advance rapidly and annihilate everything with their mechanized equipment. There are almost no drugs, and but little in the way of dressings, on this North Hupeh front. Men often die of pain or bleeding. Absolutely none of the medical supplies sent to China by American and British organizations have reached the Chinese front—unless there is a missionary hospital in the region. There is but one such hospital, two weeks from the front, in North Hupeh. So my lectures in all armies include the problem of the care of the wounded and a well-trained medical service as one of the great needs if China is to be victorious.

For weeks I have been in the mountains of Central Hupeh, with the Chinese offensive in full swing, and the wounded coming on stretchers down the paths, leaving a trail of blood after them. General Chang Tze-chung, the highest commander here, was himself killed in action. There is a tale to go down in history.

"To eat bitterness" is a Chinese expression for deep suffering. We ate bitterness. In the guerrilla detachment north and west of Hankow we ate bitterness week after week. War profiteering and Japanese depredations have driven rice prices very high, and there are few vegetables. Where the Japanese have been, they have destroyed everything—all animal life, all poultry—and destroyed or captured the rice crops. They have even taken away every bit of metal from agricultural implements or cooking vessels. So the troops have too little to eat. Night blindness blinds men when dusk falls—and the Chinese must fight at night. Sub-nutritional disease victims are more than the wounded in some regions. The troops do not have enough to eat. Where are all those vitamin extracts of which we have heard so much in Western lands? Where is the American and British medicine? Where is the quinine to wipe out the scourge of malaria that kills countless people each year? And, above all, why is it that we must constantly hear the roar of Japanese planes run by American gasoline; why must Chinese soldiers be torn to bits by American ammunition? Why must Japanese troops be transported on American trucks with American gasoline, to fight the Chinese Army which is holding the fort for democracy in the Far East?

Often when I speak in armies, soldiers have ridden great distances to borrow an American flag from some mission. It is crossed with the Chinese flag as I speak—and I could sink into the dust with misery. Soldiers going up to fight, listening to me tell them about their foreign friends and sympathizers, always ask:

"Why do Americans sell war material to the enemy to kill us with? We have done you no harm."

The American flag over me—and enemy bombers with their cargo of American death over me—but above all, over all China. Where is our friendship for China? So far as I have seen, it has been chiefly oratorical—and it is against the will of the American people. American foreign policy is still dictated by the private interests of a small class of American merchants of death. China has lost over two million soldiers since this war began; 85 percent of them have been killed by American war materials.

The greatest lesson in humanity for an American is to be at the Chinese front.

Malaria has me—malaria and all it brings, has me down and I must leave the front.

In the vast region I have traversed a few general facts stand out from the mass of material I have gathered: (1) The Japanese do not control their rear at all—their rear is a Chinese base and a Chinese front. (2) Chinese resistance and morale are much stronger than in the first period of the war—the armies and guerrillas have learned much and are confident of victory. (3) There is much development of national consciousness in all armed Chinese forces and among the common people—a consciousness varying in degree, but in armies such as the guerrillas and mobile forces under Communist control it is national and international in character, and deeper and broader than in others. (4) Many parts of the country remain unorganized, some conservative authorities still fearing for their own future power if the people are organized and educated about their rights as citizens. (5) The actual fighters of the nation are primarily peasants, with some workers and hand-workers. The poor of the nation are doing the fighting. A few new lower officers are former students, but students or other educated elements are never fighters. Wherever a fringe of educated men is to be found in any army or region, it is as political workers only. Conscription applies to the poor, not to the "better classes," not even to medical workers, who are so badly needed. (6) Japanese goods are found everywhere in the lower Yangtze valley, often masquerading under foreign or Chinese labels. Industrial co-operatives are in North Hupeh only, though there is a growing consciousness of their need everywhere. Some officials fear industrial co-operatives because these place economic power in the hands of the people.

There is a general improvement in the hospital equipment of the Army Medical Service, and an inadequate though steady supply of drugs. But the technical knowledge and methods of the medical personnel have not improved. The Army Medical Service has built up a good stretcher-bearer service from the front to the rear. I have seen the stretcher bearers, in the dead of winter, remove their jackets and cover the wounded they carry.

My own general attitude after the trip is this: a vast respect for the soldiers and commanders at the front, but a most critical attitude toward much that I hear about the life of people in the rear, particularly war profiteers and politicians.

Stimulated by Germany's blitzkrieg methods, the Japanese have repeatedly tried a similar technique in Hupeh. They succeed in occupying a number of towns and cities, only to be driven out again. The waves of bombers sent with the land forces achieve nothing of permanent value to the invaders. China is not France. It remains a vast agrarian, decentralized country, with great mountain ranges in which motorized enemy columns cannot operate; a land in which, for weeks, torrential rains turn even the few roads that exist into quagmires that make tanks and trucks useless.

Whatever may happen, however many evacuated, burned cities the Japanese may occupy, the Chinese still hold the countryside even within a mile or two of enemy garrison points. The countryside can always provide Chinese fighters with food, and, if further developed and properly administered, the famous mobile industrial co-operatives can provide them with clothing and many other necessities, including arms and ammunition to a certain extent. Even if Chungking and Kunming should be occupied (which would seem a disaster to the possessing classes), a truly democratic, revolutionary China could continue to exist and fight and eventually destroy the Japanese.

General Chiang Kai-shek still declares that China will not listen to peace terms until the Japanese are driven out of the country. He says that China is on the threshold of victory. But within the Chinese government there are Fifth Columnists working for capitulation. They bemoan the future inability of China to get arms and ammunition, medical supplies, and other necessities from abroad, or to export her products, if Japan holds the south-west routes of communication with the outside world. Many of these "surrender elements" are in high positions, while Japanese spies appear to sit high in the Government—high enough to keep the Japanese informed of almost every movement of the Government and its leaders and the exact locations of their places of work.

However, the action of these elements is held in check by Chinese armies in the field. Many of these national armies would oppose any peace with the Japanese, and if such a peace were declared would refuse to accept it—and, in co-operation with the Communist-led armies, continue to struggle.

ANNA LOUISE STRONG

Fighters for Women's Rights

Nowhere on earth today is the social clash more picturesque and startling than in the fight for women's rights in China. In this ancient land, with its primitive peasantry, where parents to get food still sell their daughters, and where respectable women remain indoors in retirement, there has arisen a generation of "bobbed hair girls" who declare that both sexes are equal citizens. They marched behind the Nationalist armies as propagandists in uniform; they aroused the countryside; they formed women's unions. Many of them today are martyrs because of their activities. From time to time news despatches from China describe the execution of a dozen or a score of women, who are condemned as revolutionists on the evidence of their bobbed hair alone.

The first group of women revolutionists whom I met were the trade union delegates in Hankow. Some twenty of them sat in the All China Labor Congress, chiefly textile workers from Shanghai and Wuchang. Notably among them I remember Wang Yeh Kin, the child-faced orator who led the Shanghai women's delegation. She was a textile worker toiling twelve hours a day in the spinning mills. Slight, with soft round face and soft bobbed hair, she seemed like a fourteen-year-old child in a grammar school as she bent smiling over her seat in the Congress. But she held two thousand workers spellbound by her fiery denunciation of Chiang-Kai-shek.

Later, when I gave a luncheon to the twenty women delegates, and asked Miss Wang to take the head of the table, I saw her as a most gracious and efficient chairman. Her gentle nod hushed all private talk at the end of the table and held my guests silent while each in turn answered my many questions. She rose at the end, with the gracious dignity of her twenty years, and gave me formal thanks for the luncheon, begging me to tell the workers and women of America that "we also, the backward workers of China, are part of the World Revolution." I forbore to tell her how little the workers and women of America felt themselves part of this World Revolution which stirred her ardor.

Yet Wang Yeh Kin, like most of the textile workers, had only recently learned to read a little, and could not write at all. She had gone to work in the mills at the age of eight, "when my parents could no longer feed me." At first she got no wage at all, as apprentice; after six months she got six cents (gold) a day. Now as a skilled worker she was making twenty-one cents for her twelve hours labor. "When I was young and made mistakes," she said, "the foreman beat me. When I grew up, he did not beat but fined me. But lately the union has protected us from both fines and beatings."

"Before the union came," she continued, "we could none of us read at all. But the union sent teachers to the factory at lunch hour. These teachers said: 'Hurry your food and have a lesson.' So we learned to read a little at lunch time, but we did not learn to write. For there are no desks and paper, and we have no time. Now again the reading lessons also are closed since the union was suppressed."

I asked Miss Wang to tell me more of the union. "Before the Nationalists came to Shanghai," she said, "there was not a union in every factory. But afterwards we had them everywhere. Our meetings were public until Chiang Kai-shek began his suppressions but now we have them in secret. However, the unions still exist in all the factories. The union has an agreement about wages; those beginning as apprentice now get eight cents a day (gold); after six months they get a five-cent increase. But the British factories do not live up to this agreement since Chiang has come. . . . We got no change in working hours. The British factory where I work is modern; it has two shifts of twelve hours each. But in old-style Chinese factories women work sixteen hours a day from four in the morning till eight in the evening. There is also one British factory where the weavers work seventeen hours, till nine o'clock in the evening."

She told me the method of union organization. "We elect committees in our mass meeting. If anyone really can fight for the benefit of others, we elect that person. The officials of the union are elected by delegates whom we send from the factory. Our union dues are ten cents a month. The union has also abolished shameful punishments. Formerly when a girl made a bad mistake, the foreman could shut her all night in a wooden cage; it is a very small cage; you cannot lie down there." Young Wang's gestures as she described the narrowness of the cage were as graceful as those of a dancer; her voice was as softly melodious as that of a singer, strangely contrasting with the facts she was describing.

Two of the delegation were described as "students." Young Sze, who worked in the office of the Central Textile Union, had studied four and a half years in a government school where she learned ancient Chinese literature, arithmetic, natural science, gymnastics, and a little English. She had learned nothing whatever of modern China, till she came last year to visit a relative in the Shanghai labor movement. Through him she got a job in the labor movement. . . . Young King, who worked in the union office of Chapei district, had studied a year in a special school of the Kuomintang, learning the "women's movement, labor movement, modern Chinese language, and natural science."

In spite of the small amount of education among the Shanghai delegates, they knew quite well what they expected of the union and the Nationalist government. Four or five of them contributed parts of the answers when I questioned them on this subject. "From the Nationalist government we get the union," they said, "for without it the union is always suppressed and the leaders shot. . . . The union is all of us, so it fights for what we need. . . . We expect an eight-hour day and better wages. . . . This is especially needed for women, who are most oppressed of all living beings. Not only must the woman work twelve or sixteen hours in the factory, but she must wash and sweep and cook at home, and also comb her hair and look after herself. . . . How can she manage herself with such long hours? . . . We expect the Nationalist government to make the factories have schools for us to learn in. And also a special room to feed babies in. And hospital care when we are sick, because we are all too poor to pay for a doctor. And also vacation with pay before and after babies are born. Also to abolish all cruel and shameful punishments." They had learned very well the revolutionary labor program, largely modeled on the conditions already obtained by the workers of Russia.

All of these girls faced capture and possible death if they should return to Shanghai under Chiang Kai-shek. They smiled when they spoke of their chances; they were too full of life and of the sense of being part of a great world movement to take the thought of death very seriously. Yet girls as young as these have already gone bravely to death at the hands of the counter-revolution in Shang-hai and Canton.

A dark little girl from Canton was among the delegates, dressed in the long blue trousers and blue tunic which mark the country districts of China, very different from the modern skirts and white blouses of the Shanghai textile workers. She told me that conditions in Canton were much the same as Shanghai.

"But the match factories in Canton are even worse. And the sack factory makes small children carry sacks which are much too heavy for them; so they suffer much from this."

She begged me to tell the workers of the world to support the Chinese revolution, "since it is part of the World Revolution." The most difficult question in China, she said, is the woman's problem. And so far, she added, "we have got nothing yet from this Nationalist government." It was the first word of discontent I had heard. Coming from Canton she had had a longer time to expect revolutionary changes and to be disillusioned by betrayals.

A girl whose glowing face I had noticed below the platform proved to be a textile worker of Wuchang, named Kiang Win Hsia. She had begun work at the age of thirteen for five cents (gold) a day. When the union came in October of 1926, she had joined immediately.

"The suffering in past times was very great," she said. "No need to speak of it now. The factory used to take women workers because they are cheaper than men. The young and beautiful girls got better treatment for a time, because the foremen and managers liked them; the ugly ones got worse treatment. Not only the foremen and managers betrayed the girls, but also the former Tupan and his officers and soldiers. So women are always worse treated than men.

"Our union was started by the workers in the factory itself without any organizers. Six men began it, but it was secret in those days. They reported it to the Hupeh Federation of Labor and it was accepted by them. Then the Nationalists came and it began to be open. The union got some benefits for us. Those who had only five cents a day got another five cents; while those who had twenty cents a day got only two cents more. The union did most for the poorest. But the union is not strong yet. The working hours are still twelve both before and now. We demand eight hours but have not yet secured it. However, the treatment from foremen has changed very much."

Other delegates from Hupeh told the same story. There were older women among them, with long hair drawn tightly back over their heads, who had had many children and had seen all their children die from the hard, unsanitary conditions of their lives. Some of them remembered the day when "you had to pay five thousand cash" (the vast sum of one dollar gold, but meaning much to a Chinese worker) to get a job as apprentice. Later, as the traditions and handicraft days became more remote, one could become an apprentice without paying. And now, through the might of the unions, even apprentices were to get money for their labor from the very beginning!

Three textile workers of Wuchang joined to tell me the wrongs of women—an earnest-faced weaver in a blue blouse with a sickle-and-hammer pin fastening her collar; an old woman in a black sleeveless jacket with graying hair, who had lost all her children; and happy, glowing young Kiang, full of the excitement of being part of a union. They added statement to statement, reechoing each other like a chant.

"By the old custom, women were not permitted to walk out of the house. Her feet were bound very small, otherwise she could not get a husband. They were forced into marriage, so the marriage relation became embittered. When they worked in a factory, they were oppressed by foremen. They also have housework to do after factory work. Today if they join the union, their husbands oppress them. They are oppressed also by their own ignorance and illiteracy. They are oppressed by the sisters and brothers of their husbands. Formerly the only way to get free from family oppression was to cut one's hair and become a nun. But this meant only a new oppression. . . . There was no liberty at all for women until the Nationalist armies taught them to organize."

After reciting this list of oppressions they began telling some of the changes. The weaver with the sickle-and-hammer pin grew especially earnest.

"Small feet," she said, "are already abolished among most of the workers, though they still remain in the country districts and among the old families. Even the husband treats his wife better since the Nationalists came. But there is no true freedom till there is economic freedom. The Chinese woman is the most oppressed creature in the world. We have no education and no time to study. We must demand shorter working hours so that we may study. Tell your comrades in America and in other lands to walk in the revolutionary path and get true freedom. Tell them that we also are part of the World Revolution. Tell them that if Chinese women are not free, then the whole world is not free either."

Besides the labor organizations, into which women entered with men, there were in the Nationalist territory three organizations fighting especially for women. These were the Women's Sections of the Kuomintang, under Mrs. Liao Chung Kai, the widow of a famous martyr of Canton's labor movement; the women propagandists with the army, under Tang Yen Ta's department; and the women's unions, local and provincial, into which women were drawn as mass organizations to fight for women's rights.

I visited Mrs. Liao in her little apartment opposite the Kuomintang Headquarters. Two years before I had seen her in Canton, shortly after her husband's death. She had explained to me then the might of Chinese tradition, and the Chinese view of womanhood.

"In our Chinese school books there is a story of a pure young girl whose hand was touched by a man; she cut off her hand to free herself from the profanation. One also reads tales of girls whose betrothed died before the marriage; nevertheless they go to the home of their betrothed's family and live there all their lives in mourning, eating only vegetables, with always the wooden image of the betrothed beside them. These are only tales in books, but such is the faithfulness that Chinese girls are taught to aspire to. Custom is three thousand years strong, and hard to break. In Canton city there is no question now that a girl may choose her own husband. But in the villages if you mention that a girl should even see her husband before marriage she would be very much afraid of the idea."

Mrs. Liao herself, for all her understanding of the might of old custom, had violated tradition more than most of the younger women. After her husband's assassination, instead of withdrawing to an upper room to mourn for him the two years of Chinese custom, she went to mass meetings to stir up the people with the tale. Under the strain her body and mind had almost broken.

I saw her now after two years of Nationalist triumph, when the women's movement had swept the countryside of many provinces. She sat in the midst of younger women, girls in army uniform just back from the front of Honan, girls in civilian dresses who were secretaries of women's organizations in Hankow. She was not well, but she was still the same kindly gracious mother, speaking in Cantonese which had to be twice translated before it reached me, once into Mandarin and again into English. She told me that now not only the women in cities but even on farms were beginning to awake. Nearly a million and a half women, in over ten provinces she said, were in some kind of organization under leadership of the Kuomintang. The purpose of her department, the Women's Section of the Party, was to draw women into active participation in the Revolution, and to obtain from the Nationalist government the rights of women. Especially were they interested in marriage and divorce laws. Always a man could divorce his wife by sending her home to her parents; but until the coming of the Nationalists no woman could thus divorce her husband. Now there was free divorce according to the party resolution; but the law was not yet applied in many places. In some places the old laws were still enforced; in others there was revolutionary conflict. The women do not even know that the new laws exist; we must have propaganda to tell them. ". . . The question of divorce," she concluded, "is the most difficult and complicated question in China."

It was clear that the effort of talking through two interpreters was tiring Madame Liao, and I had not the heart to press her further. I invited the three young girls in uniform who were just back from the armies in Honan to come and see me and we sat for some hours talking on my balcony. They wore neat knickers and military jackets of blue gray with military belts and caps, but had neither arms nor ammunition. Their weapons were the more deadly ones of propaganda. Two of them spoke with great earnestness; the third, a small, dark, round creature from Canton, was in a constant state of joyous giggles over her attempts to utter a few English words. Yet when she interrupted the others to add to their explanations, her equally intelligent command of Nationalist principles was evident. They had been organizing women's unions in the country districts of Honan which had recently been captured by the Nationalists. In the last two months there had been enrolled two thousand members, a small number which they explained by the fact that the coming of the Nationalists was very recent, and also that the province of Honan was one of the most backward.

"We travel behind the army," they said, "but we take no part in fighting. Nor do we work much among the soldiers; they have men propagandists for such work. Of course when we see wounded men, we do all we can to help them for they are our brothers. We give them a fan or a towel; we urge peasants to carry them to hospitals; sometimes we go to the local hospitals, if there are any, to get places for them. But this is not our real work. We are attached to the Political Department of the Army, which organizes the first provisional civil government in the new territory. Our work is to organize the women. For this we go into the homes and markets, wherever women are to be found, and talk with them. When we have talked enough, we organize a local women's union and leave it to handle affairs in that district. Then we move to another district."

"What do you tell these peasant women?" I asked.

"We explain first the difference between the northern troops and our revolutionary forces. We tell them we come to save them from oppression and to bring a new way of thinking. We explain that men and women are now equal. Even though you are a woman you are still a person. We say they have a duty to society and not only to husbands. It is a good thing to ask advice of parents about your marriage, but not to let the parents decide everything concerning it. We explain the new doctrine of free choice in marriage, that young folks have the right to select their own life partners. We also explain that, by the new law, women may inherit property, and we say that the feet of young girls must not be bound."

"What do the peasant women answer? Do they get rude and throw you out of the door? Do their husbands ill-treat you?"

"Oh, no," cried the girls in surprise. "They give us tea and say, 'Yes, yes!'"

It is, however, the Chinese custom to say "yes, yes" for politeness, whatever one's real idea or intention; certainly that peasant woman would be a hardy creature who would venture to contradict a visitor wearing the uniform of an army. From other sources than these girls I learned that the propaganda trains on which they traveled were not always so easily successful. In Honan, in fact, the girl propagandists were withdrawn, because of the scandalous comment their appearance aroused in this very backward province of China.

The three or four hundred girl propagandists with the army were, however, only the shock troops of the women's movement. The movement itself was much vaster. As soon as the army propagandists secured a few score members, they formed a local women's union, and left the task of further organization to civilian secretaries and committees, who in dress and appearance were much less striking, but whose constituents were much more numerous. In Hankow, as the center of the Nationalist movement, I was able to see a women's union which had been for some time in action. I visited its headquarters and was received by two charming girls of about twenty-five years, dressed in thoroughly feminine costumes of pink and white summer materials. They were secretaries of the Hankow women's union. They told me there were ten such secretaries, all unpaid except one "recording secretary" who got five dollars (gold) a month and her board and room for being constantly on duty.

There were seven district women's unions in Hankow, with a total membership of more than three thousand. All these women were supposed to pay membership dues, but very few actually did so. They had a budget of $150 (gold) a month from which to pay rent, servants, handbills, and food for the secretaries. They had six departments of work: Administration, Social, Recreation, Propaganda, Organization, Treasury. Special campaigns, like the anti-foot-binding campaign, were organized by many departments together.

"We started our work against foot-binding in the cotton mills," they told me. "These women stand all day on their feet; they realize that they did wrong to bind them. For many of them it is too late to change, but they are willing to save their daughters. Formerly a daughter was more profitable if she had 'golden lilies,' for they could get a better marriage price for her. But now she is more profitable for work in cotton mills if she has normal feet. Economic pressure is against foot-binding. Nevertheless it took the sudden blast of Revolution to destroy established custom. Once the drive starts against foot-binding, thousands of women join. There was such enthusiasm against foot-binding in one cotton mill in the British Concession that the streets were littered with bandages which the women tore off. Those who were convinced tore off first their own bandages and then compelled the others to do likewise. But the women's union does not urge such sudden action for it is very painful. It is better to make the bandages shorter each day and at last remove them altogether without too sudden pain. Also it is no use to unbind the feet of older women, for they can never be normal."

The women's union constituted itself the protector of women in all kinds of difficulties; it even at times claimed the right to issue divorces. It gave legal aid of many kinds. One startling case was that of a young prostitute sold into slavery by her parents. In the house where she was confined she met an honest, decent man whom she loved and who wanted to marry her. Her attempts to secure freedom were blocked by the matron of the house. Under old Chinese custom such a girl, fleeing, would be returned by the police to her owner. Under the modern Nationalist law she fled to the women's union, who took the case into court and secured her legal release, enabling her to marry the man of her choice.

Several other stories the secretaries of the women's union told me. "There was a girl of Hankow of good education whose father gave her years ago to a country fellow. Her husband suffered from tuberculosis and at last died. By country custom the parents-in-law may sell a daughter-in-law if they prefer to have money instead of her labor. The girl learned that such was their intention. So she ran away to the women's union. We put her for a time in the Women's Training School, and now she is one of the propaganda officers with the army." . . . Still another girl, the graduate of a mission middle school, was sold by her father in marriage to a village carpenter for fifty dollars. On the sixth day before the wedding she ran away from home and came to the women's union, which gave her the chance to study to become a woman propagandist. Many of the other propagandists had similar histories.

The outer insignia of all these women was their bobbed hair. This has become in China a flag for which women die. Already the women's union has had its martyrs, able and energetic girls killed in backward villages during some militarist reaction. But out of this torment, a womanhood which has slumbered for centuries untouched by the gentler influences of education is awakening suddenly, painfully, to its wrongs and its need for freedom.

Front Trenches—Northwest

Three days I visited front lines around Madrid with Carlos. He went every day to a different front, inspecting, organizing, carrying news to the forces, who hailed him informally with comradely greetings. The first day we ran into a shower of mortar bombs at Pozuelo. I knew that this northwest sector expected attack, for Franco had given up hope of direct assault on the street fortifications of Madrid and was trying instead to encircle the city, testing one part after another of a sixty-mile-long front.

As we drove out the Escorial road, the only signs of war were the trucks hurrying past us with supplies and the guards who stopped us at the turns of the road. But Carlos said: "The enemy is now on three sides of us. Some of his forces are between us and Madrid. The lines bend back and forth; Pozuelo is a long peninsula jutting out into the enemy."

We were walking along the muddy street of a little ruined village to the steady rat-tat-tat of machine-guns on the slopes of the hill below. These, of course, were the guns of our own forces; they were so loud that it was difficult to talk. Suddenly I saw men running for cover, but I couldn't see why. A house on the hillside three hundred feet away began flaming; I heard an occasional thin whistle somewhere in the air. Then Carlos grabbed my arm.

"Get down into that gutter! Those are mortar bombs."

The gutter was uncomfortably damp and I couldn't see anything to hide from, but I got down. Other people were running behind walls. The street emptied magically except for four of us in the gutter. Beneath us on the hillside still sounded the machine-gun rat-tat-tat.

In fifteen minutes or so Carlos let us get out of the gutter. Meantime he had explained. "Mortar bombs go high in air and then come down, explode and scatter. They are not very direct in their aim. If one of them comes down where you are, no gutter will help. But the chances of that are small. It is fairly likely that one of them will land within a hundred feet or so, and scatter bits of iron in all directions. When that happens, it helps to be below the surface of the ground or protected by a wall."

The men at Pozuelo had no time for conversation; the exchange of firing kept them busy. Carlos finished his errands and took us away. Next day on the Boadilla front there was more leisure. We approached by peaceful-looking hills where peasants were ploughing and sheep were pastured in the sun. We were gradually approaching the top of a ridge.

"Don't go to any place where you can see over," said Carlos, "or the enemy can see you too." The crest of the ridge, I saw, was roughly fortified. Beyond it, across the valley, was the enemy.

Just under the edge of the hilltop stood an ancient tower of stone—the castle of Villafranca, Carlos said a fort from the year 700. Inside we found an open fire, a pile of soldiers' equipment and a litter of newborn pups. "Born yesterday," smiled the sergeant who rose to greet us. "The firing doesn't seem to disturb them. But the castle is considerably older. And here"—he struck a cheerful pose, as of a host showing off his possessions—"is an authentic gramophone of the time of Don Quixote." Again, as often, I marveled at the Spanish sense of humor and of history, which survives at battlefronts, among untutored men.

Along the crest of the ridge soldiers were basking in the sunlight, drawing in warmth to resist the cold of the coming night in these hills. Some were cleaning their guns for the next attack; others showed us their trenches—rough ditches protected on the outer edge by sand-bags. I looked through the slit of a machine-gun emplacement and saw a smiling sunny valley beyond. Yet those sunny slopes were doomed to be strewn with corpses, in some not-far-distant attack.

A sign posted over a dugout read "Villa de los Intrépidos." I went seven steps down and then ducked under the hill. Underground was a fine plate-glass mirror and a couple of coat-hangers, and bedding of several men laid out neatly on piles of straw.

"You've a fine house," I said, "but the first rain will ruin it, running right down those steps to flood you out."

"Rain comes in March," they smiled in answer. "By March we'll be in Seville." But long before January ended, I heard of the heavy rains in Madrid, and even earlier of the desperate fighting on the slopes near Pozuelo and Boadilla, where Franco launched a main attack, drove forward and was again beaten back. And I knew that some of the boys who had talked to me so gaily were left on that valley and hill.

Some of them were Catalans from Barcelona, coming now to defend Madrid, once the hated capital of the oppressor, now the center of their common People's Front. I asked them for what they were fighting.

"For the cause of liberty and to snuff out fascism," said a nineteen-year-old peasant boy.

"They made me suffer as a miner at the age of eleven," said another. "But now begins good life for all workers."

"All peoples in the world are listening," said another, "to what we do in Spain. "It is very sure that we shall have the victory and we are glad, for this will help the whole world's fight for freedom."

Another said: "I have seen people in Barcelona and in Madrid who were hungry because they had no work. I have seen tillers of the soil who were hungry, while rich men kept the good land out of use. I think we fight for the good of all humanity, that all may work and eat."

Among them was a company of international fighters, who had enlisted in the early days in Barcelona, before the forming of the International Brigades. One of them was an older man, a German. "I came because I know what fascism is," he said. "I have lived three years in emigration. Spain took me in and gave me work, so I fight to protect my Spanish comrades from fascism. I should not wish these friends to know the bitterness of exile that I have known."

Two Italians sat on the edge of a trench moving bits of stone about on the soil. "We are planning a counter-offensive against Mussolini," they said.

All of this group was well informed and angry on the subject of foreign nations, and their knowledge and wrath was passed on to their simpler Catalan friends. It was not Germany and Italy alone that drew their wrath: they expected fascist nations to be foes. But the attitude of England and France was to them like a knife in the back from an expected friend.

"It is a mock to democracy and to international law, what they have done," a French boy from Barcelona said to me. "Yet Blum calls himself a Socialist. What he does is the death of socialism and of democracy! Can they not see that on this Madrid front we also defend France?"

"The reactionaries know it well enough," said a Belgian, "and the democrats don't care. If it were not for the indirect help the democratic governments thus give the fascists, we could long ago have finished them. But these big countries do it with impunity, disregarding the lives of thousands of men. Now there will be a long hard war and heavy cost to all of us before we finish." Never once did they doubt that they would finish, however long the war and hard the cost.

"What message do you want me to take to America?" I asked them.

"Tell them," said a youth with a red-tasseled militia cap of Catalonia, "that if they don't fight their oppressors they'll be all their lives exploited. Tell them"—here he sent a grin at Carlos and the brigade commander who was with us—"that if they want good things to eat at Christmas such as we have, they also must fight as we do."

"Did you have good things to eat at Christmas?" I asked them, puzzled at his meaning.

The youth puffed out his chest and made a grandiloquent gesture. "Magnífico!" he said. Then he laughed and hit his commander on the back, saying: "I think I must give her a good impression, what!"

Carlos explained: "This bunch is the only one that got no Christmas. It was a bad bit of organization. The presents from Catalonia went to another place where most of the Catalans are. And the presents from nearby went to men all around them. But this little bunch of Catalans—they were forgotten men! This is their way of protesting. Of course we'll see that they get something now. But it won't quite be Christmas!" . . . Such was the spirit of these front-line fighters, making the loss of Christmas cheer into that ironic boast.

Most of all on this northwest front I remember a Catalan boy of nineteen years, who was uneducated and yet so wise. When I repeated to him my question as to what message I should take from him to America, he began to thank me for the help the Mexican government had given.

Carlos began to explain to him that I came from a big, strong country north of Mexico. Others tried to tell him what sort of a land the United States was, but they grew a bit confused on this, for the role of the United States in this whole conflict was certainly far from clear.

The nineteen-year-old Catalan boy cut through their dilemma, brushing aside their irrelevant doubts.

"Wherever you are, you'll have to fight fascism. You help us now; we'll help you then."

ELLA WINTER

Woman Freed

Woman will first attain justice . . . when . . . she builds the socialist state.

—Anatol Lunacharsky

For the first time in the history of the world, a country is abolishing all discrimination on the ground of sex between women and men.

Russian women in the past, except the women of the upper classes, were as unfree as women in the East. They belonged to their fathers till they belonged to a husband, to whom they were frequently sold. They had no title to land, little education, no separate passport; they could not study at the universities nor enter professions. The way in which women were regarded in China as described in Pearl Buck's novel *The Good Earth* compares in many ways with the attitude to women in old Russia. Economically, legally, politically, socially, they were subordinate to men. They could not enjoy even the simplest biological functions of womanhood. Babies were brought into the world by unlicensed midwives, among the cockroaches and pumpkins on the stove or—since birth was unclean— outside in the shed. An American woman long resident in Russia has described the many disabilities women of all classes in old Russia suffered. The wife was obliged to follow the husband wherever he went. If a wife left her husband he could send the police to bring her home.

> . . . The unfaithful wife could be put in jail. . . . Divorce was available only to the very rich. It was a common occurrence for an innocent woman to be adjudged unfaithful by the court and have her children taken from her. . . . On marriage all of a woman's property and money came under her husband's control. . . .
>
> The peasant women grew old and ugly and ill-natured under the double burden of work and abuse. . . . You see them still, little girls of eight and nine, their child faces weirdly old. At the earliest possible moment they join the family in the fields at work. There was little romance or sentiment involved in peasant marriages.

Folk sayings and proverbs fill out the picture. "The woman's road— threshold to stove." . . . "A chicken is not a bird and a woman is not a person." . . . "Beat your wife for dinner and for supper too." . . . "Long hair, short sense." . . . "I thought I saw two people but it was only a man and his wife." . . . "For what reason should one educate a woman?"

Though middle- and upper-class women were not so badly treated, nor left so ignorant or uneducated, still life held little more spiritual freedom for them.

> The girl of the upper classes was given a grounding in art, music, and poetry; she was supposed to know a great deal about books, nothing at all about life. Any possibilities for original thinking were strangled. . . . There was a flavor of indecency about going to college.

Many examples of the old way of life are still to be found in present-day Russia. On a motor trip I visited many cottages in outlying villages; the women stood while the men sat down and ate; kept their heads bent and their hands folded, not speaking until they were spoken to. In one hut when I asked the peasant woman a question, the husband repeated it to his wife, the wife answered him, and he returned the answer to me. The baba did not talk to me directly the whole evening.

Many peasant women still worship icons and curse their Bolshevik or Red Army sons for turning on the faith of their fathers; and some are still beaten by their husbands. One peasant mother said that she was afraid her son-in-law did not love her daughter because he did not beat her. "I could not live if my man did not beat me," she said.

In Siberia women were even of less account. In some of the Central Asian republics a woman does not exist as a person at all; she is an article of trade and pleasure. Her face is hidden behind a long horsehair veil and at home she is locked up in the harem. She is subject to the Shariat, the sacred law of Mohammed, and the common laws of the land, which decree that she has no right to study, speak in public, or agitate. She may marry at nine and be taken by force by her suitor. In parts of Central Asia some parents will kill their daughters rather than send them to school. . . .

One of the strongest agencies of oppression, say communists, is religion. Why are there always more women than men in church? "Because women have no time for study, they believe everything the priest tells them," says Krupskaya. She analyzes the causes of the extraordinary hold the Church had over women:

> Her lack of free time for education makes woman an easy prey to any superstitions. A woman told me a certain lecturer had spoken very well. I asked what he said. "Do you think I have enough leisure to remember what was spoken at that meeting?" she asked. "I had some washing to do." The monotony and drudgery of housework forces women to look for recreation

near at hand; religious ceremonies provide this. A young peasant asked me whether I did not believe in God, the devil, or Holy Spirits, and when she heard my answer, "Oh," she said thoughtfully, "it must be very lonesome for you to live!" The church is thus a woman's recreation and refuge from loneliness also.

Now therefore communists must furnish moral equivalents for all these cravings of woman which heretofore the Church satisfied. Art must be made more accessible. Mass concerts should be arranged, colorful pageants, parades, and demonstrations. Dry propaganda does not make an emotional appeal.

Movies, theaters, puppet shows should be provided "to render the Church and its ceremonies superfluous to the working woman." Red christenings, marriages, and funerals, festivities and dances on Soviet holidays, will help take the place of the colorful saints' days and church holidays. These active equivalents take the place of church ceremonies today. Krupskaya relates how a traveling cinema came to a village on a Sunday. The church suddenly emptied and everybody rushed to the movie. "Was it religious feeling that had brought those people to church?" she asks, and answers, "No, merely a thirst for spectacle."

The oppression of women by religion throughout the ages is illustrated in the Museum for the Emancipation of Woman in the Novo Devichy (New Virgins) Monastery outside Moscow. A walk through this picturesque old church today gives one a panoramic view of the history of woman in photograph, poster, and slogan. It is a model of Russian propaganda. There are not many facts, but those that are told are repeated over and over, briefly, vividly. . . .

The museum is divided into two sections. The first, Woman and Religion, houses a collection of mementos of the old days. Rich purple and gold embroideries the women used to stitch for the monastery, altarcloths, priests' robes, vestments. Icons, silverware, pewter, precious chests intricately and beautifully carved, bear witness to the occupation of women in those days.

On the walls hang records and photographs of the activities of sects that tortured themselves on earth to be saved in the hereafter, women who cut off their breasts, flagellated themselves, and so on. Political prisoners were brought to the monastery as a punishment for infringements of laws. Old documents state their misdeeds. Three women did not go to the holy sacrament and were put away for three months "to work, preach, obey, and fast." In 1794 a general's wife was incarcerated because she would not obey her husband; she remained for seven years. Others were fed on bread and water.

On one wall hangs a picture of a gross priest riding on the back of a peasant woman and holding an icon on a pole before her face, which is distorted to look like a pig's snout. She is crawling on all fours while he laughs fatly. The title of the painting is: *Religion is the Enemy of Woman.* There are illustrations of the various punishments for adultery—the worst sin in a society in which the husband's power over his wife was absolute.

Under paintings of women sitting at their benches embroidering runs the slogan: *This Is How They Spent Their Day.* Huge gold letters strung across the aisle of the church spell: *Religion Is the Enemy of the People.*

The church housing the Emancipation of Women division of the museum has an exhibition of copies of old paintings in the entrance hall. Above one showing the crowned Madonna and Child runs the legend: *With Prayers to the Czar of Heaven They Learn to Honor the Earthly Czars.* Below another of the richly crowned Christ on his throne, runs the inscription: *Christ on His Throne—an Exact Copy of a Byzantine Emperor.* Close by is a brightly colored poster of drunken people playing the concertina, clinking glasses over gravestones in a cemetery, making love across a table laden with food and wine. The poster reads: *Religious Holidays Were Necessary for the Exploiting Classes as a Means of Soothing the Masses.* Above a crucifix is printed: *Jesus Suffered and Told Us to Do Likewise: This Is What They Tell the People.*

Another poster all in red shows a girl with a rake over her shoulder. In the distance a line of tractors drives intently up a wheatfield; in the bottom corner priest and kulak are indulging in an orgy. *In Our Kolhoz There Is No Place for the Priest and the Kulak.*

White marble stairs lead up to the museum door. At the top of the stairs a bronze bust of Lenin stands, and under it the legend: *Every Cook Should Learn to Govern Russia.* Nearby under a picture of Krupskaya, *Make Way for Woman!* Photographs of well-known women Revolutionaries, women soldiers, generals, naval captains, and of battle scenes adorn the walls, and above a shelf of models of gas masks, military textbooks and weapons, first-aid books, and pictures of women shooting runs the slogan: *Working Women, Strengthen the Protection of Your Country.* Airplane wings are strung across the ceiling and on one wall is pinned a large cross-section of a Red Cross airplane showing all its inner works.

Under the Bourgeois Régime the Least Rights of All Were Held by the Servant. A poorly dressed maid sits in a drab attic peeping through a door at the family dining. Models under glass portray self-centered women talking to their husbands while kerchiefed serving women stand humbly with heads bent in the doorway. Gentlemen on sofas leer out of old prints. *So you are here alone: send out for a bottle of beer!* they order the servant. Another picture left over from the old régime shows a girl talking to a soldier. The comment is: *You like to keep company with a soldier, and count it an honor when he chats with you, foolish one!*

Other sections show the actual old spinning, carding, and weaving machines, the difference between old and new forms of work. The women's hopeless faces lend color to the slogan, *The Factory under Capitalism Enslaved Woman.*

And now—Today. Charts showing health and strength, modern posters of factories and reapers and binders, up-to-date living-quarters, lines of women marching forward. Women busily fixing motors, gay and energetic tractor-drivers, smiling lathe-operators, militiawomen directing the traffic. A woman director of a silk-weaving factory, poised and self-assured, receives a report from a respectfully saluting Red Armyist. Strung across the wall run bright gold letters: *The Emancipation of Woman Was the Biggest Gain of the October Revolution. . . . The October Revolution Turned Woman Toward the Construction of the New Life.* And admonitions: *We Must Draw into Constructive Work Millions and Millions of Women.* And history: *Under the Direction of the Communist Party Woman Emerged from Slavery and Became a Conscious and Active Fighter for Her Rights and for All the Toilers of the World.* Photographs of girls in sports shorts at parades, at gymnastics, diving, racing, fencing, jumping.

And last, domestic and legal emancipation. Wrinkled skeletons of women, bending over washtubs; laundry trucks hurrying from mechanized laundries. Scenes in the law courts where *The Old Law Did Not Protect the Woman,* young girls were forced into loveless marriages with old men, women crossed themselves before the priests, vie with poster representations of ZAGS,* the Soviet People's court, a husband dauntlessly paying his alimony, a Comsomol wedding. *The Enfranchised Emancipated Woman Has Become a Real Social Being.*

And childbirth and health and education. How the baby used to be born, in a dirty hut with a pig and chicken at the trough and an old midwife in attendance, and the way it is born now, in the clean bright hospital with the cheerful, scientific, antiseptic nurse. The new toys that Soviet babies should play with are pictured, the crêche and nursery school. *By Strengthening the Protection of Mothers and Children We Help the Working Women to Become Active Constructors of Socialism.*

Would any peasant woman's head not turn dizzy with such progress? . . .

A peasant woman of sixty-two spoke eloquently at a recent conference on the changes the Soviets had wrought:

---

*The initials of the Russian name of a Bureau for the Registration of Marriage and Divorce. Every district has one.

Do not think that I am old. It is true that I am sixty-two, but I don't count the fifty years I lived under the Czar. What sort of life was that? After fifty years I did not know how to read or write. Now under the Soviet Government I have learned to read. I cannot write, the pencil does not stay in my fingers. But I write to the newspapers. When I find something wrong, I dictate to my grandson and they print it in the newspaper. I have two small windows in my izba [hut] and I can see through them how socialism is being constructed in our country. I see mothers carrying their children to crêches in the village! I see separate beds and towels for children appearing in some izbas. Is not this a bit of living socialism?

The biggest revolution has come to woman in her personal life. No longer need she live in fear of her husband. The husband not yet rid of old prejudices may be furious at his wife for taking part in public life, as was the husband in Neverov's story "Marya the Bolshevik," but he cannot do much about it (unless it be to hide ignominiously under the bed as the husband did when Marya entertained the Commissar). The wife of today may refuse to bear her husband children year after year. "What can he do? If he should beat her, she might go away. And that's not all. She'd drag him to court and the Bolsheviks would certainly put him in the jug."

Amusing stories are told of the stolid muzhik, used to absolute possession of his wife, now having to face her freedom and her new powers. At the Eighth Soviet Congress it was proposed to include peasant women in the Soviets. There was a sudden uproar in the hall. A strong young peasant jumped on to the platform, knocked his fist on the table, and shouted: "I will not let my wife be taken into the Soviet! I have eight children. How can she go into the Soviet?" A large section of the congress noticeably sympathized with the man. This was in 1922. In 1927, at the Thirteenth Soviet Congress, a group of women delegates were discussing the nomination of a woman president of a village Soviet to the All-Russian Central Executive Committee. The woman's husband, a social worker in his village, declared:

"I'll have to divorce my wife."

"Why?"

"What if I have to 'teach my wife reason' [the Russian phrase for beat] and she in the Government?" One of the woman delegates proposed the anxious peasant challenge his wife's candidature. "What! Do you want me to expose myself to general mockery? How can I oppose my wife's election? I should be called an advocate of serfdom, I, a social worker. How could I ever go back to my village?"

On one occasion the women of a village, resentful of their ill-treatment by their menfolk, collected in the schoolhouse and refused to come out and attend to cows, pigs, or children until the men signed a paper promising not to beat them, call them names, or subject them to any other humiliations. First incredulous, then unwillingly, sheepishly, the men signed. "Forty years I've lived under the sun," cried one, "and nothing like this has ever happened!"

In the East the fight against women's emancipation takes more tragic forms. Powerful male relatives and masters have taken violent revenge on their womenfolk. Removal of the veil has been made the political issue of emancipation and women have been tortured and shot for uncovering their faces. The author Boris Pilnyak relates:

> One of my comrades spent the night in a hill village. During the night he heard the voice of a woman. At first it seemed as if she were singing some melancholy song. Then he remembered that the women lament over the dying. Suddenly there was noise and confusion; then the village slept again. In the morning a Tadjik came to the village Soviet and announced that he had killed his wife in the night because she had removed her horsehair veil.

In a Tadjik theater two women of a troupe were killed, one by a relative, who hacked her to pieces, the other by a jealous husband because on the stage she kissed another man.

Kulaks in European Russia frequently behaved almost as savagely to women who took part in public affairs. A woman delegate from Tver to the Fourteenth Soviet Congress told how peasants reviled her in the street. "Ah! My respects to the Baba Commissar! How do you do, Domnushka [a term of contempt]? There will be a decree telling men and women to bear children in turn. Ha-ha, why do you turn tail, you cholera?" After a year's successful work, the peasants' attitude toward this woman changed. She reported to the congress that now she enjoys full respect.

Such cases could be multiplied endlessly. I talked to a buxom woman worker in a candy factory. "I was a servant," she said, "and was beaten by my master. My mistress said I was no good for anything because I was clumsy and broke dishes. I slept in a tiny foul attic with no windows. Nothing I did was right. I ran away to this factory."

"And in her first month she packed eight times as many boxes of candy as any other woman in the department," said her foreman proudly. "We made her a shock-brigade worker, and she has set a standard for the others."

"And last week I was elected a member of the Moscow Soviet," added the woman shyly, "and I used to believe my mistress when she said I was no good for anything!"

The new sexual morality has helped complete woman's emancipation. The heroine of Panteleimon Romanov's "Letters from a Woman" in *Without Cherry Blossom* describes a wife's feelings, why it was necessary in the past to lie and deceive her husband, her lover, herself.

Even the most free-thinking woman is generally so crushed by the unwritten moral law that she is afraid to admit to herself her real feelings.

This continuous division of the stream of life into the allowed and not-allowed leads to a woman's representing in herself one huge lie. She expresses not her own personality but some other approved by public opinion and the opinion of her husband.

Eventually the real and active life in a woman dies.

Women have had only a "mutual life," no life of their own. And I do not want the virtues of bygone days, however beautiful. I do not want married life if it doesn't give me "life"; I do not want to purchase the blessings of family life at the cost of my freedom. I want to have the means whereby to live.

Servants, peasants, household drudges, housewives, are now girl judges, editors of newspapers, foremen, radio engineers, Red Army officers—citizens. And where they are lathe-operators, bus conductors, textile workers, tractor-drivers, or unskilled workers, they are still independent, self-respecting, proud, the equal of any man.

At the Treugolnik rubber plant in Leningrad I ran across a girl of twenty-two, dressed in a shiny blue serge skirt, a worn jumper, a red kerchief over her head. She was head of her shop and was to be made a Red section director the next year. She was working sixteen hours a day, taking extra courses that she might fill the post well. Tired, white-faced, looking older than her age, she yet glowed with energy and plans. She was married and had a child in the factory nursery. "I'm afraid many of our women still find their happiness in staying home," she said. "We must make a yet more determined drive to get them into the factories. No woman should sit at home any more. No woman should be missing—this!"

RUTH GRUBER

Finding Women

"Why have you come?" They asked it of me, too. . . . "What is it you seek here?" Could I tell them it was people? But we have people at home, people who ride in streetcars, people who sit in parks, people who love the counted hours of work and dinner and the radio. Why climb 10,000 miles to see people?

"What sort of people," they asked, "do you think to find here? Gods? Supermen? Pioneers hewn out of stone, immortalized already? But we are no different from you," they said, "in the things that count. We too are looking for happiness, craving for love. We too want human understanding. Don't look at us like creatures from another world."

But I had come in search of people—in search, especially, of women. The study I was making for the Yardley Foundation had made me particularly conscious of the women; but their activity would have made any stranger stop and take notice. They presented such a sensational contrast to the women I had found in most of Europe that I decided to step extra-cautiously before I came to any conclusions. "She may be the exception," I warned myself when I met Ostro-umova, the Stalin of Igarka. "Just an emergency; labor is scarce," I argued, when the weather bureau experts I met were women, when most of the wireless operators who transmitted my articles were women. "After all, this is a woman's job," I cautioned, when I went to the kindergartens and nurseries and found that a woman was in charge of them all. "Careful, careful, careful," I shut out the thought I wanted most to welcome.

For the idea was steadily taking hold that nothing was as strange and new and admirable in this pioneer city as its women. Igarka was almost a woman's town. Here were women actively at work, leading, directing, planning, turning the wheels of the city's political and social life. And women were not only leaders in Igarka; they paved streets, built houses, sawed wood, hauled lumber, and loaded ships, working side by side with men.

There was a bright road these women seemed to be treading; a road I wanted thoroughly to understand. Its goal was simple and clear: they wanted absolute equality and emancipation in political, industrial, and family life. Women in the West had been struggling toward that goal for many years. It was the human problems along the way for which I wanted explanation: the shadows that loom up before the Western world.

I saw and spoke to one woman who stood at the docks strangely exultant, flinging her arms out toward the river and saying, "Some day the whole world will understand our sacrifices. Some day soon, all the workers in the world will live as we live, lifted up from darkness, freed from the crushing wheel of exploitation. That is what counts: that we are no longer tools and slaves, born to live and die in poverty. It does not matter that we have not all the things you have in America; it matters only that we are free, that no man can oppress us."

But I also saw and spoke to women who sat huddled in poor sweaters, rubbing their hands over the samovar and muttering, "What have I? Bread; do they think that's enough? A person can't live on bread alone. A woman wants clothes and a good home. So they're developing their heavy industries—why don't they give us the things we need, not machines. Will I have an automobile? No—my husband's not a Party member. They talk of the beautiful future; a woman can't live on talk."

I remember especially a seamstress in Igarka's sole tailoring establishment. I remember her not because of the questions she asked, or for anything she said, but because her own life threw a sharp light on one aspect of the city. She uncovered a world that was almost overshadowed by the startling growth of industry, by the feverish construction, by the solicitude and the admirable protection of those usually least protected. But we know of that bright world through moving pictures and well-documented books. It was the slow, drab, lagging world we see clearest in the speeches of Stalin himself which she revealed; the world of people who cling to the old and familiar, who complain and grumble with the things they have, but who balk like mules at the first sign of change. The world of inefficiency and slovenliness, to whose natives industry means sweatshops, and politics only corruption and greed.

I do not mean that she said it, or that she was even aware of it. But it was in watching her stitch slowly (and rather badly I thought, though I am no expert to judge) that I felt I was really seeing the astounding good and bad in the city. In the day nurseries, children were being cared for by expert nurses and trained to eat properly, to use their own towels, hang their coats in their own little closets, blow their noses and brush their teeth. In the clinics, women were receiving free care, birth-control information, contraceptives, and prenatal attention. They bore their children in free sanitary hospitals attended by doctors and qualified nurses. In the sawmills they worked swiftly and efficiently in bright airy lofts that would have satisfied most of the demands of our Department of Health.

Yet on a side street near the river was this tailor shop that reminded me of sweatshops in a tenement in New York. About fifteen women sat in a damp, dimly lit wooden house that looked like a converted barrack. They were sewing on old-fashioned Singer sewing machines, a kind I had not seen since I was a child; sewing with the indolence and perpetual fatigue you see on pictures in old Russian novels. A few were making skirts and blouses and even a rather stylish silk dress, but most of them were working on long khaki coats for the NKVD* and the Red Army men. It was ironical and a little depressing to see these slow, fretting women in the least efficient shop in the city making the uniforms for Igarka's strongest and most efficient men. I asked one of the leaders later how they expected women to accomplish anything in that dismal, unhealthy, grumbling atmosphere. He agreed that the shop was far from ideal.

"But we haven't had time," he said, "to build a sewing factory. We didn't think we'd need one so soon, since most of our clothes are sent from Leningrad and Archangel by ship. As usual, our demands far surpass our supply, and we've had to install the sewing machines in the only house we could find available."

I could accept that reason—it was obvious that the city was growing so rapidly that all sorts of emergency houses had to be thrown up and used. But how could he explain the slowness, the lack of spirit, the old-fashioned methods they used? There was one scene especially that seemed to strike the keynote of the place. A woman was standing over a long ironing board, taking swigs from a bottle of water and spurting it over the clothes in an incredibly far-reaching shower. Four or five babies, hardly able to walk, tugged at her long skirt. But she paid no attention to them and soon they left her and crawled over to a man making a pair of fine leather boots. He shooed them away, and now they began to scream disconsolately. The women all scolded at once but did nothing, and finally the shoemaker who was putting lifts on my shoes dropped his work, pulled the babies up by their dark dresses, and took them off to the kitchen, where he dumped them.

Perhaps because that scene was the only one of its kind I saw in the city was why it stood out so sharply against the clean crèches and the modern sawmills—the one black cloud in a clearing sky. It seemed historically significant that this pioneer Arctic city had a shop that was almost a throwback to the old regime. It seemed to prove that you can't change a

---

*The People's Commissariat of Internal Affairs.

whole people overnight; you can't pull them all up by the bootstraps. And you marvel, as thousands of foreigners are doing, that the majority of the Russians—slow, plodding, lazy, wanting an hour's rest after fifteen minutes of work—have been able to adapt themselves to the machine age, harness themselves to a second Five-Year Plan, and so thoroughly revolutionize the country that a shop like this one, which must have been perfectly acceptable in old Russia, stands out in the Arctic like a sore thumb.

I have said I wanted to understand the road Igarka's women were traveling, the life they led, and the shadows that are still disturbing the Western world. There they were, part of that vast horde of Soviet men and women, that nameless humanity stretching across the Arctic tundra to the mountains of the Caucasus on a road which was to lead, their leaders said, to a better life, to the future brotherhood of men. Most of them were conscious, I knew, of being trail blazers. In their propaganda, in their statistics of the present and the future, they told you proudly where they wanted to go—too proudly, we sometimes feel. Yet at least they put up definite signposts you could read along the way. You could follow the direction they wanted to be going in. There was no vast confusion, none of that bewildering conflict between political theory and the life the masses are living which baffles us when we visit most of Europe or America. In the Arctic, theory and practice were, for the most part, one; and where they split even a little, the split was made hard and clear because you knew which of them, the theory or the practice, had gone astray.

One of the signposts they put up was "Equal pay for equal work." In America and Europe, feminists have made that phrase one of their important slogans; but they stress the equal pay rather than the equal work. And when they travel to Moscow and Leningrad, they stand appalled to see women digging ditches and paving streets. Yet books on the early labor movement in Russia show that women were doing heavy work for years. Their short muscular bodies are not the sudden fruits of the Revolution. And in Igarka these women worked as long and as hard as men. Labor conditions were difficult—a seven-hour day became twelve in the summer when ships of the Kara Sea Route had to be loaded before the river froze. They suffered equal privations—men could buy no shirt collars here, and women no fine clothes.

"I don't see how the poor creatures stand it," an English captain said to me one day while I was visiting his lumber ship. "It's perfectly horrible to see these women and kiddies working on the wharves, dragging wood for twelve and sometimes twenty-four hours a day."

It was the same complaint you hear from foreigners in Moscow, salted with a seaman's exaggerations. How could the Russians treat their women so brutally; how could they permit them to do heavy masculine labor? Didn't they know it was harmful for women's bodies? Women should be kept soft. This work would ruin any feminine loveliness Russian women might have.

I didn't try to convert the captain to feminism, nor did I tell him it was nothing new for Russian women peasants to work as hard or harder than their men. But I did tell him that it was obvious there was still a shortage of labor, and that, if either of us returned next year, we might find the long hours shortened considerably.

"I'd rather see this town blown up first," he said fiercely.

"But why?" I hadn't heard anyone speak so violently against Igarka.

He reeled his complaints off hotly. "I don't like their drainage system. There's bad city planning; the houses are strewn all over. There are no single streets like Nome was before the fire. Terrible food. And awful labor conditions."

There was nothing new about his complaints. The Russians were the first to admit them. The difference between their attitude and that of the English captain was that the Russians were sure these problems would be cleared up as soon as Igarka had a little time to concentrate on herself instead of on supplying lumber to the world. They realized that Igarka's shortcomings were those of almost any Arctic boom town; but they pointed out that Igarka had economic compensations you found in few cities. It gave its women not only "equal pay for equal work," but higher wages than in any other part of the country, premiums for overtime, and free vacations to houses of rest and culture.

It seemed inevitable to me that a new philosophy of life would follow this application of equal pay for equal work. Women would plan their lives not in terms of marriage, as so many did in the Western world, but in terms of work. But would they marry if they devoted so much time to work? Could marriage and a career go hand in hand? . . .

. . . Igarka's women were essentially working women. And if women worked and had their own careers, would they still want children? Was the family really breaking down? What about divorces and abortions? Old questions, but they were being argued heatedly in the Western world. Experts had written about them after studying in Moscow and European Russia. What about the Arctic?

Divorces were easy in 1935—the postcard method was still in force. You went to *Zags* [the registry bureau for births, deaths, marriages, and divorces], registered, paid three rubles, and sent a postcard to your spouse saying you were divorced. Whether the card came or was lost in the mails made no difference. It was as legal as six weeks in Reno and a decree by a white-haired judge. Yet, throughout the year, Igarka had had only six divorces.

"What broke the marriages of the six who were divorced?" I asked the young blond registrar [at *Zags*].

"One man was lazy," she said, "and his wife grew tired of making him get up to go to work. Another one drank too much and beat his wife. But we've never had a case due to adultery yet."

She showed me the little slip of paper one of the women had filed for divorce. The woman had written simply, "I can't live with this man any longer. His character is terrible." She was granted her divorce.

"But what if the husband doesn't want a divorce?" I asked.

"Nothing can be done about it. We do try to hinder divorces though, in order to protect the women and children. If the man wants the divorce, he must pay for the education of the children. But if the woman is earning more than he, she pays too. Men usually pay about 25 percent of their salary for one child; and for two or three children, they pay between 25 and 50 percent. The amount is written into their passports and taken right off their wages by the organization for which they work."

I asked her if the children usually remained with their mother. She shook her head, "No, about an equal proportion go the father. But then we've had so few divorces here, that it's hard to generalize."

That phenomenon of only six divorces a year in a city where marriages were so frequent, and divorces so easy to get, was hard to account for. Perhaps the lack of rigid laws had the effect of making people feel free. Perhaps people don't fret and pull against a marriage tie which is absurdly simple to dissolve. Of course, since then the divorce laws have become tighter, and it will be interesting to see how Igarkans are going to react. Now both husband and wife must appear at *Zags* and sign the divorce papers. If one of them has deserted, the other must wait six months before the official decree is granted. Alimony must still be paid; and men who are lax in paying alimony are sentenced to two years in prison, instead of six months. The amount they must pay is put into their passports (every free citizen in Soviet Russia carries a passport) and the alimony is automatically taken off their wages and sent to their ex-wife or children.

Today Russians no longer dare to marry and divorce in haste and repetition. Local newspapers, as well as the two Moscow dailies, *Pravda* and *Izvestia,* which are read all over the country, devote front-page articles to the "antisocial" men, the bureaucrats, who think they can win the hearts of innocent girls, marry them, and in a few days, after tiring of them, get a divorce.

Yet, despite the new attitude toward divorce, many of the reasons Igarka's men and women gave me for their marital happiness and their lack of incompatibility will still remain. They spoke of the romance of the city; they spoke of the cold nights and the full days of work and study. They pointed out that women worked, studied, danced, went to the moving pictures, as well as married and bore children. Men worked, studied, danced, went to the moving pictures, married, and helped bring up their children. The urgency of construction and the love of holiday seemed to have so engulfed them that they had no room for personal differences. Their feverish pioneer pace left no time for the petty frictions which come in an older, well-grooved society.

As for abortions, although they were legal in 1935, they were being frowned upon. Not only was a woman's health at stake, the doctor pointed out to me constantly, but children should be wanted since motherhood was much easier under socialism than in a capitalist society. Igarka's women had four hospitals and two clinics; they were given maternity leave with pay before and after pregnancy. They had nurseries, playgrounds, and kindergartens with trained women with whom to leave their children while they worked. Abortions were, of course, performed for women who were physically unable to bear children. But the economic reasons for limiting families by abortions, reasons such as low salaries and insufficient food and clothing, were fast disappearing, and more than a year before abortions were finally declared illegal, doctors and social workers had discouraged almost 70 percent of the women who applied for them. On the polar station at Dickson Island, the doctor told me he had had to hold a conference with about five of the local leaders before he could perform the single abortion of the year.

Thus, throughout the country, in the Arctic as well as the Ukraine, the Russians were clamping down on indiscriminate abortions, hasty marriages, and easy divorces. And the young radicals in the Western world who had been disgusted with the marriage customs and morals of a bourgeois society tremble to see Russia reaffirming the old code. In twenty years the pendulum has swung from complete personal freedom which permitted licentiousness, one-day marriages, and postcard divorces, to the old restrictions where divorces are now difficult, abortions prohibited, and hypocrisy probably once more inevitable. The old code of marriage seems essential for the propagation of the race. In all the swinging social changes, love alone remains untouched.

Yet the Arctic is not the country of love that the tropics are. You don't see the wild ecstatic orgies you look for in the African jungles. You don't see couples sitting outdoors holding hands tenderly as you do in Hyde Park or Central Park or Riverside Drive. You see harmless flirtations at a party; young men will call to take a girl for a walk or to the movies. You hear of courtships, and you meet young people who ask you for the same advice they do in the temperate zone—would I be more attractive to men if I learned how to dance better? Will I be happy if I marry Anya now? But beyond seeing a Russian walk along the street with his girl friend, his arm so firmly caught in hers that he practically carries her, you see little of love-making in the open. The only unemployed person in Igarka would be a keyhole reporter. The town has no privacy. Everyone knows where you go, whom you go with, and, for the most part, what you do. Scandals and gossip are rare but inevitable even in a socialist city where you might have expected indifference to private life.

"I was told to be careful," a married woman who had come alone on a two-year contract once confided to me. "Friends warned me in Moscow that there'd be a lot of temptation. But if I wanted to keep my good name, I'd better live a chaste life. Remember there are no bad women, no street walkers, in Igarka."

Perhaps the Arctic was to blame; perhaps the coolness gave people morals; perhaps the Soviets had really wiped out prostitution. I looked in vain for a red-light district such as I had seen in almost every city I had lived in. I had long given up the idea that Igarka might be like the boom-towns in Alaska, with wide-open honky-tonks where the ladies known as Lou had held their sway. Igarka had no saloons; liquor could be sold only in bottles at regular commissaries, and at exorbitant fees. And the women who made their living from the oldest profession in the world were conspicuously absent. Actually, Igarka was the first town I had visited where prostitution seemed unknown. In Cuba, your walks at night through almost any of Havana's picturesque streets took you past half-opened grilled gates. And as you passed the door, a girl as darkly beautiful as only Cubans can be started rocking in her wooden rocking chair and smiled beckoningly. If you were a woman alone, she would go on smiling. If you were with a man whom she recognized as a tourist, she would sing or call out, "Very cheap." To many it made no difference that you were a woman. Every human was a potential customer whose pennies meant bread. Competition was keen in this profession to which girls drifted from every class; there was little other work to be had.

In Igarka you saw no half-opened doors, no hunted-looking girls walking the brown streets or docks. The women told me there was no need for prostitution. Everyone had a job. Why should anyone sell her body when she could earn more money working in the sawmills or the lumberyards or on the docks?

"Sometimes," one of the women leaders told me, "we find one of the girls going with a foreign sailor. The first time we warn her, but if she pays no attention, and we find her with the sailors frequently, we send her to Novosibirsk. They have a prophylactorium there where prostitutes are cured and rehabilitated."

I had seen the prophylactorium in Moscow together with about a hundred tourists who had been divided into German-, English-, and French-speaking groups. The bedlam of three interpreters speaking at once and the nauseating spectacle of a mob of curious sightseers walking through gynecological and surgical operating rooms, and then in the textile shop staring vulgarly at some twenty girls weaving sweaters, had sickened me. The retrieving thing was that the girls looked much better than the tourists. One or two of them used make-up, but the others looked more natural and even more wholesome than the carefully rouged tourist women and the slightly smirking men. There was little question that the prophylactoria were doing a marvelous job. Under the slogan of fighting prostitution and not prostitutes, they were offering the girls a physical cure and a gainful occupation. The cure was given them during the day, and in the evening, when habit might make them want to go out, they worked in the small textile factory set up inside the prophylactorium. . . .

. . . The Arctic was not love's own country, where you could sing and play and find romance beneath the flowers and moonlight. There is beauty in such a world, but in it woman is easily enslaved. She becomes man's mistress; she surrenders something of her strength and dignity to the pleasures of the moment. In the Arctic this could never happen. By its very nature the Arctic demanded strength and perseverance. There might have been pitfalls for women here too. The Arctic might easily have become a man's world. But the Russians made that pitfall impossible as soon as they wiped out sex prejudice, gave women equal rights with men, and restored their dignity to them. Less than a century ago, brave American women trekking across the country in covered wagons or sailing around the Cape to San Francisco had held a position as splendid and almost as exalted as they did now in the Arctic. But when the last frontiers were conquered, American women began slowly to take second place. Would this happen when the Soviet Arctic had been conquered? Would the daughters of Igarka's pioneers have to go through the old sex struggle again?

Time alone can show, though the signs augur well. Igarka's women had done as much as the men in tearing down the wilderness, in fighting against the real and imaginary hardships of the Arctic. They were leaders now in making the Arctic an industrial and very habitable country. If they could continue to find happiness in that work, continue to show that they were as fully equipped as men to carry on, there was no reason why they should lose the place they now held. They wanted neither to become amazons nor serfs again. They wanted only to walk hand in hand with men, building this Arctic world.

TILLIE OLSEN

The Strike

Do not ask me to write of the strike and the terror. I am on a battlefield, and the increasing stench and smoke sting the eyes so it is impossible to turn them back into the past. You leave me only this night to drop the bloody garment of Todays, to cleave through the gigantic events that have crashed one upon the other, to the first beginning. If I could go away for a while, if there were time and quiet, perhaps I could do it. All that has happened might resolve into order and sequence, fall into neat patterns of words. I could stumble back into the past and slowly, painfully rear the structure in all its towering magnificence, so that the beauty and heroism, the terror and significance of those days, would enter your heart and sear it forever with the vision.

But I hunch over the typewriter and behind the smoke, the days whirl, confused as dreams. Incidents leap out like a thunder and are gone. There flares the remembrance of that night in early May, in Stockton, when I walked down the road with the paper in my hands and the streaming headlines, LONGSHOREMEN OUT. RIOT EXPECTED: LONG-SHORE STRIKE DECLARED. And standing there in the yellow stubble I remembered Jerry telling me quietly, ". . . for twelve years now. But we're through sweating blood, loading cargo five times the weight we should carry, we're through standing morning after morning like slaves in a slave market begging for a bidder. We'll be out, you'll see; it may be a few weeks, a few months, but WE'LL BE OUT, and then hell can't stop us."

H-E-L-L C-A-N-T S-T-O-P U-S. Days, pregnant days, spelling out the words. The port dead but for the rat stirring of a few scabs at night, the port paralyzed, gummed on one side by the thickening scum of prostrate ships, islanded on the other by the river of pickets streaming ceaselessly up and down, a river that sometimes raged into a flood, surging over the wavering shoreline of police, battering into the piers and sucking under the scabs in its angry tides. HELL CAN'T STOP US. That was the meaning of the lines of women and children marching up Market with their banners— "This is our fight, and we're with the men to the finish." That was the meaning of the seamen and the oilers and the wipers and the mastermates and the pilots and the scalers torrenting into the river, widening into the sea.

The kids coming in from the waterfront. The flame in their eyes, the feeling of invincibility singing in their blood. The stories they had to tell of scabs educated, of bloody skirmishes. My heart was ballooning with happiness anyhow, to be back, working in the movement again, but the things happening down at the waterfront, the heroic everydays, stored such richness in me I can never lose it. The feeling of sympathy widening over the city, of quickening—class lines sharpening. I armored myself with that on National Youth Day hearing the smash and thud of clubs around me, seeing boys fall to their knees in streams of blood, pioneer kids trampled under by horses. . . .

There was a night that was the climax of those first days—when the workers of San Francisco packed into the Auditorium to fling a warning to the shipowners. There are things one holds like a glow in the breast, like a fire; they make the unseen warmth that keeps one through the cold of defeat, the hunger of despair. That night was one—symbol and portent of what will be. We League kids came to the meeting in a group, and walking up the stairs we felt ourselves a flame, a force. At the door bulls were standing, with menacing faces, but behind them fear was blanching—the people massing in, they had never dreamed it possible—people coming in and filling the aisles, packing the back. Spurts of song flaming up from downstairs, answered by us, echoed across the gallery, solidarity weaving us all into one being. Twenty thousand jammed in and the dim blue ring of cops back in the hall was wavering, was stretching itself thin and unseeable. It was OUR auditorium, we had taken it over. And for blocks around they hear OUR voice. The thunder of our applause, the mighty roar of it for Bridges, for Caves, for Schumacher. "That's no lie." "Tell them Harry" "To the Finish" "We're with you" "Attaboy" "We're solid." The speeches, "They can never load their ships with tear gas and guns," "For years we were nothing but nameless beasts of burden to them, but now. . . ." "Even if it means . . . GENERAL STRIKE," the voices rising, lifted on a sea of affection, vibrating in twenty thousand hearts.

There was the moment—the first bruise in the hearts of our masters—when Mayor Rossi entered, padding himself from the fists of boos smashing around him with sixty heavyfoots, and bulls, and honoraries. The boos had filled into breasts feeling and seeing the tattoo of his clubs on the embarcadero, and Rossi hearing tried to lose himself into his topcoat, failing, tried to puff himself invincible with the majesty of his office. "Remember, I am your chief executive, the respect . . . the honor . . . due that office . . . don't listen to me then but listen to your mayor . . . listen," and the boos rolled over him again and again so that the reptile voice smothered, stopped. He never forgot the moment he called for law and order, charging the meeting with not caring to settle by peaceful means, wanting only violence, and voices ripped from every corner. "Who started the violence?" "Who calls the bulls to the waterfront?" "Who ordered the clubbing?"—and in a torrent of anger shouted, "Shut up, we have to put up with your clubs but not with your words, get out of here, GET OUT OF HERE." That memory clamped into his heart, into the hearts of those who command him, that bruise became the cancer of fear that flowered into the monstrous Bloody Thursday, that opened into the pus of Terror— but the cancer grows, grows; there is no cure. . . .

It was after that night he formed his "Citizens Committee," after that night the still smiling lips of the Industrial Association bared into a growl of open hatred, exposing the naked teeth of guns and tear gas. The tempo of those days maddened to a crescendo. The city became a camp, a battlefield, the screams of ambulances sent the day reeling, class lines fell sharply—everywhere, on streetcars, on corners, in stores, people talked, cursing, stirred with something strange in their breasts, imcomprehensible, shaken with fury at the police, the papers, the shipowners . . . going down to the waterfront, not curious spectators, but to stand there, watching, silent, trying to read the lesson the moving bodies underneath were writing, trying to grope to the meaning of it all, police "protecting lives" smashing clubs and gas bombs into masses of men like themselves, papers screaming lies. Those were the days when with every attack on the picket lines the phone rang at the I.L.A.—"NOW—will you arbitrate?"—when the mutter GENERAL STRIKE swelled to a thunder, when everywhere the cry arose—"WE'VE GOT TO END IT NOW." Coming down to headquarters from the waterfront, the faces of comrades had the strained look of men in battle, that strangely intense look of living, of feeling too much in too brief a space of time. . . .

Yes, those were the days crescendoing—and the typewriter breaks, stops for an instant—to Bloody Thursday. Weeks afterward my fists clench at the remembrance and the hate congests so I feel I will burst. Bloody Thursday—our day we write on the pages of history with letters of blood and hate. Our day we fling like a banner to march with the other bloody days when guns spat death at us that a few dollars might be saved to fat bellies, when lead battered into us, and only our naked hands, the fists of our bodies moving together could resist. Drown their strength in blood, they commanded, but instead they armored us in inflexible steel—hate that will never forget. . . .

"It was as close to war . . . as actual war could be," the papers blared triumphantly, but Bridges told them, "not war . . . MASSACRE, armed forces massacring unarmed." Words I read through tears of anger so that they writhed and came alive like snakes, you rear in me again, "and once again the policemen, finding their gas bombs and gas shells ineffective poured lead from their revolvers into the jammed streets. Men (MEN) fell right and left." ". . . And everywhere was the sight of men, beaten to their knees to lie in a pool of blood." "Swiftly, from intersection to intersection the battle moved, stubbornly the rioters refused to fall back so that the police were forced. . . ." "and the police shot forty rounds of tear gas bombs into the mob before it would move. . . ."

Law . . . and order . . . will . . . prevail. Do you hear? It's war, WAR—and up and down the street "A man clutched at his leg and fell to the sidewalk" "The loud shot like that of the tear gas bombs zoomed again, but no blue smoke this time, and when the men cleared, two bodies lay on the sidewalk, their blood trickling about them"—overhead an airplane lowered, dipped, and nausea gas swooned down in a cloud of torture, and where they ran from street to street, resisting stubbornly, massing again, falling back only to carry the wounded, the thought tore frenziedly through the mind, war, war, it's WAR—and the lists in the papers, the dead, the wounded by bullets, the wounded by other means—W-A-R.

LAW—you hear, Howard Sperry, ex-serviceman, striking stevedore, shot in the back and abdomen, said to be in dying condition, DEAD, LAW AND ORDER—you hear and remember this Ben Martella, shot in arm, face and chest, Joseph Beovich, stevedore, laceration of skull from clubbing and broken shoulder, Edwin Hodges, Jerry Hart, Leslie Steinhart, Steve Hamrock, Albert Simmons, marine engineer, striking seamen, scaler, innocent bystander, shot in leg, shot in shoulder, chest lacerated by tear gas shell, gassed in eyes, compound skull fracture by clubbing, you hear—LAW AND ORDER MUST PREVAIL—it's all right Nick, clutching your leg and seeing through the fog of pain it is a police car has picked you up, snarling, let me out, I don't want any bastard bulls around, and flinging yourself out into the street, still lying there in the hospital today—

LAW AND ORDER—people, watching with horror, trying to comprehend the lesson the moving bodies were writing. The man stopping me on the corner, seeing my angry tears as I read the paper, "Listen," he said, and he talked because he had to talk, because in an hour all the beliefs of his life had been riddled and torn away—"Listen, I was down there, on the waterfront, do you know what they're doing—they were shooting SHOOT-ING—" and that word came out anguished and separate, "shooting right into men, human beings, they were shooting into them as if they were animals, as if they were targets, just lifting their guns and shooting. I saw this, can you believe it, CAN YOU BELIEVE IT? . . . as if they were targets as if . . . CAN YOU BELIEVE IT?" and he went to the next man and started it all over again. . . .

I was not down . . . by the battlefield. My eyes are anguished from the pictures I pieced together from words of comrades, of strikers, from the pictures filling the newspapers. I sat up in headquarters, racked by the howls of ambulances hurtling by, feeling it incredible the fingers like separate little animals hopping nimbly from key to key, the ordered steady click of the typewriter, feeling any moment the walls would crash and all the madness surge in. Ambulances, ripping out of nowhere, fading; police sirens, outside the sky a ghastly gray, corpse gray, an enormous dead eyelid shutting down on the world. And someone comes in, words lurch out of his mouth, the skeleton is told, and goes again. . . . And I sit there, making a metallic little pattern of sound in the air, because that is all I can do, because that is what I am supposed to do.

They called the guard out . . . "admitting their inability to control the situation," and Barrows boasted, "my men will not use clubs or gas, they will talk with bayonets" . . . Middlestaedt . . . "Shoot to kill. Any man firing into the air will be court-martialed." With two baby tanks, and machine guns, and howitzers, they went down to the waterfront to take it over, to "protect the interests of the people."

I walked down Market that night. The savage wind lashed at my hair. All life seemed blown out of the street; the few people hurrying by looked hunted, tense, expectant of anything. Cars moved past as if fleeing. And a light, indescribably green and ominous, was cast over everything, in great shifting shadows. And down the street the trucks rumbled. Drab colored, with boys sitting on them like corpses sitting and not moving, holding guns stiffly, staring with wide frightened eyes, carried down to the Ferry building, down to the Embarcadero to sell out their brothers and fathers for two dollars a day. Somebody said behind me, and I do not even know if the voice was my own, or unspoken, or imagined, "Go on down there, you sonovabitches, it doesn't matter. It doesn't stop us. We won't forget what happened today. . . . Go on, nothing can stop us . . . now."

Somehow I am down on Stuart and Mission, somehow I am staring at flowers scattered in a border over a space of sidewalk, at stains that look like rust, at an unsteady chalking—"Police Murder. Two Shot in the Back," and looking up I see faces, seen before, but utterly changed, transformed by some inner emotion to faces of steel. "Nick Bordoise . . . and Sperry, on the way to punch his strike card, shot in the back by those bastard bulls. . . ."

OUR BROTHERS

Howard S. Sperry, a longshoreman, a war vet, a real MAN. On strike since May 9th, 1934, for the right to earn a decent living under decent conditions. . . .

Nickolas Bordoise, a member of Cooks & Waiters Union for ten years. Also a member of the International Labor Defense. Not a striker, but a worker looking to the welfare of his fellow workers on strike. . . .

Some of what the leaflet said. But what can be said of Howard Sperry, ex-serviceman, struggling through the horrors of war for his country, remembering the dead men and the nearly dead men lashing about blindly on the battlefield, who came home to die in a new war, a war he had not known existed. What can be said of Nick Bordoise, Communist Party member, who without thanks or request came daily to the Embarcadero to give his fellow workers hot soup to warm their bellies. There was a voice that gave the story of his life, there in the yellowness of the parched grass, with the gravestones icy and strange in the sun; quietly, as if it had risen up from the submerged hearts of the world, as if it had been forever and would be forever, the voice surged over our bowed heads. And the story was the story of any worker's life, of the thousand small deprivations and frustrations suffered, of the courage forged out of the cold and darkness of poverty, of the determination welded out of the helpless anger scalding the heart, the plodding hours of labor and weariness, of the life, given simply, as it had lived, that the things which he had suffered should not be, must not be. . . .

There were only a few hundred of us who heard that voice, but the thousands who watched the trucks in the funeral procession piled high with fifty-cent and one-dollar wreaths guessed, and understood. I saw the people, I saw the look on their faces. And it is the look that will be there the days of the revolution. I saw the fists clenched till knuckles were white, and people standing, staring, saying nothing, letting it clamp into their hearts, hurt them so the scar would be there forever—a swelling that would never let them lull.

"Life," the capitalist papers marveled again, "Life stopped and stared." Yes, you stared, our cheap executive, Rossi—hiding behind the curtains, the cancer of fear in your breast gnawing, gnawing; you stared, members of the Industrial Association, incredulous, where did the people come from, where was San Francisco hiding them, in what factories, what docks, what are they doing there, marching, or standing and watching, not saying anything, just watching. . . . What did it mean, and you dicks, fleeing, hiding behind store windows. . . .

There was a pregnant woman standing on a corner, outlined against the sky, and she might have been a marble, rigid, eternal, expressing some vast and nameless sorrow. But her face was a flame, and I heard her say after a while dispassionately, as if it had been said so many times no accent was needed, "We'll not forget that. We'll pay it back . . . someday." And on every square of sidewalk a man was saying, "We'll have it. We'll have a

General Strike. And there won't be processions to bury their dead."
"Murder—to save themselves paying a few pennies more wages, remember that Johnny. . . . We'll get even. It won't be long. General Strike."

Listen, it is late, I am feverish and tired. Forgive me that the words are feverish and blurred. You see, If I had time, If I could go away. But I write this on a battlefield.

The rest, the General Strike, the terror, arrests and jail, the songs in the night, must be written some other time, must be written later. . . . But there is so much happening now. . . .

VIVIAN DAHL

Them Women Sure
Are Scrappers

"Them women sure are scappers," says a State Trooper. And how! A beet truck was coming down the road. Scab beets. The women knew that scabs in Seabrook's canhouse would wash and can those beets unless they stopped the truck. The women thought of their babies at home. Lil's youngest was nursing and only three months old. Should scabs keep milk from their babies?

As the truck drew up to weigh in, the women saw "red." It was three colored women who started pulling the beets off the truck. It didn't take long for one of those rich farmer-vigilante friends of Seabrook's to swing his pick-axe handle. Smash, down on the eye and forehead of Ella Roberts, young colored girl who never missed a day on the picket line and volunteer relief duty.

That started things. For an hour and a half, the women, colored and white, joined by their husbands and children, put up such a battle as the cops and deputies and whatnots never saw.

Battling against scabs, trucks, blackjacks, pick-axe handles, water from the fire engine and tear gas, the valiant strikers wore out the cops and deputies who got as much tear gas back as they threw.

Not content with trying to smash the picket line with tear gas and clubs, the cops and deputies and Seabrook's son, Belford, shot tear gas into houses, setting fire to one and burning down an out-house.

Helen Bitterelli, vivid with her yellow dress and snapping eyes, tells how her two children, overcome by the gas, had to be taken to the hospital. The gas bomb was shot into her house and exploded as it hit the bed, setting fire to and burning the bedding and the mattresses. As the strikers were putting out the fire, the deputies came with more tear gas and drove them away.

Another girl was badly burned on the leg when a gas bomb hit her. The burn shows clearly that there was powder or acid in the bombs as well as tear gas.

Yet all the tear gas in the world couldn't stop the strikers. They battled on to victory against the 50 percent wage cut.

There were over sixty arrests during the strike, many were women. Elinor Henderson, fiery leader of the strike and secretary-treasurer of the District Council of the Agricultural and Cannery Workers Industrial Union, was arrested several times and finally jailed until the strike was settled. Lil Young, mother of a three-months-old nursing baby was illegally held in the Bridgeton Court House along with twenty-four others overnight, in the attempt to smash the strike with mass arrests. I was arrested on five different warrants and jailed twice. Margaret Cepparulo, fearless young Italian girl, called "Joan of Arc" of the strike, was arrested and later released. I remember hearing her ask the deputies why they didn't protect the strikers instead of the scabs? And when the cops and deputies lamely answered that they were there to "Preserve law and order," she won the support of the entire picket line by telling them, "Whose laws? They are Seabrook's laws!"

Mary Karisko, short, stout Russian woman who had worked in the canhouse, was dragged off the picket line for questioning. The detectives and deputies tried to frighten her. "Why did you come on the picket line? You will not get your job back if you stay on the picket line." She answered, "I come on the line, I stay on the line." They threatened to arrest her. She told them, "Go ahead. Take me to jail. And take my eight kids with me!" She and her eight kids and her husband were right there on the picket line until the strike ended!

Scrappers they were and the women had plenty to do with winning the Seabrook Farms strike. For two weeks, the ag-workers on the biggest corporation farm in the east battled for a decent scale of wages after Seabrook had served notice of wage cut and breaking the contract with the Union.

When you look at the houses where the workers live and realize that even at twenty-five and thirty cents an hour when there is no work on rainy days and only for a few months at the most, you can understand why the whole family, men, women, and children, are ready to fight to a finish against lower wages. The houses are falling to pieces, the rain sweeps in from all directions. Smoky stoves, one pump for fifty to seventy-five people. Two toilets for the same number. Open sewers, breeding mosquitoes and disease. Undernourished children. Such is the picture of the Seabrook Farm workers. Seabrook himself lives in luxury and gets quarter-million-dollar loans from the United States Government in order to starve his workers.

Last April, before the first farm strike, even children had to be taken out of school to work. They got five cents an hour. Women received twelve and a half and men fifteen cents an hour. They struck for higher wages and for recognition of their Union. They won 100 percent of their demands and child labor stopped. So when Seabrook tried to break their contract which he had signed April 10, the workers voted strike. And they won; going back to work only when Seabrook agreed to keep the original contract, for twenty-five and thirty cents an hour and recognition of their Union.

ELAINE ELLIS

Women of the Cotton Fields

Another cotton picking season has opened in the South. On the farms and plantations, tenants and croppers are harvesting the gleaming white crop with the hope that this year they will get enough from their share to live through the winter. In the cities, the relief agencies are following their annual custom of commanding thousands of undernourished families to go to the cotton fields and pick for what they can get, or starve.

Scenes showing pickers at work in these fields can be secured on postcards throughout the South. Chambers of Commerce and other civic bodies use such pictures quite often in pamphlets which invite the summer tourist to visit Dixie and learn something about the picturesque region that formed the background for "My Old Kentucky Home" and other folk songs that will never be forgotten. The average tourist will drive through some of these states, visit a few capitols, shake hands with a few governors if he gets a chance to see any, and return home. The cotton fields will cease to be of much interest, for he will have seen too many of them.

Tourists are not told by the big-shot advertising agencies that these cotton fields tell the story of what Norman Thomas calls "probably the most depressed body of workers in America." The men, women, and little children who work in these fields under the blazing Southern sun create the great Cotton Kingdom for which this region is famed. In return for their labor, they receive only poverty, ignorance, and disease.

And it is the woman, Negro and white, on whom the burden is heaviest. In every cotton field one can see her type—a stooped woman dragging a heavy cotton sack. Usually she wears a slatted sunbonnet, and her arms and neck are swathed with rags to protect them from the blistering heat.

This is the woman whom civilization has passed by. But it is from her loins, no less than from the earth itself, that the world's greatest cotton industry has sprung. A slave, and a breeder of slaves, hundreds of thousands of her kind have been crushed in its gigantic and merciless machinery. And as long as the tenant system continues, she must be sacrificed to its greed.

In the past, this woman was compelled to reproduce a large number of children because a large labor supply was in demand. Large families also mean a cheaper form of labor; for children, as well as women, generally represent labor that does not have to be paid. Consequently, the "overhead" falls upon the family instead of the landlord. The landlord himself has enforced this monopoly by letting his farm go to the tenant or cropper having the largest family.

Now the tenant-croppers are charged with "over-population" by economists and agriculturists who disregard the unwholesome economic factors that have caused an increase in farm tenancy. This increase has amounted to 60 percent since 1930 despite the fact that the AAA drove approximately 300,000 tenants and sharecroppers from the land.

STERILIZATION PROPOSED

As one solution to this "over-population," proponents of the sterilization racket are endeavoring to work up an agitation for sterilization of these cotton workers. The now ex-governor of Arkansas, J. M. Futrell, and H. L. Mencken, the writer, have expressed themselves highly in favor of such a measure. Sterilization, one of the tenets of Fascism, makes women its chief victim. One can readily visualize its vicious application as a means of controlling the labor supply.

On the other hand, birth control information has been denied these women, although in some sections of the South there is a plan to introduce it by means of traveling clinics. Now that there is a surplus labor supply, this method that would be such a boon to women is beginning to be viewed in a most favorable light. But the most simple medical attention is still denied them. Even during pregnancy, a woman must work in the field. The fact that she is carrying a child does not excuse her from dragging and lifting the heavy cotton sack. Frequently, when the child is born, she does not have the assistance of a physician. Women in the neighborhood, or a midwife, must help her through her confinement. Very often she does not have even this inadequate aid. It is a common occurrence for a woman who is pregnant to pick cotton until the labor pangs strike her. She may be able to drag herself to the shade of a tree, or to the wagon or car, to give birth to her child. But sometimes it is born among the cotton plants. After it is a few weeks old, it will be taken by its mother to the field. There it will sleep on a pallet with brothers and sisters too young to pick. As soon as it is old enough to carry a sack, it, too, will go into the field.

The mother, in addition to working in the home field, will "hire out" to a neighboring landlord as soon as this crop is harvested. In addition, she has the upkeep of the house, and further outside work. Her hours average from about twelve to fourteen a day, each being one of extreme toil.

There is an equally bad situation existing for young girls. Many have their health ruined for life because they are forced to drag and lift the heavy cotton sacks during puberty. While the landlords' daughters attend universities and join sororities, these daughters of the croppers help to pay the cost of their dinner dances, rush weeks, and dissipations.

In the lives of these illiterate farm women, there is mute evidence of a capacity for creation. During planting time, they will sow the seeds of zinnias along the outer cotton rows. After the day's drudgery, which ends late at night with the housework, they will return with buckets of water for the seeds. Often one of these women can be seen standing idle for a moment during the busiest part of the day to gaze across the even rows to where gaily colored zinnias flame among the white cotton. And the change in her is miraculous. This woman is suddenly straight and clear-eyed, and pushing back her bonnet, she shades her eyes with her hand as she looks across the field shimmering in waves of heat. But just as suddenly, she will droop, and turn again to her task. The cotton must be picked!

GRADUALLY BEING ORGANIZED

But the women of the cotton fields are awakening. It began back in 1931 when Estelle Milner, a young Negro girl, brought the tenants and share-croppers of Camp Hill, Alabama, a little paper called *The Southern Worker*. The organization of the Sharecroppers Union that followed, and the bloody battles of Camp Hill and Reeltown will never be forgotten. In the years that have followed, the Sharecroppers Union, Southern Tenant Farmers Union, and the Farmers Union have organized more than 300,000 tenants and sharecroppers throughout the South.

The bloodshed that planters and deputy sheriffs caused at Camp Hill and Reeltown, when mangled croppers were forced to flee for their lives, marked only the beginning of terrorism that breaks out wherever unions of these workers demand better conditions. But undaunted, they struggle on, frequently adding victories to their score.

MARY GUIMES LEAR

Bessie: A Garment Strike Story

I was numb with cold. The pain in my frost-bitten fingers brought tears to my eyes; and each time the penetrating wind raised a gust of snow, a cold chill passed through me, and my teeth chattered. But with a desperate effort, I walked on.

I was a striker. Nor was I alone. There were sixty of us—men, women, and girls—walking two-by-two in a long line. At the end of the block the line would curve, and we would turn slowly, silently, and pass the entrance of the building, where a squad of policemen and a number of detectives were watching alertly every move we made.

Ours was a peaceful demonstration. To approach the strikebreakers who took our places in the dress-factories was impossible—the police would drag us away the minute we came near them. Day after day dozens of pickets were arrested. Others took their places. Our solidarity was our strength.

It was after five on a gloomy February afternoon, and it was rapidly getting dark.

"Look at the machine that's comin' for the scabs!" the girl next to me in line suddenly exclaimed. She was a young thing of seventeen or eighteen, small and slender. Her face was blue with the cold, and so were her gloveless hands, which she tried to warm in the pockets of her old, worn coat.

"We're freezin' here like dogs, an' them scabs who took our jobs comin' an' goin' home in machines!" she flashed out angrily. "Wait, I am goin' to speak to them drivers! They ain't got no right to carry scabs!"

Before I had time to interfere, she was off. I ran after her, but it was too late. A big, heavy policeman was holding her.

"Please, leave her alone!" I protested. "She hasn't done anything wrong!"

"You think so, eh?" he grumbled. "Come along, too!" He grabbed me by the arm.

It was useless to argue. Besides, a crowd of strikers began to gather around us, and I knew that more arrests would follow.

"Let them go! Let them girls alone!" indignant voices came from the crowd. "Why do you arrest them?"

The police became busy. . . . There was a scuffle . . . Someone shrieked . . . someone shouted . . . someone fell and was dragged over the muddy snow . . . clubs rained blows right and left . . . a man with a blood-streaked face, fighting a policeman, yelled with rage. . . .

The patrol wagon arrived. There were twenty of us, frightened, hysterical, many bleeding, shoved into it and taken to the nearest police station. . . . I was locked up in a cell together with other girl pickets.

"The cop hit me with the club . . ." one of the girls showed a bruised arm. " 'Cause I didn't move on quick enough for him. . . ."

"Did you see the way they dragged Mollie? . . ." a girl in a torn coat cried. . . . "An' look at my coat," she wept. "Sleeve torn n' all . . . I only bought it before Christmas. . . ."

I didn't escape unhurt. The policeman's iron grip on my arm left a blue and black mark, and my arm was swollen. But I wouldn't let him drag me.

"Easy, officer!" I protested. "No need to break my arm! I don't refuse to follow you!"

"Shut up!" he answered roughly, but he eased his grip.

A few days later we were arraigned in the Jefferson Market Court, and fined five dollars each. The same union lawyer who had bailed us out the evening we were arrested paid the fines for us.

"Five dollars for the first offense; ten for the second; and workhouse sentences for anyone of you who is arrested the third time!" the judge warned us.

Thus began the third week of the garment strike.

"But I signed the agreement," argued Mr. Hesser, when the strike was declared. "Why should you walk out on me? You want forty-four hours? All right! I'll give you half a day off on Saturdays. I don't want no strike in my place!"

In vain did Bessie, one of the machine operators, who was our union representative, explain to him that we must go out on strike out of solidarity.

"We'll be out a few days only," she tried to pacify him. "An' we surely ain't goin' to picket your place, Mr. Hesser," she assured him.

We did not picket Mr. Hesser's factory, but we picketed the large dress houses on Madison Avenue, where strikebreakers were employed.

"Who is volunteering for picketing duty today?" the union organizer called out every morning when we reported at the strikers' hall. "Girls! It's your chance to show what you can do for your union! Come on, girls! You'll soon be off half a day Saturdays!"

Together with Bessie and other girls I was sent to picket non-union places. One evening as we walked back and forth in front of a building, I suddenly saw Margaret, Stella, and the colored matron Elsie, with whom I had worked in the Klein dress house, step out cautiously from a vestibule and hurry along the street. The minute they saw us, they began to run.

"We ain't goin' to strike!" Margaret threw at us defiantly. "We're satisfied! . . . Get along, girls, don't be afraid of them!"

I appealed to Stella. "Don't you want to be off a half day Saturdays? Think what it will mean to all of us!"

"Don't I? I should say, I do! Only we ain't got much of a chance with Clara. . . . We've been out long enough. . . . It's only a short time since we've been taken back. Say, I'm married, you know. . . ."

"Really? I am awfully glad to hear it, Stella!"

"Yes . . . I'm goin' to work for a while though. . . . To give John a better start. . . . Say, it'd be great to work less hours. I'd have time to do my housework Saturdays, so I could be free Sundays. . . . Only, as I said, we ain't moved to this Madison Avenue place, she's been doin' all the bossin', and you know what that means. . . . Margaret is scared stiff to lose her job again—you can't talk to her—she makes me sick! . . ."

"Come on, Stella! Don't you let her talk to you! Come on this minute I say! We ain't goin' to strike! . . ." Margaret called to her. "You leave us alone!" she snapped at me, as they ran to the subway station.

"Well, I'll talk to them in a different way next time!" Bessie said angrily. "Slavies! . . . It's because of the likes of them that we can't win the strike!"

Bessie, the robust, heavily built dress operator wasn't afraid of anything or anybody. She entered fearlessly into non-union places, and ordered the workers to join the strikers.

"Come on!" she told me one morning. "You come with me. Here!" she said, as we walked up endless flights of stairs, avoiding the elevators, and reached the sixth floor of a building. "It's here they want scabs! Say you want a job."

"What's youse girls want?" asked the man who owned the small dress shop, looking at us suspiciously.

"Lookin' for work," Bessie answered.

The man scrutinized us for a while. He didn't trust us, but he needed help badly.

"All right," he said at last. "Take your hats and coats off. There's the coat room," and he motioned to the right. But Bessie didn't stop to take her things off. As soon as she entered the workroom, where twenty workers were making garments, Bessie went straight to the machines and turned off the electric power.

"All out and join the strikers!" she commanded, her eyes flashing.

"Every one of you! There's more of us downstairs waitin' for you, see? Come on, girls and fellows! This is your chance to join the strike and get your union books! Don't be scabs! . . ."

The frightened workers followed us. We brought them triumphantly to the strikers' headquarters.

The strikers' halls were situated on the Lower East Side—on Fourth Street, Eighth Street, and Eleventh Street, near Second and Third Avenues. There the men, women, and girls of the dress industry met every morning, waiting for the results of the negotiations between the union officials and the manufacturers. The dingy, stuffy meeting rooms, with floors on which saw-dust was strewn, were packed with agitated workers, who came and went, talking and shouting excitedly to each other. Amidst the deafening noise and tumult union officials were addressing the strikers, trying to keep up their courage.

"It's all right to work shorter hours," grumbled an unshaven individual one morning, stopping Bessie, our chairwoman. "It's all right for youse girls. . . . But when a man's got a wife and four kids to feed, it ain't no fun to strike for weeks. . . ." He sighed despondently.

"We ain't goin' to be out long," Bessie assured him. "Your own kids'll be better off if we win this strike! And we're goin' to win, don't you worry!"

But after the third week of the strike more and more disconsolate faces could be seen. The men, whose families were beginning to feel the consequences of the strike, looked dejected. The smaller manufacturers were willing to grant the union's demands, but the big dress houses locked out the union workers and were employing non-union help. The union's hope was chiefly in the girl workers, who bravely took upon themselves the task of picketing. The police brutally attacked the men pickets; but they were easier on the girls after much publicity had been given in the papers to the fact that the girl pickets were maltreated.

Bessie was on her post from early in the morning till late at night. After the morning picketing was over, she would come to the union hall where the Hesser workers were assembled in one of the corners of the large meeting place.

"Grace ain't here again," she frowned one morning. "I ain't goin' to stand it no longer! Either she's here with us, or she can't go back to Hesser's!"

But Grace defied her. She appeared once in a while for an hour, and went off again, a fellow or two accompanying her.

"So you think you can go to the movies every day, and we'll do the picketin' for you?" Bessie accosted her furiously late one afternoon.

"I'll do as I please!" Grace pouted her pretty mouth.

"No, you won't, if I can help it! Here!" and Bessie tore into pieces Grace's union-card which she, as chairwoman, had for every worker of the Hesser dress house.

"Go," she said. "You can enjoy yourself with your beaux all you want!"

Next morning, when Grace claimed admittance to the hall, she couldn't get in without her striker's card. She demanded to see Bessie.

"Very well," Bessie said. "I'll give you another card if you promise to go picketin' with the rest of the girls. We need some pretty faces to smile at the cops, so they won't be so hard on us!"

And Grace went picketing. Policemen were men after all, and she tried her best.

"Say, officer," she addressed one of them as she passed back and forth in front of the building we were picketing.

"Move on!" he answered roughly.

"Don't be so hard on a poor girl . . ." she pouted, throwing him a swift, smiling glance. "Gee, but you're a handsome fellow . . . I like handsome fellows. . . ."

"Move on!" he grumbled, straightening up, and his voice sounded less harsh. "Move on, girlie! . . ."

In a day or two Grace nodded in a friendly fashion to all the policemen. The number of arrests diminished. In fact, there were almost no arrests made in front of that building after Grace came picketing.

"Well, Gracie," Bessie said, smiling broadly. "You certainly saved me this time. . . . They're after me the minute they see me, them cops. . . . An' if I am locked up the third time, it's workhouse for me, see. . . ."

We returned to Hesser's in a jubilant mood, after having been out for six weeks. The strike hadn't been won altogether. Half of the workers were still out, and suffering and starvation were rampant among them. Those who returned to the factories were pledged to contribute part of their earnings toward the support of the strikers' families.

"Well, girls!" Bessie announced when we came back. "Now that we've won the forty-four hours, we've got to see that the rest of the strikers get it, see? That means picketin' with them in the morning and in the evening, before and after work. That's what the union expects us girls to do! We's got to win this strike for everybody, or we'll lose what we've gained!"

"What?" Mr. Hesser threw up his hands. "Didn't you have enough yet? Here I am stocked with work, an' all you're thinkin' of is picketin' an' trouble! . . . Do you want to be locked up again, you crazy-head? You're just runnin' into fire! See if they don't send you away across the water yet!" the little man wailed.

His prophecy came true. Two weeks later Bessie was arrested in front of Hesser's place while picketing with the girls from an upper floor. The employer, who had strikebreakers in his place, had hired thugs to keep the pickets away from his girls. Big, husky, degenerate-looking individuals, the very scum of the slums, they stood at the entrance of the building, ready to knock down any girl who came near the strikebreakers; while the police looked on and immediately arrested the girls the thugs pointed out to them. Whenever the union and non-union workers came within hearing distance, none too cordial epithets were exchanged between them.

"Scabs!" the strikers called out bitterly. "Jail-birds!" the strikebreakers jeered.

"You're gettin' fat wages now. Let's see what you'll get after we win the strike!" Bessie accosted the strikebreakers one evening, as we were picketing together.

"Shut up!" one of the thugs shouted.

"Shut up, you'self! Got an easy job, ain't you? A dollar a day for knockin' down girls! Why don't you go and work like we do?!"

"You——!" the man threw at her a dirty word.

Wild with rage, Bessie shot out of the picketing line and slapped the man's face. He knocked her down with one blow. The policeman's whistle brought the patrol wagon and Bessie was taken away. She was sentenced to the workhouse for a month.

The strike was over at last. The day Bessie came back from the workhouse was celebrated by everyone in Hesser's factory. With a collection we had taken among ourselves, we ordered some flowers; and when Bessie entered the workroom, she was greeted enthusiastically, and led to her machine, which was all covered with red carnations.

"Thank you, girls," she said simply. She was thinner, and her serious, honest eyes had an introspective look, as if she saw us, and yet we seemed far away. . . . But little by little, the nightmare she had been through began to wear off, and she became her normal self again.

"Well, we won the stike, didn't we, girls?" she reminded us now and then. "Next time we strike it will be for forty hours. . . ."

"What, strike again?" Mr. Hesser, who overheard her once, exclaimed. "My God, Bessie! . . ."

ELLA FORD

We Are Mill People

This is the story of a Gastonia striker. No effort has been made to improve the literary quality of the story. It is a simple narrative of a mountain woman; her first experience in a highly developed industry, her first contact with vicious speed-up methods and the resulting struggle. At this moment fifteen men and women go on trial for their lives in Gastonia for fighting against such slavery. This story we believe is an important social document. It is an indictment of conditions as brutal as those in England a hundred years ago.—Editors of *New Masses*

1. MOUNTAIN PEOPLE

I am one of the strikers in the Gastonia textile strike. It was the first strike I ever was in. I was raised in the mountains of the western part of North Carolina. It was near the Balsam mountains. My parents died when I was small and I was raised by my grandparents. They rented land and raised corn, beans, and such things, and had chickens, cows, and hogs to make meat for the winter.

Then I was married at an early age. My husband and I took up some land in the mountains but it was hard living. You can get enough to eat, but not enough for clothes. That's why we went down to the cotton mill one winter. Many of the mountain folks did that. They worked in the mills winter to get their clothes and shoes then went back to the farm for the summers. Sometimes the mills sent men up to the mountain towns and farms. They would go around and make all kinds of promises and ship off a whole trainload of farmers and their families to work in the mills. They said it was free transportation, but when we got there they took the fare out of our first week's wages.

They liked to ship off big families, because then there'd be lots of children for the mills. At first none of the farmers would go down to the mills. They didn't like to leave the farms. They called the people who went the "poor trash." But as times got hard everyone started going to the mills.

Once people were down in the city they got into the habit of living there. They liked the movie shows and the radios, and being surrounded by people. And they got to buying dresses and things on the installment plan, and that kept them working, too. So fewer and fewer mill people went back to the mountains.

I worked in the Loray Mill for seven years. My first job was in the spinning room, but it was hot and there was too much noise. It made me sick, and I quit after two and a half days. But they just kept coming after me, and they gave me a place in the spooling room, so I went there and liked it better. I spooled for about two years. Sometimes I spooled, sometimes I untangled yarn. I made about twelve dollars a week.

One of my boys worked a few days and quit too. It was too confining for him in the mill. He was beginning to look bad, so one day I told him to get work elsewhere. He worked in a grocery for some years but then went back to the mill because there was no other work for him.

Then I was given a beam clerk's job. I worked on that job for four years. I had to talk to most of the warpers and creelers in the mill. Lots of times they worried when they could not make a week's pay. It was piece work, and things often went wrong, and then they had to work faster and faster. Children work in the mills. I have seen small boys not over ten but they said they were fourteen. They work a twelve-hour shift. In the morning you will see whole families going to work. The families run big down our way. When a mother works in the mill and has a small baby she takes off time to nurse it. The company has a community house for the small children. Of course the mother loses time by the nursing and doesn't draw pay.

In 1927 they first began closing in on us. A new manager came out there, but we finally got him away. He was scared. He thought we would do something with him and he left town. Then we celebrated and the streets were full of people going around the town.

But other managers came. That's when the stretch-out system began. It wasn't long before two beam boys were doing the work of seven. They doubled up all over. They put in new machinery and that knocked out a lot. They put in automatic spoolers and warpers. Sixteen new warpers could do the work of seventy-two old warpers. One man was doing the work of about three under the old system. They cut all thru the mill.

Jobs got hard to find. Lots of times the hands would get talking about a strike.

2. STRIKE

The first time I knew anything about this strike is when one of the men who was running a warper asked me if I would join a union if there was one. I said I could not do anything different. "Well, here," he said, "sign this card. Be quiet, don't say anything."

That was the beginning of the strike. On Saturday I went to the open meeting and on Monday I went out. I never did go back.

Along that evening about four o'clock on nobody worked. We waited until the whistle blew and then went out.

That night the girl that got my job came in to work. I asked her not to go in. She never answered me. I could have stomped her.

There was a tremendous crowd around the mill. Only a few went in.

On Wednesday we were not allowed to picket. They roped us off and would not let us get to the gate. Then the National Guard came and we were not allowed to get nearer than two blocks from the mill.

I got to the employment office once when I was trying to get to the manager to see him about our union. I went with two men of the National Guard who were sent with me. I did not get to see the head manager. He sent word that if it was anything about the union he did not want to see me.

It was the night after that that a mob of 100, from the mill, the deputies, and the police, tore up the headquarters in splinters. Then they went to the store of the Workers International Relief, broke the windows, threw out the food in the streets, and wrecked the building. Later we found police badges, blackjacks, and some tools from the mill in the wreck.

They broke up the picket line every time we went out. The National Guard would not beat up the people, but the police and deputized police were the ones who did the dirty work. The National Guardsmen had guns with fixed bayonets. They just drove the crowd.

At this time about 1,700 were out on strike. One evening they drove the people from the picket line up to the store. I got up on top of the counter so I could see what was happening. They were driving the men with bayonets, guns, and clubs. There was one old man who kept saying that he hadn't done anything. They twisted his arm and put the old fellow in a car. Chief Alderholt was shouting "get the hell out of here." There was a very old woman standing close to me when I went out of the store and one of the deputies kept jumping her with his bayonet. Her back showed blood where he kept sticking the bayonet. Then three policemen came to her and grabbed her by the arms and twisted them around and they took her to jail where she was beaten terribly. Her face was an awful sight when she came out.

All these things only made the strikers stronger. Most of our American people are proud and they won't be driven like in slavery. The use of the guns, bayonets, and police clubs, and the wrecking of the W.I.R. relief store made us stick. It made people see things more clearly. There are over 100 cotton mills in Gaston County. We got people from all of them to join the union.

Nobody would rent us a store for relief or for headquarters. Everyone was afraid it would be burned down.

Then they began throwing people out of the homes. There was no place to go. Some of the things lay in the streets for a week. Some fixed their beds on the street and they would cook the food there that they got from the W.I.R. We finally got a place just to store things away.

We were looking out for the women and children first. The W.I.R. sent us tents and moved the families in them so the children would have somewheres to stay.

One night some of the millmen on the Committee of 100 came down to the open meeting and began to throw rotten eggs at our speakers. The police did not take a single one of them to jail.

3. GUNS, BAYONETS, AND BLACKJACKS

Then the strikers formed a picket line to march on the mill. The police broke it up. Soon we learned that the chief of police and his men were going to raid the place. We had some men and boys guarding the headquarters. When they came down in cars, the police started firing and Chief Alderholt was killed. No one knows who killed him but police shots were flying everywhere.

Our people had to run. The mob from the mill did not tear down the headquarters but they destroyed all the union books and the little groceries we had. Then they went over to the tent colony and searched the tents all night.

They took the men to jail and told the women they would also be arrested if they would not go. Some of the women took their children and walked for miles that night.

The tents were scattered and the floors were taken up. Some of the strikers had their furniture scattered and were never able to find it.

Early the next morning I went with Caroline Drew to get relief for the people who were hungry. Her check was refused for groceries and as it was only 8:30 in the morning we started out for the bank in town. On the way we stopped for coffee. While we were there the police walked in. They knew Caroline was in charge of relief and they were after her. They twisted her arm and threw her into a car to take her to the station. I was also arrested.

Four of us were packed into a tiny cell. Three of us were kept there for a couple of nights. From Saturday until Wednesday following we were kept without water to wash our face in. They gave us two sandwiches in the morning, nothing for dinner, and two sandwiches for supper. We all had to drink water out of one rusty cup.

Long after midnight we could hear the police abusing the boys. We could hear them knocking them around while they were handcuffed. I saw them when they were led away to court. One was being hit with a blackjack and the blood was all down his back.

The women were not taken. But on Wednesday night just outside the window we heard a man telling another how to hold his hand and the way something was to be thrown into the union hall. Just then a tear bomb was thrown through our window. The gas was in our eyes and ears and throat and my eyes smarted terribly. We finally lay down to sleep under an old blanket.

On Thursday we were taken to the county jail where we had a good supper of corn bread and milk. They put us in a big room with plenty of beds and blankets and I did not wake up until the next morning.

I was finally released after being held on charges for carrying a deadly weapon with intent to kill. Those who were guarding the tents were all held.

4. FRED BEAL, OUR LEADER

There are many down there who would like to railroad all those workers to the electric chair. They know that would bust up the union in the South. The South would not be organized; we would have to go on working like before.

We would not be able to do anything if it was not for the people in the North from whom we get our food. We think if we could get one meal a day we could fight and stick it out until we won. We are getting our shelter from the tents the W.I.R. sent us.

At first the bosses talked a lot about the Communists. They kept saying the Bolsheviks and Reds were free lovers. We were told that Russia was an awful place. This was new for us at first. You have to realize and study about these things before you understand them.

Not many Negroes work in the Loray Mill where I was. In Bessemer City, 150 Negroes work in the waste department.

At first the members of the union did not understand how to deal with the Negro workers. Now they are working side by side with them. Everybody realized they had to be organized with the whites. If we stood apart the boss would get the benefit.

The mill owners were especially after our leader Fred Beal. They printed leaflets saying that he was a Bolshevik and that he did not believe in God. Most of the workers are Methodists and Baptists. But they would pay no attention to the leaflets. They tore them up. Everybody there likes Fred Beal. We know the people that are working for us.

The majority of the people are for the strikers. The workers are all back of the people on trial now. But they are broke and they can't do much unless the people in the North will help them.

The strike would go on forever if only the children did not suffer so much. So many have Pellagra, they eat too much of one kind of food. Their arms and their bodies break out, they get thin and they waste away. In the mountains we never had clothes but there was always enough to eat. We had canned beans we picked in the fall and sauerkraut we had made.

Sometimes people got to wishing they could go back to the farm but they don't have certain pay days there. Once you get in the mill it is pretty hard to get out.

You work from six in the morning until six at night. There are always payments to be made. Sometimes we can go to the movies.

For the last two years I only missed a day and a half outside of Sundays. I would get one or two days off for Christmas. You don't get any holidays. Even on the fourth of July you work all day until six o'clock and the mill has fireworks in the ball park in the evening.

We are used to another kind of life now. I think most of us will never go back to the mountains. We are mill people now.

FACING THE ELECTRIC CHAIR

In the Gastonia Trial the following are charged with murder: Fred Beal, Louis McLaughlin, Amy Schechter, Wm. McGinnis, Vera Bush, George Carter, Sophie Melvin, K. O. Byers, Joseph Harrison, J. C. Heffner, Robert Allen, Russell Knight, N. F. Gibbons, K. Y. Hendricks, and Delmar Hampton. Eight others are held on charges of conspiracy. The International Labor Defense is conducting the defense of these men and women. The American Civil Liberties Union is assisting.

ANONYMOUS

My Life: A True Story by a Negro Worker of the South

Dadeville, Alabama

Dear Comrades:

I am a working woman of the South. Before I begin my life history, I want to tell you that I am thirty-four years of age. I have been working all my life on the farm. I am a mother of three children, two boys and one girl. The girl died before she was a month old. That left me two boys. Their father is farming though now I keep house and also work among the women since 1931. I became acquainted with the share-croppers' union in 1931 and ever since I learned of it I have been running about trying to study the best way to organize the farm workers.

I was born in Tallapoosa County and raised here and have never seen the day that the boss would give us poor Negroes anything, as far back as I can remember from a little child up to now. They worked my father and mother like convicts and always at the end of the year they could not get us little ones clothing and just enough food to keep us alive.

Although there were about nine of us in the family, mother worked hard to try to raise us and did so as long as she could. But at last by going clothed part of the time as well as barefoot, she took sick the spring of 1909, and died and left us little kids with no clothing, no shoes, no food and nothing. My father made a good corn crop that year and the boss man he worked with sent wagons. Down there we had two mules and he took them and the two fatting hogs which we had to kill and all of this was supposed to be used to take care of us little kids.

Then I became acquainted with this organization and found that the Communist Party fights against all such rotten stuff as that. I do wish that we workers had found it out years ago.

What I hated most was that mother left a nine-months-old baby. And my older sister married and lived with us a year and then she moved out. Then my father decided that he would marry because he had to work hard in the field and see after us and it was dangerous for us girls to go around because when we would go to the field to carry water the boss man we lived with made it his business to come back with us girls and pick at us and tell us we better not tell about it. But we told father about it and he was afraid to get after him because lynching would be the next thing.

Then he married a woman although she was fourteen years old at that time. We girls could not get clothes like we wanted because the boss would take everything away from us and father. Every winter we were forever hungry. I hate to think of it. It was misery. Although our school term was short, we had to stop. See, the boss had taken everything. As long as mother lived she managed some way and kept us in school, but the boss took everything away from father until he would be so worried he would not know what to do.

So in 1916 during the World War I married. Still it was not any better and much worse because I began raising children and let me tell you raising children in this capitalist system is hard and the boss cheated us workers out of everything we could get and therefore it was still worse.

*   *   *

Note: This comrade wants to say that her life story is so long that she will send us the rest in her next letter.

And Mine: A True Story by a Negro Worker of the North

New York City

Dear Comrades:

I had to go to work as a servant when I was just a child in the South. We weren't driven quite so hard there as domestic workers are in the North but we got almost no money for our work. Later on I went to Detroit where sometimes I got real good jobs, and sometimes bad ones depending on the people I had to work for. I had one good one for instance where I got eighteen dollars a week with good food, a good room, and short hours. I kept that a long time and I was able to make a nice home for my mother and begin to save a little money.

Then times got bad. I couldn't get a decent job anywhere. I had to give up my home and put my furniture in storage. Then I came to New York. Wages were a little higher but the "Madams" expected an awful lot of work. For instance, I got a job in a rich family for twelve dollars a week but I had to cook, wash, clean, iron, and wash windows from seven in the morning till ten at night. When I told the woman the work was killing me and she ought to get a laundress, she fired me and after all that work I had to put up a terrible fight to get my money.

Pretty soon there were almost no jobs at all. I lost my furniture because I couldn't pay the storage and I couldn't keep up my payments on my life insurance. I had to go up on the corners in the Bronx to look for work. I used to stand around or sit on cracker boxes with the other women waiting for someone to come along and offer me a job. Most of the women up there expected you to work for twenty-five cents anyhow. I was even offered ten cents an hour for general housework! And they worked you just like dogs for that money.

I used to pass by the speakers on the soap boxes in Harlem without paying any attention, but after one day when they evicted me and my seventy-five-year-old mother, I listened. I went to the Unemployed Council and they helped me fight for relief. At first the bureau wasn't going to give me relief for my mother because she didn't have a birth certificate. I told them my mother was born in slavery and in those days there weren't any birth certificates for slaves. I told them that my mother had worked for years and as a child they had even hitched her to a plow and made her plow the fields while the master sat in the shade and watched her, and that if they didn't give her any relief now when she was old I was going to tear up the damned city! That's how I got my relief.

No More Helling! A True Story by a Working Woman

There are thirty women here working under the most miserable conditions. For twenty cents an hour women work there, and the men get twenty-five cents an hour. They work twelve and fourteen hours. In 1933 the women worked for ten cents an hour. They assort papers and must work with backs bent because of lack of chairs or tables. You must be skilled and understand the quality of paper. Some women have worked in this junk place for fifteen and sixteen years. One related to me the following: "Look at me. I entered this shop young, beautiful, and healthy. Now I am only forty years old and I look like sixty."

It was true. She had rheumatic pains in her legs and arms, she dragged her legs when she walked.

In the winter the place is not heated. The workers are forced to wear as much clothes as they have to keep from freezing. The paper comes in, in the winter time, damp and frozen. The women are not permitted to wear any gloves, and they have to pick the paper with their bare hands. Their hands bleed from cuts in their fingers. They eat their lunch where the garbage is. The waste paper comes from hospitals, doctors' offices, and waste paper receptacles in the alleys, which are full of germs and diseases. One woman while assorting the paper got a piece of wire in her eye. She lost her eye and after three years the cavity is not yet healed.

Around this factory are company-owned shacks where the factory workers live with their families. Most of the workers are Negroes. For these shacks Mr. Levine charges five dollars a week. This money is taken out of the wages. A Negro worker who worked there for nine months contracted consumption and still lives in one of the shacks with his wife and one-year-old child.

One day the women in the plant decided to stop the cursing of the foreman. Constantly listening to him say, "If you don't like it here get the hell out and go back where you came from." He would also throw things at them. They declared a strike and it's worth mentioning the militancy of these women.

For two weeks at 6 A.M. they were on the picket line. Women of forty-five and fifty years of age. They were an inspiration to younger ones. It was encouraging to see the awakening of women, fighting for better conditions.

Each one telling the story of her life. One woman related how she was forced into the factory when her husband went to the hospital ten years ago with a paralytic stroke. He is still there and the woman had to support the children and herself on ten cents an hour. Out of this pay came her carfare and lunch.

Those who had worked sixteen or seventeen years for Levine told how they had built up the factory from a tiny place, how they had built his summer and winter homes, while they themselves were always threatened with evictions. They could hardly give their children milk. Those women had to work because their husbands were unemployed or made hardly enough to support their families.

The women on strike prevented any scabbing through their splendid solidarity. Those women cannot read or write. They told us how anxious they are to go to school, but after a day's work they must go home and take care of their houses and families. Mr. Levine takes advantage of this when it comes to counting hours and wages.

During the strike Mr. Levine came down and offered individuals better wages if they would go in. He smiled and acted very cordial. One woman said, "I know Levine for sixteen years, he never smiled or said good morning to us. Since we are on the picket line we are ladies. He smiles and greets us because there is no one to pick up his trash and garbage."

These are the demands they have won: Two and a half cents increase an hour; no work on Saturday; eight hours a day; no helling by the foreman (the offensive foreman was shipped to another factory); no waiting for work (stagger system); recognition of the shop committee.

This junk and paper scrapping as it is called is used for some kind of war materials, so Mr. Levine is anxious for another war so he can make money. He has promised to give the workers five cents more if prices go up on paper. That means war prices. Those women were talking of war with such horror. They said that their lives were wasted, but they did not want to waste the lives of their sons and loved ones. And they mean what they say.

MOLLIE V. LEWIS

Negro Women in Steel

"Perhaps you are a Negro woman, driven to the worst part of town but paying the same high rent," writes Jenny Elizabeth Johnstone in her challenging little pamphlet *Women in Steel.* "You are strong. There is nothing new in suffering to you," she continues. "Your man is driven even harder than the white workers, but your man gets lower pay—hired the last and fired the first."

I know these women of the steel towns of which Miss Johnstone writes—these women living dreary lives under the domination of powerful and impersonal corporations. I have been one of them. The conditions under which they live, the excessive rents demanded for cramped and inadequate shelter, the uncertainty of employment for their men folk, and the disruptive inconvenience of the mill shifts all combine to make life a hard and uneven road for them. It is because of such conditions, faced by the women of every mill worker's family, that the Steel Workers' Organizing Committee, of the Committee for Industrial Organization, has sponsored the formation of women's auxiliaries in the campaign for the unionization of the industry.

Last summer I revisited Gary, that hard and unbeautiful metropolis of steel upon the banks of Lake Michigan. In the mills which line the lake shore, furnaces were going full blast, twenty-four hours a day. Steel was pouring from them in molten streams. Thousands of men of both races and many nationalities, sweaty and grimy, were tending the furnaces and conducting the ore through its processes to the finished product.

Something new had come into the lives of these men. Thousands of them had joined the union. For the first time it was possible for them openly to be union men in the mills of the United States Steel Corporation. For the first time this vast corporation for which they worked had recognized their union and entered into an agreement with it.

Only a few miles distant, however, in Indiana Harbor and South Chicago, Little Steel had taken a bitter stand against the union and against the spirit of the New Deal and had engaged in a costly fight which was climaxed by the Memorial Day Massacre. The strike was now over and the men were returning to work without the recognition which had been negotiated with Big Steel.

Hand in hand with the campaign to organize the mill workers went the drive to bring the women folk of these men into active participation in the labor movement. The agency for organizing the women was the Women's Auxiliary of the Amalgamated Association of Iron, Steel and Tin Workers of North America. The objectives of the campaign were to organize the women "to lend aid to the union in all possible ways," to help them to maintain the morale of the steel workers, to educate them in the principles of trade unionism, and to weld them into a force for social betterment.

BRINGING RACES TOGETHER

In the matter of race relations, Gary and the adjacent steel towns are by no means utopian. From time to time bitter racial animosities have flared, not only between Negroes and whites, but also between native citizens and the foreign born. In addition many of the foreign born brought with them to this country nationalistic enmities rooted in Old World conflicts. To induce the women of such diverse groups to join the same organization, even for their own benefit, has been no easy task.

In Gary I talked with Mrs. Minneola Ingersoll who was in charge of the organization of women's auxiliaries in the Chicago-Calumet district. Mrs. Ingersoll is a young southern white woman and a graduate of the University of Alabama. Together we visited the homes of members of the auxiliary of both races and various nationalities.

"Our policy in the auxiliary, as in the union," Mrs. Ingersoll said, "is to organize all regardless of their race, color, creed, or nationality. When it comes to exploitation, the mill owners draw no color line. They exploit the native white workers just as they do the Mexican, Polish, and Negro workers."

In Indiana Harbor where Inland Steel had forced its workers into a long and bitter strike rather than grant their demand for recognition, a number of Negro women had been drawn into the auxiliary. In Gary, however, Negro women seemed more reluctant to join and the campaign had been less successful among them. Along with the women of other groups, Negro women were represented on the picket lines of the struck plants.

During the strike they cooperated with others behind the lines in the preparation and serving of hot meals to the strikers. They were members of the various committees which sought contributions of money and food to keep the strike going.

NEGROES AIDED IN STRIKE

In her pamphlet, Miss Johnstone calls attention to "the swiftness with which Negro women have taken the leadership in our chapters. There is not one auxiliary where the staying power of these courageous women has not carried the organization over some critical period, especially in the first days of unseen and unsung organizing drudgery before the body took form. They were undaunted and gave great moral strength with their persistence."

The organizing of white and Negro women in the same units has naturally had its by-product in the field of race relations. While the auxiliaries have by no means eliminated racial barriers in a district where jim crowism flourishes, they have for the first time made it possible for the women of both races to get to know one another on friendly terms.

While the municipal government of Gary continues to keep the children apart in a system of separate schools, their parents are getting together in the union and in the auxiliary. And after school hours, the children meet jointly in a junior lodge under guidance of an instructor. It is noteworthy that the only public eating place in Gary where both races may be freely served is a cooperative restaurant largely patronized by members of the union and auxiliary.

These, it may be true, are of minor importance. But they represent steps toward inter-racial cooperation on a mass basis. When the black and white workers and members of their families are convinced that their basic economic interests are the same, they may be expected to make common cause for the advancement of these interests. Women of both races have, for traditional reasons, been inclined to be more stand-offish than men when it comes to organizing in a common body. The efforts of the auxiliary to bring the women together may ultimately prove to be a significant factor in overcoming racial barriers which still retard the advance of the labor movement in this country.

DOROTHY DAY

A Good Landlord
(An Interview with
Our Janitress)

She is brown-eyed and cross-eyed, the little janitress in a tenement on East Thirteenth Street. And she is very young, painfully, pathetically young. But thank God she has a job! That's what she says. She has only had the job for the last few weeks. Before that she and her husband were only janitor's helpers. Now she and her husband do it all themselves. They are the whole thing. They haven't any one to boss them, and they haven't any one to boss. This is how it came about.

Just three weeks ago Bessie was sweeping out the hallways when her labor pains began. She had one kid already, lying in a crib in the little dark apartment down in the basement. That one was only a baby too, just a year old. She said to the janitress,

"Gee, missus, I feel my pains on me."

"Fer Cripes sake, Bessie, quit your stalling. If you don't want to do the work, my husband can get plenty as would want it. Git to the dumb waiters and start taking off the garbage!"

But Bessie was doubled up. She couldn't. She could hardly move, could only hang on to the broom and lean against the walls of the narrow halls.

She leaned there for a moment, her funny little grotesque body pressed close against the wall, trying to shrink, "But gee, I was big," she said. "I took up most the hall. I was trying to get out of the way so one of the tenants could get by. 'What's the matter, Bessie?' she says.

" 'It's my pains,' I told her. 'And Missus, the janitor's wife says to get down and empty the garbage.' The lady tole me to get to bed but by then the pains had left, and I could finish the hall. Maybe only a false alarm, I said. And then they started again. You know how they come. First minute you feel fine. I was all ready to get down to the basement and dump the garbage. Then another pain.

"But I thought—they're pretty far apart. Maybe I'll have time to tend to one dumb waiter while James does another. There's three you know, one for each building. This is three buildings, not one.

"So I went downstairs. 'James,' I said, 'My pain's started.' 'Jeze, Bessie, get to bed, can't you?' he kept saying.

"But we just got the job a few months ago, and him out of work for six months. I felt I had to keep going. 'I'll help you with this dumb waiter,' I said.

"So he took off the heavy cans and I took the paper. And I'm not saying anything against the people in the house, but gee, they're in a hurry. We have to keep the dumb waiters locked, padlocked all day, or else they throw their packages of garbage right down the six stories to the basement. And some times when we used to open the door we'd almost be buried in it. So now we keep them locked. But then at five and six when we're emptying, people are all in a rush, getting the old man's supper and all, and do they yell down at us!

"We worked like hell, but sometimes I had to sit on the floor with my knees up to my chin. It was something fierce.

"And then a big rat, a foot long, jumped out of the dumb waiter. I screamed. It seemed to start the pains all the faster. I couldn't help but moan. Everything all at once was too much.

"And there was Jenny, lying in the crib in the apartment, yelling her head off for supper, and me moaning on the floor and Jim a cursing and the sweat pouring in his eyes.

"It got so they could hear me up the shaft. They were all yelling what's the matter.

" 'And of course she had to go have her baby right now,' " I heard the missus saying.

"So Jim, he was mad. He just picked me up and took me into the apartment and put me to bed. He left everything, and put me into bed and ran out and got the woman to come in—we couldn't afford a doctor—and then he got Jenny's supper, and I seen him crying in the kitchen. Gee, it was hell.

"Well, we was fired. They came down and told us so, before the kid came, that was. . . .

"But there's decent people in the house. They heard about it and they called up the owner—he lives in Brooklyn—and he come over the next day and come in and seen me and the new kid. He fired the old lady, he told me, and made a present of the job to me and my husband."

Bessie's apartment is one of twelve basement apartments. There are three buildings, with four apartments on a floor, and the buildings are six stories high. Bessie's work is to clean the halls which are tiled, sweep the side walks front and back, help her husband with the garbage and trash from seventy-two apartments, show the empty apartments, and collect the rents.

She hasn't much time for her own rooms. They are sparsely furnished fortunately, so the rooms seem bigger than they are. It means more room for little Jenny to crawl ape-fashion, when she is released from her crib, from one dark end to the other. Bessie has to shut her up alone with the tiny new arrival most of the time when she is working around the house. Jenny is precocious and if she had her way, she'd climb up and fall down the stairs in an effort to keep up with her busy mother.

When I saw Bessie it was Sunday morning. She was pridefully showing her apartments, gallantly telling their virtues—"The rats ain't bad up-stairs, but my husband killed eleven down in the kitchen one night. He just sat by the cupboard under the sink and hit them on the head with a club as they came out. But now we got a big black cat that goes after them. She's wonderful at killing them. . . . Y' see how nice they're all painted up. Not a bug in the house when you keep them painted this way. It makes it lighter too. Steam heat and hot water and bath—all for forty dollars a month. You can't do better."

Down in her own dark little unpainted kitchen where the breakfast dishes were still unwashed and dirty clothes were piled by the tub—"A nice white tub, see?"—she showed me the children.

Jenny had been crying till there were lavender shadows under her blue eyes. She lay in the crib and looked at us resentfully. The baby, Marie, a pale basement baby, slept heavily in the middle of a double bed in the living room. "She hasn't been out yet. She's only three weeks old. But you ought to pass by this afternoon and see how she looks. She'll be out in her carriage then."

So later in the afternoon, I passed again the high barracks of seventy-two apartments where Bessie, three weeks after her confinement, is up and toiling. Little Jennie, in a pink silk dress, and spotlessly clean white shoes, was trying to escape from the arms of one of the other tenants. Marie lay in her carriage sleeping still, but she did not look quite so ghastly since her unnaturally heavy crop of hair which accentuated the pallor of her face was covered by a little lace bonnet. Over her was spread a silk embroidered coverlet, surmounted by a vast pink satin bow.

Bessie, her hands still wet and soapy from some inside work, stood there in a dirty white overall, contemplating with pride the two little ones she was helping support by scrubbing out who knows how many square feet of tiled hall, and emptying untold quantities of garbage.

But after all she has a job. A swell job! Sixty apartments. Sixty pails of garbage. Sixty boxes and baskets of trash. And it was a good kind landlord who took the job which used to be handled by four and handed it over to Bessie and her husband.

THYRA J. EDWARDS

Chicago in the Rain
(Relief for Negro Homeless Men
on the South Side)

If you know Chicago in the rain you have the setting. Rain and an unnaturally warm winter's night, close, ominous, bedraggled, hopeless. Fine old mansions leer in sullen dilapidation. On such a night we went to share a meal at one of the South Side shelters for "unattached" men.

The mess hall occupies the full basement of the old Unity Club at 3140 Indiana Avenue. The upper floors now house a political organization. Fraser Lane, veteran social worker and a genial sympathetic soul, directs the feeding station. This evening a long queue of men trailed out into the alleyway in the rain, edging themselves inside to warmth and food. (They formerly came in at the front, but crowding the walks with shabbily clothed men annoyed their comfortable neighbors.) Feeding begins at 4:30 P.M. It was 7:00 when we came. Fourteen hundred men had already passed through the line and the queue still extended out into the alley. A queue of grim, sullen, hopeless, inert men who presented their cards to the "clocker." (Blue cards for "regulars" and white for newcomers whose cases have not been cleared.) No man is turned away hungry pending clearing and investigation. Without eagerness or haste they shuffled up to the counter. Accepted each in turn a pan of beef stew, four slices of bread, white and rye, and a huge aluminum mug, choice of coffee or milk. Then the heavy, dull saunter to a place at one of the long scrubbed pine tables.

And the men—some torn and dirty, a few gray and old, aware that for them this is the jumping off place, the final scene. For even with a normal revival of industry these will be scrapped and replaced by men in earlier strength. Here and there smooth, carefully groomed men with intelligent faces evidencing education and good living. A thin-faced West Indian bearing himself with British hauteur; a graduate of a Boston law school; a handsome brown man with iron gray hair, formerly a college professor; the pampered son of a one-time "policy king"; several university students and a meager sprinkling of Mexican, Polish, and American white huddled together in the helplessness of a common dilemma. For the past months I have been working at a Relief Station for the service of families and married couples. The men cling to their traditional status as family head and bread-winner so make the applications and subsequent complaints of delays or shortage or renewals. Discouraged and restless—not unjustly— as they become they yet have their families and wives and a room— eviction imminent—to turn toward at evening. They are yet a little way removed from the bottom of the bottom. Not so finally emasculated and reduced to the complete infantile dependence into which our economic system has forced "men without families," men and their families following close.

There was a dreary absence of conversation among the more than 800 men then at "mess." The Negro in this present strait has lost his traditional readiness either to laugh or to sing through a difficulty. With a history precarious always, for the first time he is hopeless. Under slavery there was freedom to be prayed and sung and hoped for. "Massa" this time is too remote and intangible to be shaped into prayers. Then there was the War and simultaneously the trek north and their subsequent disillusionment. Negroes ceased their prayers when they returned from the War pursuing the mirage of a democracy fought for and heralded as won. For a gay, extravagant decade, desperate in its excess, Spirituals gave way for the "Blues." The "Blues" expressing a nostalgia for loved things of the southland coupled with a realization that never again could there be complete submission to its accompanying oppression. This present dilemma is incomprehensible and the voluble, laughing Negro silent and inarticulate.

We chatted with the chef while he cleaned a huge pot over a diminutive sink. From New Orleans, he said. He had cooked at an infirmary there, and at Julia King's in Chicago; had seen "hard times up and down the river but never caught in a crack like this." Here was neither humor nor drollery even when he learned I knew and loved New Orleans and we shared opinions on the charm of the old city. From a table a man called, "Didja come to git me outta the bread line?" and further a particularly dejected lad supported his head in his hands staring nowhere while an old man opposite pleaded comfortingly, "Have some of mah beans." Pathos—drab tragedy lacking the color and drama and romantic heroism of war.

And after supper the long hours until morning with breakfast the only event to anticipate.

It is a few blocks to the "shelters" and we passed many of these former men, now helpless children, shuffling over for cots. The Wabash Avenue Lodge includes a cobbler shop for the service of the district shelters. The cobbler was amiable. He had been withdrawn from the ranks of the unemployed and now receives three dollars a week in cash. That means meals outside at will, cigarettes sometimes, and even an occasional "movie." "I used to preach to save souls," he laughed (the only laugh we encountered all evening), "but now I have two soles in view."

On 31st Street the old Royal Gardens Cabaret has been converted into a shelter. Incognito under its chaste green and white paint the ornately carved ceiling and deep stairway betray its frivolous, gaudy past. Ten years gone and fewer, here was the center of Chicago's "night life." A favored rendezvous of young white women from the gold coast and sleek, brown men. A jazz orchestra wailed nightly and there was never floor space. Tonight I somehow felt wickedly glad that for one brief interval black men had lived gaily, extravagantly, lewdly perhaps. Fed, tailored, groomed, perfumed, loved lavishly. Many, of course, saved carefully only to lose in crashed banks or in homes sold to them at an inflated market. Chuck Lewis, a Fisk letter man with an interesting army record, is host here where 800 men sleep. Long rows of army cots and to each man two sheets, two blankets, and a nightie. Upstairs the former gala ball room and stage furnishes a boxing ring and workout floor. Checkers, cards, and dominos are available. And a service on Sunday in which men from two shelters join. It was only 8:00 but most of the men had retired though curfew is at 9:00. But a bad night out and nothing to do until breakfast.

For many of the men the bread line is a step up physically. Regular meals, sleep, baths, fresh linen. But there is none to whom it is not wholly devastating to personality, to manhood, to the essential self. Men who have never had or known how to use leisure find themselves literally stifled with time. And still no program for the direction that might lighten a little the tedium of interminable idleness. In the melee of administering physical relief we have been tardy in recognizing how urgent it is that we salvage, it is now too late to preserve the morale of the unemployed.

MARY HEATON VORSE

School for Bums

April 29, 1931

They took a census of the floating unemployed on the East Side, which covered the homeless men. In the Municipal Lodging House, in the missions and shelters, in flop houses and speakeasies where a man can stay all night, sleeping on sawdust, if he buys a drink, they took a census.

The regular salaried census takers had a force of between two and three hundred volunteers, divided up into teams. Each captain had working under him a team of six or more people, flung across the Bowery, down Doyers Street, through Christie Street, on to the waterfront.

They are rounding up the misery of the East Side. Doing it "intensively" as one census taker puts it. This is a queer census. It is a census of misery. It is the count of despair. In New York City for future reference they will tabulate the hopeless and put between covers of books how many men are wandering around shelterless, no prospect of jobs, no place to stay in the daytime, no place to sleep at night. How many are there—the wanderers from Municipal Lodging House to Salvation Army shelter, to flop house, to speakeasy? How many are there sleeping in the subway or under the bridge at 184th Street?

Well, at this writing the figures are being compiled. They are not yet accurate, but it looks as if there are about 15,000 homeless men in New York—which would include a couple of hundred homeless women.

The unemployed homeless do not take so kindly to the count. Social workers reported that in the flop houses and twenty-five-cent-a-bed hotels they were hard to talk to—different from what they had been two years before when a similar count had been taken. Some men did not answer at all. Nor did the social workers wonder at this.

Everyone said the missions were the easiest places in which to take the unemployed census. Take the mission in Doyers Street. It is where the Chinese Theatre used to be. You come into a large irregular room. They hold the mission service where the Chinese actors used to play their interminable plays. Go down a flight of stairs. Here is an underground place. Toward one end, a counter, men in aprons behind it. This is where the men get their food. After that, after they have praised God with hymns, after the prayers, the beds stacked up high against bricked-in arches will be spread down in this space, which holds perhaps three hundred.

The line, before the men are fed, shuffles patiently in front of the census takers. One is a young girl in a raccoon coat, with a clear-cut profile. Her eyes are open with surprise. She has never seen anything like this before. She is embarrassed asking questions—name, age, where born, what trade? They file along, the men in the mission, a long shuffling line. A patient line. Weary feet, broken shoes, worn clothes, unshaven faces.

Very few young men in the missions now. The young men don't go in so much for religion. Many of them over forty, comparatively few under thirty. They crawl along, glad enough to answer the questions and get on. They shuffle along like men already accustomed to waiting, easing themselves on one foot, then on the other. After a couple of hours they get their handout.

A queer census. What happened to John Bentley, twenty-nine, house painter, born in Kansas of American parents, union member? Well, there was this depression in the building trades, and he heard of a job farther east. He had a job for a short time. Now here he is in the line. His face is clear-cut, English, with a long upper lip. The type of man who should be upstanding and brisk. His shoulders sag, his shoes are broken. Defeat and bitterness are in his expression. The slight defiance in his answers is of the man who dares you to ask him how he happened to come on a breadline. There are hundreds more with his story.

The beds are being spread out. The girl in the raccoon coat cries out, "My God, they're lying on the floor!" There are not beds enough for everyone. Enough handouts, enough free food of a kind "that don't stand by you," all the drifters will tell you. But not enough flops.

A group of some twenty well-dressed people suddenly appears on the stairs. "Ladies and gentlemen," chants a guide, "this was one of the underground resorts of old Chinatown. This used to be the place where Chinatown came to hit the pipe. You would find white people and Chinese together sodden in opium dreams. Behind those bricked-in arches was where the plutocrats and the society people used to come to smoke their pipes in privacy. . . ."

"My Lord!" says the girl in the raccoon coat. *"Tourists!"*

The people from the sightseeing bus peer at the men rolling themselves in blankets. They peer at the bricked-in archways behind which in the old days "plutocrats and society women" supposedly came for an opium debauch. Then they go on.

The census is over. No one else will be allowed in tonight. They are taking care of all they can.

The groups of census takers go on from the mission to the speakeasies. In some of these there is a free lunch. Here, if you buy a drink, they let you stay and sleep on the sawdust or on a chair. In some of them there is a drink of free whiskey all around at midnight.

It is not hard to understand why a man would rather sleep in the filthy sawdust than at a mission or in that place of massed misery, the Municipal Lodging House—where there is a somewhat ghastly moment after a man has given up his clothes to be sterilized. After his shower, he stands naked, with all his other naked and miserable comrades, waiting for a nightshirt. The speakeasy, after all, has a touch of home about it, a place where a man can keep his personality, what there is of it.

A group of volunteer census takers meet, men and women. They have together accumulated a series of nightmare pictures of our civilization. They have seen where the men sleep and how inadequate the beds of New York are for the homeless. One social worker sums it up as he exclaims:

"It's a school for bums."

It is a school for bums—crawling breadlines—81,000 free meals daily. No certain place to sleep, no organized shelter.

If you want to know how to make a bum out of a workingman who has had trade, home, security, and ambition taken from him, talk to any of the young fellows on the breadline who have been in town long enough to have become experienced in misery. Say a man in this town goes to the Municipal Lodging House for his first night. Until lately, he would have been routed out at five in the morning. Now he can stay until six. He is given breakfast, then he must leave, blizzard or rain. He can go next to a Salvation Army shelter for a handout, and get down to the City Free Employment Bureau before it opens. Or he can find shelter in subways and mark the Want Ads in a morning paper.

If he decides on the Employment Bureau, he is wise to arrive there before the doors open. He will find himself in the midst of a huge company which augments all the time until the opening of the doors. He may have spent two hours there—from nine to eleven. After that, he will not have eaten since his handout at seven at the Salvation Army, and he will have walked quite a lot. The next thing to do will be to put himself on some other breadline. It will take him one and a half or two hours to get his noonday meal.

In the afternoon there isn't very much use hunting jobs; yet there may be a chance at something; at some of the agencies, or perhaps by looking through the scanty Want Ads in the afternoon papers. There is a question then as to how and where to spend the rest of the time. If he has good enough clothes he can kill some time in the library. With discretion, hours can be spent in the terminals of stations. He can go to a museum. If he has a nickel, he can "ride the subways." But if he can panhandle some money, he can at least stay indoors in a speakeasy or Bowery hotel.

It will take him an hour and a half or two hours for his evening meal, and if he is going to the Municipal Lodging House again, he had best be early on the line.

Until recently the Municipal Lodging House was open only one night a month to non-residents and five nights to residents of New York. This restriction has now been removed. There are 3,300 people sleeping at the Municipal Lodging House, of which 100 are women. The beds are full, and they are sleeping on benches, on the floor.

In the life of this drifting worker there is never any security. He is never sure where he is going to sleep. It is easy to learn to panhandle twenty-five or fifty cents for a night's flop. Between the agencies who help homeless men—the Salvation Army, Municipal lodging houses, the Y.M.C.A., and missions—there are not enough beds. Make a count of all the agencies, even including the new pier, which furnishes shelter for 700 more, and the Salvation Army boat that gives lodging to 600 seamen, besides its other shelters. There is still a slack of thousands for whom there is no free accommodation at present in the city.

The present situation is indeed a school for bums. A thing to sap moral and physical strength. A situation which in a few weeks would make most employable men unemployable, and which puts a premium upon panhandling. It is the deadly frustration of each unsuccessful day of job hunting when, tired and footsore, a man again stands in the long gray queue of the breadline only to seek an uncertain shelter. It is astonishing how soon a newcomer learns the ropes, how quickly it spreads from mouth to mouth where food is better, where flops are to be had.

Usually when times are hard and people are out of work, Fifth Avenue and Broadway know nothing about it. This is the first time these streets have lost their glittering shine. The shabby, shifting, ebbing men out of work have taken it from them.

On a street corner near 50th Street was a store which had been turned into a free restaurant for the unemployed. Well-dressed young ladies were cutting sandwiches for all who wanted to come in and get one. In the middle of each table stood a pot of mustard. There were men with well-brushed clothes, men who looked like old bums, young white-collar men, all engulfing enormous sandwiches, cheese spread with mustard—three sandwiches to a person and coffee.

There were men whose faces made a spot of yellow, famine color. They had been starving. The men eating behind the plate-glass windows of the corner store were being gaped at by a crowd. Outside two men discussed them.

"That's to keep 'em from riotin'; it's to keep 'em quiet that they're feedin' 'em" said a man who talked like a play by Upton Sinclair.

"Har! Ye talk like a radical," said a man with an English accent. "That's fir hadvertising that they're feedin' 'em, them's society girls in there."

"It's to keep 'em quiet, I say. If they didn't feed 'em, they'd come marchin' down to the markets. They'd break the windows and loot 'em and help 'emselves. An' what's to prevent 'em from takin' what they want? They's a million of 'em in the city; if they was to march they'd make a procession!"

What if they should march, one wonders—all of them. What if having had their census taken and their misery compiled, they should give an exhibition of their numbers? What then? Tear gas and clubs and arrests, no doubt.

There are other sides to the avalanche of despair. As a part of the widespread slump, the people who thought themselves secure have been thrown into it. The people who have been able to have a college education suddenly find themselves out of a job. No one can take the census of this misery. It doesn't walk the street. It sits and shivers in cold houses. It hides itself.

They hunt in vain for jobs. Or, if they have homes to go to, they return, defeated, to be dependent. Or perhaps, having no home to go to, these people, too, may slip gradually downhill where they must apply for charity.

And what about such people as a friend of mine told me of recently? She was working in one of the emergency employment bureaus on the East Side where daily men came to get the Prosser jobs which are now nonexistent. Daily the little crowd of people gathers outside and waits in vain.

I watched this flood of people who had been once well-to-do, judging by their clothing. People used to steady work, coming in vain with their stories of five children, no work, savings gone.

"It's not nearly as hard as the employment agency I used to work with in Queens," my friend told me. The first day she worked there, she went to nine houses, which had in each case been lost by the young people who were in the process of buying them. Here was a little suburban community where young people, many of them with college educations, had come to found homes, to live where their children could be brought up healthfully.

"There was something more desperate in Queens," my friend told me, "than there is on the East Side, where people are used to the idea of insecurity. The car goes first: the furniture goes; then the house goes; confidence in life goes."

Of the number of people losing their all, because they cannot raise a few dollars, there is no record as yet. Maybe there will never be. One can only generalize and say that the white-collar class is suffering today with the mechanic. The man who has spent thousands upon his education is no more secure than a laborer. The misery, doubt, and defeat pile up, an incalculable mountain. There is no census yet of these.

Hard-Boiled

The trial of Haywood Patterson, one of the Scottsboro boys recently sentenced to death for alleged assault on Victoria Price, exposes how corrupt the capitalist society is in which we live. It spread open the sore of the class dominion of the courts thru the violation of the Fourteenth Amendment by excluding Negroes from all Southern juries. It indicted the South by proving that there is no such thing as justice for a Negro in a Southern court. A county official said to me:

"The trial was over soon as a white woman said the nigger was guilty. That jury didn't need to know anything more." It was a sure thing that as they heard that, they were going to bring in a conviction with the death sentence. A woman who had proved herself a perjurer, who had three convictions against her on the police records of her home town, who had a motive for her crime of both revenge and self-preservation, opens her mouth and accuses a Negro; and he is as good as dead, unless the workers of the county mass themselves behind him.

Victoria Price by her unsupported word condemned Haywood Patterson to death. Her companion, Ruby Bates, has recanted and has sworn no Negro was ever near them. Haywood Patterson, however, was accused and condemned by something far more terrible and far greater than Victoria Price. His real accuser and would-be executioner is poverty and bad conditions—the frightful conditions which surrounded every footstep which Victoria Price has taken during the short years of her life.

As you go thru the railway yards of Huntsville, there are acre on acre of mean two-room shacks and a lean-to behind, perched over the mud on brick posts. Instead of flowers, mud and litter. Instead of any green thing, festering garbage piles and tin cans. Not far away are the high towers of the mills. It was along such streets Victoria Price and Ruby Bates walked. Here in the mills they worked for a few dollars a week, ten and twelve hours a day. And then the work stopped, and there was work only a day or two a week. So these two girls, Ruby Bates and Victoria Price, who had never had a chance, who had lived without a glimpse of loveliness, who did not know there was such a thing as aspiration and beauty in the world, had their shabby love affairs promiscuously in the jungles and hobo camps. They got diseased, they got jail sentences. That was all that the great capitalist country of America had to give these girls. All that this great country and the great State of Alabama had for Ruby Bates and

Victoria Price was such frightful conditions that it was a relief to put on overalls over three dresses and catch rides on freight trains, and sleep with boys in freight car boxes, and arrive penniless in a hobo camp while their light-o'-loves went off "stemming" for food, while the girls planned how they would go West and "hustle the towns."

The conditions under which Victoria Price lived were so hard, the vice with which she was confronted so low, that in her twenties she is harder than any product of city streets; so cruel, so pitiless that a New York tart would seem a model of soft womanliness beside her. Yet she was made of firm enough material. Dimly one can see an outline of what her life might have meant if there had ever been a ray of hope, a small chance for her. There never was.

So this act of injustice is not that of one vicious girl. It is that of the vicious system behind her, that of relentless grinding of a breaking-down civilization which is squeezing out into the hobo camps and jungles 200,000 boys and girls.

MYRA PAGE

"Leave Them Meters Be!"

"Just look at that!" Ann called Mary over to the window. Together they peered angrily at the husky giant loosening dirt around a water meter. Alabama's July sun sizzled across his wet shoulders, danced merrily on the heads of the little Negro babies making sand pies on a wobbly porch nearby. Beyond the dingy shacks reared the rust-colored furnaces of the enormous Tennessee Coal and Iron Company's steel mills.

"That gas bird's aiming to dig 'em all up. Blest if he ain't!"

"Damn company!" Ann snorted. "Right in the hottest time. How we-all's gona get along without water?" Three meters were already leaning against the side of the company truck."

"You telling me!" Mary jerked at her apron. "And everybody sitting home cross-legged. It's a shame!" At this rate, soon all the colored families of Morseville would be running with tin pails to the dirty creek. If that water company had its way. "With all the lay-offs now, how they expect us to have a dollar every month?"

Ann looked glumly at her friend. "We gotta do something, that's all."

"But what?"

"Get them women outa their kitchens."

"Just try it—they're scared of their own shadow!"

"Now you listen here," Ann grinned. Black eyes stared into black eyes as the plan grew. With a snicker, Mary agreed.

Suddenly Mary made for the porch, arguing at the top of her voice.

Ann ran after her, calling down the walk, "You black-faced hussy, you!" She flapped her apron, "I'll learn you to sass me!"

Mary walked with a swagger, calling back. Heads appeared at windows, the children dropped their game. Still quarreling, the women edged slowly up the street. Some neighbors came out on their porches.

The man digging meters stopped to wipe his face and watch the fuss.

Mary leaned to pick up a rock. "Shut your loose mouth woman, or I'll—"

Ann reached for a clump of dirt. Two women grabbed her, as the meterman pinned Mary's arms behind her.

Seeing the women crowding around, Ann gave a vigorous shake to her shoulders, freeing herself. Quickly she stepped into the circle. "Fellow workers! Women! Ain't you shamed? Letting this no-count shut off your water!"

Amazed, the women stared, drew closer. Somebody giggled. Mouth open, the company man loosened his hold on Mary, fell back. "Well, I'll be—"

"Sitting home on your stumps," Ann went on, "mourning your hard times. That won't get us nowhere—you ought to know that!"

"We sure ain't nowhere now," one woman muttered, "that's the Lord's truth."

"You said it!"

"How you gona get along without water?" Ann demanded, "Tell me that? How you gona cook your cornmush?

"But only trouble comes of kicking up a fuss," her neighbor argued.

"Depends on who kicks up the fuss and how," Ann retorted. "One or two alone don't mean nothing. All together, it means the water turned back on. Now tell me, how you gona wash the white folks' clothes? How you gona scrub your floors?"

"Oh, lawsy," one listener mourned, "but we ain't got no dollar!"

"My man ain't had a day's work since doomsday. He's wore his shoes out looking—just don't look like the steel mill's ever going to hire again."

"What we gona do?"

Ann turned on the water meter agent, who was digging like mad. "Stop that man! That's the first thing." As he saw the women turn on him, he dropped his shovel, backing off. "Now lookahere, ladies," he begged, "I ain't done nothing. It's company orders."

"Just drap them meters back where they belong," said Mary kindly, "and skiddoo."

As his empty truck chugged hurriedly down the road, Ann looked at the women. "You see?" Everybody was grinning, eyeing their meter. She went on, "this ain't all. We gotta put a stop to this water business, once for all. There's plenty more families in Morseville ain't got the dollar either."

"That's right," a woman near her spoke up, "my bill's overdue and so's all on my block. Any day we been thinking that truck'd come."

"You telling me!" Mary jerked. Ann told them, "We gona sign up in an organization right now, an Unemployed Council. And when your mens come home, you gona sign them up too. Who-all wants to give in names?"

Some hung back and Ann went on, "We gona chose a committee right here and now," Ann said, "and go down to that water company office in Birmingham and tell them we gotta have water in their houses and for them to leave them meters be. I'm going and Mary's going, and who else's going along?" Three others were chosen out of a dozen hands. . . .

Well, in telling this, which is no made-up story, but something that actually happened, Ann ended with a twinkle in her eye—"And that's how we come to get free water in Morseville for the unemployed."

"Water!"

Ann toiled slowly up the hill, puffing as she went, for the day was sultry and the sun's glare on the yellow dirt hurt her eyes. In the distance loomed Red Mountain, bristling with coal and iron, its sides dotted with mining camps. Along the valley below ran the big Tennessee Coal and Iron Company and Republic Steel Company mills, some stacks smoking, others dead.

Ann was on her way from the company steel town of Morseville, to a mining camp up the valley. A hilly, six-mile hike under the molten steel of Alabama's sun. But shoe leather and hoofing—it came easier than nickels. Every copper these days had to be saved for food and leaflets.

As she climbed she hummed.

"Oh, we're from Alabama.

And we shall not be moved—"

And she thought of many things, while the crickets buzzed in the grasses nearby, lazily protesting the heat. Swiftly her green gingham moved past the many-shaded greens of earth's late summer.

As she rounded a curve, her humming stopped.

Some of the white women busily filling their pails turned quickly at her approach. Seeing who it was, they went back to their work, unconcerned.

Ann slowed her pace. Dressed in ginghams as washed-out as her own, the women were taking their turns before an improvised water spout. Somebody had sprung a leak in a watermain running near the path, sprung it with an axe. A board had been placed over it to slant the water's flow back to the earth where the pails could catch its gurging splash.

Ann smiled ruefully, taking it all in at a glance. Free water!

Moving closer, she noticed the thin little woman, her belly swollen with child, slipping dangerously in the mud. She jumped to catch her, help fill her pail.

"Lawsy!" Ann exclaimed, "what all you doing here?"

The woman looked up blankly at the raw-boned dark woman who had helped her. "Can't you see, getting water! All Glenspeak's toting water from here."

"How's that?"

"Company's turned off all the water in town."

"You don't say, now that sure is bad." Glenspeak's shacks lay a good quarter-mile from there. "Don't you-all ladies know," Ann continued cannily, hiding her real feeling, "don't you-all know this here's against the law?"

"But we gotta have water," one woman retorted irritably, "you can't cook or wash or live nohow without water."

"That's right," Ann agreed, "but busting a water main can land somebody in jail."

"Good land," someone whispered, "that's what I been saying."

"Let 'em try it!" a gaunt figure muttered, "I ain't scared."

"Never see our chillens again!" The filled pails clattered noisily.

"You got a right to this water," Ann suddenly veered, "you don't have to sneak it. Make the company turn it back on. She paused. "Like we done in Morseville."

"Turn it back on! How's that?" A couple of her listeners looked at her with real interest. "We heard tell of that." If the colored folks had done it, well the whites surely could. They stepped closer. "Tell us how you did it."

Ann told them. They laughed about the company's man being run off by the women when he tried to dig up the meters. And when they heard how the Unemployed Council, that they with their men had organized in Morseville, had won free water, they said, "By gorry, we can do that too."—"No sense in having to sneak and tote this water so far."—"And winter-time coming on."

"Maybe," the gaunt woman in a faded morning glory print who had said she wasn't scared, spoke hesitantly, "Maybe you'd show us how to get started?" True, Ann was a colored woman and she was white. But this came first. They had to have water. "Water, water," an old refrain burred through her head, "—the stream of life by which all things live—"

"Sure I will," Ann agreed. And waited. She knew she mustn't rush them.

The white woman named Marge looked around at the others. "We need a meeting?" They nodded. "All right, in my house, tomorrow." She looked again at the women, they turned to Ann. "Will you come?"

"Sure," Ann replied, "Sure, if you want me, I'll come."

As they started down the path, Ann helped the pregnant woman with her pails. She might be a little late for her miner's meeting, but this was worth it.

Marge slowed down to drop back by Ann. "How come you-all knew how to organize and all? You got some papers and books, maybe?" Ann nodded cautiously. "Well, maybe I got one or two papers at my house. Why?"

"I was just thinking," Marge said, "I been reading in the *Birmingham News* about unions and reds and things." They walked on.

"Your man work at the T.C.I.?" Marge asked.

"When there was work," Ann told her.

"Mine too," Marge grunted, "when there was work." They walked further. "I kinda figured," Marge continued with a soft drawl, "what the *News* says is bad, can't be so bad. Not for us poor working class of folks."

"That's right," Ann agreed, "the *News* is for the company, not us."

As they reached the edge of Glenspeak, Marge asked, "Could you bring me some of your reading along tomorrow?" "Yes," Ann said, she reckoned she could.

The women's voices and their pails tingled with a new key. They were going to have water again. The stream of life.

And Marge, as she looked after Ann's strong figure, re-climbing the path, smiled at the thought of the fresh streams soon to be flowing through Glenspeak, Morseville, and all of Red Mountain Valley.

MERIDEL LE SUEUR

The Fetish of Being Outside

In times like these, points of view are important; they represent what you will be called upon to act from tomorrow. They are not static or simply curious parlor flora any more. I would like therefore to give my position too on some of the problems brought up by Horace Gregory in a recent issue of *The New Masses.* I have also been struggling with these problems and look forward to the impetus of a communal discussion of them at the Writers' Congress in May.

Every point that Horace Gregory raises is extremely vital and indicates a middle-class malady I believe, a sickness common to all of us nourished on rotten bourgeois soil. These are important because it may be from these peculiar maladies that we break the old forms of psychic reaction to an old society and create a new nucleus of communal interaction.

I would like to say first that I believe an act of full belief very difficult to the bourgeois mind, a reflex from nineteenth-century romanticism, Darwinism, etc., and that this belief is the action, the function of the writer, this is his peculiar and prophetic function to stand for a belief in something that scarcely exists, as Mr. Gregory points out, but the writer must create from this belief the nucleus of a new condition and relationship of the individual and society and all the problems involved in that new orientation. Of course this is moving in the chaotic dark of a new creation, admittedly, but it is exactly this movement that is the "action" of the creative worker. This I believe pertinently brings up the various points Mr. Gregory states and is related to them all, the individual and the group, the objective fetish of the old literature, being outside and at the same time inside, being above or removed from "splits" and party lines, etc., and left and right "deviations."

As for the individual and the group: Joining has always been obnoxious to the bourgeois artist because of his false orientation to the middle-class groups and because such groups in an exploiting world are spurious and false groups, an accretion of individuals. An organic group pertaining to growth of a new nucleus of society is a different thing. You do not join such a group, you simply *belong.* You belong to that growth or you do not belong to it. As a matter of fact you cannot simply attach yourself to the Communist philosophy. It is a hard, difficult, organic growth away from old forms, into entirely new ones. You cannot "join" it in the ordinary middle-class sense as you can join the Rotarians or Kiwanis or any similar group. There are no organic groups in middle-class society because all groups are a subtle hypocrisy since capitalism is based upon the exploiting ability of every individual against every other one. So I feel strongly that this holding off of the artist from a group is artificial, a hangover from an old society.

Growing from this subtly and connected is the assumption that the creative worker is not an economist and cannot understand deviations, and political theory. This again is something entirely different from under-standing or participating in the political theory (if any) of say Hoover and ilk or the economics of the donkey or the elephant. This again I believe is a hangover, a curious infantilism and exhibitionism of the bourgeois artist. (These are instinctive in us and difficult of removal and should be looked at, I believe, in a clear light as being tendencies of us all.) We have put on this infantilism as a cloak because we could not function in the merchant world, or rather didn't care to function, and had to keep ourselves out of it by appearing childish or strange or macabre creatures, like Hawthorne going out only at night, or Poe taking refuge in strangeness or the Stein infantile inarticulateness—these of course are extreme, but the extreme is the only way to prove the fallacy of middle courses. If you have to have some excuse for not entering the counting house, being a child or eccentric are both good. Why shouldn't the artist be in the vanguard in a well-integrated society, the most mature, with the greatest powers of psychic synthesis and prophecy and the fullest grasp of vital tendencies toward life or toward death in that society?

In this crisis political and economic activity are no longer specialized and theoretic classroom sociology. They represent an accumulation of forces, a direction of energies and tendencies that show whether you are going to get enough to eat, get married, whether your child will be born alive or dead, or whether you are going to be thrown out on the streets tomorrow. They have become highly integrated emotional, contemporary facts, happening to a lot of people, making the contemporary composition. The artist can no longer take refuge in infantilism, or the supposition that he has not the kind of mentality to understand economic thought because this is the dynamic stuff of the composition of our time and he cannot take a double course and be part of it and still apart from it. It is impossible and the closer we approach the crisis where these elements come together in dynamic clash the more this will be so. You cannot be both on the barricades and objective or removed at the same time. I suppose you can but you are likely to receive the bullets of both sides.

For myself I do not feel any subtle equivocation between the individual and the new disciplined groups of the Communist Party. I do not care for the bourgeois "individual" that I am. I never have cared for it. I want to be integrated in a new and different way as an individual and this I feel can come only from a communal participation which reverses the feeling of a bourgeois writer. What will happen to him will not be special and precious, but will be the communal happening, what happens at all. I can no longer live without communal sensibility. I can no longer breathe in this maggotty individualism of a merchant society. I have never been able to breathe in it. That is why I hope to "belong" to a communal society, to be a cellular part of that and able to grow and function with others in a living whole.

This leads of course directly to the problem of objectivity. This also has something to do with the writer's precious naivete about party lines and splits, comes possibly from his fetish of being an outsider. I feel strongly that this being outside the demarcations of economic and political positions (which directly had to do with the betrayal of the Austrian workers, with men tramping over the snow, with women shooting from the roofs of the Karl Marx House in Vienna and all these undoubtedly individuals, and perhaps even objective individuals to themselves) represents a real deviation of emotional and psychic hangovers and difficulties of a new orientation to the writer who has always been alone in a merchant society, which boils down to a desire real and definite enough to take a middle course, very dangerous and from which our life and death of the future will emanate. Objective writing can never provide will or purpose and is related to the liberal formal ideal of neutrality and disinterestedness. This of course is only carrying Gregory's position to its dangerous conclusions.

I cannot understand or sympathize with the subtle equivocation that exists in Horace Gregory's entire position. Why want to be an outsider when you see and admit sight of the promised land as Gregory does; why choose to walk around the walls of Jericho merely? Yes, it seems equivocal and dangerous and I mention it bluntly because I am sure he, like the rest of us from the middle class, has a difficult orientation to make; but it seems very dangerous to me to want at the same time to be in and to be out. . . . You must accept the discipline of the party and yet you must be objective and individual and outside. You must act and yet *you* must not act, you must be individual and again objective. This is like saying I will fall in love and I will not fall in love, I will remain outside, cunning, keep my head, etc. And just as disastrous to any final heat of creation or action. He says also he cannot write in the heat of conflict. I don't think anyone demands this but what we do demand is heat. You can't hatch anything without heat. "Objective" removed "individual" writing at this time doesn't give birth to anything.

It seems to me Gregory's position shows a dangerous hangover integration with his class still. Not actually of course but these half equivocations lead by a devious route straight back to all the old alignments. Even nationalism. He says he is a nationalist. Believes in America. So do I, not knowing any other breast for nourishment, but to believe only in difference smacks too much of the nineteenth-century scientific thought that disassociated and dissected every living organism and left us a horror of parts and broken pieces and—equivocations.

Double entendre, equivocation, a subtle hypocrisy under an apparently frank ideology seems to me dangerously akin to the habits of the middle class.

My stand is that I feel that all this old ideology is dead. I have always felt this subtly, internally, but now it is proven, stands in broad daylight, as an actual physical decay. I see it now. It is known. Everyday I see people rotting, dying in this dead class like plants decaying in a foul soil. I feel I, myself, have rotted and suffered and threshed in this element of the bourgeois class like an organism in a decaying pool with the water evaporating about you and the natural elements of your body and desires in stress and your hungers decaying and rotting and stinking to high heaven.

I have felt the impossibility of growth both as an individual and a creative worker in that class, and how all these ideologies are reversed now and do nothing but strangle one and diminish the possibilities of integration and growth.

I, too, like Gregory, have wanted to be a writer of fine poetry. So do we all, like a fine bloom but you cannot grow a fine bloom by equivocation, by only half growing a fine bloom. This is where the "action" of the writer or creative worker of any kind comes in. It is an action of belief, of full belief. There is some kind of extremity and willingness to walk blind that comes in any creation of a new and unseen thing, some kind of final last step that has to be taken with full intellectual understanding and with the artist, a step beyond that too, a creation of a future "image," a future action that exists in the present even vaguely or only whispered, or only in a raised arm, or a word dropped in the dark but from these, because of full belief, he will produce a movement, even a miraculous form that has not hitherto existed. Even the lowest forms of life are able to step out in this belief into a new element and grow a new orientated fin or organ that makes creative alignments.

It is difficult because you are stepping into a dark chaotic passional world of another class, the proletariat, which is still perhaps unconscious of itself like a great body sleeping, stirring, strange, and outside the calculated, expedient world of the bourgeoisie. It is a hard road to leave your own class and you cannot leave it by pieces or parts; it is a birth and you have to be born whole out of it. In a complete new body. None of the old ideology is any good in it. The creative artist will create no new forms of art or literature for that new hour out of that darkness unless he is willing to go all the way, with full belief, into that darkness.

You cannot blow a trumpet by only half putting it to the lips or even a fraction of an inch away from the lips. You can only blow a trumpet by putting it completely to the lips.

Of course as Gregory says we see no strong victorious worker. Most of the time in the past we have seen nothing but the horizon of prairie out here with Chicago, the hog butcher of the world, thrusting a bloody head out of misused Illinois corn soil. Our song is as he says "broken, truncated," but important to the writer is to go off the deep end (heaven knows it ought to be as easy as stepping off a rotting Ward liner that is sinking a mile a minute).

To be willing to do any less leads to an abortive birth, to fascistic tendency in writers, to reformism, back into the old ideology, into the enemies' camp, into preserving a stinking individualism, objectivity, retreat, and even leads finally to the abortive creation of oneself as an artist and individual.

You can't have a unity with the nether world and the dangerous dust that falls from bourgeois ideology.

Belief is an action for the writer. The writer's action is full belief, from which follows a complete birth, not a fascistic abortion, but a creation of a new nucleus of a communal society in which at last the writer can act fully and not react equivocally. In a new and mature integrity.

MARY INMAN

Manufacturing Femininity

There is no evidence that woman's biological function as a childbearer reacts on her mental processes in such a manner as to fit her better to become a chambermaid than an engineer. What evidently does react to produce more women who are chambermaids than engineers is not woman's nature, but her environment.

Women are influenced by their physical surroundings, both as members of society and as members of a particular group in society which, in general, has had a particular kind of work allotted to it. It is natural that they should so react, and there is nothing here about which to object, except the kind of work women do.

But, women, like members of other subject groups, such as workers and Negroes, have had part of their behavior cut to a particular group pattern and forced upon them, often from birth.

These groups react to this purposely made environment in much the same manner as certain varieties of grapes, when exposed to dry heat, turn into raisins.

Deliberately manufacturing characteristics by this artificial process is neither more natural nor mysterious than the deliberate manufacture of sauerkraut. All that is necessary to do is take certain elements and do certain things with them.

In making kraut, the cabbage is shredded, or chopped, then packed into a wooden container with alternating layers of salt and cabbage. The cabbage is pounded down and a weight is added to keep it submerged.

To manufacture femininity, about one minute after a baby is born you determine whether it is male or female. After that has been established you are ready to begin, for there are already set up and operating two well-defined sets of rules to guide you. One governing the conduct of males, the other that of females, and the attitude of persons toward each. So, if the new baby is a girl the making of femininity begins at once. If a boy the making of masculinity starts.

Little boys are trained to be confident and independent; little girls to be cautious and dependent. Boys are taught that they can achieve their ambitions; girls that they must have some one achieve their ambitions for them.

He has toys and games designed to cultivate his intellect. She has playthings to develop her emotions. He is taught to build a tower. She to pin on a diaper.

He must be daring and brave; she restrained in deportment, meek and submissive. Little girls must grow up to obey and follow men. Little boys to command and lead women.

If it were just a matter of training a child to live life, one set of rules would suffice for all children, because all children have to be taught to live life.

But, instead, we find that boy and girl rules are made to serve an altogether different purpose than teaching a child to wash its hands, blow its nose, wipe its feet, keep away from fire and out from under automobiles, or anything else making for survival.

Neither are they ethical rules covering such necessary social training as sharing one's apple, or toys, or coming to the rescue of another in danger, or playing fairly, because these things apply to children of both sexes.

The two opposite sets of rules, into one of which every baby is inducted before it can walk, talk, see, hear, or think, have only one purpose. To regulate the relations between subject group and overseers.

To this end, rules which govern him are calculated to bring out and emphasize those traits useful to a petty strawboss and submerge and atrophy those traits which would interfere with the successful pursuit of such a role. To this end also, rules taught her are calculated to aid him in a successful consummation of his strawboss rule over her.

In view of this training it is rather absurd to say that women have less brains than men. If men are smarter than women, then the dullest man is the mental superior of the most intellectual woman. The dullest male has maleness, and if maleness is made the measure by which we estimate intelligence then the rest necessarily follows.

Say women are smarter than men and you merely reverse the rule. Femaleness is made the measure by which we estimate intelligence and if we should insist on this measure it would label the most stupid female the intellectual superior of the most brilliant man.

How illogical to insist on attaching particular sex characteristics to the human brain. Negroes come in for the same sort of discrimination. A mulatto writes a brilliant book. Some newspaper reviews attribute his skill to his white blood.

This is often carried to the extreme of insisting, when there is no evidence or proof that a Negro who excels has any white blood, that he must have a little, for it is said to be hard to always know, or be sure. So they insist that brains not only possess sex but color and race as well.

The surprising thing is not that woman has achieved so little, but that she has accomplished so much, handicapped as she has been by her training. One reason she has escaped to the degree that she has is because those who make the molding rules do not have complete control over the manufacturing environment.

Those nearest and dearest to her were assigned the task of crushing her spirit and arresting any tendency toward independent thinking. The task has been a repulsive one and they have not always done it well.

Then, too, children's resistance has helped to save them from the full effects of this training. It has been said that a child is a natural rebel. Certainly they know many times when something that their trainers insist upon is harmful to them, and they not only disobey the socially conflicting sex rules on occasion but often contest them verbally and give logical arguments why they should not be applied.

One other factor operates in woman's favor. In addition to complicated housework, embodying some twelve or so kinds of skilled and semi-skilled work, she has other tasks to perform, such as teaching, keeping books, answering the telephone, and holding her own with tradesmen, who on occasion would cheat her. For these necessary tasks she must have an independently functioning brain, and it is impossible to keep her from using this brain to solve her problems embodying survival and escape.

Yet, it is not merely woman's restricted work and the peculiar manufactured "feminine" characteristics that causes all the trouble.

Women, like members of other subject groups, have been slandered and charged with weaknesses and faults which they do not possess, but which it is convenient for the subjectors to have believed about them.

Human nature, manufactured characteristics, and falsified characteristics have all been lumped together and labeled feminine nature.

A woman who several years ago gained much publicity from lecturing on the subject of sex expression and repression makes the charge in the published story of her life that women are to blame for their subject status.

Her indictment is based on the theory that women, as trainers of children, could wipe out in one generation the discrimination against women, merely by teaching their children to have theories of equality and freedom toward women.

Woman's children can unquestionably be a vital factor in her emancipation. But, to expect them, as this woman does, to do the job alone is to pit them against an entire economic and social process, armed only with an idea about a single issue. They would be unaided by their fathers, and have only the coaching of women to guide them.

Furthermore, her estimate glosses over the fact that in the training of children, it is not just women who train just children, but subject women who train subject children, and back of these women are successive generations of subject parents.

This does not mean that these subject parents did not pass on training and traditions from their struggles to their children that are helpful to them, for they did, but they also passed on theories of the subjectors, who had laid their cuckoo eggs in the parental nest.

Boys and girls, today, are not trained by their parents into such strikingly different patterns as they were, say, thirty years ago. This modification of the training of children came as a result of the people attaining a fuller, more rational life. With their increased economic and political power they were able to resist the most oppressive measures applying to their children and themselves.

However, if we should have fascism, or black reaction, in the United States, the training of children will return to its old repressive forms.

The Pivot of the System

It may be difficult for the woman doctor, lawyer, teacher, or other professional or business woman to seek the solution to the particular discrimination she meets in the nature of the work housewives do, and see the importance of this work and its relation to social production and, in turn, its importance to her.

The woman doctor who finds her life and work affected by the attitude of fear with which many persons regard her cannot escape the conclusion that her troubles key to the opinion that women are incompetent, and that woman's conduct is liable, even in treatment of the sick, to be erratic and unpredictable.

In other words these persons see when they look at her, not primarily a doctor, but primarily a woman and secondarily a doctor. And not even a woman as she is, but as she is said to be, so no wonder they distrust her.

The handicaps under which business and professional women live and work were levied upon women before there were any business or professional women. Basically they were levied upon women as productive workers, and basically they continue because, under capitalism, housewives' work, in a majority of cases, is necessary to the process of producing and distributing commodities, and we must first take into account the base to understand deviations from the base.

"Capitalism does not without reason make the economic institution of the family, or the family household, with its subjugation of women, the pivot of its system," wrote R. Palme Dutt in an essay, "Women and the Class Struggle," published in "Woman's Coming of Age," a symposium.

In the subjugation of women the aim of the subjectors is the same as that toward any other subject group: the acquisition of labor products, or surplus values, created by others; gold, wheat, cotton, or other wealth, or a service such as cooking, nursing, hairdressing, etc.

No one would give up to another, either knowingly or unknowingly, what they themselves created, nor perform menial tasks for an idle class they despised, except for one reason: because that class controls their means of subsistence, their jobs, their feeding grounds so to speak, the lands and the means of production.

Now, while the reason for subjugation is simple—the acquisition of surplus values; rent, interests, and profits—and simple also the fundamental thing on which it rests—expropriation—there is nothing else simple

308/Mary Inman

about the arrangement, on the contrary, it is very complex, and it is more complex in the case of woman than any other subject group.

The acquiring of surplus values has become complex chiefly because the means of creating this wealth has changed, and many persons who do necessary social labor in relation to the production of wealth no longer come directly into contact with the owners of the means of production, and some of these persons are often unaware of the very existence of the class of "takers" for whom they work.

Of this group who have no direct contact with their exploiters are housewives who work only at home, and the means of exploiting them is clear only when we take into account the entire *system* of production.

Another reason subjugation is more complex with women is that sex has been injected, not only as an actuality, but it has been injected in theory far beyond its importance in reality, and there is a very pronounced tendency to seek the answer to woman's enslavement in a sex use.

It is in her status as a bearer and trainer of subject children, and as a worker, whose work is related to the creation of profits, that we will find the answer.

The following news item, from the *Los Angeles Times,* December 9, 1936, indicates woman's role as household worker, producing children for cheap labor and plenty of cheap soldiers for imperialistic armies:

Tokio, Dec. 9, (A.P.)—Baroness Shizue Ishimoto, editor of the Woman's Encyclopedia, shocked a large audience with the assertion Japanese women frequently were treated with no more respect than idiots or lunatics. . . .

Even the women of superior classes are not free, she declared, citing her own inability to get a passport to visit the United States, until her husband applies for it. "History reveals Japanese women occupied a much higher position in society before the advent of Buddhism (552 A.D.) in Japan. The present reactionary regime decrees women shall become household machines producing human bombs or to meet the demand for cheap labor."

We emphasize subject woman's role as a bearer of subject children and not just children because a great deal of confusion centers around the claim that woman's subordinate status is necessitated by a biological difference, that of childbearing.

For this reason we call attention, as sharply as we can, to the important difference, and the fact, that it is not just the bearing of children, but subject children, that is responsible for what biological basis exists for woman's subjugation.

If woman's subjugation arose simply from a biological cause, uncomplicated by a class reason, then it would be useless to try to change it because women will continue to bear children. But it is not the case. Women throughout history have borne children and there is proof that during part of the time they were everywhere socially and economically the equals of men.

Neither the woman question, nor the man question which arises from it, is primarily a sex question, but an economic question, although no part of their personal lives, including sex, has escaped being involved.

It is true that a group of women are held to sex enslavement. These sex serfs perform no useful work and are held to their social parasitism by most cruel methods, and are terribly oppressed both in their persons and in their civil liberties; but this group in actual numbers is small compared to the great majority of women.

Yet most of the things written about women of ancient and medieval times that attempt to trace woman's past life center around this very small group, or outstanding individuals of this type, and give practically no space to the important majority group of women who were performing socially useful work, yet were held to oppression.

Nor would a description of the working women of such historic eras alone have been sufficient, but an adequate account of their lives must also have included the conditions and method of work of the entire toiling and producing populations, with which their status was indissolubly linked.

On the other hand there is another tendency to seek the answer to woman's enslavement in the lower pay women wage workers, especially those in production, receive below that of men.

Women, according to this latter theory, are discriminated against so employers can work them cheaper. This situation exists, but it is not the cause of woman's subjugation, on the contrary, is an effect of it.

Women do not prefer to work for lower wages, nor are they unaware of the fact that they do work for less than men are paid. So some strong reason impels them; and it is the pressure of circumstances arising from the fact that all the discriminations they meet key back to a second-hand economic status applying to subject women.

A status on woman reaching her allotted economic sphere through marriage, taking a subordinate position to man, and as a consequence being labeled inferior to perpetuate her subjugation by turning persons against her, as well as causing her to conduct herself in the manner of a subordinate.

It should not surprise us greatly to see that business and professional women do not correctly estimate the importance of housewives' work and its relation to their problems, when we observe that ordinarily the housewife herself does not suspect that the key to the mystery has been so close to her. That it was as close as the dishes she washed and the meals she cooked; as close as the clothing she mended and washed and ironed.

She knew the importance to her family of this work she did, but she had no idea that it was important to persons whom she had never seen and would never see.

She perceived the importance of this work when applied to each of her neighbors, and to each individual household everywhere, but the significant thing she did not know was the importance of the work the totality of some 22 million non-wage-earning housewives in the United States did when taken in relation to the entire system of production.

Out of the 23 million married women listed in the 1930 U. S. Census, who have no earnings or income of their own, perhaps 22 million do all, or nearly all, of their own housework.

The Code of a Class

Men are trained to guard women, especially those of their immediate family, and to a considerable extent women not of their family, and women also receive training to act as guards of other women. But in the background of these men and women who function as guards is a group of mercenary propagandists, novelists, newspaper columnists, and speakers. They play skillfully on all the emotions of doubt, fear, and jealousy, and make sex feeling in a woman appear synonymous with irresponsibility in sex conduct.

When man helps perpetuate the fraud of woman's subjugation he is assisting in the perpetuation of a fraud against himself, for their interests are so inextricably bound up together that he cannot hurt or degrade her without hurting or degrading himself.

Notwithstanding this, support of enough men is secured to comprise the largest single group that assists in holding women to some form of segregation or isolation. The activities of such men are a great handicap to women, since they wield, because of their position, both personal and economic power over the individual woman, and their activities are felt at home and in general outside the home. Such a man becomes a sort of private policeman for the subjectors.

Theoretically, any man may attain an economic status that makes possible a life that includes a wife and children and a well-run household, where he can take his friends and associates. Successful in his business, work, or profession he supposedly has all the comforts and almost all the luxuries. In addition he supposedly has the opportunity for full sexual freedom with a large group of women maintained especially for this purpose, the no-rights group, toward whom he has no responsibility whatever.

There are many reasons why such a method of life is not now, and cannot be, a reality to the majority of men. In a country where the male population has not been decimated by war, the number of men and women average about the same. So how could every man of marriageable age have a wife to whom he had exclusive use and title, yet also have access to a group of women of marriageable age owned in common? Where would these women come from?

In order to have a group of public mates, many men would have to go without private mates. And this is exactly what we have today: a large group of men denied private wives, and restricted to occasional association with public women.

The would-be private wives of these men have been delivered up by the method for public use and thus instead of the exclusion of the use of their mates by other men, there is inclusion and no privacy.

Manifestly such a scheme, under any economy, would be inoperative for all men on account of numerical factors, and would therefore mean the victimization not only of that group of women set aside for public use, but the would-be husbands of these women deprived by this method of wives.

But the fraud involved in the promise of exclusive use, supplemented by unlimited promiscuity, goes even deeper than outlined above. The vast majority of the male population, made up of working- and middle-class men, have not and can never have, under the present economic arrangement, the means to maintain a family household and support as many persons as this plan involves.

As it is, the average man never has enough funds to satisfy the most elementary needs of his household: money for housing and foods; doctors and dentists and recreation of some sort; clothing for himself and the expense of at least partly keeping up with constantly changing fashions for his wife, and an unending supply of clothing for growing children. Pocket money is needed for the children to pay for entertainment for themselves and their associates on occasion.

At least some expenditure is necessary for books, magazines, lectures and shows, and an occasional dinner for friends. Gas, water, and electric bills, and taxes of some sort, must be paid and daily carfare and other transportation costs met. Besides, a certain amount of voluntary contributions to various funds is inescapable if he is to maintain the good will of those around him.

If his wife does not do all the cooking, house cleaning, laundry work, and shoe shining then these are further sources of expense which must be met and nothing has yet been set aside for old age, and no emergency fund has yet been created to take care of unexpected expense, due to accidents, death, or a loan to a friend or relative in distress, or for various other reasons which if not observed will lead to spending ahead, or going into debt.

None of these things are extravagant, but are necessary for even a modest amount of comfort and joy. They clamor for attention and first place and the average man cannot even meet them, so where is he going to acquire the money to live a double life?

He may occasionally associate with an ordinary prostitute. In most cases she will not want him, nor will he generally have any special affection for her. And he will have to do this associating in a hidden and surreptitious manner.

The grocer, the real estate owner, or landlord, and various tradesmen will want their money and will not look with favor upon his spending if their pay is not forthcoming. In the event he cannot pay them, they refuse service and he is faced with the clamorings of his household.

He may possibly associate with a woman whom he cares for and who wants him for himself, but everything will be in league and conspiring to make them miserable.

And he will find that life becomes a round of pretense and hiding if he goes out to collect his double-standard bride which propagandists of subjugation have led him to believe the present method of woman's subjection guarantees if he will support the method.

The April 1937 issue of the *American Mercury* makes it very clear from what economic strata males who really are to practice the double-standard are to be drawn. It selects an employer of labor, who has a wife and maintains a household, and associates with obvious prostitutes on whom he spends money, and with women whom he employs and whose labor he exploits, "like pretty Miss Tompkins, who does the filing" in the office.

For these women with whom the husband exercises his freedom of the double-standard, and are considered to be of a lower social class, there is expressed only contempt. But there is also only contempt for the virtuous wife who is of the same social class as her husband, and she is referred to as "chief concubine . . . the matrix of his legitimate heirs."

So, when all is said and done, and the whole theory is boiled down, we get back to the same old formula of Wieth-Knudsen's wherein men are to oppress women and then a small group of rich men is to oppress them all, including women of their own class.

The double-standard is fascism in the bedroom. Even owning-class women are treated with contempt and have a status of sex slaves, under the double-standard.

What is the most significant thing about the double-standard? Not that women are restricted, because every time a man has sex relations with a woman, a woman of necessity must have sex relations with a man.

No, restriction of the woman is not the main point, but *punishment for her participation,* which participation is unavoidable if he is to exercise his "right." If she is not already an outcast for similar reasons, such participation makes her one.

Now, on the contrary, it is not the code of a man to attack and punish a woman for having had intimate relations with him, or to set the sex vigilantes upon her and have her hounded into the ground. It is the code of a man to protect a woman from such hounding; to shield her.

The double-standard then is not the code of men, but the code of a class. And its asserted restriction of women's sex practices and its asserted nonrestriction of men's sex practices are only a part of this code and not the largest part either, but the framework on which to hang a whole contemptuous philosophy of women.

REBECCA PITTS

Women and Communism

In the case of female education the main stress should be laid on bodily training, and after that on development of character and last of all on intellect. But the one absolute aim of female education must be with a view to the future mother.

Hitler, *Mein Kempf*

Let German women breed warrior men and take pleasure in breeding them. Woman is to be neither comrade, nor beloved, but only mother.

Spengler, *Years of Decision*

The Soviet Union is the first state in the world in which the government authorities and the whole public are consciously working at the solution of the woman's question.

Clara Zetkin

There is a specific dilemma involved in being a woman, and few ever solve it triumphantly. In general it may be stated as a conflict between *sex* (with its biological needs and social demands) and our *humanity*. There are certain powers and possibilities latent, we assume, in every human being; they achieve clear expression, however, only in very highly conscious individuals. Important among these powers is a capacity for impersonal creative living—by which I mean no renunciation of private and personal experience, but a transcending of such experience: a conscious participation, that is, in the processes of nature and history. Without doubt this relation to the world is an important condition—a rich soil, so to speak—for the growth of genius. But in women there has existed (ever since the development of *property*) a tragic battle between the demands of personal life and this capacity for impersonal living.

The conflict has been sharpened rather than eradicated by our recent gains in freedom. Formerly only the woman of "genius" was aware of it—trying to reconcile her needs and duties as lover, wife, or mother with some urge toward a more conscious human development. But today the difficulty is widespread among cultivated middle-class women, who have a leisure and intellectual awareness not yet reached by working-class women. We have—theoretically—every political and cultural advantage open to our brothers. Nevertheless it is still bitterly hard for us—whether we are geniuses or not—to find a personal, emotional fulfillment and at the same time live a creative social life. The dilemma still exists.

As a result we have heard a good deal recently about the "biological tragedy" of being a woman. Women—so the theory goes—have at last been granted complete freedom to develop. If such a life were really natural, therefore, women would combine some socially creative work "outside the home" with the functions of sex and motherhood. But what has been the case? To begin with, there has been no great flowering of genius in any field, in spite of all hopeful prediction. Individual women may have achieved, perhaps, at no tragic personal cost, a degree of genuine eminence; but such women are exceptions. Ordinarily the division among us is bitterly distinct: on the one hand a growing army of restless, unsatisfied women—sometimes neurotic, often emotionally sterile—who do not, of course, admit that when they chose a "career" they chose ill; on the other hand an even greater army of those whose *real* talents—within the framework of marriage—are never used. So much for the bourgeois woman. For working-class women the problem has a more deadly simplicity. Most of them have no choice; they are forced into productive work "outside the home"—but with heart-breaking results for their own health and the welfare of their children. These facts make an impressive case for the theory that our sex is a disability: that "genius" is rare among us and a personal tragedy when it appears; that for the vast majority fullness of life is to be attained *only* in marriage; and that married women ought never to be obliged to work.

Now if we were content (in spite of our theoretical freedom) to accept the old restrictions, women could be regarded as unfit *by nature* for independent (productive) activity. But we do not accept this doom as inevitable. In spite of a personal cost that is often tragic, thousands of women demonstrate what a vital urge drives them—married or single—into creative effort: in science, the arts, or the professions. On such a large scale the very presence of desire indicates the presence of a capacity crying to be used. Quite as much as men, then, women need (for keen and conscious living) to do some kind of socially productive work.

As a matter of fact, we realize now that the root of our dilemma is *social* rather than biological. This becomes clear as we see women everywhere stirring in discontent. Even the relatively free middle-class woman is coming to suspect that it is her *status in society*—not her sex in itself—that makes it hard to lead a balanced life. But the factor of social tyranny is laid bare, in all its ugliness, only by the plight of women in the working class. These women, who are usually married, have been driven (not by a need for wider arenas but by a simple hunger) into socially productive work in industry. And what is the result? Savage discrimination against their sex, although often they work better than men; and a vast complex of conditions making it impossible for them to do their necessary work without endangering their health and their children's welfare. In their case two brutal facts are clear: that women today are an exploited group in society, and that the competitive wage-system offers them no hope of better things. The suffering of working-class women, then, arises from the fact that they are exploited as workers and doubly exploited as *women*. It is also true—and I shall make it clear—that, *for every woman in capitalist society,* the suffering, defeat, and frustration too often involved in womanhood arise wholly out of our enforced status in society.

The question of the status of women, all over the world today, is a bitterly living issue. Obviously this is so in Nazi Germany, where women are denied higher learning and degraded into breeders of cannon-fodder. Not so obviously but just as truly is it an issue for us. For in our so-called "emancipation" (as I shall indicate later) we cherish only the husk, not the reality, of a truly human freedom. But even this husk is not guaranteed forever. *When we drift toward Fascism, we drift inevitably toward a degradation of women.* The reason is clear when we analyze our real status today—historically tied up with property and the psychology of property.

The continued subjection of women was necessary to early capitalism: there was need of the primitive family to bring up children, to support the aged and the unemployed, to consolidate property, and to perform those tasks of "domestic" labor that society could not yet conveniently take over. Hence women were forcibly compelled to marriage as the one honest way to get a living. (In this way society merely italicized the treatment it had accorded women since the age of barbarism.)

At a certain stage in its growth, however, capitalist society had to take a progressive stand with regard to women. In the search for more workers to exploit, industry began to hire female labor. In spite of brutal discrimination against us (on the theory that we have no dependents) women have, nevertheless, gained a foothold in the economic order. Political "rights" and cultural "opportunities" reflect this basic economic fact; they are impressive—although theoretical—concessions. To this extent, then (and because a thriving capitalism found it profitable), women have been set free.

Now, however, capitalism is falling into decay: it no longer needs a large labor-army; it does, on the other hand, need to spread poverty—so that as many dependents as possible may live on the wretched pay of one worker. The political expression of this decaying economy is, of course, Fascism— a reactionary and brutal dictatorship set up solely to preserve the profit-system. It is quite logical that Fascism (in its effort to enlarge the circle of one worker's dependents) should reverse history with regard to the status of women. Woman as cook, domestic toiler without pay, breeder of Fascist Storm Troopers: that is the new ideal, and signs of its approach are not wanting even in this country. It is no longer profitable for capitalism that women should be free; as the system decays, then, we must lose—like the workers—our hard-won rights.

In the light of these facts, it is now possible to define the real position of women under capitalism. And the definition is not pleasant. In spite of political "rights," cultural "opportunities," and every other pleasant fiction about equality we delude ourselves with, one fact emerges clearly. Capitalist society has granted us a relative liberty for precisely the same reason that it "freed" the Negro slaves. In other words, women *constitute a reserve labor-army maintained in the interests of the employers.* So that all labor may sell itself cheaply in the open market, there must be some who are discriminated against and forced to sell themselves much too cheaply. In industry there are two such groups: Negroes—and women; and this basic discrimination is reflected also in the professions. Capitalist society could free neither women nor Negroes until it became *profitable* to free them. And as soon as a dying profit-system finds it more profitable to degrade us to our former position (for reasons I suggested in the preceding paragraph), we shall lose, as in Germany, our relative and illusory liberty.

We find ourselves thus bound to an evolving capitalism because of one simple fact: since the beginning of history *women have been degraded and oppressed.* Even folk-lore and fable reflect that in the days of the heroes women were subject to men. It would seem, therefore, that a good reason for discrimination is given by our innate "inferiority." Bourgeois law-givers could enjoy, in fact, a glow of generosity in liberating us, while all the time maintaining the old oppression in all important respects. Of course the process has worked out without reference to the will or desire of individuals; but the interests of capitalism have been well served by our historic status as inferiors.

Women were not always oppressed, however, as the evidence of anthropology reveals. In primitive times, and, indeed, until shortly before the dissolution of tribal communities, women were free, productive members of the group. But during the late Neolithic period (the Middle Status of Barbarism, as Lewis H. Morgan called it) they were enslaved. It is very interesting and important to notice that women lost their liberty precisely when primitive communal life broke down and *private property* developed. Only then was the ancient "mother-right" destroyed.

This primitive dignity of woman—this mother-right—was rooted in the collective form of barbaric society. The wholly promiscuous herd-family of savagery had evolved into the *tribe* with its minor sub-division, the *clan.* The tribe was a "political" unit; the clan (really an enlarged family) was an economic unit, resting upon an absolute community of property. Within the clan all were considered brothers and sisters: hence, to avoid incest, one had to marry someone from another clan in the tribe; and, by an equally severe rule, no property could be taken out of the clan. Inevitably, according to such rules, there were only two alternatives: to reckon descent through the mothers and expel men from the clan when they married; or to reckon descent from the fathers and expel women upon marriage. Now in this early communal life both men and women were free; they all held their property in common; and they all shared in the labor of the clan. No one, in other words, had any motive for constraining another; neither men nor women had anything to gain or lose. Naturally, therefore, they reckoned descent through the mothers, for the obvious reason that maternity cannot be doubted. (So when a man married, he entered his wife's clan.) A few peoples—for example the Lycians, whom Herodotus mentions—persisted in this custom after the beginning of history; and to this day there are traces of it in many primitive tribes.

But the development of agriculture put an end to the mother-right nearly everywhere. Increased wealth brought more leisure and a division of labor; and the upshot was that the *men* came into possession of farm-tools and means of production. At the same time the various clansmen (who had formerly hunted, or tended herds, in common) began to acquire their own plots of ground. Thus by slow degrees *private property* arose, and the economic basis for clan-life was undermined. In many parts of the world, however, (for instance, Rome), the clan was retained as a means of reckoning descent, but with one very significant change. Since property now belonged to the man, the *father-right* was set up so that his wealth could be handed down to his own heirs; and—in order that the children be unquestionably his—he forced upon his wife the command of absolute faithfulness. In this way women were slowly degraded—from a position of freedom and productivity in the community to a completely subject role. Of course they did not suffer this shame without resistance; the legend of the Amazons has a basis in fact. But they were doomed to defeat: the long upward spiral of conscious history had begun; and only by means of property and class-division could a part of human energy be released for progress. Through the evolution of private property, therefore, woman herself became the property of man: from an end in herself she became a sexual commodity and a means to an end.*

Today all women under capitalism bear the marks of this servitude in their lives. It is hard for us to be clear about this; the forces that mold us

---

*The reader is referred to: Bebel, *Women under Socialism,* chap. 1. Fannina Halle, *Woman in Soviet Russia,* chap. 1. Friedrich Engels, *The Origin of the Family.*

are too subtle and pervasive. It is not merely a matter of economic discrimination; although that alone is bitter. Equally, in our so-called "feminine" reactions to the world, in our frustrations and baffled struggle, in our failure to attain genius—we are stifled by the old historic bondage. Not one of us has reached (nor *can,* conditioned as we are) the stature that ought to have been ours. For if a man or woman is to develop his capacities to the full, he must take his part in the two chief functions of mankind: *work* and *sex.* The tragedy of woman, however, is that society has denied her a free creative part in the world's work; and that as a result even sex, about which her life has centered, has been warped for her and unnaturally twisted.

In the communal life of barbarism women shared, as free individuals, the productive work of the clan. There is abundant anthropological evidence that the focal values of that time lay in the group, not the individual; that all early culture arose out of *group* needs—whether statue of Fertility, spring rite for adolescents, or majestic animal fresco in the caves of Altamira. Un-self-conscious, impersonal as Nature is impersonal, these early peoples must have felt an organic unity with the world that civilized men have not recaptured. Up to a certain point their growing cultural complexity (their richer productive forces) merely made life more human and more conscious. In these last stages of pre-history, then, *work* must have had a very great dignity and importance for every person in the clan. It was man acting upon his environment—creating, discovering, growing— and not only for himself but for the group. In this creative activity women shared to the full.

With the further development of tools and agriculture, however, and the rise of private property, all this was changed. Women were gradually degraded, imprisoned in the "women's quarters," and denied all participation in community life. And not only *women* were enslaved, of course, but great masses of toilers who had lost out in the scramble for wealth. Work—for the few—became personal, ambitious, acquisitive; for the masses—meaningless drudgery.

Now for happiness in work, people need to feel that what they toil at has some value and meaning beyond a mere subsistence. In actual practice only society can confer this value upon anything; that is, we need to feel our work (even if it is revolt) as integral to the social process. No doubt many medieval craftsmen shared this happiness—taking pride in their contribution to the community and in an honest job well done. Genius itself (burning with an intense flame) is only this same double passion: a love of one's craft and an imaginative sense of larger wholes. But since the beginning of history women have been shut off from a vital contact with society. Only with capitalism have we entered a wider arena; and yet, we are not free. Nor do the chaotic, egoistic values of capitalism permit—to most people—any real happiness in work. With the rise of property and class society, then, women were robbed of their dignity as productive workers.

But this was not all. At the same time, and in the same way, women were robbed of their *sexual* dignity. Sex may be a very personal matter, but our reactions are shaped by the social psychology about us; and this psychology, of course, reflects the basic economic structure of the period. Under primitive communism the sexes were equal, all members of the clan were productive workers, and value resided not in the atomic person but in the organic group. In a very real sense the individual found his happiness and liberty in the communal whole. This absence of egocentric aims must have deeply colored their attitude toward sex—rendering it less personal than it is today, and free of jealous obsessions. With the rise of private property, however, there was a great change. The seizure of economic goods by the individual gave rise inevitably to conflicting aims and a psychology of *power*. In man's fight to amass wealth and give it to his legitimate heirs, he compelled woman to a faithfulness based not on desire but on necessity. No longer was mating a free choice of equals; man had come to regard woman as his own property, made for his personal use and pleasure.

Throughout history, then, women were *owned*—and kept at home—until factories needed their labor. Today, however, the property-theory is absurd among the working classes; too often the woman—not her husband—feeds the family. It is quite true, however, that even among the middle classes a new woman is emerging—and a more comradely ideal of marriage. But we need not delude ourselves. The historic view that women are property still fosters the myth of our "inferiority"—employed so usefully today in unfair discrimination against us. And now with the decline of capitalism, as Fascism invokes again our old servility, we see clearly that we are still used as property.

Upon this view of women, indeed, bourgeois society founds its whole theory of marriage: that in return for the use of her body (to give him pleasure and to breed his children) a man is obliged to support his wife at home. (As I have pointed out, the theory seems not to operate among working-class people. But the bourgeois woman is a sexual commodity; and to be respectable her husband must demonstrate his ability to pay for her.) Hence the opposition even yet between marriage and a "career," which in practice condemns most wives to domestic slavery. And from the same theory of purchase stems the man's right to woo, to select, to impose his own taste upon women who bid for his approval.

This view of marriage is enforced by three factors—deriving from a competitive system. First, for most men an early marriage is impossible. Second, by unfair discrimination society renders productive work unattractive in itself to a majority of women. Third, for economic reasons there are always more women than men who are eligible for marriage. It is impossible to overestimate the pain and injustice inflicted upon women by these circumstances. The economic necessity for late marriage implies (if not prostitution) the brief liaison; and no matter how we glorify or become used to such compromise affairs, they have tragic shortcomings. The fact that women are discouraged by unfair discrimination, moreover, means that most of them look forward to *marriage* rather than *work* as the principal end in life. And the fact that marriageable women greatly outnumber the men who can marry means simply this: that from early youth the competition for male favor is fierce and of primary importance. This implies for every woman an intense preoccupation with sex.

But sex itself—in the civilized world—has been twisted into an ugly mockery of conscious living. Except for a mature minority, human sexual behavior is based largely upon egotism, self-worship, and personal conquest. With the rise of private property, value shifted from the *group* to the *individual*—where it has stayed ever since. Of course barbaric society was crude and simple, and evolution could occur only by means of this development; but at the same time a violent dislocation took place in human personality. The sex-relation was altered; the element of autocratic preference on the man's part, and submission on the woman's had been introduced. Upon a psychology of power and egotism, therefore, civilized man has built his vast complex of attitudes on sex and love. *Sex* has been transformed into *sexuality;* from an impersonal end (participation in life) it has become a personal means. Sometimes, transmuted by an elaborate ritual of romance, this ego-sexuality becomes the "in love" state so characteristic of our culture: naively greedy in popular songs and screen plays; subtly disguised in the lamentations of a Byron or De Musset. Whether "in love" or not, however, each sexual partner desires in the other the mirror and gratifications of his own self-love. So widespread is this personalism that we crown it with social approval and call it "normal."

If women are to escape celibacy, therefore, they must play incessantly and with passion at this game of conquest. For a man, sex may be a means to personal pleasure; but by virtue of his power to choose a woman when he will, he can forget this personalism and become absorbed in larger interests. For women, however, there is no such easy solution. At all times—since husbands are won by clever angling—women must be "alluring." Confronted by an imperious sexual need (often complicated by economic need) no wonder the majority find work to be secondary, and ambition hollow.

Woman under capitalism, therefore, finds herself not only oppressed as a worker, but kept (by means of this basic tyranny) in a position of *sexual* servility as well. Daily she is told, of course, that she is the equal of the male; but daily the quiet, inexorable force of social reality shapes her tragic dilemma. If she is to escape celibacy and lead a "normal" life, she is forced, in most cases, into a definite pattern. To get a husband (even lovers, even admirers) she must please the dominant male—"normally" an undeveloped egotist who regards her as a means to his own pleasure. It becomes her business, therefore, to arouse desire; to play by means of sex-allurement, dress, and personal charm upon male ego-sexuality. Instead of being a rounded, creative personality she is warped and twisted (by this overemphasis upon sex) into a creature who really is inferior to man. Vain, spiteful, personal, petty: so often these epithets are well deserved. It is proof of a strong urge in woman that so many really do—in spite of this terrific pressure from bourgeois society—lead creative lifes.

From even so brief a scrutiny, we see that the tragedy of womanhood is not biological at all—but *social*. To begin with, we are confronted by a false and warped choice between marriage and work. The mother who leaves six children to work in a factory is no exception. She has been forced by need and exploitation; her work is drudgery and her family life precarious. The young middle-class wife who ekes out her husband's income with her own is likewise no exception. For in her case, too, the work has neither meaning nor independent integrity: it is something to do one season and drop the next. *The fact remains that most women are unable to marry, to have children, and still pursue any absorbing, satisfying work.* This is partly a result of discrimination; more frequently, however, it is the consequence of their early conditioning that women are literally ruined for such work. But the necessity for such a choice is vicious and unnatural—as a growing rebellion among women indicates.

Even more vicious than the fact of choice, however, are the alternatives themselves. If a woman prefers marriage she is driven, in most cases, to be "normal" with a vengeance; to become absorbed, that is, in a highly personal, self-regarding manipulation of sex. But if her urge to work is deep and strong, she is confronted by an even more deadly alternative. Discrimination is very real, for one thing, against married women; and for the right to persistent, sustained effort in science or the professions a woman must almost take a vow of celibacy. As a result of discrimination, therefore, and the difficulties of celibacy, many talented women are denied real satisfaction in their work. Just as the poison of individualism has withered sex into sexuality, so the poisons of unfair competition, anxiety, and denial of natural instinct warp and shrivel the creative urge.

From the beginning of history, then, society has denied to women the reality of life. From the experience of those who have learned to live consciously, we can understand what life *ought to be:* a conscious cooperation with—participation in—the process of universal growth; not any infantile "happiness" or "security," but a great awareness of the world and the will to labor for the unfolding of its possibilities. But to live at such a level the individual must be free. His experience of sex cannot halt at self-adulating romance or sensuality; it must mature into an identification with life. His productive labor cannot remain mere drudgery; it must be integrated in some real way with the labor of society—so that he feels it to have value and dignity. It is unnecessary to point out that although most men have never been able to reach this level, they have had far more chance than women have had to do so.

Denied this reality of conscious living, women have, broadly speaking, adjusted themselves to their dilemma in two ways: by acquiescing in their socially imposed fate they have become "normal" or "feminine"; by rebelling against it they have substituted some kind of more obvious compensation. It is important to realize, however, that the "normal" adjustment is just as false—just as empty a shadow of reality—as any of the varieties of rebellion. The "normal" is approved for purely statistical reasons; but the term carries no implication whatever of the *natural* or organically *right*. It is as much a mockery of life for woman to be vain, petty, and personalistic, as for her to erect any other system of replacement.

A sturdy minority, indeed, *have* rebelled in one way or another—repudiating with pain or violence this servile necessity to "please." Of course we cannot guess how many wives have instinctively desired a richer and more honest relation with their husbands; or how many (failing, perhaps, to hold their men) made motherhood and religion compensate for the loss. And it would be equally hard to estimate how many women— married or single—have dashed themselves into fanatical reform movements because their desire for creative work had been frustrated. Modern psychology, however, is very suggestive on these points.

But a more intense (although unconscious) repudiation of social tyranny takes place in the nightmare pain of the neurotic. In both men and women this conflict arises when a highly sensitive personality fails to become organically adjusted to the world. Only a rare minority, of course, ever do attain any wholeness, any depth, any reality of experience; but the "normal" person accepts a set of facile substitutes, a shallow pasteboard imitation of organic life. From this falsity the neurotic recoils with horror—his fear of life arising from a sense of its mocking emptiness, and from his own failure to reach a three-dimensional *participation* therein. Thus painfully aware that life is slipping by, he clutches at shadows and symbols and weird replacements of his own; all the while, of course, cutting himself off the more sharply from reality. Now it is the custom to deal with neurosis and insanity as if they were isolated cases; as if, in short, the disorder arose in the individual and could be healed there. Nothing could be farther from the truth; it is *society* which thrusts mental anguish upon so many. By denying to human beings a valid sense of the dignity and meaning of their toil, society creates in sensitive people a feeling of frustration and strain. And by fostering (on a basis of economic individualism) a collective psychology of shallow cruelty and warped display, society destroys our power to find creative self-realization in sex. And of course economic worry is a source of terrible tension. In the light of these facts, we need not be surprised that a great majority of neurotics are women.

Whether "normal" or neurotic, however (and in spite of the fact that a few women can transcend these limitations), most of us stagger today under a crushing inner burden imposed not by nature, but by the social order.

By now it should be clear to every woman that *within class society* she has nothing to expect but a return to slavery. Women were enslaved to begin with by the rise of property and class divisions, and they have been regarded ever since as inferiors and sexual commodities. Our "liberty" today is not true freedom: freedom hardly exists, in class society, even for many men; and I have labored to show the added burdens (economic, sexual, and psychological) which are thrust upon women. Our emancipation is merely the right to work—if we can—thereby driving down *all* wages for the fat profit of the owners. From this one fact it is plain that while the profit-system endures women cannot be free: we are too useful in a servile position. With their usual bluntness the Nazis have made this brutally clear.

Only when exploitation, therefore, is destroyed—and the psychology of power and profit—can women be free. We all need to see this: the oppressed industrial worker, to be sure; but also the professional woman, the ambitious college girl, the wife who has stifled her native talents in domestic slavery. For in a classless society—a democracy of free workers—we shall have for the first time the conditions for a truly human development. Only Communism offers woman the right to be an *independent productive worker:* recognizing that sex and parenthood are important for women and men alike; but that while they *are* important they do not fill every need nor exercise every capacity. Only Communism, likewise, offers woman another right (so closely related to that of independent work): the right to a freer, more natural sex happiness.

In the Soviet Union we already find proof that to liberate woman as worker means to liberate her also as *sexual being.* For since women can enter any work they choose (except the heaviest physical labor) and are not discriminated against in any way, no economic need can turn marriage for them into a means instead of an end. And since even very young people can be self-supporting, they do not need to endure the pain and frustration of chastity, or the brief pathos of a clandestine affair. An early marriage may prove unstable, but it can be decently dissolved; meanwhile the very naturalness and ease with which it has been formed are safeguards against unhealthy obsessions. And as for the strictly "biological" problem of womanhood—adequate contraceptive aid, so that when a child comes it is *wanted;* four months' leave from work, with pay, for the mother; and nurseries where young children are cared for during working hours: these provisions *by society* are a sane solution. Of course all these factors make for a freedom and honesty in sexual matters (and therefore a new happiness for women) that we merely dream of under capitalism.

We have reason to hope, however, for an even deeper change—under Communism—in our attitude toward sex: a change arising from the basic revolution in property relations. I have already hinted at the unity of the barbaric clan: its simple, organic sense of communal interests that transcend those of the individual. This unity was based on a common ownership of productive goods and was therefore shattered with the rise of private property. Now, after a history of conflict and bloody greed, humanity returns (but on a higher, more conscious level) to *another* communal ownership of wealth. When no individual—no class—can exploit another; when all resources are owned by society, the very idea of private interest will disappear. Rid of this age-old mental burden (like insanity dividing man from man) people can live natural lives again. It will no longer be reserved for saints and sages to experience the unity of life; every member of society will find his own happiness in serving a truly human whole. In such a world sex, too, must inevitably take on new meaning.

In recent years there have been many prophets of a sexual "transvaluation of values." Of these D. H. Lawrence was undoubtedly the greatest— by virtue of the loathing he poured upon a petty generation; and by virtue of his terrible vision of sex itself, as an *impersonal plunging into life,* a rebirth into the natural order. Instinctively he knew that beneath the experience of civilized men lies the great perversion: that in seeking "love" (no less than pleasure) we use life for personalistic ends. But he could not understand the emergence of *mind* as a creative force, so he rejected it; and he failed to see that men are social beings as well as biological. In his effort, therefore, to avoid ego-sexuality he sought identification with "Nature" in a mindless, sensual darkness; but such a quest for reality was only a more strenuous form of the very perversion he wished to escape. This was inevitable, since in rejecting mind and society he came to Nature as a naked atom, looking for his own salvation. Thus his fate is a paradox: he felt the stale horror in the property-perversion of sex; and yet throughout his work we find prophetic hints of the cruelty and lust of Fascism. The men of the future will not follow Lawrence in his rejection of mind and society; they will, on the contrary, see Nature risen to supreme self-consciousness *in the human community*. But will they not find in sex (as he confusedly prefigured) a means of identification with the natural order? Not personal pleasure; certainly nothing mystical; but an experience that is natural and deeply real. This can come, however, only when the economic and psychological foundations have been laid. And any such revolution in sexual attitudes cannot fail to affect women (since they have been slaves, historically, of sex) far more than men.

Today, of course, it is impossible to prophesy in detail—to say that women will be like this or that in a classless society. An attempt at any such forecast would be an attempt to make a blueprint for one phase of the future—a most un-Marxian procedure. It is even impossible to state categorically that women are not inferior to men. From a social point of view, however, these questions are merely speculative: the one essential thing now is to give every human being, regardless of race or sex, the chance to develop freely, to grow, to live to the limit of his capacity. And from the foregoing analysis it is clear that in class society every women bears a heavy load of disabilities imposed by that society: a burden of economic discrimination, psychological strain, and sexual inferiority, all of which are a wholly adequate explanation for our apparent failures in the field of productive work. Only in a classless society, then, only under Communism, can we free ourselves as workers and as women. Meanwhile the Soviet Union gives embryonic hints of the future: hints of rich growth in personality, and socialist virtues—courage, tenacity, self-subordination—which ennoble the new woman as well as the new man.

GRACE HUTCHINS

Women under Capitalism

Freedom. What do the women of the middle and upper classes mean when they speak of freedom and equal opportunity with men? They mean freedom to enjoy the rights of property and the rights of citizenship on an equality with men. They mean "getting the opportunity to do the interesting and important work at any scale of pay." They mean freedom to pursue a career, to do creative work, to study for any one of the professions they may choose and to practice that profession without being hindered by sex discrimination. Much of this freedom has already been won by women of the privileged class. Legal disabilities and disqualifications have for the most part been removed in the United States. Most of the institutions of higher education are now open to women. The professions have yielded a grudging recognition of women's intelligence and ability and achievements. An Amelia Earhart flies alone across the Atlantic; a Madame Curie discovers radium; and their success is hailed as a remarkable achievement or as an outstanding contribution to the sum of human knowledge.

In the privileged groups mothers have been able to hire some one to help in the housework at home; they have had information on how to space and limit the number of their children; they have parked the smaller children in private nursery schools or employed a mother's helper or a nursery governess, and thus have been almost as free as single women to work outside the home without neglect of the house or children. In this special group of the middle and upper classes, married and single women alike have had the opportunity to do creative and interesting work, to write books and articles on every imaginable subject; to do original, scientific research; to hold responsible positions in the business and professional worlds.

But for women of the working class in capitalist society, this freedom of women in the comfortable middle classes is a mockery. Working women have no such freedoom. While still in their teens, they are forced to work long hours in the mills, in domestic service, or in the fields, in order to add a few dollars to the meager family income. When married, they are bound down by the labor of the house and the kitchen, "that little penitentiary," and then by the care of children. Throughout their lives they are exploited, haunted by the fear of unemployment, of illness, of old age, of destitution. A girl earning twelve dollars a week or less in a mill or shop has about as much "freedom" and "opportunity" as a rose-bush in a desert of sand. . . .

STATUS OF WOMEN UNDER MODERN CAPITALISM

Karl Marx and Friedrich Engels were the first scientific thinkers to examine the Industrial Revolution and the development of modern capitalism with its effects upon the workers from the viewpoint of the working class. They included in their analysis the first basic treatment of women's status under capitalism and their statements are as true today as when they were made some eighty years ago. It remained for Lenin and the Soviet Union to point the way with inescapable clearness toward the true freedom of women in a socialist society.

Already in 1848, Marx and Engels had seen that capitalism would introduce increasing numbers of women into the process of production. They wrote in the *Communist Manifesto:*

> The less the skill and exertion of strength implied in manual labor, in other words, the more modern industry develops, the more is the labor of men superseded by that of woman. Differences of age and sex have no longer any distinctive social validity for the working class. All are instruments of labor, more or less expensive to use, according to their age and sex.

Since machines do not usually require heavy work, women and children could be used by the capitalists and could be paid lower wages than men workers were supposed to receive, thus making more profits for the owners of the machines. Marx in the first volume of *Capital,* published in 1867, explains more fully the reasons for this use of women and children in the mills and shops:

> The labor of women and children was, therefore, the first thing sought for by the capitalists who used machinery. This mighty substitute for work and workers speedily transformed itself into a means for increasing the number of wage workers by enlisting all the members of the working class family, without distinction of sex or age, to bring them under the direct sway of capital. . . .
> To buy the labor power of a family of four workers may perhaps cost more than it formerly cost to buy the labor power of the head of the family; but the purchaser buys four working days in place of one, and the price falls in proportion to the excess of the surplus labor of four over the surplus labor of

one. In order that the family may live, four persons must now not merely work, but supply surplus labor for capital.

But it costs more in cash for the worker's family to live under modern capitalism, since many of the things formerly made at home must now be bought outside. This means an increased expenditure of money, in order to buy at the shop the food and the other things needed for the family. The cost of maintaining the working class family thus increases.

Marx was the first to point out that with all the brutality of modern capitalism in its treatment of women workers—underpaid, exploited, ruined in health and then cast out on the scrap heap of unemployment and old age—yet modern capitalism itself has created the conditions for women's final freedom. By drawing increasing millions of women and girls into social production it has opened the way for a wider and fuller life for women which, however, can never be secured under capitalism. . . .

ECONOMIC BASIS OF WOMEN'S SUBJECTION

The working-class housewife is supposedly dependent upon her husband's earnings; yet if he has a job at all his wages are totally insufficient to provide for a family's needs. The wife and mother has the daily struggle to make ends meet. Her days are full of a great burden of work; as cook, dishwasher, scrub-woman, laundress, chambermaid, seamstress, errand girl, and nurse, to say nothing of the skilled profession of a mother with little children. Almost a dozen trades, skilled, semi-skilled, and unskilled, are represented in the housewife's work. She must also be ready to serve her husband whenever he wishes to use her. She is subordinate because she has no money of her own. Of these unpaid housewives there are still 23,000,000 in the United States, according to Wm. M. Steuart, director of the Census Bureau.

Nor does the working woman who goes out to earn her living in capitalist industry find that her earnings bring her freedom and equality with men. The employer can buy a woman's labor power at even less than a man's, and the woman therefore remains subordinate. The capitalist class is of course interested in buying women's labor power at the lowest possible price and therefore wishes to keep the masses of working women in this position of submission.

Propaganda to this effect is seen everywhere in the capitalist world, in advertisements, in the daily press, in the schools and churches, on the radio, and in the "talkies." Take, for example, a hundred advertisements in the press or on the billboards and see what a high percentage of such "ads" are addressed to women as subordinate to men, simply as vehicles of sex charm, as if their sole end and aim in life should be to attract and please the man.

Kept on unskilled or semi-skilled jobs, the girl worker still has less chance than the boy to be a machinist, for example, or to learn any one of the more skilled trades. She is expected to stay in the "inferior," less well-paid occupations and every influence is against her earning more. The man who is her fellow-worker has been taught by boss class propaganda since his earliest childhood to regard girls as less important than boys and he does not usually encourage the girl to learn a more skilled job. It is only as he becomes class conscious in the workers' own movement that he recognizes the interests of all workers, men and women, white and Negro, as bound up together.

Petty bosses, superintendents, and capitalists insist upon women's subordination in order to forestall the demand for equal pay for equal work. It is a common practice to fire men workers and hire women for the same work at lower pay, and so the myth of women's inferiority is kept alive. Whether the boss is a factory foreman, a restaurant manager, an office executive, or a hospital physician, his girl worker, his waitress, his typist, or his trained nurse must be kept subordinate.

American Federation of Labor officials have been as ready as the employers to preach and teach women's subjection. Jealous of women's coming into the more skilled trades to take men's jobs, these officials of the craft unions have steadily opposed equal opportunity for girls and have established restrictions against taking women into the A. F. of L. unions on any equal basis.

Women workers themselves react to this propaganda in different ways. Often it has been effective in creating a submissive attitude on the part of girl workers who have been too docile to revolt against conditions. Taught to expect marriage and motherhood as a sufficient life work in itself, girls have thought of the outside jobs as temporary and have usually been less ready than men workers to organize and demand wage increases. Many girls have what might be called an "inferiority complex" as the result of the capitalists' teaching and it is only as they have been made bold in strikes or in other struggles of the workers' movement that they overcome this sense of inferiority to men and take their place in the ranks of active workers, striving to improve their conditions.

As a result of the ruling-class propaganda, among some of the men workers who should know that their strength lies in working-class solidarity, there still exists an attitude of superiority toward women workers. And just as white workers may not recognize in themselves the "white chauvinism" toward Negro workers which is felt keenly by Negroes, so also the men workers may not recognize in themselves their attitude toward women. The result is that women have not been encouraged to take positions of leadership and the workers' movement has been weakest on the very front where it might be strongest—among the masses of unskilled and semi-skilled women workers. When once aroused to class consciousness and to the possibilities of organization women have proved themselves among the best and most active fighters in the labor struggle.

Every word that is said about the exploitation of white American-born women workers is doubly true for Negro and foreign-born women of the working class. White women's wages are lower than men's, but Negro women's wages are lowest of all. They are discriminated against in every imaginable way and the discrimination is by no means confined to the southern states. Negroes everywhere have been forced to submit to the white ruling class. Jim-crowism runs through every phase of capitalist society in every part of the United States. . . .

Capitalism depends for its very existence on a large body of surplus labor power ready to be bought at the lowest possible price. It is therefore to the interests of employers to keep these Negro and foreign-born women workers in a condition of "inferiority" ready to underbid white workers, just as it is to the interests of employers to keep women to underbid men in the labor market. One group of workers is played off against another group—foreign-born against American, Negro against white, women against men. So long as the boss can point to a body of workers ready to work for still lower wages, he has the whiphand over his employees. . . .

IN THE CRISIS

Since the crash of 1929, women of the working class have suffered from the effects of unemployment even more intensely than men workers. This crisis of 1930–33, the greatest crisis in the whole history of capitalism, has driven an ever greater number of mothers, with little children at home, out into the labor market in an effort to find work and thus replace the men breadwinners, now jobless. If the man has had part-time work for a day or two during the week, the women has tried to earn a few dollars to make up at least a small part of what the family formerly had for the week's expenses.

Unemployment means evictions, breaking up of homes, undernourishment, starvation, and all these results destroy the very life of working-class women. Mothers have asked desperately if some way cannot possibly be found to keep their children in the home with their mother and father. Whole families are barely existing in shanty-towns on the city dumps, feeding themselves only from garbage pails. The general press has presented plenty of evidence to prove that undernourishment to the point of starvation exists in every industrial center of the world's richest country. . . .

These years of crisis have merely intensified the suffering of working-class women under capitalism. Even in times of so-called "prosperity," the total income of a working-class family is barely enough to provide for the most immediate needs of life, and the burden of work, of trying to get food enough for the children, falls with deadly effect on the woman, making her old before she is middle-aged, breaking her health and her spirit. The worker's family cannot save to meet the unemployment, illness, and old age that are sure to come. Never under capitalism can a working woman find adequate social provision for her needs, for maternity, for the proper care of the children, or for her own protection and health at home and at work.

Revolt is beginning. Spontaneous strikes of industrial women workers against wage cuts and speed-up have been followed by rent strikes and bread strikes of working-class tenants and housewives. Farm women and agricultural workers have engaged in a series of notable struggles. Negro women have shown what solidarity between Negro and white workers can accomplish.

This story of organization and struggle must be told . . . of women workers at home and on the farms, in domestic service, in offices, stores, hospitals and restaurants, and in factories; how many there are and what they are doing, how the work affects their health, what they earn; their grievances, their demands, their aspirations for a classless society; the story of their struggles—their defeats and their victories. . . .

The Double Burden

"Fine to have a rest yesterday, wasn't it?"

It was Monday morning and we were toiling up the long flight of wooden stairs in the cigar factory. I looked at the two workers beside me and saw they did not look at all rested. I had spent a good part of the day, Sunday, in bed, trying to get over the effects of fifty-four hours' work the week before.

"Rest!" One of them looked at me with amazement. "Sunday's the only day I have to do all the washing and cleaning and cooking up for the week."

"You said it," the second one added. "I was s'tired this morning I couldn't hardly get up at all."

Each had a husband and children at home and all the housecleaning, cooking, laundry work, and marketing to do for a household of five or six, in addition to a nine-hour day in the cigar plant every day except Sunday.

Most of the two hundred women in the cigar-rolling department, where I worked, had some responsibilities before and after the day's work. It was supposedly a nine-hour day, but really longer, since we came into the plant at 7:15 A.M., and seldom got out before 5:45 P.M., with three-quarters of an hour out for lunch eaten right there at our benches. It was winter, barely light when we went into the factory in the morning and dark when we came out at night. The sun might as well never have shone for all we saw of it through the small dirty windows of the plant.

Yet many a woman worker there had already done at least an hour's work, usually more, preparing the breakfast, getting the children up and ready for school or day nursery and the beds made before she came to the factory. When she washed up, ready to leave the plant at night, each one was planning what she would buy on the way home to cook for supper, and it would be at least 7:00 P.M. before she could have the food ready. She would compare notes with neighboring workers as to what the husband liked to have cooked for supper.

"My man likes meat every night and it's slow to cook. I cook up a roast on Sunday and it lasts a few days." This was before the crisis when most workers' families were still able to have meat.

Only the young unmarried girl who had a mother at home to cook for her had not, as yet, this double burden. If the worker had children—and most of them had several—it was late in the evening before she had finished getting the children to bed, washing the dishes, and doing the most necessary cleaning and mending.

"Tired. I'm always tired. Too tired to hear the alarm clock go off at five o'clock in the morning." That is the way the women themselves express it.

CHILDREN OF WORKING MOTHERS

From the time the young working-class girl is first married, she has the problem of having children whether she wants them or not, because she has no way of getting the information that is known to practically every woman of the middle and upper classes—on how to limit the number of children. To the parents who can afford a private physician the information on birth control is given as a matter of course. But according to the present federal law, passed in 1873, it is illegal to give any information on birth control, and the violator of the law is subject to imprisonment for five years or a fine of from $2,000 to $2,500 or both imprisonment and fine. It is illegal to send information or supplies through the mails or by express or to import any article designed to prevent conception.

The effect upon the working class of this cruel class legislation may be seen in letters from workers, desperate at the thought of another baby coming. Each year from 7,000 to 10,000 such letters as these are received by the American Birth Control League from mothers and fathers seeking the information they need:

> My husband has been out of work for over a year and no help is in sight. I am 31 years old, have a girl of 11 and a boy of 8. I can't afford more children. I have practiced homemade methods to no use, and I average at least two abortions a year, which I do for myself, and which are ruining my health. I asked the Health Bureau in our city what to do, but so far find no place to get information.

And from a father:

> A year ago I lost my job because the man I was working for failed in business. I've had no steady work since and on top of all the rest of the troubles, my wife has had an abortion and is expecting a baby now. We got scared of another abortion, so we went through with it this time. I've tried hard to find out about birth control, but people put you off with stuff that's no good, and where I live they say it's against the law. I bet my boss who laid me off gets it all right from his private doctor and his wife doesn't have to go through such hard times. . . . It gets one sort of upset to see something you need so badly held back for the rich.

There are 145 birth control clinics operating in the United States (1933), but their work is still limited by many restrictions. The New York clinics turn away thousands of applications for information each year, because the New York law forbids the giving of information except where further motherhood would endanger the health of the mother. The Pittsburgh birth control clinic found that about three-quarters of the 450 women applying for information in the year lived in overcrowded quarters. Half their husbands were jobless and another 20 percent were working only part-time. One family of fifteen lived in four rooms.

Workers do not expect that information on safe methods of birth control will end unemployment or end any other basic evil of the capitalist system, but they have the right to such knowledge that they may space the period between the births of children in consideration of the mother's health, the family income, and the future welfare of the children. As one mother exclaimed, after having eight miscarriages:

"Why in the name of heaven can't they tell us so we won't slip into the grave before our babies are weaned!"

Ten thousand mothers in the United States die needlessly each year in childbirth, authorities maintain. Of the 16,000 who die annually from this cause, over 60 percent might be saved through adequate maternity care. Dr. Louis I. Dublin, statistician of the Metropolitan Life Insurance Co., points out that the United States, with its maternal mortality rate of 7 per 1,000 live births in 1929, occupies an unenviable position in relation to other nations that keep maternity death records. According to a recent study the maternal mortality rate in New York City *increased* from 5.33 in 1921 to 5.98 in 1932.

One contributing factor in this excessively high death rate of mothers in childbirth is that the necessary knowledge has not been available to the working class on the spacing and limiting of births. In the vicious circle of poverty the working-class mother has too many children because she has not money to buy the information she needs on how not to have babies; she cannot afford, under the conditions of capitalism, to give even one child the care he should have for his health and welfare; in the effort to give the children the necessaries of life, she goes back to work to earn a few dollars each week, and in so doing must neglect the children and her own health.

She has no time to secure the specialized knowledge of child care which makes for the health and advantage of the children, nor can working-class parents afford to provide any expert care for their children in any other way. The working mother is always tired and this tiredness reacts on the children, making a continual nervous strain in the household. Overcrowding, lack of privacy, ill health, anxiety, and insecurity, all the attendant evils of the worker's economic situation, make the life exactly the opposite of what child welfare experts say children should have for normal and healthy development, and these evils react usually on the health of the working mother herself.

Children die for lack of the care which working-class parents want of course to give them but cannot. The U.S. Children's Bureau has made studies of infant deaths under one-year-old in many different cities and states and has revealed the fact that in low-wage, working-class families, the infant death rate is nearly three times as great as in the families of the well-to-do. The more money the fathers earn, the fewer babies die. In jobless workers' families where the fathers have "no earnings," more than a fifth—one in every five—of all babies die before they are a year old. But for the well-to-do the rate is only one in seventeen.

Under the pressure of post-war capitalism, greater numbers of mothers are driven to seek work outside the home even when it means forced neglect of small children. Thus, in Philadelphia, in 1928, it was found that one-fifth of 12,000 mothers with children under sixteen were working out to help support their families. A similar study of a similar working-class district at the close of the war had shown only one-seventh of the mothers so employed. Yet the year 1928 was one of comparative "prosperity." In reporting the results of this special study, the U.S. Children's Bureau noted:

> The indications are that mothers of children who require constant supervision and mothers of large families do not go to work except as a last resort. They then try to obtain work at night, or at hours that interfere the least with their duties as mothers. *Mothers who must earn to keep the family together, however, will work even if the children are neglected.* It is a choice between food and clothing for the children and their adequate supervision. (Our emphasis.—G. H.)

Mothers who were the principal breadwinners for their households were employed mainly in factories or in domestic service, this survey showed. Cleaning of offices, stores, and other buildings occupied about half the mothers who had to supplement the husband's meager wage, but this work, mostly done in night hours, pays miserably low wages. Its advantage to the working mother is that it gives her daytime hours at home with the children whom she can then leave with the father or with an older child for the evening hours.

Among Negro women the necessity of working outside the home is far greater than among the whites, as this report revealed. Negro widows received less benefit from relief agencies, state or private, than did the white, for 88 percent of Negro widows were working. In fact among Negro mothers the necessity of working was general; as a rule the only ones who were not employed were those with a number of young children requiring constant care.

Thus, on top of a long day's work in the home, the working mother goes out for another stretch of five or six hours' work, scrubbing and cleaning floors and stairs and toilets. If her job is night work in a mill, the hours are often twice as long. Such night work is especially common in the South, but by no means unknown in the North.

CONTRIBUTORS

The three *Anonymous* workers' narratives reprinted here all appeared first in *Working Woman* magazine. "My Life: A True Story by a Negro Worker of the South" and "And Mine: A True Story by a Negro Worker of the North" were published in the October 1934 issue; "No More Helling! A True Story by a Working Woman" appeared in the September 1934 issue.

Lucille Boehm was a songwriter as well as a fiction writer. Her story, "Two-Bit Piece," appeared in *Opportunity* in 1939.

A graduate of Radcliffe College, *Marita Bonner* (1899–1971) published dozens of stories in the *Crisis* and *Opportunity* between 1925 and 1941. "The Whipping" first appeared in the *Crisis* in 1939. A collection of her work, *Frye Street and Environs,* is forthcoming from Beacon Press.

Eleanor Clark (1913–) is the author of numerous works, including fiction, essays, memoirs, and travel books. During the late 1930s, she edited (with Horace Gregory) *New Letters in America* and contributed to *Partisan Review,* where "Hurry, Hurry" was first published in 1938. The story was later reprinted in her collection *Dr. Heart: A Novella, and Other Stories* (1974). A recent novel, *Camping Out,* was published in 1986. She is married to Robert Penn Warren.

Vivian Dahl contributed "Them Women Sure Are Scrappers" to the *Working Woman* in 1934.

Joy Davidman won the Yale Younger Poets Award in 1938 for *Letter to a Comrade,* her first collection of poems. During the 1930s, she contributed reviews and commentary to *New Masses.* Her other works include a novel, *Anya* (1940).

Journalist and social activist *Dorothy Day* (1897–1980) is best known today as cofounder with Peter Maurin of the Catholic Worker Movement. In the 1920s she contributed to radical publications such as the *Masses* and published her first book, *The Eleventh Virgin,* a novel, in 1924. Following her conversion to Catholicism, Day began to publish the *Catholic Worker* in 1933 and devoted the rest of her life to social activist causes, including the founding of numerous homes and shelters for poor people. Her other books include *From Union Square to Rome* (1938) and *The Long Loneliness* (1952), an autobiography.

Little is known about *Edith Manuel Durham* except that her story "Deepening Dusk" stirred considerable controversy when it appeared in the *Crisis* in 1931.

Thyra J. Edwards was a social worker with the Joint Emergency Relief Service in Chicago when "Chicago in the Rain" was published in *Opportunity* in 1932. She also reported on the Spanish Civil War for that journal.

Elaine Ellis contributed "Women of the Cotton Fields" to the *Crisis* in 1938.

Ella Ford was a striking mill worker in Gastonia, North Carolina, when she described her experiences in "We Are Mill People" for the *New Masses* in 1929.

Mary LeDuc Gibbons published her poem "Mothers" in 1930 in *Opportunity,* which reported her as familiar to readers of that journal and other poetry magazines.

Ruth Gruber (1911–) is an international journalist and writer whose books include *I Went to the Soviet Arctic* (1939), from which the excerpt in this anthology is taken; *Haven: The Unknown Story of 1,000 World War II Refugees;* and *Raquela: A Woman of Israel* (1979).

Opportunity described *Gladys Casely Hayford* as "a young African girl who frequently contributes to *Opportunity* and other magazines." Hayford's poem, "The Palm Wine Seller" was published in *Opportunity* in 1930.

Born in the Midwest, *Josephine Herbst* (1892–1969) migrated to New York and then to Europe where she was one of many American expatriate writers living in Paris and Berlin during the early 1920s. Back in the United States, Herbst struggled as a writer throughout the depression, establishing herself as a respected novelist and journalist. Her best-known work, *Rope of Gold* (1939; The Feminist Press, 1984), the concluding volume in her fiction trilogy, is deeply rooted in the personal and political passions of the 1930s.

Grace Hutchins (1885–?), labor historian, is the author of *Women Who Work* (1934), a survey of women's labor in the United States from which the two excerpts—"Women under Capitalism" and "The Double Burden"—in the present work are taken. Hutchins also wrote about women in the silk industry, black and white women workers in the South, and children under capitalism.

Little is known about *Mary Inman* other than that her 1939 series in the *People's World* (later collected by the Committee for the Advancement of Women under the title *In Women's Defense*) sparked a major controversy among Communist party theorists about the productive value of women's domestic labor.

Aunt Molly Jackson (1880–1961) was a midwife in Eastern Kentucky during the 1920s and 1930s. She and her half-sister Sarah Ogan Gunning were eventually driven out of the Kentucky mountains for their union activity, which included writing some of the most moving lyrics about working-class struggle to come out of the 1930s.

Josephine W. Johnson (1910–) was born in St. Louis, Missouri. She is the author of eleven books, including short stories, poetry, novels, and essays. *Now in November* (1934), her novel of farm life in the depression, received the Pulitzer Prize. The poems reprinted here are from her 1937 collection *Year's End.* Her more recent work, *The Inland Island* (1969; reprinted 1987), a journal, and *The Circle of Seasons* (1974), an essay in text and photographs, are about nature. According to Johnson, "only a *world* point of view that includes all of nature as well as humankind will save us and our children's children for a life worth living. I believe in writing *green.*"

Mary Guimes Lear wrote "Bessie: A Garment Strike Story" for the *New Masses* in 1937.

Ruth Lechlitner (1901–) published poetry and reviews in the *New Masses* and other journals during the 1930s. A collection of her poems, *Tomorrow's Phoenix,* was published by Alcestis Press in 1937.

Meridel Le Sueur (1900–) developed her talents as a writer by living and working with unemployed women in St. Paul, Minnesota, where she still lives and writes. A prominent figure in the literary left of the 1930s, Le Sueur published widely in radical journals of the period. A collection of her writing, *Ripening: Selected Work, 1927–1980* (Feminist Press, 1982) encompasses the range of her poetry, fiction, autobiography, and reportage. Other works include *The Girl,* a novel written in 1939 but not published until 1978, and *Rites of Ancient Ripening* (1975), a collection of her poetry.

Mollie Lewis reported on "Negro Women in Steel" for the *Crisis* in 1938.

Ramona Lowe published her story "The Woman in the Window" in *Opportunity* in 1940.

Ruth McKenney (1911–1972), best known for her memoir, *My Sister Eileen* (1938), is the author also of two proletarian novels, *Industrial Valley* and *Jake Home* (1943). An excerpt from *Industrial Valley* (1939; Greenwood Press, 1969) is reprinted here.

Novelist *Toni Morrison* (1931–) is the author of *The Bluest Eye* (1970), *Sula* (1973), *Song of Solomon* (1976), *Tar Baby* (1979), and *Beloved* (1987). She was appointed Schweitzer Professor in the Humanities at the State University of New York at Albany in 1984.

Charlotte Nekola (1952–) received her Ph.D. in English language and literature from the University of Michigan, Ann Arbor. She received a Schweitzer Fellowship in Humanities from the State University of New York at Albany to support, among other projects, the compilation of *Writing Red*. She is also a poet, and has published poetry in *Massachusetts Review, New Letters,* and *Calyx.*

Tillie Olsen (1913–) began a promising writing career in the 1930s, when she contributed frequently to such journals as *Partisan Review* and the *New Republic*. The demands of supporting and rearing a family forced her to put aside her writing for many years. She is the author of *Tell Me a Riddle* (1962), *Yonnondio* (1974), and *Silences* (1978), and editor of *Mother to Daughter, Daughter to Mother* (The Feminist Press, 1984), and *Life in the Iron Mills and Other Stories* by Rebecca Harding Davis (The Feminist Press, 1985).

Myra Page (1897–) was an active novelist and journalist during the 1930s. Two of her novels, *Gathering Storm* (1932), about the cotton-mill workers' strike in Gastonia, North Carolina in 1929, and *Moscow Yankee* (1935), about the experiences of an American worker in the Soviet Union, were hailed as examples of proletarian fiction by critics of the time. A third novel about an Appalachian coal-mining family was written in the 1930s, published in 1950 under the title *With Sun in Our Blood,* and reissued in 1986 under the title *Daughter of the Hills* by The Feminist Press.

Rebecca Pitts was a member of the Indianapolis John Reed Club when she wrote "Women and Communism" for the *New Masses* in 1935.

Paula Rabinowitz (1951–) received her Ph.D. in American culture from the University of Michigan, Ann Arbor. She is currently Assistant Professor of English at the University of Minnesota in Minneapolis. Her poems have appeared in *Moving Out, Greenfield Review,* and *Passages North.*

Florence Reece (1900?–?) wrote her famous song, "Which Side Are You On?" while she was living in Harlan County, Kentucky. Her father and husband were coal miners and she was active in organizing for the United Mine Workers.

Muriel Rukeyser (1913–1980) began a lifelong career as a poet and political activist in the 1930s, when she traveled to Alabama to protest the Scottsboro trials in 1933 and won the Yale Younger Poets Award in 1935 for her first volume of poetry, *Theory of Flight*. She subsequently published over thirty volumes of poetry, drama, translation, biography, children's books, and a novel. In later years she traveled to Hanoi in protest against the

Vietnam War and in support of the world peace movement. Her *Collected Poems* appeared in 1978.

Susan McMillan Shepherd contributed the poem "White Man's Blues" to *Opportunity* in 1935.

Tess Slesinger (1905–1945) published two major works during the 1930s: a novel, *The Unpossessed* (1934), was loosely based on her association with Herbert Solow and Elliot Cohen, editors of the *Menorah Journal;* and a collection of short stories, *Time: The Present* (1935), from which the story "The Mouse-Trap" is reprinted. In 1935, Slesinger moved to Hollywood where she collaborated with her husband Frank Davis on such filmscripts as *The Good Earth* and *A Tree Grows in Brooklyn.*

Agnes Smedley (1892–1950) whose novel *Daughter of Earth* (1929; The Feminist Press, 1973, 1987) in many ways marked the beginning of proletarian writing during the 1930s, spent most of that decade in China reporting on the revolutionary movement there. She ultimately published five books on China including *Battle Hymn of China* (1943), which combines history and autobiography, and a posthumously published biography of Red Army leader Chu Teh. "Shan-fei, Communist" originally appeared in *New Masses* in May 1931 and was subsequently collected in *Chinese Destinies: Sketches of Present-Day China* (1933) and *Portraits of Chinese Women in Revolution* (The Feminist Press, 1976). "The People in China" was published in *Clipper: A Western Review* in August 1941.

Anna Louise Strong (1885–1970) earned a Ph.D. in philosophy from the University of Chicago at age twenty-three. She worked on urban social reform projects before moving to Seattle in 1915. Here she became a reporter for a socialist paper and started a lifelong career as a political journalist. Her special interest was revolution, which she covered in Russia, Mexico, Spain, Poland, China, and later, Laos and Vietnam. She wrote over ten book-length works of international reportage and is best known today for her writing on China and for her autobiography, *I Change Worlds* (1935).

Genevieve Taggard (1894–1948) was born in Waitsburg, Washington, and grew up, except for two visits to Washington state, in Honolulu, Hawaii, where her missionary parents started and ran a public school. Her first poem was published in Hawaii, when she was sixteen. After graduation from the University of California, Berkeley, in 1919, she went east to work in New York City. Looking back to those years, she said later, "I called myself a Socialist in a rather vague way. Since then I have always been left of center." She was married in 1921, bore a daughter, founded a poetry magazine, and had her first volume of verse published in 1922. She was the author of eleven volumes of poetry and a biography of Emily Dickinson;

she also edited three anthologies and wrote many reviews and articles. She taught literature at three colleges—Mount Holyoke, Bennington, and Sarah Lawrence; was married a second time; and lived in later years in Europe, New England, and New York City.

Elizabeth Thomas contributed the story "Our House" to the *Crisis* in 1939.

Lucia Trent (1897–?) is the author of several volumes of political poetry including *Children of Fire and Shadow* (Packard, 1929), from which the poems in this anthology are reprinted. She and her husband poet Ralph Cheney edited a number of anthologies including *Unrest! The Rebel Poets' Anthology* (1931) and *More Power to Poets! A Plea for More Poetry in Life, More Life in Poetry* (1934), a collection of essays.

Mary Heaton Vorse (1874–1966) was a leading labor journalist and feminist who covered the major labor and radical struggles in the United States and abroad during the first half of the century. Vorse was a frequent contributor to the *New Republic,* where "School for Bums" first appeared in 1931; "Hard-Boiled" was written for *Working Woman* and published in 1933. A prolific writer, Vorse published almost twenty volumes of fiction and journalism.

Margaret Walker (1915–   ) won the Yale Younger Poets Award for her 1942 volume of poetry *For My People*. During the 1930s Walker was employed by the Federal Writers Project in Chicago. It was during this time that she began work on her Civil War novel, *Jubilee,* which was not completed and published until 1966. Walker taught English at Jackson State College (now University) in Mississippi for many years. She is currently working with editor Maryemma Graham to complete a collection of essays, *How I Wrote Jubilee and Other Essays,* for publication by The Feminist Press.

In the early 1930s, *Ella Winter* (1898–1980) traveled to the Soviet Union with her husband Lincoln Steffens. An accomplished journalist, Winter travelled widely, speaking and writing about radical causes. The excerpt reprinted here is taken from her book, *Red Virtue: Human Relationships in the New Russia* (1933).

Kathleen Tankersley Young contributed "All Things Insensible" to *Opportunity* in 1930. The journal described her as "among the better known of the younger poets."

Leane Zugsmith (1903–1969) published widely during the 1930s. Her novel, *A Time to Remember* (1936) recounts the events of a saleswomen's strike against Orbach's department store. "Room in the World" is reprinted from her 1938 short-story collection *Home Is Where You Hang Your Childhood and Other Stories.*

ACKNOWLEDGMENTS

We gratefully acknowledge permission to reprint the following material:

Marita Bonner: "The Whipping" from *Frye Street and Environs: The Collected Works of Marita Bonner,* ed. by Joyce Flynn and Joyce Stricklin. To be published by Beacon Press, December 1987. Reprinted by permission of Beacon Press.

Eleanor Clark: "Hurry, Hurry" from *Partisan Review* 4 (January 1938). Reprinted by permission of the author.

Joy Davidman: "This Woman," "Twentieth-Century Americanism," "Prayer Against Indifference," from *Letter to a Comrade* by Joy Davidman. © 1938 by Yale University Press. Reprinted by permission of the publisher.

Dorothy Day: "A Good Landlord" from *New Masses* 6 (October 1930). Reprinted by permission of Tamar Hennessy.

Edith Manuel Durham: "Deepening Dusk" from the *Crisis* 38 (January 1931 and February 1931). Reprinted by permission of the publisher.

Elaine Ellis: "Women of the Cotton Fields" from the *Crisis* 45 (October 1938). Reprinted by permission of the publisher.

Ruth Gruber: "Finding Women" from *I Went to the Soviet Arctic* by Ruth Gruber. © 1939, 1966 by Ruth Gruber. Reprinted by permission of Simon & Schuster, Inc.

Josephine Herbst: "The Enemy" from *Partisan Review* 3 (October 1936). © 1936 by Josephine Herbst. "Passport to Realengo 18" from *New Masses* 16 (July 16, 1935). © 1936 by Josephine Herbst. Both reprinted by permission of Georges Borchardt, Inc. and the author's estate.

Grace Hutchins: "Women under Capitalism" and "The Double Burden" from *Women Who Work* by Grace Hutchins. © 1934 by International Publishers. Reprinted by permission of the publisher.

Mary Inman: "Manufacturing Femininity," "The Pivot of the System," and "The Code of a Class" from *In Woman's Defense* by Mary Inman (Los Angeles: Committee to Organize the Advancement of Women, 1940).

Originally serialized in *People's World* in 1939. Reprinted by permission of *People's Daily World*.

Josephine W. Johnson: "Under the Sound of Voices," "He Who Shall Turn—," and "Ice Winter" from *Year's End* by Josephine W. Johnson. © 1937. Reprinted by permission of the author.

Ruth Lechlitner: "On the Wall to Your Left" from *Tomorrow's Phoenix* by Ruth Lechlitner. © 1937 by Ruth Lechlitner. Reprinted by permission of the author.

Meridel Le Sueur: "Sequel to Love" from *Anvil*, January–February 1935. "The Fetish of Being Outside" from *New Masses,* February 1935. Both reprinted by permission of the author.

Mollie V. Lewis: "Negro Women in Steel" from the *Crisis* 45 (February 1938). Reprinted by permission of the publisher.

Ruth McKenney: From *Industrial Valley* by Ruth McKenney. © 1939 by Ruth McKenney. Reprinted by permission of Curtis Brown, Ltd.

Tillie Olsen: "The Strike" from *Partisan Review* 1 (September–October 1934). © 1934 by Tillie Lerner. "I Want You Women Up North to Know" from *Partisan* (March 1934). © 1934 by Tillie Lerner. Both reprinted by permission of the author.

Myra Page: "Leave Them Meters Be" from *Working Woman,* September 1934. "Water" from *Working Woman,* October 1934. Both reprinted by permission of the author.

Muriel Rukeyser: "Ann Burlak" from *A Turning Wind* by Muriel Rukeyser, © 1938, 1957 by Muriel Rukeyser; "Fifth Elegy: A Turning Wind" from *A Turning Wind* by Muriel Rukeyser, © 1939, 1958, 1978 by Muriel Rukeyser; "Absalom" from *U.S. 1* by Muriel Rukeyser, © 1939, 1958 by Muriel Rukeyser; "More of a Corpse Than a Woman" from *U.S. 1* by Muriel Rukeyser, © 1938, 1957, 1978 by Muriel Rukeyser. Reprinted by permission of International Creative Agency, Inc.

Tess Slesinger: "The Mouse-Trap" from *Time: The Present* by Tess Slesinger. © 1935 by Tess Slesinger; renewed 1963 by Frank Davis. Reprinted by permission of Simon and Schuster, Inc.

Agnes Smedley: "Shan-fei, Communist" from *Chinese Destinies: Sketches of Present-Day China* by Agnes Smedley. © 1933, 1961 by Vanguard Press, Inc. Reprinted by permission of the publisher.

Anna Louise Strong: "Fighters for Women's Rights" from *China's Millions: The Revolutionary Struggles from 1927 to 1935* (Knight, 1935) and

"Front Trenches—Northwest" from *Spain in Arms* (Holt, 1937). Reprinted by permission of Tracey B. Strong.

Genevieve Taggard: "Try Tropic," "Return of the Native," "To My Mother," and "Silence in Mallorca" from *Collected Poems 1918–1938* by Genevieve Taggard. © 1938 by Harper & Row, Publishers, Inc., renewed 1966. Reprinted by permission of Marcia D. Liles. "Proud Day," "Autumn Song for Guitar," "Creative Effort," and "Ode in Time of Crisis" from *Long View* by Genevieve Taggard. © 1942 by Harper & Row, Publishers, Inc., renewed 1970. Reprinted by permission of Marcia D. Liles.

Elizabeth Thomas: "Our House" from the *Crisis* 46 (February 1939). Reprinted by permission of the publisher.

Margaret Walker: "For My People," "Dark Blood," and "Lineage" from *For My People* by Margaret Walker (Yale University Press, 1942). © 1942 by Yale University Press. Reprinted by permission of the author.

Ella Winter: From "Woman Freed" in *Red Virtue: Human Relationships in the New Russia* by Ella Winter. © 1933 by Harcourt Brace Jovanovich, Inc., renewed 1961 by Ella Winter. Reprinted by permission of the publisher.

The Feminist Press at The City University of New York offers alternatives in education and in literature. Founded in 1970, this nonprofit, tax-exempt educational and publishing organization works to eliminate sexual stereotypes in books and schools and to provide literature with a broad vision of human potential. The publishing program includes reprints of important works by women, feminist biographies of women, and nonsexist children's books. Curricular materials, bibliographies, directories, and a quarterly journal provide information and support for students and teachers of women's studies. In-service projects help to transform teaching methods and curricula. Through publications and projects, The Feminist Press contributes to the rediscovery of the history of women and the emergence of a more humane society.

NEW AND FORTHCOMING BOOKS

Carrie Chapman Catt: A Public Life, by Jacqueline Van Voris. $24.95 cloth.

Competition: A Feminist Taboo? edited by Valerie Miner and Helen E. Longino. Foreword by Nell Irvin Painter. $29.95 cloth, $12.95 paper.

Daughter of Earth, a novel by Agnes Smedley. Foreword by Alice Walker. Afterword by Nancy Hoffman. $8.95 paper.

Doctor Zay, a novel by Elizabeth Stuart Phelps. Afterword by Michael Sartisky. $8.95 paper.

Get Smart: A Woman's Guide to Equality on Campus, by S. Montana Katz and Veronica Vieland. $29.95 cloth, $9.95 paper.

A Guide to Research on Women: Library and Information Sources in the Greater New York Area, compiled by the Women's Resources Group of the Greater New York Metropolitan Area Chapter of the Association of College and Research Libraries and the Center for the Study of Women and Society of the Graduate School and University Center of The City University of New York. $12.95 paper.

Harem Years: The Memoirs of an Egyptian Feminist, 1879–1924, by Huda Shaarawi. Translated and edited by Margot Badran. $29.95 cloth, $9.95 paper.

Leaving Home, a novel by Elizabeth Janeway. New Foreword by the author. Afterword by Rachel M. Brownstein. $8.95 paper.

Lone Voyagers: Academic Women in Coeducational Universities, 1869–1937, edited by Geraldine J. Clifford. $29.95 cloth, $12.95 paper.

My Mother Marries, a novel by Moa Martinson. Translated and introduced by Margaret S. Lacy. $8.95 paper.

Sultana's Dream and Selections from The Secluded Ones, by Rokeya Sakhawat Hossein. Edited by Roushan Jahan and Hanna Papanek. Translated by Roushan Jahan. $4.95 paper.

Turning the World Upside Down: The Anti-Slavery Convention of American Women Held in New York City, May 9–12, 1837. Introduction by Dorothy Sterling. $2.95 paper.

With Wings: An Anthology of Literature by and about Women with Disabilities, edited by Marsha Saxton and Florence Howe. $29.95 cloth, $12.95 paper.

Women Activists, by Anne Witte Garland. Introduction by Frances T. Farenthold. Foreword by Ralph Nader. $29.95 cloth, $9.95 paper.

Writing Red: An Anthology of American Women Writers, 1930–1940, edited by Charlotte L. Nekola and Paula Rabinowitz. Foreword by Toni Morrison. $29.95 cloth, $12.95 paper.

FICTION CLASSICS

Between Mothers and Daughters: Stories across a Generation. edited by Susan Koppelman. $9.95 paper.

Brown Girl, Brownstones, a novel by Paule Marshall. Afterword by Mary Helen Washington. $8.95 paper.

Call Home the Heart, a novel of the thirties, by Fielding Burke. Introduction by Alice Kessler-Harris and Paul Lauter and afterwords by Sylvia J. Cook and Anna W. Shannon. $9.95 paper.

Cassandra, by Florence Nightingale. Introduction by Myra Stark. Epilogue by Cynthia MacDonald. $4.50 paper.

The Changelings, a novel by Jo Sinclair. Afterwords by Nellie McKay, and Johnnetta B. Cole and Elizabeth H. Oakes; biographical note by Elisabeth Sandberg. $8.95 paper.

The Convert, a novel by Elizabeth Robins. Introduction by Jane Marcus. $8.95 paper.

Daddy Was a Number Runner, a novel by Louise Meriwether. Foreword by James Baldwin and afterword by Nellie McKay. $8.95 paper.

Daughter of the Hills: A Woman's Part in the Coal Miner's Struggle, a novel of the thirties, by Myra Page. Introduction by Alice Kessler-Harris and Paul Lauter and afterword by Deborah S. Rosenfelt. $8.95 paper.

An Estate of Memory, a novel by Ilona Karmel. Afterword by Ruth K. Angress. $11.95 paper.

Guardian Angel and Other Stories, by Margery Latimer. Afterwords by Nancy Loughridge, Meridel Le Sueur, and Louis Kampf. $8.95 paper.

I Love Myself when I am Laughing . . . And Then Again when I Am Looking Mean and Impressive: A Zora Neale Hurston Reader, edited by Alice Walker. Introduction by Mary Helen Washington. $9.95 paper.

Life in the Iron Mills and Other Stories, by Rebecca Harding Davis. Biographical interpretation by Tillie Olsen. $7.95 paper.

The Living Is Easy, a novel by Dorothy West. Afterword by Adelaide M. Cromwell. $9.95 paper.

The Other Woman: Stories of Two Women and a Man. Edited by Susan Koppelman. $9.95 paper.

The Parish and the Hill, a novel by Mary Doyle Curran. Afterword by Anne Halley. $8.95 paper.

Reena and Other Stories, selected short stories by Paule Marshall. $8.95 paper.

Ripening: Selected Work, 1927–1980, 2nd edition, by Meridel Le Sueur. Edited with an introduction by Elaine Hedges. $9.95 paper.

Rope of Gold, a novel of the thirties, by Josephine Herbst. Introduction by Alice Kessler-Harris and Paul Lauter and afterword by Elinor Langer. $9.95 paper.

The Silent Partner, a novel by Elizabeth Stuart Phelps. Afterword by Mari Jo Buhle and Florence Howe. $8.95 paper.

Swastika Night, a novel by Katharine Burdekin. Introduction by Daphne Patai. $8.95 paper.

This Child's Gonna Live, a novel by Sarah E. Wright. Appreciation by John Oliver Killens. $9.95 paper.

The Unpossessed, a novel of the thirties, by Tess Slesinger. Introduction by Alice Kessler-Harris and Paul Lauter and afterword by Janet Sharistanian. $9.95 paper.

Weeds, a novel by Edith Summers Kelley. Afterword by Charlotte Goodman. $8.95 paper.

The Wide, Wide World, a novel by Susan Warner. Afterword by Jane Tompkins. $29.95 cloth, $11.95 paper.

A Woman of Genius, a novel by Mary Austin. Afterword by Nancy Porter. $9.95 paper.

Women and Appletrees, a novel by Moa Martinson. Translated from the Swedish and with an afterword by Margaret S. Lacy. $8.95 paper.

Women Working: An Anthology of Stories and Poems, edited and with an introduction by Nancy Hoffman and Florence Howe. $9.95 paper.

The Yellow Wallpaper, by Charlotte Perkins Gilman. Afterword by Elaine Hedges. $4.50 paper.

OTHER TITLES

Antoinette Brown Blackwell: A Biography, by Elizabeth Cazden. $24.95 cloth, $12.95 paper.

All the Women Are White, All the Blacks Are Men, but Some of Us Are Brave: Black Women's Studies, edited by Gloria T. Hull, Patricia Bell Scott, and Barbara Smith. $12.95 paper.

Black Foremothers: Three Lives, 2nd ed., by Dorothy Sterling. $9.95 paper.

Complaints and Disorders: The Sexual Politics of Sickness, by Barbara Ehrenreich and Deirdre English. $3.95 paper.

The Cross-Cultural Study of Women, edited by Margot I. Duley and Mary I. Edwards. $29.95 cloth, $12.95 paper.